IoT-Driven Business Transformation:

Strategy, Data, Trust, and Security

Johanna Pangeiko Nautwima
https://orcid.org/0009-0004-6153-5014
Namibia University of Science and Technology, Namibia

Asa Romeo Asa
https://orcid.org/0000-0002-7549-2949
Namibia University of Science and Technology, Namibia

IGI Global
Scientific Publishing
Publishing Tomorrow's Research Today

Vice President of Editorial | Melissa Wagner
Director of Acquisitions | Mikaela Felty
Director of Book Development | Jocelynn Hessler
Production Manager | Mike Brehm
Cover Design | Jose Rosado

Published in the United States of America by
IGI Global Scientific Publishing
701 East Chocolate Avenue
Hershey, PA, 17033, USA
Tel: 717-533-8845 | Fax: 717-533-7115
Website: https://www.igi-global.com E-mail: cust@igi-global.com

Library of Congress Cataloging-in-Publication Data

(CIP Data Pending)
ISBN13: 979-8-2600-1263-5
Isbn13Softcover: 979-8-2600-1264-2
EISBN13: 979-8-2600-1265-9
British Cataloguing in Publication Data
A Cataloguing in Publication record for this book is available from the British Library.

Table of Contents

Detailed Table of Contents

The Internet of Things (IoT) is a central pillar of digital transformation. However, many organizations still struggle to transform technological investments into strategic business benefits. This chapter tackles this issue by investigating IoT as a strategic facilitator from the perspective of organizational change and supply chain management. Based on the resource-based view, dynamic capabilities perspective, and socio-technical systems perspective, this chapter argues that IoT creates value indirectly. Furthermore, IoT serves as a dual transformation mechanism by building internal organizational agility through the enterprise's ability to sense and seize context. A dual transformation model is proposed to represent this mediating process through organizational and supply chain transformation capabilities that lead to superior business performance. The model reinforces the critical linkages between internal organizational transformation and external network performance and ultimately illustrates a strategic pathway to realizing business performance through IoT.

Preface

INTRODUCTION

In an era defined by rapid digital acceleration, the Internet of Things (IoT) has emerged as a transformative force reshaping how organizations operate, compete, and create value. Like a compass guiding enterprises through the complexities of digital transformation, IoT provides direction by connecting systems, enabling real-time intelligence, and unlocking new forms of strategic innovation. Yet, the journey toward IoT-driven transformation is multifaceted, requiring not only technological adoption but also organizational change, data governance, trust-building, and robust security infrastructures.

IoT-Driven Business Transformation: Strategy, Data, Trust, and Security brings together a comprehensive set of scholarly contributions that examine IoT from a strategic, operational, and human-centered perspective. The chapters collectively explore how organizations can move beyond mere technological implementation to achieve meaningful transformation—redefining business models, enhancing operational agility, and fostering sustainable innovation.

A recurring theme throughout this volume is that IoT's value is rarely direct; rather, it is realized through the capabilities it enables. Organizational agility, data-driven decision-making, and adaptive business ecosystems emerge as critical mediators of success. At the same time, the integration of IoT introduces new challenges, particularly in the areas of data privacy, cybersecurity, ethical governance, and regulatory compliance. These challenges underscore the necessity of aligning technological advancement with responsible and transparent practices.

This book also highlights the convergence of IoT with emerging technologies such as artificial intelligence, digital twins, and advanced analytics. These integrations are expanding the boundaries of what is possible, from intelligent healthcare systems and smart cities to real-time marketing driven by biometric data. However, such advancements further complicate the ethical and legal landscape, demanding interdisciplinary approaches and collaborative solutions.

Ultimately, this volume positions IoT not simply as a technological innovation, but as a strategic enabler of transformation that requires holistic thinking—integrating strategy, data, trust, and security into a unified framework for navigating the digital future.

CHAPTER OVERVIEWS

Chapter 1: Explores IoT as a strategic enabler of business transformation, emphasizing its indirect value through organizational change and supply chain capabilities, and introducing a dual transformation model.

Chapter 2: Examines how IoT enhances operational efficiency and drives business model innovation, enabling organizations to transition toward service-oriented and data-driven approaches.

Chapter 3: Investigates the role of IoT in fostering operational agility within smart ecosystems, highlighting the integration of real-time analytics, automation, and adaptive decision-making.

Chapter 4: Focuses on AIoT applications in healthcare, addressing both transformative opportunities in personalized care and the challenges of data governance, ethics, and interoperability.

Chapter 5: Introduces the concept of biometric-driven marketing through IoT-based systems, proposing innovative approaches to real-time consumer engagement using physiological data.

Chapter 6: Analyzes IoT-driven systemic restructuring across industries, emphasizing the convergence of digital economies and adaptive sectors alongside key integration challenges.

Chapter 7: Explores the role of digital twins in enhancing smart city IoT applications, demonstrating how real-time modeling and optimization improve urban sustainability and efficiency.

Chapter 8: Examines strategies for building trust and brand loyalty in IoT environments, positioning security, transparency, and user experience as critical competitive differentiators.

Chapter 9: Addresses ethical, legal, and security challenges in IoT markets, offering frameworks for responsible governance and trust-building in complex digital ecosystems.

Chapter 10: Investigates the ethics of big data and responsible AI in IoT-powered marketing, providing guidance on data governance and ethical decision-making.

CONCLUSION

The contributions in this volume collectively affirm that IoT-driven transformation is as much about strategy and trust as it is about technology. While IoT offers unprecedented opportunities for innovation, efficiency, and connectivity, its successful implementation depends on the ability of organizations to navigate complex challenges related to data, ethics, and security.

Trust emerges as a foundational pillar across all domains—whether in consumer relationships, organizational systems, or regulatory environments. Without it, even the most advanced IoT solutions risk limited adoption and diminished impact. At the same time, the growing reliance on data and intelligent systems necessitates a commitment to ethical governance, transparency, and accountability.

As IoT continues to evolve alongside emerging technologies, organizations must adopt integrated approaches that balance innovation with responsibility. By bridging strategy, data, trust, and security, this book provides a roadmap for scholars, practitioners, and policymakers seeking to harness the full potential of IoT in shaping resilient, adaptive, and future-ready enterprises.

Johanna Pangeiko Nautwima
Namibia University of Science and Technology, Namibia

Asa Romeo Asa
Namibia University of Science and Technology, Namibia

Chapter 1

Internet of Things as a Strategic Enabler of Business Transformation Through Organizational Change and Supply Chain Perspectives

Asa Romeo Asa
http://orcid.org/0000-0002-7549-2949
Namibia University of Science and Technology, Namibia

Johanna Pangeiko Nautwima
http://orcid.org/0009-0004-6153-5014
Namibia University of Science and Technology, Namibia

Helvi Nyete Johannes
Namibia University of Science and Technology, Namibia

ABSTRACT

The Internet of Things (IoT) is a central pillar of digital transformation. However, many organizations still struggle to transform technological investments into strategic business benefits. This chapter tackles this issue by investigating IoT as a strategic facilitator from the perspective of organizational change and supply chain management. Based on the resource-based view, dynamic capabilities perspective, and socio-technical systems perspective, this chapter argues that IoT creates value indirectly. Furthermore, IoT serves as a dual transformation mechanism by building internal

DOI: 10.4018/979-8-2600-1263-5.ch001

organizational agility through the enterprise's ability to sense and seize context. A dual transformation model is proposed to represent this mediating process through organizational and supply chain transformation capabilities that lead to superior business performance. The model reinforces the critical linkages between internal organizational transformation and external network performance and ultimately illustrates a strategic pathway to realizing business performance through IoT.

1. INTRODUCTION

1.1. Background and Context

The current business landscape is fundamentally a transformative process resulting from digital transformation. It is not just the introduction of new technology; it involves the deep transformation of a firm's strategy, culture, and operations models to establish and capture value in a digital economy (Verhoef et al., 2021; Vial, 2019). The Internet of Things (IoT) is at the heart of this transformation, an ecosystem of interconnected physical things from industrial equipment to consumer goods, with built-in sensors and software that allow for real-time data exchange (Atzori et al., 2010; Yoo et al., 2010). As IoT evolves from a simple connectedness notion into an ecosystem of intelligent and autonomous systems, it signifies an important turning point in digital innovation and our next business model (Porter & Heppelmann, 2014; Iansiti & Lakhani, 2014).

Furthermore, with the globalized IoT, the pace of development is rapid, creating massive economic impacts across the globe. The velocity of connected devices is a significant technological trend, and academic predictions indicate that this trend will continue to increase in both consumer and industrial markets (Kamble et al., 2020). This momentum is followed by significant corporate buy-in, creating a market in which economic value is expected to be revolutionary (Lee & Lee, 2015; Nagy et al., 2018). This impact is typically applied to the manufacturing, logistics, and healthcare sectors, with IoT solutions driving operational effectiveness and new business and service models (Ben-Daya et al., 2019). Smart manufacturing is an example of this. The IoT is used for predictive maintenance and process improvement. In logistics, it provides real-time traceability and transparency (Tjahjono et al., 2017; Rejeb et al., 2022).

Given this potentially disruptive nature, it is important to take a strategic perspective on the role of the IoT. Viewing IoT merely as a technological solution fails to recognize its role in facilitating systemic changes in businesses. This chapter uses a dual lens to consider IoT in the fields of organizational change and supply chain management. The premise for this is the understanding that IoT can provide value not because of technology per se but because of the way it interacts with organizational elements such as structure, culture, and processes when interacting with external relationships in a supply network (De Vass et al., 2018; Fatorachian & Kazemi, 2018). Thus, a good IoT strategy is closely connected to the change management of the organization and the development of a more visible, fast, and collaborative supply chain (Kamble et al., 2020).

Despite considerable investment and potential benefits, a persistent gulf exists between IoT implementation and business strategy transformation. Organizations typically find it difficult to move beyond isolated pilot programs or standardize business processes for only minor operational efficiency (Frank et al., 2019; Vrchota et al., 2021). Empirical research frequently finds numerous impediments to successful implementation, leading to projects that do not scale or offer the anticipated return on investment (Luthra et al., 2020; Parviainen et al., 2017). Much of the failure lies in the technical centricity of implementing solutions that weigh the balance between technology, people, and processes (Ghaffari et al., 2019; Sony & Naik, 2020). Organizations focus on technical implementation but do not worry about non-technical areas related to internal resistance to change, lack of skill development, lack of a strategic vision, or lack of developing a data culture (Saarikko et al., 2020; Gebayew et al., 2018). The issue is that the organization misaligns IoT uptake with business strategy, aligning technology to offer a new source of competitive advantage (Teece, 2018).

The primary purpose of this chapter is to examine how IoT acts as a strategic facilitator of business transformation, specifically considering its dual influence on internal organizational changes and external supply chain efficiencies. This is the concept introduced in this action-driven work, which considers realistic organization theories along with some empirical analysis, moving the conversation beyond a technical focus. To achieve this, this chapter has the following objectives:

- To establish a solid theoretical base for IoT-based transformation, theories of the resource-based view (RBV), dynamic capabilities, and sociotechnical systems have been implemented (Barney, 1991; Teece, 2007; Pasmore et al., 1982).
- To critically analyze how IoT enables organizational change by examining how it influences the architecture of business models, leadership styles, and workforce capabilities.
- To examine the multifaceted influence of IoT on supply chain management by specifying improvements in end-to-end visibility, operational agility, network collaboration, and resilience.
- To propose an integrative conceptual framework that connects organizational and supply chain perspectives, demonstrating how internal agility and exter-

nal network integration are interdependent levers of business performance outcomes.

The chapter's premise is focused on two related areas: the internal organizational changes made to exploit IoT and the external transformation of supply chain networks into intelligent, responsive value networks. Internal focus addresses internal features, such as organizational structure, culture, leadership, and capabilities. The external focus is on how IoT enhances transparency, efficiency, and collaboration between supply chain members. The chapter's contributions are the integration of organizational theory and supply chain management research in the context of IoT. There is already quite a bit of literature related to the IoT, as it relates to digital transformation or operational impact for supply chains. Research on a firm's internal readiness and whether it can leverage IoT relative to supply network performance is limited (De Vass et al., 2018; Dubey et al., 2019). The dual-lever framework presented in this chapter offers a more comprehensive and strategically meaningful view of firms that want to develop a sustainable competitive advantage. This model presents a conceptual path from the development of IoT capabilities to improved organizational agility and enhanced supply chain integration, and consequently, value delivery. This integrated view offers a succinct account of academics and practitioners interested in the challenges of technology-based business transformation.

2. THEORETICAL AND CONCEPTUAL FOUNDATIONS

2.1. The Evolution of the Internet of Things

The conceptual origins of IoT can be traced back to experiments in telemetry and networked computing. Its modern shape has only begun to take form with the advent of radio-frequency identification (RFID) technology (Atzori et al., 2010; Borgia, 2014). Initially, the paradigm was straightforward, a blend of automation and identification: linking objects to a network, mainly for tracking and monitoring. During that stage the emphasis lay in carving out visibility, gathering enough data to finally answer the question "What is the condition of this asset?" (Gubbi et al., 2013; Miorandi et al., 2012). This move leapt beyond the constraints of tracking, yet it stayed largely tethered to logistics and inventory management- contexts, where the primary aim was simply to identify objects and monitor their whereabouts (Weber & Weber, 2010).

When breakthroughs in sensor technology, computing, and network protocols finally intersect, they spark a paradigm shift. Emphasis has gradually shifted from automation to the integration of embedded intelligence (Yoo et al., 2010; Zuehlke, 2010). This turning point signaled the leap from a network of objects" to the Internet of Things, where devices no longer just broadcast their status; they now sense their surroundings, crunch data on-site, and chat with other gadgets to perform intricate tasks (Whitmore et al., 2015). The emerging paradigm pivots away from analytics, simply noting what happened, toward predictive and prescriptive analytics, which aim to forecast what will happen and prescribe what should be done. At this stage, IoT ecosystems flood the landscape with massive data streams. When these streams are paired with artificial intelligence and machine learning-, they empower systems to make autonomous decisions, adjust processes in real time, and launch entirely new data-driven- services (Lee & Lee 2015; Kolk, 2017). This shift marks a redefinition of connectivity, moving from a mere monitoring tool to a platform that actively drives intelligent actions and generates value.

2.2. Theories Supporting IoT-Enabled Transformation

The transformative capabilities of IoT are best understood by framing theories on how firms build and maintain competitive advantages. Three theories are particularly important: i) Resource-Based View, ii) Dynamic Capabilities Theory, and iii) Socio-technical Systems Theory.

2.2.1. Resource-Based View (RBV): IoT as a Strategic Capability

The Resource-Based View (RBV) states that sustained competitive advantage occurs when a firm leverages valuable, rare, inimitable, and non-substitutable (VRIN) assets and capabilities (Barney, 1991; Wernerfelt, 1984). A VRIN logic perspective views IoT as more than a technology; it is the building block of strategic capability. While an industry may be able to acquire the same technology, value arises when IoT is embedded in a firm's unique resources, such as exclusive databases, specialized analytical skills, and distinct processes (Bharadwaj, 2000; Wade & Hulland, 2004). Data collected through IoT networks, in conjunction with sophisticated analytical capabilities, can create unique market data that cannot be easily copied by competitors; thus, it is a strategic capability (Hartmann et al., 2016; Soto-Acosta & Meroño-Cerdán, 2008). The integration of IoT infrastructure and a firm's data processing and decision-making processes is an interconnected, relational, and socially complex capability that is path-dependent and causally ambiguous, satisfying the definition of a source of sustained competitive advantage (Barney, 1991; Teece, 2018).

2.2.2. Dynamic Capabilities Theory: Sensing, Seizing, and Transforming in IoT Ecosystems

In evolving environments, competitive advantage comes not only from owning resources but also from the capacity to reconfigure them. Dynamic Capabilities Theory deals with this by a firm's ability to "integrate, build, and reconfigure internal and external competences to address rapidly changing environments' (Teece et al., 1997, p. 516). The Internet of Things (IoT) directly supports all three microfoundations of dynamic capabilities (sensing, seizing, and transforming) (Teece, 2007; Helfat et al., 2007).

- **Sensing:** IoT provides an unparalleled opportunity to sense opportunities and threats with real-time information streams from products, operations, and customer contexts. This allows them to have high-resolution perspectives of deviations in the market and operations and better emotional foresight (Krotov, 2017; Kindström et al., 2013).
- **Seizing:** Organizations can seize opportunities more swiftly by leveraging real-time data. Acting on the data in real time can enable organizations to deploy data-driven services quickly, optimize prices rapidly, or reallocate supply chain resources quickly in patterns that align with shifting demand (Westerman et al., 2014; Kindström et al., 2013). Reality-based information from the IoT will ensure much faster informed investment decisions and adjustments to business models based on evidence within operating databases.
- **Transforming:** IoT sources ongoing organizational transformations by providing real-time data to reconstruct (re-design) processes, enabling potential new partnerships for resourcing new technology, and even transforming the business model as a whole. Business innovation and transformation will become a perpetual cycle of learning and adjustment to keep pace with shifting strategies in dynamic environments (Nambisan et al., 2017; Vial, 2019).

2.2.3. Socio-Technical Systems Theory: Alignment of Human and Technological Subsystems

Socio-technical Systems (STS) theory, which was originally developed from studies of worker-technology interactions, posits that the performance of an organization is maximized when social and technical subsystems are designed together (Pasmore et al., 1982; Trist, 1981). The social subsystem encompasses people, skills, organizational structures, and culture, whereas the technical subsystem comprises the tools and technologies that accomplish the work. STS theory is pertinent to IoT transformation because it articulates a major cause of implementation failure:

dedicating excessive attention to technology, and insufficient attention to human and organizational aspects (Ghaffari et al., 2019; Bostrom & Heinen, 1977). Realizing the full potential of IoT demands co-designing novel work processes, building data literacy skills among employees, creating a culture of trust in data usage, and evolving leadership styles to manage human-machine teams (Sony & Naik, 2020; Parker & Grote, 2022). When the social subsystem is ignored, resistance increases, adoption fails, and the potential of the technology is diminished.

2.3. Conceptualising IoT as a Strategic Enabler

2.3.1. IoT as a Technology and IoT as a Transformative Enabler

To appreciate the impact of IoT, it is important to distinguish between IoT as a technology and strategic enabler. IoT technology comprises sensors, actuators, network protocols, and data platforms (Atzori et al., 2010). In this sense, the value of IoT lies in its technical functions, such as data acquisition or remote control of detected objects. In contrast, IoT, as a strategic enabler, is fundamentally transformational in terms of how value is created and captured (Porter & Heppelmann, 2014; Nambisan, 2017). This distinction changes the focus from technology to new activities and outcomes that enable an organization to be capable of. For instance, IoT has sparked a shift from selling products to offering the business model of products as a service, fostered unprecedented levels of integration of supply chains, and enabled adaptive and intelligent processes in organizations (Verhoef et al., 2021; Coreynen et al., 2017). The distinction is pivotal: firms that think about IoT as a technology are likely to achieve generic or incremental efficiencies, whereas companies that embrace it as a strategic enabler are likely to achieve transformative business outcomes (Saarikko et al., 2020).

2.3.2. Strategic Alignment and Digital Maturity Models

The effectiveness of IoT as a strategic enabler depends on its alignment with a wider business strategy. In the absence of this alignment, many IoT initiatives remain ad hoc projects that do not gain traction within the organization and do not provide any competitive advantage (Chan & Reich, 2007; Henderson & Venkatraman, 1993). Strategic alignment helps ensure that an investment in the IoT is targeted at addressing a critical business challenge or significant market opportunity, thus linking the attributes of the IoT to business performance. The path to leveraging IoT as an enabler is not linear but rather evolves through the phases described in maturity models for digital technologies (Westerman et al., 2014; Gill & VanBoskirk, 2016). Maturity models typically illustrate a linear progression, beginning with limited and localized uses aimed at operational efficiency (e.g., automation). As the organization becomes more proficient in applying IoT, it moves toward more interconnected applications to maximize efficiency across siloed functional parts (Kane et al., 2017). Finally, in the later stages, the organization utilizes the IoT for business model innovation, which creates additional revenue opportunities and establishes a wider partner ecosystem (Frank et al., 2019; Westerman et al., 2014). Digital maturity models represent a path for organizations to follow, which develops situational knowledge of their current capabilities, sets appropriate goals, and implements the challenges of organizational and technical change to fully realize the strategic capabilities of the IoT.

3. IOT AND ORGANISATIONAL CHANGE

Introducing the IoT into an organization is not merely a matter of upgrading technology; it is a transformative organizational change that challenges and fundamentally alters the established core configurations, processes, cultures, and capabilities of the organization. Serving as a strategic enabler, IoT demands a systems-based conceptualization of change in the organization, where the adoption of a technology is managed alongside deep-seated internal change.

3.1. IoT-driven Organisational Transformation

3.1.1. Redefining Business Models, Structures, and Processes

The adoption of IoT fundamentally changes how companies create, deliver, and capture value, resulting in challenging business models (Porter & Heppelmann, 2014). The most apparent change is the transformation from product-centric to service-centric models, also called servitization (Coreynen et al., 2017). Continuous data streams from connected products enable firms to deliver product outcomes and improve performance. For example, industrial equipment manufacturers can offer "power-by-the-hour" or predictive maintenance services, generating not only continuous revenue streams but also upstream and one-to-one customer relationships (Lee & Lee, 2015). Such a transformation of business models requires organizational structure transformation. Traditional functional silos (e.g., R&D, manufacturing, and customer services) impede value creation in the IoT context (Vial, 2019). Real-time data should be freely shared throughout the organization to promote coordinated actions. This necessitates coordination with a more integrated, cross-functional team coalition centered around value streams or the customer's journey (Yoo et al., 2010). Thus, core business processes move from being reactive to being proactive and predictive. Instead of repairing equipment after use and failure, predictive maintenance algorithms use IoT data to allow scheduled services before a breakdown occurs. Similarly, supply chain processes have changed from periodic, forecast-based replenishment (Tjahjono et al., 2017; Fatorachian & Kazemi, 2018) to demand-sensing and automated inventory replenishment.

3.1.2. Transition from Traditional Hierarchies to Data-Driven, Agile Organisations

IoT enables a movement away from rigid, top-down hierarchies to more agile and decentralized organizational structures. Traditional hierarchical structures often lack the speed required to act on the high-velocity real-time data generated by IoT systems (Galbraith, 2014). With frontline employees and operational teams having direct access to relevant data and analytical insights, IoT enables decentralized decision-making (Mithas et al., 2011). Decentralized decision-making enables faster responses to operational issues and changing market conditions, which is a key characteristic of organizational agility (Dubey et al., 2019). Organizations have less dependence on managerial command-and-control and more dependence on data-driven protocols and empowered autonomous teams, resulting in a more adaptive and resilient organization.

3.2. Cultural and Leadership Shifts

(a) The Role of Leadership in Fostering Digital Culture and Innovation Readiness

The effectiveness of any IoT-driven transformation is challenging and contingent on leadership. Leaders should approve technology budgets and do more than simply approve them. Leaders need to create a strong strategic relational narrative about how the IoT will transform business from the present to the future (Westerman et al., 2014). This consists of explaining the "why" of the changes and reinforcing them on a continuous basis across colleagues in the organization. Leaders are also responsible for fostering a digital culture that legitimizes data-driven decision making, transparency, and learning (Saarikko et al., 2020). Data in this culture are appreciated as a main asset, and continuous experimentation and psychologically safe learning from failures are sought as a natural part of being innovative under an uncertain technological terrain (Kane et al., 2017). Leaders themselves model these behaviors, often turning decisions based on intuition to decisions driven by IoT systems, where evidence is a fact (McAfee & Brynjolfsson, 2012).

(b) Change Management in IoT Adoption

Owing to changes in existing processes, roles, and power balances, IoT can raise substantial internal resistance. Therefore, change management is an essential component of any IoT strategy (Matt et al., 2015). A structured approach to navigating the human side of the change process is necessary to subdue employee anxiety towards performance and getting on board with the change. This includes communicating the objectives, processes, and outcomes of the change consistently and clearly, involving employees in the design of the new process, and providing adequate training and support (Vial, 2019). A helpful starting point to gain traction would be to have tangible evidence of success from early prototypes or projects to demonstrate potential success and convince any naysayers of why the change will have value (Westerman et al., 2014).

3.3. Capability Development and Workforce Transformation

(a) Reskilling, Data Literacy, and Cross-functional Collaboration

The implementation of IoT makes some existing skills irrelevant while requiring new ones. This implies a strategic orientation toward workforce transformation through reskilling and upskilling (Dremel et al., 2017). As repetitive manual and cognitive work become more automated, human employees value shifts to activities that require complex problem solving and critical and creative thinking. A major requirement across the workforce is data literacy: an employee's ability to read, interpret, create, and communicate data as information (Gebayew et al., 2018). This skill is no longer specific to data specialists; it is required for employees in all roles to consider and interpret whether the information derived from the IoT might inform their job duties. It also necessitates a large-scale increase in cross-functional teamwork that obliterates some of the separation between departments, operations, IT, and marketing (Nambisan et al., 2017).

(b) Human-Machine Integration and its Organisational Implications

The integration of humans and intelligent machines in the workplace is accelerated by the Internet of Things (IoT). This is clearly more than automation; it is augmentation, whereby technology aids human performance. Augmented reality glasses add digital content to a technician's view or to collaborative robots ("cobots") that operate with humans in manufacturing and logistics (Dwivedi et al., 2021). The implications of this study for organizations are significant. Job roles should be redefined to create the best combination with machines, avoiding the pitfalls of both human and machine performance (Parker & Grote, 2022). Performance management systems, workplace safety systems, and ethical guidelines should be developed and revised for hybrid work. Emphasis has shifted from managing people to managing a collaborative system of people and machine actors.

3.4. Barriers and Enablers

(a) Internal Resistance, Cybersecurity Concerns, and Integration Complexity

Despite their potential, there are serious obstacles to the IoT transformation. Internally, resistance to change continues to be a major challenge owing to the fear of job loss, loss of power or authority, and/or a simple unwillingness to abandon ingrained behaviors (Ghaffari et al., 2019). Cybersecurity is a top priority in terms of technology. Each connected device offers an entry point for nefarious individuals, vastly extending the organization's attack surface and exposing it to high-risk exposures for data privacy and operational risk (Al-Fuqaha et al., 2015). Another significant technical hurdle is the complexity of integration. Many organizations have difficulty integrating a new IoT platform with their legacy IT systems, such as Enterprise Resource Management (ERP) systems and/or Manufacturing Execution Systems (MES). This problem is aggravated by the inherent lack of interoperability standards, which leads to fragmented and siloed IoT applications (Frank et al., 2019).

(b) Success Factors from Empirical Evidence

Empirical research has highlighted several important enablers that make IoT-based transformations more likely to succeed. Consistently, the most prominent enabler is unyielding top management support, as it provides strategic alignment, the needed resources, and helps legitimize the change effort (Luthra et al., 2020). A salient enabler of management support is the explicit alignment between IoT initiatives and strategic business goals, which circumvents technology-led initiatives without business value. A gradual, iterative implementation starting with a pilot to learn and show value conversion before scaling works better than a big-bang high-risk initiative (De Vass et al., 2018). Creating strong internal capabilities, particularly in data analytics, is critical for converting raw IoT data into actionable insights (Dubey et al., 2019). Additionally, successful firms tend to form ecosystem collaborations with syndicates of technology vendors, startups, and research universities for the diversity of expertise needed for complex IoT solutions (Nambisan et al., 2017).

4. IOT AND SUPPLY CHAIN TRANSFORMATION

IoT serves as a key accelerant in the transformation of supply chain management from a linear, sequential function to a highly interconnected, intelligent, and responsive ecosystem. IoT delivers unparalleled levels of real-time data and connectedness, which allows long-standing issues of visibility and coordination to be addressed while developing new capabilities for efficiency, collaboration, and resilience.

4.1. Digital Supply Chain Evolution

A modern supply chain is viewed as the sum of its stages. Supply Chain 3.0 saw the first wave of digitalization and focused on internal process control automation through technologies such as Enterprise Resource Planning (ERP) and Warehouse Management Systems (WMS) (Butner, 2010). This increased functional performance, although operations still behaved in silos and were based on historical data and forecasts. With the introduction of Industry 4.0, including the Internet of Things (IoT), Supply Chain 4.0 was designed. Supply Chain 4.0 is characterized by hyper-connectivity, where cyber-physical systems cooperate to form an intelligent data-driven network (Tjahjono et al., 2017). Supply Chain 4.0 takes advantage of the Internet of Things, big data analytics, and artificial intelligence for real-time visibility, predictive capabilities, and a greater level of automation and integration across network partners (Ben-Daya et al., 2019). Supply Chain 4.0 shifted the focus from the operational optimization of singular functions to the end-to-end optimization of the value chain. Recently, Supply Chain 5.0 emerged as an extension of Supply Chain 4.0, based on the technology folks of 4.0, but re-established themes regarding human-centricity, sustainability, and resilience in supply chains (Frederico, 2021). This newly evolved setting is intended to have supply chains that are efficient, intelligent, socially responsible, and agile enough to survive major disruptions. IoT remains the foundational enabler of Supply Chain 5.0, as it enables data to support circular economy models, improves worker safety through human-machine interactions, and builds the adaptive capacity necessary to achieve resilience (Ivanov, 2021).

4.2. IoT-enabled Visibility and Integration

One longstanding issue in supply chain management is limited visibility beyond an organization's immediate tier-one suppliers and customers. The IoT addresses this issue directly by creating a seamless digital thread to facilitate end-to-end visibility. IoT sensors affixed to products, pallets, and shipping containers report the location, status, and condition (e.g., temperature, humidity, and shock) of goods throughout the supply chain (Zhou et al., 2017). This represents more than periodic updates from traditional barcode scanning; it provides continuous real-time information. In the context of data-driven analytical models, this allows predictive analytics regarding more accurately estimated times of arrival and early alerts for potential delays (Dubey et al., 2019). Through the use of a shared platform to synchronize data, each partner in the supply chain, from raw material suppliers to end retailers, works from a single source of truth, thereby minimizing information asymmetries and alleviating the bullwhip effect; that is, demand variability increases as the supply chain moves up (De Vass et al., 2018). High-fidelity data creates transparency that was not possible before. Transparency differs from visibility in that it entails mutual awareness of processes, inventory levels, and risk levels among all network participants (Kamari et al., 2019). For example, a manufacturer can view the production status of a material at a supplier's facility, a logistics provider can see a shipping container's condition in real time, and a retailer can precisely monitor inventories arriving onsite. This mutual awareness allows for the proactive joint resolution of problems that may arise and promotes increased trust and accountability among partners.

4.3. Operational Efficiency and Decision Agility

IoT, which provides granular and real-time data from the physical world, leads to a major transformation in operational efficiency and faster and better decisions. In manufacturing and logistics, IoT sensors on machinery, vehicles, and equipment enable the monitoring of operational health and the prediction of failures before they occur. Transitioning from reactive to predictive maintenance can reduce unplanned downtime and supply chain disruptions (Lee & Lee, 2015). In warehousing, IoT-enabled smart shelves and automated guided vehicles enable accurate real-time inventory counts, saving cycle counting, reconciling stock discrepancies, and safely inventorying less safety stock while lowering carrying costs (Ben-Daya et al., 2019). In logistics, real-time tracking and the use of traffic and weather data lead to the dynamic routing of shipments to minimize fuel consumption and improve lead times (Rejeb et al., 2019). Real-time data fundamentally change the way supply chain decisions are made. Decisions can no longer be based only on historical patterns and static plans; they can now be made dynamically in real time based on live events (Wamba et al., 2017). For example, if a quality problem is detected by sensors at a supplier's facility, the manufacturer is automatically notified and can make changes to production schedules or use a different supplier's source. The use of sensors to quickly detect and respond to events is decision agility, which is essential for competing in uncertain, volatile markets (Dubey et al., 2019).

4.4. Collaboration and Value Co-Creation

IoT enables inter-organizational relationships to evolve from transactional exchanges to cooperative partnerships in a wider digital ecosystem.

(a) IoT Ecosystems and Inter-organizational Networks

To realize the full potential of the IoT, one should be a part of the ecosystem that connects beyond the traditional buyer-supplier network. Organizations should collaborate in an ecosystem comprising technology companies, analytics companies, and others from their supply chain, all working off the same platform through data and information sharing (Nambisan et al., 2017). Value is co-created in this ecosystem. For example, a manufacturer may gather data on customer usage of its product and then share it with its suppliers to enhance the design of the part, or even with their logistics provider to optimize the idling of spare parts. This value is beneficial to each organization (Rymaszewska et al., 2017).

(b) Combining IoT Ecosystems with AI, Blockchain, and Digital Twins

The real disruptive potential of IoT arises from its combination with complementary advanced technologies.

- **Artificial Intelligence (AI):** AI and/or machine learning algorithms are required to make sense of the vast amount of information generated by IoT devices. AI can recognize complex patterns, perform automatic repetitive decisions, and generate predictive insights that are impossible for humans to identify while turning raw data into strategic intelligence (Dubey et al., 2019).
- **Blockchain:** Coupled with IoT, blockchain technology can provide a safe, immutable, and transparent ledger for all transactions within the supply chain. It enhances tracing, deters fraudsters, and creates trust between organizations that may not have a direct relationship; it is valuable in intricate, multiple-tier supply chains (Saberi et al., 2019; Kshetri, 2018).
- **Digital Twins:** An ultra-realistic digital twin indicates a representation of observable attributes from a physical supply chain asset, process, or network, and is constantly fed with updated primitive information from IoT-sensed attributes. This allows managers to estimate the impact of their decisions, test immediate contingency protocols, and leverage customer demand in a risk-free virtual environment before entering a scarce constrained physical world (Fatorachian & Kazemi, 2021).

4.5. Sustainability and Resilience

In addition to efficiency and cost savings, the Internet of Things (IoT) is a major enabler of two strategic imperatives that are becoming increasingly relevant: the sustainability and resilience of the built environment.

(a) IoT in Circular Economy Models and Carbon Footprint Reduction.

IoT enables tracking and monitoring capabilities that are invaluable to a circular economy. By applying sensors to products, organizations can identify an asset's lifecycle, assess its state, and know when to retrieve, recover, or recycle it (Kamble et al., 2020). IoT also advances environmental sustainability by optimizing resource usage. Smart logistics reduces emissions from fuel, precision agriculture minimizes water and chemicals, and smart building systems improve energy consumption in warehouses and factories (Rejeb et al., 2022).

(b) Adaptive Supply Chains with Resilience after COVID-19

Global disruptions due to COVID-19 have revealed the fragility of optimized but brittle supply chains (Ivanov 2020). Consequently, the strategic shift has focused on resilience - the capacity to forecast, absorb, and bounce back from disruptions (Choi et al., 2020). The IoT is a fundamental component of smart cities. Real-time visibility acts as an early warning agent, enabling firms to identify disruptions more rapidly. Timely insights allow firms to react to contingency plans, such as rescinding production to a different location or rerouting products, thereby continuing their adaptive capacity and flexibility in managing uncertainty (Dubey et al., 2020).

5. INTEGRATIVE FRAMEWORK: IOT AS A DUAL TRANSFORMATION LEVER

The previous sections discussed the effects of IoT on organizational change and supply chain transformation as distinct but related areas. The true strategic value of IoT occurs when these two areas of transformation are viewed and managed as a combined, mutually reinforcing system instead of two separate transformations. This section presents an integrative framework that uses the IoT as a double lever, driving internal organizational change and external supply network integration to deliver superior business performance.

5.1. Linking Organisational and Supply Chain Transformation

Although the progression from internal organizational change to external supply chain performance is not linear, it is cyclical and interdependent. The development of internal capabilities is a necessary precursor to external collaboration; however, the expectations of a connected supply chain can often be an impetus for internal change. Without first establishing the necessary internal capabilities and structures, organizations will not achieve deep supply chain integration. For example, real-time data produced from IoT-enabled supply chains are essentially worthless if an organization does not possess a data-driven culture and analytical capabilities to analyze and act on data (Saarikko et al., 2020). Furthermore, cross-functional teams and agile system processes should share common internal pathways to leverage the end-to-end workflows that IoT will unlock across the supply network (Galbraith, 2014). Without an internal agile structure, the organization would not be able to turn external data into timely, overarching actions, making technological deficiencies yield the worst interest. Consequently, internal changes are required to enhance external network performance (De Vass et al., 2018).

In contrast, externally connected IoT ecosystems generate an internal transformation process. Being connected to supply chain partners on common data platforms requires new protocols, standards, collaborative technologies, and more transparent work processes, thereby pushing the organization to further integrate and eliminate internal functional silos. This allows for greater transparency and visibility of supplier production schedules and customer inventories, thereby developing internal networks to act more quickly and efficiently. Thus, external forces on supply chain connections are a massive catalyst for internal organizational change, allowing both internal capabilities and external performance to co-evolve (Fatorachian & Kazemi, 2018).

5.2. Conceptual Model of IoT-Enabled Business Transformation

The proposed conceptual model, depicted in Figure 1, shows the strategic pathway for business performance, where IoT serves as a source of dual transformation, influencing internal organizational processes and external supply chain relationships. The model incorporates elements of the Resource-Based View (RBV) and Dynamic Capabilities View (DCV). IoT capabilities serve as valuable, rare, and inimitable technological resources that are strategically used when enacted through agility (dynamic capability) and integration (relational capability). The sequential mediation of IoT capabilities on organizational agility, supply chain integration, and business performance illustrates how firms transform technological investments into sustainable benefits. This depicts Teece's (2018) statement on the need to engage in sensing, seizing, and transforming activities to achieve performance benefits from digital potential. It also supports Dyer and Singh's (1998) relational perspective, which emphasizes collaborative routines and trust to achieve superior inter-firm performance.

The model features a layered capability architecture in which technological, organizational, and relational dimensions are interfaced to create business value. The model demonstrates that IoT investments should be aligned with agility and integration initiatives to achieve sustainable competitive advantage.

Figure 1. Conceptual Model of IoT-enabled Business Transformation

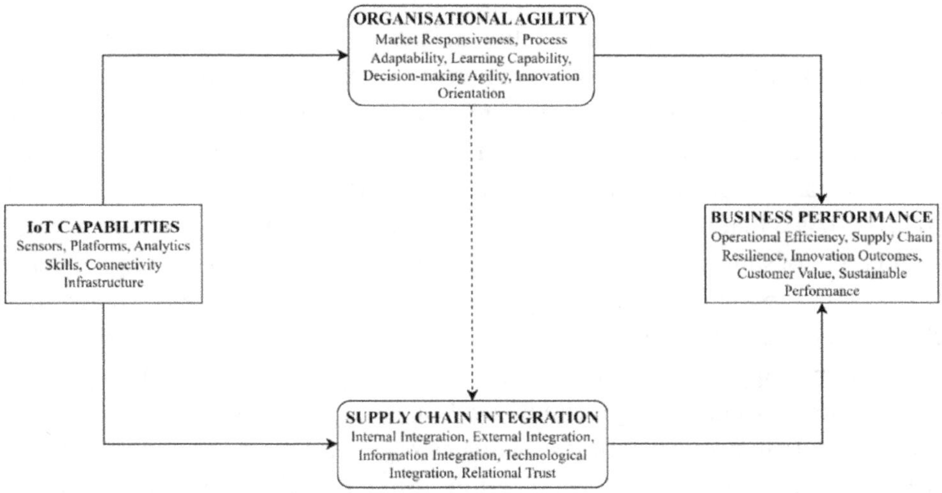

Source: *Authors' work (2025)*

5.2.1. IoT Capabilities and Organisational Agility

IoT capabilities represent a firm's digital competence in connecting assets, collecting real-time data, and analyzing data for decision-making. These capabilities include sensors, analytics platforms, digital skills, and connectivity infrastructure, which together form the basis of visibility and automation across business processes. Firms with an established IoT foundation can continuously monitor their operations, anticipate disruptions, and adapt accordingly. This enables organizational agility, which consists of market responsiveness, process adaptability, learning orientation, and innovativeness. Empirical studies have validated that IoT firms are agile and adaptive. Ahmed et al. (2022) found that IoT capabilities enhance process adaptability and decision-making agility in a manufacturing environment. Sullivan et al.

(2023) further demonstrated that IoT-enabled analytics also increased firms' ability to dynamically reconfigure operations and drove agile learning loops. Framed within dynamic capabilities, IoT serves as a sensing and seizing mechanism to enable firms to identify market opportunities and configure resources for a quick response (Teece, 2018). IoT capabilities provide a technology-based foundation to realize agility to increase real-time situational awareness, enhancing learning capability and decision process quality, which forms the basis for organizations to adapt effectively to environmental turbulence.

5.2.2. Organisational Agility and Supply Chain Integration

Agility is an organizational capability that helps firms convert the informational advantages of IoT into action within the organization and with other actors. Agile firms can enhance communication, synchronize preparatory activities, and coordinate supply chain actors using digital information. Agility also allows firms to manage uncertainty and respond relatively quickly to supplier or customer needs. Niu et al. (2022) revealed that organizations with a high level of agility were able to achieve greater types of supply chain integration because they understood the data and made swift changes to operations to bring together supply chain partners. Trocin et al. (2023) found that agility facilitates relational trust, transparency, and collaborative action among supply chain firms and encourages integration. Thus, agility serves as a behavioral bridge linking technological capability and inter-organizational coordination. Organizational agility strengthens supply chain integration, as it allows organizations to turn digital responsiveness into collaborative synchronization, both in steady internal processes and for actors in a network that come together and work as one by using anticipatory adaptation and thrusting forward with knowledge sharing.

5.2.3. Supply Chain Integration and Business Performance

Supply chain integration (SCI) includes internal, external, technological, and relational integration, which aligns partner firms' information systems, goals, and processes. Applying SCI effectively improves efficiency, resilience, and innovation, making information flow and collaborative decision making between inter-organizational partners seamless. Mashat et al. (2024) established that supply chain integration enabled by the Internet of Things (IoT) improves firm performance by enabling better coordination, information flow, and innovation outcomes. Niu et al. (2022) similarly noted that in coordinated supply chains, resilience is higher and customer satisfaction is even higher when continuous real-time data drive supply chain decisions. With a relational view (Dyer & Singh, 1998) of supply chain integration, relational rents are created as advantages that flow from one firm to another through trust, mutual access to information, and shared learning. Supply chain integration operationalizes the constructs of agility through inter-organizational collaboration, thereby enabling technological and behavioral capabilities to convert into real economic value for the business: efficiency, innovation, and resilience.

5.2.4. Organisational Agility and Business Performance

Organizational agility directly supports business performance by allowing organizations to sense and act on environmental changes faster than their competitors do. An agile organization can change its business strategies, quickly redeploy resources, and continuously innovate, creating greater value for customers and competitiveness in the marketplace. According to Gao et al. (2020), agility can enhance a firm's performance by creating flexibility as process structures modify and swift innovation, specifically in the context of digital transformation. Ahmed et al. (2022) also concluded that above-average agility promotes firm performance through increasing operational efficiency and responsiveness features for sustainable performance. Thus, agility becomes a meta-capability that develops firm performance by providing capability conditions to create measurable performance outputs, such as profitability, customer satisfaction, and innovation. Agility asserts performance through timely adaptation to strategies, innovations, and optimal processes. Firms that leverage advanced technologies and agility outperform those that focus on static efficiency.

5.2.5. IoT Capabilities and Supply Chain Integration

IoT capabilities have a limited direct impact on supply chain integration because they also provide real-time visibility, interconnectivity, and automation between network partners. IoT infrastructure can coordinate with less than complete agility by uniting supplier, production, and logistics data throughout the value chain. Moyne and Iskandar (2017) showed that industrial IoT increases inter-organizational visibility and technological interoperability, making it easier to digitally connect partners. Trocin et al. (2023) showed that IoT capabilities can enhance both information and technological integration through real-time data communication. However, IoT-based integration will only deliver full strategic benefits if agile management coordinates and facilitates full data interpretation and action. It is important to note that agile management makes sense from a strategic perspective, but may not always be the case from a tactical standpoint. IoT capabilities set the technological foundation for integration, whereas agility structures the foundational strategic capacity. Therefore, companies that implement favorable technology coupled with agile management are likely to establish deeper and more effective integration.

5.2.6. IoT Capabilities and Business Performance

The relationship between IoT capabilities and business performance is mainly indirect through organizational agility and supply chain integration. IoT technologies alone do not yield better performance. When IoT readiness and data are utilized in the agile decision process and through integrated supply chain processes, performance benefits are obtained. Ghobakhloo and Iranmanesh (2021) found that the effect of digital transformation on firm performance operates primarily through indirect effects comprising intermediate capabilities such as agility and integration. Mashat et al. (2024) also showed that the impact of IoT on performance is completely mediated through supply chain integration, providing evidence that the potential of technology requires complementary capability development. Therefore, IoT capabilities improve business performance through a series of improvements. Technology delivers data and connectivity, agility facilitates the utilization of data to generate actions, and integration incorporates these actions as part of collaborative networks to increase performance.

5.3. The Strategic Pathway

IoT-enabled transformation is not a one-time change; it is a planned journey that proceeds through incremental stages of maturity, as shown in Table 1. As an organization acquires IoT capabilities and traverses the linkages in the proposed conceptual model, it moves from simple automation to full autonomy. The strategic journey represents a relationship between IoT maturity and internal/external capabilities to take the organization through incremental improvements to systemic change.

- **Stage 1: Automation (Operational Efficiency):** In the early stages, organizations implement IoT for isolated, localized activities that drive operational efficiency. The emphasis is on automating current activities, such as applying sensors to achieve predictive maintenance on a production line or tracking assets in a warehouse. In this early stage, the scope of the impact primarily occurred in the functional silos.
- **Stage 2: Integration (Process Optimization):** With increased maturity, organizations seek to integrate IoT data across several functions and key external partners. The focus shifted from automating activities to optimizing the entire process. For instance, production data can be obtained and shared for logistics and procurement to create a more synchronized flow of materials. This stage requires organizational agility to manage new integrated cross-functional workflows.

- **Stage 3: Transformation (Business Model Innovation):** At this advanced stage, the organization utilizes rich, integrated data streams to transform its business model. Servitization begins when organizations employ connected product data to provide value-added services and value propositions (Coreynen et al., 2017). This demands a high level of organizational agility and integrated supply chains within a collaborative ecosystem of partners (Westerman et al., 2014).
- **Stage 4: Autonomy (Intelligent Ecosystem):** The highest level of maturity utilizes IoT and AI-enabled autonomous decision-making in the supply network. At this stage, the supply chain can be self-optimized. A network can automate delivery changes as a result of disruption, follow patterns, and adjust production schedules as demand signals arise or even issue procurement orders autonomously without any human input. This is a manifestation of a truly intelligent, adaptive, and autonomous supply ecosystem (Ivanov, 2021).

Table 1. The Strategic Pathway

Stage	Focus	Description
Stage 1: Automation	Operational efficiency & task automation	IoT-based control of very discrete operational activities
Stage 2: Integration	Cross-functional and partner process optimisation	Inter-organizational synchronization of data and resources
Stage 3: Transformation	Business model innovation & servitisation	Very agile, integrated service models with digital leadership
Stage 4: Autonomy	AI + IoT-enabled intelligent ecosystems	Complete automation, real-time optimization, self-adjusting decision making

Source: Authors' work (2025)

6. DISCUSSIONS

This section identifies the principal strategic, operational, and policy-level implications taken from the analysis of the IoT as a dual lever for transformation will be discussed in this section. The implications do not represent prescriptive advice; rather, they aim to offer realizable guidance for leaders in organizations, supply chain leadership, and the public sector and governmental stakeholders responsible for building the digital economy.

6.1. Strategic Implications for Organisations

The effective use of IoT as a means of transformative business development requires a purposeful and strategic approach to establish new organizational capabilities and leadership. Managers need to understand that competitive advantage comes not from the technology itself but from the dynamic capabilities that the IoT enables the firm to develop to adjust and adapt to environmental changes. This requires purposeful efforts to develop the three primary micro-foundations of dynamic capabilities (Teece, 2007). Organizations should first establish higher-level sensing capabilities by implementing data analytics initiatives to better analyze the information generated by IoT devices and identify market changes and operational issues (George et al., 2014). To act on the opportunities uncovered by these insights, managers should establish cross-functional teams and utilize agile organizational structures that support quicker and more decentralized decisions (Galbraith, 2014). Finally, leadership should have a continuous transformation capacity that draws on IoT insights to question current business models, promote experimentation and idea experimentation, and strategically allocate resources to innovative data-based services (Nambisan et al. 2017).

The most important contribution to the success of organizations in this journey is clear leadership. Senior management should take early ownership of the transformation work and support the change effort by defining an organization-wide vision that outlines the transformation of IoT into business outcomes and engages senior management to collectively support and enact the vision across the organization (Westerman et al., 2014; Vial, 2019). One primary role of leadership is to establish a digital culture that encourages data-based decisions, which rely on establishing expectations of transparency and psychological safety for ideas to be tested (Saarikko et al., 2020). One barrier to understanding adoption is a recognized skills issue; thus, leadership should commit to genuine investment in human capital. Organizations will benefit from implementing extensive re-skilling or up-skilling training focused on data literacy-based analysis or similar competencies, so that the employee base is on par with the technology utilized (Dremel et al., 2017).

6.2. Supply Chain Implications

The key implication for supply chain professionals is the transition from linear management to managing a dynamic, interconnected, and responsive value network. A connected supply chain can provide a full degree of value only by improving data interoperability and real-time responsiveness. Managers should support common data standards and shared platforms to negate technical fragmentation and data silos that degrade end-to-end visibility (Ben-Daya et al., 2019). Interoperability is a precondition for responsiveness because real-time data are only relevant if timely actions can be executed. Thus, the first step in redesigning supply chain processes is to be more agile rather than depend on rigid long-term plans to facilitate dynamic planning cycles. Second, operational teams should be empowered to make local decisions using live information and automated alerts to establish supply chains that sense and respond to disruptions and opportunities in real time (Durvey et al., 2019).

6.3. Policy and Ecosystem Implications

The successful implementation of IoT across sectors is not simply reliant on a network of individual firms engaging in IoT but instead relies heavily on a supportive ecosystem influenced by government policy, joint industry efforts, and common standards. Policymakers play an important role in creating an IoT-friendly environment by investing in the necessary digital infrastructure, such as 5G, and through clear and uniform regulations for data privacy and cyber security to establish trust in public perceptions and offer legal certainty to businesses (Weber, 2010). Industry alliances and standards organizations are required to overcome the hurdle of interoperability. By establishing common technical standards and protocols, the devices and platforms of different vendors can communicate effectively (Al-Fuqaha et al., 2015). Collaboration in this manner reduces vendor lock-in, creates a more open and competitive market, and is an important step toward realizing the eventual network benefits of a connected economy.

7. CONCLUSION

This chapter conceptualizes the Internet of Things (IoT) not just as a technology, but as an organizational-wide transformation strategy. The transformation opportunity is due to the IoT's unique capability of enabling both extensive internal organization transformation and transforming external supply chain networks. The findings suggest that the path from technology investment to sustainable competitive advantage is not straight or even guaranteed; it is dependent on an organization's adaptive capabilities and the agility of that strategy. This chapter suggests that the value of IoT in a strategic sense is founded on organizational agility and a reinterpretation of the ecology of structures, cultures, and capabilities to enable data-driven decision-making and response. This agile internal action is a critical precondition for achieving advanced supply chain integration, which enables better visibility, collaboration, and resilience in network ecosystems. The framework here integrates this journey by summarizing agility and integration as the leading facilitating capabilities for harnessing IoT technology resources into actual/bottom-line performance. In modern terms, sustainable competitive advantage does not come from technology but from the enforced synergy of technological systems, human capabilities, and organizational processes. However, achieving this synergy would require an integrated socio-technical model that considers IoT as part of the overall strategy of digital economy-oriented organizational transformation.

REFERENCES

Ahmed, A., Bhatti, S. H., Gölgeci, I., & Arslan, A. (2022). Digital platform capability and organizational agility of emerging market manufacturing SMEs: The mediating role of intellectual capital and the moderating role of environmental dynamism. *Technological Forecasting and Social Change*, *177*, 121513. DOI: 10.1016/j.techfore.2022.121513

Al-Fuqaha, A., Guizani, M., Mohammadi, M., Aledhari, M., & Ayyash, M. (2015). Internet of Things: A survey on enabling technologies, protocols, and applications. *IEEE Communications Surveys and Tutorials*, *17*(4), 2347–2376. DOI: 10.1109/COMST.2015.2444095

Atzori, L., Iera, A., & Morabito, G. (2010). The internet of things: A survey. *Computer Networks*, *54*(15), 2787–2805. DOI: 10.1016/j.comnet.2010.05.010

Barney, J. (1991). Firm resources and sustained competitive advantage. *Journal of Management*, *17*(1), 99–120. DOI: 10.1177/014920639101700108

Ben-Daya, M., Hassini, E., & Bahroun, Z. (2019). Internet of things and supply chain management: A literature review. *International Journal of Production Research*, *57*(15-16), 4719–4742. DOI: 10.1080/00207543.2017.1402140

Ben-Daya, M., Hassini, E., & Bahroun, Z. (2019). Internet of things and supply chain management: A literature review. *International Journal of Production Research*, *57*(15-16), 4719–4742. DOI: 10.1080/00207543.2017.1402140

Bharadwaj, A. S. (2000). A resource-based perspective on information technology capability and firm performance: An empirical investigation. *Management Information Systems Quarterly*, *24*(1), 169–196. DOI: 10.2307/3250983

Borgia, E. (2014). The Internet of Things vision: Key features, applications and open issues. *Computer Communications*, *54*, 1–31. DOI: 10.1016/j.comcom.2014.09.008

Bostrom, R. P., & Heinen, J. S. (1977). MIS problems and failures: A socio-technical perspective. Part I: The causes. *Management Information Systems Quarterly*, *1*(3), 17–32. DOI: 10.2307/248710

Butner, K. (2010). The smarter supply chain of the future. *Strategy and Leadership*, *38*(1), 22–31. DOI: 10.1108/10878571011009859

Chan, Y. E., & Reich, B. H. (2007). IT alignment: What have we learned? *Journal of Information Technology*, *22*(4), 297–315. DOI: 10.1057/palgrave.jit.2000109

Choi, T. Y., Rogers, D., & Vakil, B. (2020). Coronavirus, supply chains, and the future of manufacturing. *Harvard Business Review*.

Coreynen, W., Matthyssens, P., & Van Bockhaven, W. (2017). Boosting servitization through digitization: Pathways and dynamic resource configurations for manufacturers. *Industrial Marketing Management, 60*, 42–53. DOI: 10.1016/j.indmarman.2016.04.012

De Vass, T., Shee, H., & Miah, S. J. (2018). The effect of "Internet of Things" on supply chain integration and performance: An organisational capability perspective. *AJIS. Australasian Journal of Information Systems, 22*, 1734. Advance online publication. DOI: 10.3127/ajis.v22i0.1734

Dremel, C., Wulf, J., Goutier, M., & Brenner, W. (2017). How AUDI is navigating the digital transformation. *MIS Quarterly Executive, 16*(4), 289–306.

Dubey, R., Gunasekaran, A., Childe, S. J., Bryde, D. J., Giannakis, M., Foropon, C., Roubaud, D., & Wamba, S. F. (2019). Big data analytics and artificial intelligence pathway to operational performance under the effects of entrepreneurial orientation and environmental dynamism: A study of manufacturing organisations. *International Journal of Production Economics, 226*, 107599. DOI: 10.1016/j.ijpe.2019.107599

Dubey, R., Gunasekaran, A., Childe, S. J., Papadopoulos, T., Hazen, B., Giannakis, M., & Roubaud, D. (2020). Examining the role of big data and predictive analytics in the era of industry 4.0 and the COVID-19 pandemic on supply chain resilience. *International Journal of Logistics Management, 32*(1), 137–162. DOI: 10.1108/IJLM-05-2020-0205

Dubey, R., Gunasekaran, A., Childe, S. J., Papadopoulos, T., Luo, Z., Wamba, S. F., & Roubaud, D. (2019). Can big data and predictive analytics improve social and environmental sustainability? *Technological Forecasting and Social Change, 144*, 534–545. DOI: 10.1016/j.techfore.2017.06.020

Dwivedi, Y. K., Hughes, L., Ismagilova, E., Aarts, G., Coombs, C., Crick, T., Duan, Y., Dwivedi, R., Edwards, J., Eirug, A., Galanos, V., Ilavarasan, P. V., Janssen, M., Jones, P., Kar, A. K., Kizgin, H., Kronemann, B., Lal, B., Lucini, B., & Williams, M. D. (2021). Artificial Intelligence (AI): Multidisciplinary perspectives on emerging challenges, opportunities, and agenda for research, practice and policy. *International Journal of Information Management, 57*, 101994. DOI: 10.1016/j.ijinfomgt.2019.08.002

Dyer, J. H., & Singh, H. (1998). The relational view: Cooperative strategy and sources of interorganizational competitive advantage. *Academy of Management Review, 23*(4), 660–679. DOI: 10.2307/259056

Fatorachian, H., & Kazemi, H. (2018). A critical investigation of Industry 4.0 in manufacturing: Theoretical operationalisation framework. *Production Planning and Control*, *29*(8), 633–644. DOI: 10.1080/09537287.2018.1424960

Fatorachian, H., & Kazemi, H. (2021). Impact of Industry 4.0 on supply chain performance. *Production Planning and Control*, *32*(1), 63–81. DOI: 10.1080/09537287.2020.1712487

Frank, A. G., Dalenogare, L. S., & Ayala, N. F. (2019). Industry 4.0 technologies: Implementation patterns in manufacturing companies. *International Journal of Production Economics*, *210*, 15–26. DOI: 10.1016/j.ijpe.2019.01.004

Frederico, G. F. (2021). From Supply Chain 4.0 to Supply Chain 5.0: Findings from a systematic literature review and research directions. *Logistics (Basel)*, *5*(3), 49. DOI: 10.3390/logistics5030049

Galbraith, J. R. (2014). *Designing the agile organization*. Jossey-Bass.

Gao, P., Zhang, J., Gong, Y., & Li, H. (2020). Effects of technical IT capabilities on organizational agility: The moderating role of IT business spanning capability. *Industrial Management & Data Systems*, *120*(5), 941–961. DOI: 10.1108/IMDS-08-2019-0433

Gebayew, C., Hardini, I. R., Panjaitan, G. H. A., & Kurniawan, N. B. (2018). A systematic literature review on digital transformation. *In 2018 International Conference on Information Technology Systems and Innovation (ICITSI)* (pp. 260–265). IEEE. DOI: 10.1109/ICITSI.2018.8695912

George, G., Haas, M. R., & Pentland, A. (2014). Big data and management. *Academy of Management Journal*, *57*(2), 321–326. DOI: 10.5465/amj.2014.4002

Ghaffari, K., Lagzian, M., Kazemi, M., & Malekzadeh, G. (2019). A socio-technical analysis of Internet of Things development: An interplay of technologies, tasks, structures and actors. *Foresight*, *21*(6), 640–653. DOI: 10.1108/FS-05-2019-0037

Ghobakhloo, M., & Iranmanesh, M. (2021). Digital transformation success under Industry 4.0: A strategic guideline for manufacturing SMEs. *Journal of Manufacturing Technology Management*, *32*(7), 1376–1397. DOI: 10.1108/JMTM-11-2020-0455

Gill, M., & VanBoskirk, S. (2016). The digital maturity model 4.0. *Forestry Research*, *1*, 1–15.

Gubbi, J., Buyya, R., Marusic, S., & Palaniswami, M. (2013). Internet of Things (IoT): A vision, architectural elements, and future directions. *Future Generation Computer Systems*, *29*(7), 1645–1660. DOI: 10.1016/j.future.2013.01.010

Hartmann, P. M., Zaki, M., Feldmann, N., & Neely, A. (2016). Capturing value from big data – a taxonomy of data-driven business models used by start-up firms. *International Journal of Operations & Production Management, 36*(10), 1382–1406. DOI: 10.1108/IJOPM-02-2014-0098

Helfat, C. E., Finkelstein, S., Mitchell, W., Peteraf, M. A., Singh, H., Teece, D. J., & Winter, S. G. (2007). *Dynamic Capabilities: Understanding Strategic Change in Organizations*. Blackwell Publishing.

Henderson, J. C., & Venkatraman, N. (1993). Strategic alignment: Leveraging information technology for transforming organizations. *IBM Systems Journal, 32*(1), 4–16. DOI: 10.1147/sj.382.0472

Iansiti, M., & Lakhani, K. R. (2014). Digital ubiquity: How connections, sensors, and data are revolutionizing business. *Harvard Business Review, 92*(11), 91–99.

Ivanov, D. (2020). Predicting the impacts of epidemic outbreaks on global supply chains: A simulation-based analysis on the coronavirus outbreak (COVID-19/SARS-CoV-2) case. *Transportation Research Part E, Logistics and Transportation Review, 136*, 101922. DOI: 10.1016/j.tre.2020.101922 PMID: 32288597

Ivanov, D. (2021). Supply Chain Viability and the COVID-19 pandemic: A conceptual and formal generalisation of four major adaptation strategies. *International Journal of Production Research, 59*(12), 3535–3552. DOI: 10.1080/00207543.2021.1890852

Kamari, M., Ismaili, A., & Gencel, C. (2019). The role of transparency in supply chains: A literature review. In *Proceedings of the 31st Annual Conference of the Nordic Logistics Research Network (NOFOMA)*.

Kamble, S. S., Gunasekaran, A., & Gawankar, S. A. (2020). Achieving sustainable performance in a data-driven agriculture supply chain: A review for research and applications. *International Journal of Production Economics, 219*, 179–194. DOI: 10.1016/j.ijpe.2019.05.022

Kane, G. C., Palmer, D., Phillips, A. N., Kiron, D., & Buckley, N. (2017). Achieving digital maturity. *MIT Sloan Management Review, 59*(1), 1–20.

Kindström, D., Kowalkowski, C., & Sandberg, E. (2013). Enabling service innovation: A dynamic capabilities approach. *Journal of Business Research, 66*(8), 1063–1073. DOI: 10.1016/j.jbusres.2012.03.003

Kolk, A. (2017). The social responsibility of international business: From ethics and the environment to CSR and sustainable development. *Journal of World Business, 51*(1), 23–34. DOI: 10.1016/j.jwb.2015.08.010

Krotov, V. (2017). The Internet of Things and new business opportunities. *Business Horizons, 60*(6), 831–841. DOI: 10.1016/j.bushor.2017.07.009

Kshetri, N. (2018). 1 Blockchain's roles in meeting key supply chain management objectives. *International Journal of Information Management, 39*, 80–89. DOI: 10.1016/j.ijinfomgt.2017.12.005

Lee, I., & Lee, K. (2015). The Internet of Things (IoT): Applications, investments, and challenges for enterprises. *Business Horizons, 58*(4), 431–440. DOI: 10.1016/j.bushor.2015.03.008

Luthra, S., Kumar, A., Zavadskas, E. K., Mangla, S. K., & Garza-Reyes, J. A. (2020). Industry 4.0 as an enabler of sustainability diffusion in the supply chain: An analysis of influential strength of drivers in an emerging economy. *International Journal of Production Research, 58*(5), 1505–1521. DOI: 10.1080/00207543.2019.1660828

Mashat, B., Katircioglu, S., & Tanovic, E. (2024). Impact of Internet of Things adoption on organizational performance: A mediating analysis of supply chain integration, performance, and competitive advantage. *Sustainability (Basel), 16*(6), 2250. DOI: 10.3390/su16062250

Matt, C., Hess, T., & Benlian, A. (2015). Digital transformation strategies. *Business & Information Systems Engineering, 57*(5), 339–343. DOI: 10.1007/s12599-015-0401-5

McAfee, A., & Brynjolfsson, E. (2012). Big data: The management revolution. *Harvard Business Review, 90*(10), 60–68. PMID: 23074865

Miorandi, D., Sicari, S., De Pellegrini, F., & Chlamtac, I. (2012). Internet of things: Vision, applications and research challenges. *Ad Hoc Networks, 10*(7), 1497–1516. DOI: 10.1016/j.adhoc.2012.02.016

Mithas, S., Ramasubbu, N., & Sambamurthy, V. (2011). How information management capability influences firm performance. *Management Information Systems Quarterly, 35*(1), 237–256. DOI: 10.2307/23043496

Moyne, J., & Iskandar, J. (2017). Big Data Analytics for Smart Manufacturing: Case Studies in Semiconductor Manufacturing. *Processes (Basel, Switzerland), 5*(3), 39. DOI: 10.3390/pr5030039

Nagy, J., Oláh, J., Erdei, E., Máté, D., & Popp, J. (2018). The role and impact of Industry 4.0 and the Internet of Things on the business strategy of the value chain—The case of Hungary. *Sustainability (Basel), 10*(10), 3491. DOI: 10.3390/su10103491

Nambisan, S. (2017). Digital Entrepreneurship: Toward a Digital Technology Perspective of Entrepreneurship. *Entrepreneurship Theory and Practice*, *41*(6), 1029–1055. DOI: 10.1111/etap.12254

Nambisan, S., Lyytinen, K., Majchrzak, A., & Song, M. (2017). Digital Innovation Management: Reinventing innovation management research in a digital world. *Management Information Systems Quarterly*, *41*(1), 223–238. DOI: 10.25300/MISQ/2017/41:1.03

Niu, B., Dai, Z., Liu, Y., & Jin, Y. (2022). The role of Physical Internet in building trackable and sustainable logistics service supply chains: A game analysis. *International Journal of Production Economics*, *247*, 108438. DOI: 10.1016/j.ijpe.2022.108438

Parker, S. K., & Grote, G. (2022). Automation, algorithms, and beyond: Why work design matters more than ever in a digital world. *Applied Psychology*, *71*(4), 1171–1204. DOI: 10.1111/apps.12241

Parviainen, P., Tihinen, M., Kääriäinen, J., & Teppola, S. (2017). Tackling the digitalization challenge: How to benefit from digitalization in practice. *International Journal of Information Systems and Project Management*, *5*(1), 63–77. DOI: 10.12821/ijispm050104

Pasmore, W. A., Francis, C., Haldeman, J., & Shani, A. (1982). Sociotechnical systems: A North American reflection on empirical studies of the seventies. *Human Relations*, *35*(12), 1179–1204. DOI: 10.1177/001872678203501207

Porter, M. E., & Heppelmann, J. E. (2014). How smart, connected products are transforming competition. *Harvard Business Review*, *92*(11), 64–88.

Rejeb, A., Keogh, J. G., & Treiblmaier, H. (2019). Leveraging the Internet of Things and Blockchain Technology in Supply Chain Management. *Future Internet*, *11*(7), 161. DOI: 10.3390/fi11070161

Rejeb, A., Zailani, S., Rejeb, K., Seuring, S., & Treiblmaier, H. (2022). The Internet of Things and the circular economy: A systematic literature review and research agenda. *Journal of Cleaner Production*, *350*, 131439. DOI: 10.1016/j.jclepro.2022.131439

Rymaszewska, A., Helo, P., & Gunasekaran, A. (2017). IoT powered servitization of manufacturing–an exploratory case study. *International Journal of Production Economics*, *192*, 92–105. DOI: 10.1016/j.ijpe.2017.02.016

Saarikko, T., Westergren, U. H., & Blomquist, T. (2020). Digital transformation: Five recommendations for the digitally conscious firm. *Business Horizons*, *63*(6), 825–839. DOI: 10.1016/j.bushor.2020.07.005

Saberi, S., Kouhizadeh, M., Sarkis, J., & Shen, L. (2019). Blockchain technology and its relationships to sustainable supply chain management. *International Journal of Production Research*, *57*(7), 2117–2135. DOI: 10.1080/00207543.2018.1533261

Sony, M., & Naik, S. (2020). Industry 4.0 integration with socio-technical systems theory: A systematic review and proposed theoretical model. *Technology in Society*, *61*, 101248. DOI: 10.1016/j.techsoc.2020.101248

Soto-Acosta, P., & Meroño-Cerdán, Á. L. (2008). Analyzing e-business value creation from an RBV perspective. *International Journal of Information Management*, *28*(1), 49–60. DOI: 10.1016/j.ijinfomgt.2007.05.001

Sullivan, Y., Wamba, F., & Dunaway, M. (2023). Internet of Things and Competitive Advantage: A Dynamic Capabilities Perspective. *Journal of the Association for Information Systems*, *24*(3), 745–781. DOI: 10.17705/1jais.00807

Teece, D. J. (2007). Explicating dynamic capabilities: The nature and microfoundations of (sustainable) enterprise performance. *Strategic Management Journal*, *28*(13), 1319–1350. DOI: 10.1002/smj.640

Teece, D. J. (2018). Business models and dynamic capabilities. *Long Range Planning*, *51*(1), 40–49. DOI: 10.1016/j.lrp.2017.06.007

Teece, D. J. (2018). Profiting from innovation in the digital economy: Enabling technologies, standards, and licensing models in the wireless world. *Research Policy*, *47*(8), 1367–1387. DOI: 10.1016/j.respol.2017.01.015

Teece, D. J., Pisano, G., & Shuen, A. (1997). Dynamic capabilities and strategic management. *Strategic Management Journal*, *18*(7), 509–533. DOI: 10.1002/(SICI)1097-0266(199708)18:7<509::AID-SMJ882>3.0.CO;2-Z

Tjahjono, B., Esplugues, C., Ares, E., & Pelaez, G. (2017). What does Industry 4.0 mean to supply chain? *Procedia Manufacturing*, *13*, 1175–1182. DOI: 10.1016/j.promfg.2017.09.191

Trist, E. (1981). The evolution of socio-technical systems. In Van de Ven, A. H., & Joyce, W. F. (Eds.), *Perspectives on Organization Design and Behavior* (pp. 19–75). Wiley.

Trocin, C., Mikalef, P., Papamitsiou, Z., & Conboy, K. (2023). Responsible AI for Digital Health: A Synthesis and a Research Agenda. *Information Systems Frontiers*, *25*(6), 2139–2157. Advance online publication. DOI: 10.1007/s10796-021-10146-4

Verhoef, P. C., Broekhuizen, T., Bart, Y., Bhattacharya, A., Dong, J. Q., Fabian, N., & Haenlein, M. (2021). Digital transformation: A multidisciplinary reflection and research agenda. *Journal of Business Research, 122*, 889–901. DOI: 10.1016/j.jbusres.2019.09.022

Vial, G. (2019). Understanding digital transformation: A review and a research agenda. *The Journal of Strategic Information Systems, 28*(2), 118–144. DOI: 10.1016/j.jsis.2019.01.003

Vrchota, J., Řehoř, P., Maříková, M., & Pech, M. (2021). Critical success factors of project management in relation to Industry 4.0 for sustainability of projects. *Sustainability (Basel), 13*(1), 281. DOI: 10.3390/su13010281

Wade, M., & Hulland, J. (2004). The resource-based view and information systems research: Review, extension, and suggestions for future research. *Management Information Systems Quarterly, 28*(1), 107–142. DOI: 10.2307/25148626

Wamba, S. F., Akter, S., Edwards, A., Chopin, G., & Gnanzou, D. (2017). How 'big data' can make big impact: Findings from a systematic review and a longitudinal case study. *International Journal of Production Economics, 165*, 234–246. DOI: 10.1016/j.ijpe.2014.12.031

Weber, R. H. (2010). Internet of Things – New security and privacy challenges. *Computer Law & Security Review, 26*(1), 23–30. DOI: 10.1016/j.clsr.2009.11.008

Weber, R. H., & Weber, R. (2010). *Internet of Things: Legal perspectives*. Springer Science & Business Media. DOI: 10.1007/978-3-642-11710-7

Wernerfelt, B. (1984). A resource-based view of the firm. *Strategic Management Journal, 5*(2), 171–180. DOI: 10.1002/smj.4250050207

Westerman, G., Bonnet, D., & McAfee, A. (2014). *Leading digital: Turning technology into business transformation*. Harvard Business Press.

Whitmore, A., Agarwal, A., & Da Xu, L. (2015). The Internet of Things—A survey of topics and trends. *Information Systems Frontiers, 17*(2), 261–274. DOI: 10.1007/s10796-014-9489-2

Yoo, Y., Henfridsson, O., & Lyytinen, K. (2010). The new organizing logic of digital innovation: An agenda for information systems research. *Information Systems Research, 21*(4), 724–735. DOI: 10.1287/isre.1100.0322

Zhou, W., Piramuthu, S., Chu, F., & Chu, C. (2017). RFID-enabled flexible warehousing. *Decision Support Systems, 98*, 99–112. DOI: 10.1016/j.dss.2017.05.002

Zuehlke, D. (2010). SmartFactory—Towards a factory-of-things. *Annual Reviews in Control*, *34*(1), 129–138. DOI: 10.1016/j.arcontrol.2010.02.008

Chapter 2

Strategic Business Transformation Through IoT:

Enhancing Operational Efficiency and Business Model Innovation

Sankar
J.N.N. Institute of Engineering, India

P. V. Raja Suganya
Velammal Engineering College, India

R. Abitha
Vel Tech Multi Tech Dr. Rangarajan Dr. Sakunthala Engineering College, India

N. P. Ponnuviji
R.M.K. College of Engineering and Technology, India

K. Saravanan
http://orcid.org/0000-0002-0672-1568
SRM Institute of Science and Technology, India

A. Maheshwari
http://orcid.org/0009-0009-7357-8536
SRM Institute of Science and Technology, India

V. Nivaskumar
http://orcid.org/0009-0003-6080-3999
R.M.K. Engineering College, India

ABSTRACT

The Internet of Things (IoT) is transforming the strategic landscape of modern enterprises by enabling enhanced operational efficiency and driving innovation in business models. This chapter explores the foundational components of IoT, its integration into enterprise systems, and its role in real-time monitoring, automation, and predictive analytics. It highlights how IoT empowers organizations to shift from product-centric to service-oriented models, create new revenue streams, and improve customer engagement. The chapter also examines cross-industry applications,

DOI: 10.4018/979-8-2600-1263-5.ch002

including manufacturing, healthcare, retail, and agriculture, while addressing key challenges such as data privacy, interoperability, and organizational resistance. Looking ahead, the convergence of IoT with AI, blockchain, and 5G points to a future of autonomous, ethical, and sustainable deployments.

1. INTRODUCTION

1.1 Background of Digital Transformation and the Fourth Industrial Revolution

The fourth industrial revolution (4IR) is the new period of evolution that significantly alters the lifestyle, working and interaction processes(Gadre, M., & Deoskar, A. 2020). Fourth Industrial Revolution contrasts other industrial revolutions that have been characterized by mechanization, electrification and automation in the fourth industrial revolution, technologies are becoming fused to produce what is termed as a fusion of technologies that are blurring the lines between the physical, digital and biological worlds. It is being driven by the pace of growth of novel technologies such as artificial intelligence (AI), robotics, the Internet of Things (IoT), blockchain, augmented reality and big data analytics(Javaid, M et al 2022). Such technologies are not existing in a vacuum and are converging to create smart, networked systems that can act independently, in real time. The core of this transformation is the digital transformation that involves using digital technology by organizations to transform everything in their business. It is not only about getting new tools or platforms but also re-evaluating and re-engineering business models, processes of operation, mechanisms of value delivery, and approaches of customer engagement. Digital transformation enables organizations to be flexible, creative and more responsive to the changing market patterns and customer demands. It empowers the business to ensure that they utilize resources to the fullest, allow them to make improved decisions using data inspired findings and allow them to offer more personal customer experiences(Ghobakhloo M 2020).

The digital transformation is not a problem inside the corporate sector only. This digital transformation is transforming governments, medical institutions, learning and even simple social life. An illustrative case is the digital revolution that has led to smart cities, e governance, telemedicine, online education etcetera in order to make them more accessible, efficient and user friendly. The fourth Industrial Revolution is distinct in its rate as well as scope that keeps on rising exponentially. It is not a slow, linear process, but a rapid, disturbing transformation that challenges the current business ways and calls on a strategic reinvention. In the current competitive and technologically dynamic global economy, which is fast changing, organizations that never adopt digital transformation will be obsolete. Digital transformation is no longer a fad or even a choice, it is a strategic need. To remain relevant and win in this new industrial age, organizations and companies will have to take the initiative and invest in technology, revise their basic strategy and develop an environment of innovation and lifelong learning. The fourth Industrial revolution needs a more proactive strategy, and technology should be introduced in all operations so that the world becomes more connected, intelligent and adjustive.

1.2 Definition and Boundary of the Internet of Things (IoT)

The IoT is a massive network of all the physical objects that are interconnected with sensors, software and other technologies that allows them to collect, share and process data through the internet(Gokhale, M et al 2018). These are known as the smart devices or objects which can be as straightforward as refrigerators, thermostats and wearable fitness watch and as complex as industrial equipment, agricultural machines, medical devices and autonomous vehicles(Kumar et al 2020). IoT bridges the physical and digital divide when these devices become a part of one digital environment. The ability to transform passive objects into active members of a network is a feature of IoT. Smart devices are constantly generating massive data that can be analyzed to extract meaningful information, enable the company to make superior decisions, and enhance its functioning. As an example, a smart thermostat may learn about the preferences of the user and automatically adjust the temperature or an industrial IoT (IIoT) sensor on a production line may detect a machine outage end of life product in advance and trigger a massive downtime(Gubbi et al 2013). IoT is making the internet to be extended widely beyond the conventional computing devices such as desktops and smartphones. It helps us develop intelligent systems that can be operated with very limited human resources by developing intelligent systems that can be operated in varied environments hence making them automated, monitored and controlled. Thus, IoT has no particular sector or application, but it is a big number of domains. Some of the notable areas are smart homes, smart cities, healthcare, agriculture and logistics. Real time visibility of operations and environments is also considered one of the primary advantages of IoT. It makes stakeholders more aware of the situation and allows them to respond to the alterations in the conditions in a timely manner. IoT systems can be applied to add transparency and responsiveness to things like monitoring air quality in cities, to tracking the movement of assets along international shipping paths. IoT as an enabling technology is increasingly gaining significance to both businesses and the societies, as they depend on the connected technologies to transform digitally. It allows coming up with smart services and data-driven solutions that will subsequently deliver a base of automation, innovation and improved customer experience.

Technologically speaking, the IoT is simply that: a technological innovation, yet it is also a model of creating smarter and more adjustive systems on the other end of the modernity spectrum of life(MAY P et al., 2025).

1.3 The Role of IoT in Transformation of Strategic Business

IoT is the one which is redefining the strategic path of the contemporary businesses. The possibilities of IoT in terms of operational improvements (i.e. automation, efficiency gains, cost reduction) are not very new, however the effects of IoT are far(Soumyalatha S. G. H 2016). It is a catalyst because it enables deep change in organizations to push the companies to abandon the reactive, traditional ways of working towards more proactive and predictive methods of decision making. IoT contributes to smarter hopefully data driven enterprises through the introduction of intelligence into products, processes and services. As an illustration, in the manufacturing industry, predictive maintenance through IoT enables the forecast of mechanical issues before they occur after real time measurements of equipment sensors. It minimizes downtime that is unexpected, extends the life of machines and greatly decreases the cost of maintenance. IoT smart shelves and In store analytics in the retail business are used to help businesses engage with their customers through personalized experiences, manage inventory and enhance store layouts with customer behavior. Similarly, remote patient monitoring is applicable to healthcare as a form of continuous monitoring of health, to intervene on patients and prevent hospitalization before it is too late, to enhance patient outcomes at low costs.

These are some of the ways in which IoT has changed whole value chain of designing products up to the customer support. And it is not just that it makes processes better, it transforms business models. In IoT, the shift is made to the service centric approach also known as servitization instead of the product centric approach. The service business can use the data regarding the usage of smart devices to offer customized services like performance based maintenance or subscriptions based services, which create new revenue sources and result in more customer loyalty. Moreover, IoT makes organizations agile and creative. Connected devices give real time insights, which allow prompt reaction to the market change and customer demand. This is responsive and this breeds the culture of constant improvement and innovation that is highly significant in the current competitive and fast world. Notably, IoT is not about a technological upgrade only, but is a strategic facilitator of sustainable competitive advantage. It helps it develop differentiated offerings, to act with efficiency and develop stronger customer relationships. Reliable use of IoT by companies has the potential to create new areas of productivity, customer interaction and innovation; enabling them to dominate the digital economy. The aspect of IoT in business change is complex. It supports the capability of new business models and data driven strategies that enable enterprises to be more responsive, competitive and future ready as a fast changing marketplace(Kuppusamy, P. 2019).

1.4 Objectives and Organization of the Chapter

This survey chapter has tried to provide a general image of how IoT is assisting strategic business transformation by enhancing the operational efficiency and innovation of business models. I have structured the chapter to mention the technical foundations and strategic uses of the IoT in other industries. It begins with the description of the significant elements and structure of IoT systems in a business frame. It then proceeds to describe how IoT has resulted in improved operational efficiency due to automation, predictive maintenance and efficient resource consumption. The chapter goes on to explain how the IoT has changed the business models and the shift of the business models towards data-driven services and new value propositions. Case studies of industries show the actual application of IoT and the outcomes that can be determined. Lastly, the chapter discusses the key challenges such as security, interoperability and organizational resistance, and develops future trends that will set the future of IoT in business. In this way, the survey, conducted in the form of a structured analysis, is aimed at giving the researchers, practitioners, and decision-makers deeper insights into the strategic implications of IoT.

2. FOUNDATIONS OF IOT WITHIN THE BUSINESS CONTEXT

2.1 Key Components of IoT

The IoT is anchored on an excellent system of inter-dependent components that enable easy collection, transportation, processing, and analysis of the data. At the back of any IoT system, there are sensors and actuators. Actuators transform digital signals into physical actions whereas sensors record physical world (temperature, pressure, humidity, motion or location) data in real time. It is these gadgets that act as the primary point of contact between the real and the virtual world. One of the enablers of connecting these sensors and actuators to computing resources and cloud services is connectivity. Communication technologies like Wi-Fi, Bluetooth, Zigbee, LoRaWAN, cellular (4G/5G) and Ethernet enable secure data transfer between different devices and systems. In the case of different use cases, various communication protocols are used in order to strike a balance between factors such as range, power consumption and data rate(Sathya et al., 2024).

To cope with the huge streams of data coming from IoT devices, cloud computing offers scalable storage and computing power. However, because of latency issues and the lack of bandwidth, edge computing has become a complementary solution. By processing data near the source (on gateways or local servers) edge computing makes it possible to achieve faster response times and minimise the load on central systems. This model of distributed computing is particularly useful in the industrial setting, autonomous vehicles, and real-time monitoring applications.

Lastly, raw sensor data needs to be extracted value from which is facilitated by data collection and analytics frameworks. There are data lakes, stream processing engine, machine learning model and visualization tools which allow organizations to extract actionable insights from the data in the data lake. However, in an IoT environment, with a good data governance and integration, IoT is a powerful asset for informed decision making and process optimization(Jaffrin et al 2025).

2.2 IoT Architecture for Enterprise Applications

For achieving complexity management and interoperability, a structured IoT architecture is needed in enterprise environments. Usually, there are four main layers of IoT systems, namely: device, network, platform, and application.

The device layer consists of all physical hardware that comprise of sensors, actuators, embedded devices and edge nodes. These are for sensing and the interaction with the environment. These devices are connected to the processing units and platforms with the help of the network layer through the communication protocols. This layer guarantees secure and reliable data transmission and can consist of LAN, WAN, or low-power networks, depending on an application.

The platform layer acts as the middleware, which gathers, stores and processes data. It consists of device management, identity and access control, data integration tools, and analytics engines. Major cloud providers provide enterprise-grade infrastructure that can scale, is secure and offers real time processing(Qian et al 2009).

The application layer delivers user-facing interfaces and decision support tools. These applications include dashboard applications for monitoring the performance of equipment to mobile applications for controlling smart homes or logistics.

To be successful in enterprise deployment of IoT, there is a need to integrate with the existing IT (Information Technology), OT (Operational Technology) infrastructure. This integration will mean that data from physical systems can be made compatible with business systems like ERP, CRM, and SCADA. A convergence of such is critical to deliver end to end digital visibility and automation through the value chain.

2.3 IoT Ecosystem Stakeholders

The deployment and success of IoT initiatives are dependent on a complex network of stakeholders creating, deploying, governing and using IoT systems. Successful deployment of IoT initiatives and success with IoT initiatives depend on a complex web of stakeholders involved in the creation, deployment, governance & use of IoT systems. Between this ecosystem are technology providers such as hardware manufacturers, software developers, cloud service provider and system integrators. These players are building core elements and platforms for rollout and sustenance of IoT. IoT technology is the main player and the main beneficiary of the businesses and organizations. IoT solutions are used to improve operations, reduce costs and deliver better customer experience and to create new business models. They have to find use cases, spend on infrastructure and make IoT initiatives strategic. Customers as well as end users are becoming active participants of the IoT ecosystem.

Their interactions with IoT-enabled products provide the companies with useful feedback and usage information that helps in enhancing services and personalizing offerings. Trust and privacy of the user are also important in the success of many consumer IoT applications. Lastly, standards organizations and regulators play a significant role in making sure that the implementation of the IoT technologies is safe, secure and ethical. This involves the making of policies governing data privacy, cyber security, use of spectrum as well as interoperability. The governments and international organisations are also coming up with structures that facilitate innovation whereas they minimise the risks. This is a collective set of stakeholders and comprises a dynamic and interdependent ecosystem that shapes the way the evolution and influence of the IoT is formed in business.

3. ENHANCING OPERATIONAL EFFICIENCY THROUGH IOT

3.1 Real-Time Monitoring and Predictive Maintenance

Some of the greatest contributions of IoT in the operating of businesses include the capacity to offer real-time tracking, and predictive maintenance. The IoT sensors installed in machinery in such industries as manufacturing can give a continuous stream of data that includes temperature, vibration, pressure, etc. of the machinery operation. The operators can use this data to present the health of equipment on-demand and detect anomalies that might be evidence of a failure that is about to happen. Rather than relying on the scheduled routine maintenance, which could be inefficient and expensive, predictive maintenance uses analytics and machine learning to predict a component's failure. This approach allows the businesses to schedule repairs only when there is a need to it which helps to reduce unplanned downtime and increases the life of the equipment.

In logistics, GPS and telematics enabled IoT devices enable firms to monitor the condition and location of vehicles and goods throughout the delivery chain. This will maximize fleet utilization, wastage of time and ensure timely interventions in case of route deviation or mechanical failures. Likewise, in the energy sector, utilities use IoT-enabled smart meters and sensors to track infrastructure in real-time so that they can identify faults early and reduce service outages. As a whole, the IoT-based monitoring and predictive maintenance contribute to the reduction of the costs of operations, improvement of safety, and the provision of a consistent level of the service delivery.

3.2 Process Automation and Optimization

One of the most significant forces of process automation and optimization of business processes is IoT, particularly to the complex environment, like a factory or huge service processes. One of the ways in which IOT can streamline and automate the industrial processes is the introduction of the so-called smart factories a hallmark of the Industry 4.0. The IoT networks enable the real-time coordination, adaptive control and autonomous decision-making of machines, robots and control systems. The IoT also contributes greatly to enhancing the workflow automation. Sensors can give rise to automatic behavior - such as automatic re-ordering of raw materials when the stock falls to a dangerously low level, or automatic re-driving of merchandise on a belt depending on quality inspection information. Such improvements are lean in character wherein waste is minimized and value is maximized. The IoT systems can ensure continuous monitoring of such KPIs as production rate, machine utilization and energy consumption and enable the managers to make decisions based on data allowing optimization of the processes and removing the inefficiencies. In addition, the IoT can be integrated with enterprise resource planning systems (ERP) to ensure that the operational activities are in line with the business goals. For example, the real-time production data can be used to make financial projections, plan workforce schedule and coordinate the supply chain. This degree of synchronization was hitherto hard to attain and is now a strategic strength in cut-throat markets.

3.3 Supply Chain and Inventory Management

IoT is changing supply chain and inventory management to allow more visibility, traceability and responsiveness along the value chain. Asset tracking using RFID tags, GPS units, and IoT sensors ensures that businesses are able to have up to date information on the location, condition, & status of inventory items, vehicles, and containers. This minimise the risk of lost goods, theft and spoilage, especially important in industries such as food, pharmaceuticals and high value manufacturing.

Demand forecasting also becomes better by the analysis of historical data along with live market indicators and trending in consumption. As an illustration, online payments with IoT-based point-of-sale system will provide real-time insight into customer buying behavior which can be utilized to forecast future demand more accurately. This understanding allows business organizations to mobilize dynamic resource management whereby, they can adjust the inventory levels and route of distribution real-time. Smart warehouses utilize automated guided vehicles (AGVs), robots and internet of things-based administration to control and enhance the inventory flow with minimum human interference. This results in more agile, efficient, and responsive supply chain that is capable of responding to the changing demands of customers and disruptions around the world.

3.4 Energy and Resource Efficiency

The IoT technologies are very significant in matters of energy and resource efficiency that on the other hand gain more importance towards the costs reduction and the sustainability of the environment. Smart buildings have lighting, HVAC, and water consumption systems, which are controlled by the IoT-enabled systems depending on the occupancy and environmental conditions. When nobody is in the room, sensors decide and take settings to conserve energy without compromising comfort. The smart grids apply the IoT to balance the supply & demand in real time, incorporating the renewable energy sources, and improving the load distribution. This decreases energy wastage and improves the grid reliability. In industrial environment, IoT solutions are used to monitor emissions, water consumption and waste generated, to ensure compliance with environmental laws and corporate sustainability objectives.

Environmental monitoring via IoT is also critical in such industries as agriculture, where soil moisture sensors, weather stations, and drone-based imagery help to develop accurate irrigation and fertilization strategies. These technologies conserve the usage of resources while maximizing yield. IoT helps to make the use of resources smarter, reduces operational costs and helps to create a more sustainable business model in all sectors.

4. BUSINESS MODEL INNOVATION DUE TO THE IOT ENABLED

4.1 From Products to Services

One of the most revolutionary changes that can be brought by IoT is the revolution of selling products to selling services, a trend that is commonly known as servitization. Companies in the past used to only make money from one-time sale of physical goods. However, with the help of IoT, it is possible to track the product usage and performance at all times and hence, pay-per-use, subscription-based, or outcome-based service models are possible. For instance, a manufacturer can provide compressed air as a service whereby it is charged on actual use and gives uptime assurance through predictive maintenance instead of selling an industrial compressor outright.

This transformation is not only able to generate recurring revenue streams but also develops long-term customer relations. With a fixed collection and analysis of data on the use of products, companies can offer proactive support, ensure the optimal functionality, and reduce downtime by customers. During the process, businesses are made into solution providers, where they will add value in the performance and results and not merely the physical assets. Internal change is also prompted by the change and it requires service management capabilities, new pricing model and real time support system to develop.

4.2 Data-Driven Value Creation

IoT generates massive data, and a possibility to monetize this data is one of the strongest business implications of IoT. Organizations can derive insights out of the operational data and the behavioral data in order to enhance internal decisions and in order to generate marketable assets. To give just an example, a smart city infrastructure provider has the chance to sell the data on traffic pattern to ride-hailing organizations or city planners. Similarly, the IoT players in the agricultural sector will be able to offer climate report, and soil report to insurance companies or the supply chains. This creates platform-based business models where businesses create digital ecosystems of device manufacturers, developers, and end-users. Such platforms enable third-party integration, sharing of data as well as development of applications, promoting innovation and extending the value proposition beyond a single firm.

This ecosystem thinking creates network effects and allows co-creation of value, and several stake holders benefit from the shared use of data and services. Companies that will implement this model will need to pay attention to governance, data ownership, and interoperability standards to create a fair and functional environment for participants.

4.3 Customization and Customer Engagement

IoT allows businesses to shift from the standardized offerings towards highly personalized products and services through the use of real time & historical data in order to customize experiences for individual customers. In the consumer domain, smart devices like wearables or connected home systems learn the preference of users as time goes by, modifying functionalities and providing recommendations. In B2B environments, it is possible to remotely customize industrial machines to perform to client-specific performance objectives or environmental conditions.

In addition, IoT enables real-time customer feedback loops, which enables companies to track the use of products and the response of customers in real-time. This constant feedback loop facilitates the faster cycles of innovation as companies can release updates, enhancements, or even new features based on live data of users. It also builds customer service because problems can be detected and addressed beforehand and thus enhance satisfaction and loyalty.

Such dynamic involvement generates opportunities for value co-creation where the users co-create products and services. As customers get more involved, businesses will have to invest in user-friendly interfaces, data privacy measures, and open communication to gain the trust of the users and improve the user experience.

4.4 New Revenues Streams and Market Opportunities

IoT brings new revenue streams as a result of product extensions, digital add-ons, and foray into adjacent or new market. For example, an automotive producer can complement the sale of a traditional car with telematics services, in-car entertainment subscriptions or insurance depending on behavior in car. Similarly, companies that used to be only physical product space players can become data and analytics players, using insights from IoT deployments.

This ability allows businesses to exploit cross-industry partnerships, where their data/platforms apply to other industries. An example of an enterprise that specializes in industrial equipment may discover new areas of application in energy management, optimization of facilities, or logistics, based on the universality of data streams in IoT.

Also, IoT assists companies to recognize untapped market segments, make applications and even scale solutions across various geographies. The ability to find emerging markets at high speed is highly crucial in the modern dynamic business environment and it can enhance the competitiveness and growth prospects in a grand manner.

5. CASE STUDIES AND INDUSTRY APPLICATIONS

5.1 Manufacturing (Industry 4.0)

The IoT plays a leading role in the implementation of the Industry 4.0, the fourth industrial revolution in the manufacturing industry. Such transformation occurs through the linking the conventional manufacturing processes and the recent digital technologies into creating smart factories. They are all highly developed production settings which are typified by the real time communication that is smooth between machines, systems and human operators. IoT supports this transformation as machines and equipment are becoming smart, as well as, connected and capable of gathering, disseminating and acting upon information. Smart factories have sensors installed in all parts of the production lines to measure a great number of parameters including the temperature, pressure, vibration and equipment condition. The real time information is inexhaustible and manufacturers may continuously monitor the processes and make some changes on the spot to ensure efficiency, avoid failures and make the most of resources. The outcome is a more responsive, agile production system, able to make the required changes very fast to fluctuation in demand or conditions. One of the most radical application of IoT in the manufacturing industry is the use of digital twins. A virtual model of an object, machine or process that spans the life cycle of the object, including data collected by sensors, people and other devices that reflects its behavior over time, is known as a digital twin. Digital twins rely on the sensor measurements of IoT to model the behavior and predict the wear and tear and experiment with other operational conditions without exposing the actual machinery to dangers. One such application might be a digital twin of a turbine that evaluates patterns of stress in various conditions and engineers might operate using a design for proactive maintenance or may design to modify the design. It reduces downtime, enhances the life of equipment and lowers overall price. Another large scale innovation that can be effected by IoT involves predictive quality control. When you had to get to quality control, you had produced a product, and you ended up with garbage and scrap. IoT is allowing manufacturers to study the sensor data produced during the manufacturing process to realize early indicators of errors or deviations outside the quality standards. Since manufacturers are able to detect issues in their time, they are able to initiate corrective measures to address an issue prior to a product completion. It minimizes production wastage, enhances output, minimizes cost and time to market. Moreover, the supply chain is more transparent and traceable with the help of the integration of the IoT. Manufacturers are able to monitor the product lifecycle that includes the raw material and the delivery of the product to the customer making the process more accountable and trustworthy with customers. Concisely, the IoT is transforming how businesses are being manufactured, shifting towards more efficient and smarter, as well as data driven operations. Such innovations as digital twins and predictive quality control are useful to manufacturers who tend to reach greater productivity, reduce downtimes and enhance product quality, which are the marks of the Industry 4.0 age.

5.2 Healthcare

As the IoT revolutionizes the healthcare industry, the remote monitoring process is improving, diagnosis becomes more precise and patients become more involved. IoT is utilized in such a way that health related data is gathered and sent continuously and over connected devices and sensors and the healthcare providers can monitor their patient in real time and intervene in advance. One of the most notable and most common applications of IoT in healthcare is wearable devices, e.g. Smartwatches, fitness trackers and health bands. They will be able to constantly track such parameters as heart rate, body temperature, oxygen level, sleeping pattern and physical activity. These real time health data can be transmitted to healthcare professionals so that they can identify issues such as arrhythmias, breathing issues or irregular sleep patterns at an early stage. Early symptoms can be identified and appropriate interventions can be undertaken in a timely fashion to prevent the development of medical complications. Remote Patient Monitoring (RPM) systems have become an indispensable part of long term care for patients with chronic illnesses. Digital blood pressure monitors, glucose meters, ECG monitors and smart inhalers allow patients to monitor their health from home. These are IoT enabled devices which allow you to send data to the healthcare providers without regular in person visits and make sure that any aberration from normal health parameters is treated quickly. The good thing is patient convenience is increased, there are fewer hospital visits and clinicians are able to provide more individualized care. Also, IoT is being used by hospitals and healthcare facilities to enhance internal operations and resource management. Medical asset tracking, environmental condition management and patient and staff movement are all enabled by connected hospital devices. For example, smart beds are adjusted to the patient, so the bed will automatically adjust to give them the most comfortable, pressure relieving sleep possible, reducing the risk of bedsores. Real Time Location Systems (RTLS) are also used to track vital equipment like ventilators, infusion pumps and wheelchairs so when they are needed, they are available. Integration of IoT in healthcare leads to high efficiency in operations, clinical outcome and cost reduction. Instant supervision, early identification and preventive treatment can be used to deliver superior patient experiences and superior healthcare provision by IoT. To conclude, IoT is changing healthcare by introducing intelligent, interconnected solutions to real time monitoring, decisions made with data and effective management of healthcare. It is beneficial both to patients and providers, results in improved health outcomes, reduces resource stress and less sustainable healthcare systems.

5.3 Retail

IoT is transforming retail industry to help in increasing operational efficiency and revolutionize the way customers shop. We are linking the devices and smart systems to provide more data driven responsive environments, both in the back end operations to the front end customer engagement. Smart shelves are one of the best IoT applications in retail. These include RFID tagged shelves which are weight sensing and record inventory in real-time. It will also provide an automatic alert to the store workers when an item is out of stock or low in order so that they can replenish the stock before they lose out on a sale because a product is out of stock. Assists in ensuring the shopping experience with the customers is smooth and fulfilling. Automated checkout is another IoT technology. With IoT sensors and computer vision and machine learning, we can identify the products that our customers steal shop. It automatically charges the accounts of customers as they leave the store, and they do not have to wait in line. The technology eliminates the traditional checkouts, reducing the time of waiting and introducing convenience to the customer service. Besides this, retailers can have helpful customer analytics using IoT. Retailers can develop profound insights into shopping habits by tracking the movement patterns, the dwell time, and the interaction products. These understandings can be applied in tailoring marketing campaigns, store architecture and in store interaction. In addition to that, online and offline data can be combined using IoT and thus, customers get the same levels of services and personalization across all frontline experiences of the retailer. This integration is all seamless and promotes strengthening customer loyalty and sales. In short, IoT in retail facilitates inventory management, simplifies the checkout process and supplies data driven insights that make the shopping experience more enjoyable. The retailer is empowered to be more efficient in its operations, yet deliver personalized, engaging and convenient service to its customers.

5.4 Agriculture

In agriculture, the IoT supports the development of precision farming, data and automation are used to achieve the maximum in all the processes of management of crop and livestock. In fields, sensors monitor soil moisture, temperature and nutrients and the farmers apply water and fertilizers only where necessary no waste, maximum yield.

Livestock monitoring includes wearable IoT devices that are used to monitor the health, behavior, and position of the animals. These systems warn farmers about indications of illness, the change in eating habits, or calving events, so that they are able to intervene in time to enhance animal welfare and farm productivity.

Smart irrigation systems utilize real time weather information and soil sensors in controlling the delivery of water with a high degree of precision such that crops get the precise amount of water they need. These developments improve productivity and contribute to the implementation of sustainable practices in the context of climate change and resource shortage.

5.5 Smart Cities and Utilities

The use of IoT technology is important in the creation of smart cities whereby interconnectivity of the infrastructure enhances the city-life. Smart transportation systems depend on automated road sensors, GPS, and adaptive lights to congestion reduction, route optimization, and improved infrastructure of the public transportation. Smart bins in waste management are fitted with sensors that measure the amount of waste in the bin and alerts the collection services that the bin has to be emptied therefore minimizing unnecessary collection and efficient resource distribution. Smart grids combine IoT to equate the supply and demand of energy and distribute energy resources such as solar panels and address outages in a more efficient manner. Utility companies also leverage the use of IoT in leak detection of water networks, predictive maintenance of their electrical infrastructure as well as dynamic pricing models depending on the real-time consumption.

These IoT applications support cities in becoming more efficient and sustainable, as well as responsive to the needs of citizens, which leads to the better quality of life and urban resilience.

6. CHALLENGES AND RISKS

6.1 Data Privacy and Security

With more and more businesses embracing the IoT solutions, data privacy and security are some of the most important and difficult issues to overcome. IoT devices produce massive quantities of data, which can be in real time, from the user behavior to sensitive operational metrics. When not secured, this data is vulnerable to cybersecurity threats such as unauthorized access, malware & distributed denial of service (DDoS) attacks. The IoT ecosystems are heterogeneous and decentralized in nature and this makes them appealing to the attackers. IoT devices can be quite serious in case of data breaches. As an example, privacy laws, and trust may be broken in healthcare by breaching privacy through the release of personal health information through compromised healthcare monitoring devices of the patients. Manipulation of sensor data in a factory may disrupt the work or, further, jeopardize the safety. To add to all of that, businesses have to deal with a complicated system of data protection rules that must be supported by efficient data governance and insight into the data processing and usage and user consent. These threats can be done away with encryption and other secure communication protocols, frequent updates and authentication of devices, but at the steep cost of doing so.

6.2 Interoperability and Standards

The primary issue is that the IoT devices and platforms do not interoperate and are not premised on the standardized protocols. The market is fragmented with vendors all around with proprietary technologies and different communications protocols, thus integrating devices with them is typically custom development and inflates the cost and technical expenses. The outcome is that there is data siloing that prevents data from flowing seamlessly across systems and eventually eliminates the aspiration of integrated analytics and seamless automation. In the enterprise settings, where IoT systems need to interoperate with legacy IT and operational technology (OT) infrastructures, lack of standardized APIs and protocols becomes a critical challenge.

Industry group and standards organizations, such as the Industrial Internet Consortium (IIC), IEEE, and ISO, are moving toward more standardization, but adoption is still varied. Until there is a broad agreement on the standards of communication, both data formats and security protocols, companies need to be very careful about interoperability when they are designing or scaling IoT solutions.

6.3 Scalability and Infrastructure Readiness

Scalability is one of the major technical issues in deployment of IoT. With the increase in the number of connected devices, the organizations are facing a high demand on their network bandwidth, data processing and storage. Most of the legacy systems were never designed to deal with the large volume, velocity, and variety of data generated by IoT, and hence, there is need to upgrade the network infrastructure and computing architecture significantly.

One of the key trade-offs in deploying the IOT is to decide between the cloud computing and the edge computing. Although cloud-based platforms provide centralized processing and scalability, they introduce latency and might not be able to satisfy the real-time demands, especially in the case of the critical applications such as autonomous vehicles or remote surgery. On the other hand, edge computing handles data closer to its source, i.e., on the device or nearby gateway, and latency is minimized with less strain on the central networks. Nevertheless, it also requires distributed processing power and more advanced management of the devices.

Organizations have to evaluate the preparedness of their infrastructure for scale, such as 5G connectivity, edge capabilities, and data integration tools. Lack of proper investment and planning in scaling the IoT solutions can cause performance bottlenecks, additional costs, and an unreliable system.

6.4 Change Management and Organizational Resistance

Deployment of IoT is not a technical exercise but one that demands major organizational change. Many companies are subject to the resistance of change from the employees who do not know or do not believe in new technologies. This cultural inertia may affect the adoption, limit innovation, and diminish return on investment.

There is a need for new skills in data analytics, cyber security and systems integration in most cases of IoT adoption. Thus, to achieve a successful transformation, one has to heavily upskill the existing staff, hire new talent, or build partnerships with the technology providers. If not trained and supported, employees may find it hard to adjust to new workflows and tools, which will result in frustration and inefficiency.

Leadership buy-in is critical for the implementation of the changes that the organization needs to make for IoT success. Executives need to put into clear perspective the strategic value of IoT investments and align them with the overall business goals & create a culture of innovation & agility. Some of the change management strategies that can be used to deal with resistance and gain momentum in the organization include stakeholder engagement, pilot programs, and iterative implementation.

7. FUTURE DIRECTIONS AND EMERGING TRENDS

7.1 Merging of IoT With AI, Blockchain and 5G

The next stage of the evolution of the IoT is its integration with other revolutionary technologies, including AI, blockchain, and 5G networks. Each of these technologies has its own set of capabilities that when combined with IoT increases the ability of IoT to transform business.

AI and ML are becoming more and more integrated into the IoT systems in order to allow smart decision-making (Rezazadegan, R., & Sharifzadeh, M. 2022).

AI algorithms process huge datasets obtained from sensors and connected devices to detect patterns, forecast the outcomes, and automate procedures. This turns IoT systems not only reactive, but actively adaptive, for the best of the predictive maintenance to the customer personalization(Jagatheesaperumal et al 2021).

The blockchain technology enhances the IoT by addressing significant issues on the security, trust and transparency of the data. In a multi-stakeholder environment (such as a supply chain or an energy grid), blockchain may provide an immutable decentralized registry of IoT transactions: in such a system, no one can modify the data and trust can be established in the absence of a central entity. Smart contracts also allow the IoT devices to reach out to agreements automatically based on the stipulated conditions. Simultaneously, the implementation of the 5G connection opens a new dimension of speed, reliability, and low latency to the IoT networks. It is particularly important in the applications that demand real time response such as autonomous vehicles, remote surgery, and industrial robots. The ultra-low latency and massive device connectivity offered by 5G will drive the IoT ecosystems to become more scalable and high performance, and further drive the uptake in all sectors.

7.2 Autonomous IoT Systems

Autonomous IoT systems networks of devices that sense, process, decide and act in a manner requiring minimum human intervention is one of the new trends in the IoT environment. These systems are driven by the progress in edge computing, AI and self healing networks and are a shift from central control to distributed intelligence. For example, in smart manufacturing, IoT self-governing systems can track machine health, change production schedules and manage logistics without a human input. Similarly, IoT sensor-based drones and AI algorithms can provide us with the condition of crop health and treat it automatically in fields of agriculture. There are numerous benefits of this system, efficiency, reduced response time and human error. However, they are also challenging in new ways for accountability, governance and fail safe mechanisms of systems.

As machines start making decisions on their own, businesses need to be very precise in terms of setting limits for autonomy and ability to override systems.

Figure 1. Future Directions and Emerging Trends

7.3 Ethical and Sustainable IoT Deployments

As the society and business become more integrated with IoT, ethical considerations and sustainability goals are seeing the light of the day. Major issues are the proper use of personal data, the avoidance of unfair automated decision-making, and the reduction of environmental effects of massive device rollout. From an ethical point of view, companies need to guarantee that their IoT solutions comply with the principles of data privacy, consent, and transparency. This is particularly important in such industries as healthcare and smart cities where personal and behavioral data are usually collected without direct interaction. On the sustainability side, the energy use of billions of interconnected devices and the e-waste produced by the rapid hardware obsolescence is a major environmental problem. Companies are paying more attention to the design of energy-efficient IoT hardware, prolongation of device life cycles, and the implementation of the principles of a circular economy. Besides, IoT can generate sustainability through the applications that it supports, including energy-efficient buildings, precision agriculture, and smart grids, which maximize resource use and minimize emissions.

8. CONCLUSION

IoT has emerged as one of the powerful instruments that can lead to strategic business changes providing organizations with the tools they need to enhance operational efficiency and reimagine the traditional business model. IoT is able to apply connectivity and intelligence to physical assets by enabling real-time monitoring, predictive maintenance, automation of operations, and optimization of resources - making smarter, more agile operations. At the same time, the ability to gather and process massive data has led to the development of new value-generating patterns such as servitization, customized customer experience and the initiation of data-driven platforms and ecosystems. The strategic implication of the adoption of the IoT is enormous to the decision-makers. IoT is not merely a technological change but a paradigm shift on how business is done, how the organization engages with customers and also how the business is organized. To get the maximum benefits, the leaders should invest in scalable and secure infrastructures, develop a culture of innovation, and correlate IoT initiatives with the general corporate objectives. Also, to make IoT roll-out successful, inter-functional cooperation, workforce training, and learning and evolving will be needed. During the further evolution of IoT technologies, the success of future will depend on the opportunity to develop systems, which will not only be intelligent and interconnected and will be also secure, ethical, and human-centered. Data privacy, interoperability, scalability, and change management are some of the issues that organizations have to address with caution and foresight. In addition, as the world is becoming more interested in the notion of sustainability and social responsibility, the policies of IoT should be based on energy conservation, environmental consequences, and digital equity. Finally, IoT is not a fad, it is a business imperative to companies that would like to perform well in a world that is getting increasingly interrelated. Organizations that have flexible, secure and purpose driven strategies can achieve the potential of IoT in the long term.

REFERENCES

Gadre, M., & Deoskar, A. (2020). Industry 4.0–digital transformation, challenges and benefits. *International Journal of Future Generation Communication and Networking*, *13*(2), 139–149.

Ghobakhloo, M. (2020). Industry 4.0, digitization, and opportunities for sustainability. *Journal of Cleaner Production*, *252*, 119869. DOI: 10.1016/j.jclepro.2019.119869

Gokhale, P., Bhat, O., & Bhat, S. (2018). Introduction to IOT. *International Advanced Research Journal in Science. Engineering and Technology*, *5*(1), 41–44.

Gubbi, J., Buyya, R., Marusic, S., & Palaniswami, M. (2013). Internet of Things (IoT): A vision, architectural elements, and future directions. *Future Generation Computer Systems*, *29*(7), 1645–1660. DOI: 10.1016/j.future.2013.01.010

Jaffrin, L. C., Nithya, T., & Divya, J. (2025, April). IoT for Sustainable Development: Enhancing Environmental Efficiency and Resource Optimization. In *2025 5th International Conference on Trends in Material Science and Inventive Materials (ICTMIM)* (pp. 1224-1230). IEEE.

Jagatheesaperumal, S. K., Rahouti, M., Ahmad, K., Al-Fuqaha, A., & Guizani, M. (2021). The duo of artificial intelligence and big data for industry 4.0: Applications, techniques, challenges, and future research directions. *IEEE Internet of Things Journal*, *9*(15), 12861–12885. DOI: 10.1109/JIOT.2021.3139827

Javaid, M., Haleem, A., Singh, R. P., & Suman, R. (2022). Artificial intelligence applications for industry 4.0: A literature-based study. *Journal of Industrial Integration and Management*, *7*(01), 83–111. DOI: 10.1142/S2424862221300040

Kumar, K. V. R., Kumar, K. D., Poluru, R. K., Basha, S. M., & Reddy, M. P. K. (2020). Internet of things and fog computing applications in intelligent transportation systems. In *Architecture and security issues in fog computing applications* (pp. 131–150). IGI Global. DOI: 10.4018/978-1-7998-0194-8.ch008

Kuppusamy, P. (2019). Smart education using internet of things technology. In *Emerging Technologies and Applications in Data Processing and Management* (pp. 385–412). IGI Global. DOI: 10.4018/978-1-5225-8446-9.ch017

MAY. P. M. A., Savitha, V., Gayathri, S., & Mahalakshmi, S. (2025, April). Exploring Sustainable Computing: IoT, Big Data, and Energy-Efficient Solutions. In *2025 5th International Conference on Trends in Material Science and Inventive Materials (ICTMIM)* (pp. 1218-1223). IEEE.

Qian, L., Luo, Z., Du, Y., & Guo, L. (2009, December). Cloud computing: An overview. In *IEEE international conference on cloud computing* (pp. 626–631). Springer Berlin Heidelberg.

Rezazadegan, R., & Sharifzadeh, M. (2022). Applications of artificial intelligence and big data in industry 4.0 technologies. *Industry 4.0 Vision for Energy and Materials: Enabling Technologies and Case Studies*, 121-158.

Sathya, U., Hashini, S., Lakshmipriya, C., Varun, C. M., & Nalini, M. (2024, December). Emerging Trends and Future Prospects in Internet of Things (IoT) Technology. In *2024 International Conference on Sustainable Communication Networks and Application (ICSCNA)* (pp. 79-85). IEEE.

Soumyalatha, S. G. H. (2016, May). Study of IoT: Understanding IoT architecture, applications, issues and challenges. In *1st International Conference on Innovations in Computing & Net-working (ICICN16), CSE, RRCE. International Journal of Advanced Networking & Applications*, *478*, 14.

Chapter 3
Smart Ecosystems and Intelligent Enterprises: The Role of IoT in Reshaping Operational Agility

Varanasi Rahul
http://orcid.org/0000-0003-2407-7654
Jain University, India

N. Sathyanarayana
http://orcid.org/0000-0002-4185-7751
Jain University, India

A. Arunprakash
http://orcid.org/0000-0002-8025-681X
Jain University, India

L. B. Muralidhar
http://orcid.org/0000-0003-3453-613X
Jain University, India

B. U. Muthamma
http://orcid.org/0009-0001-3132-1910
CMR University, India

ABSTRACT

This chapter explores the transformative role of the Internet of Things (IoT) in reshaping operational agility within smart ecosystems and intelligent enterprises. As businesses confront dynamic market demands and technological disruptions, IoT emerges as a critical enabler of real-time responsiveness, automation, and adap-

DOI: 10.4018/979-8-2600-1263-5.ch003

tive decision-making. Anchored in Dynamic Capabilities Theory, Systems Theory, and Sociotechnical Systems Design, the chapter conceptualizes operational agility through the integration of sensor networks, AI-driven analytics, edge computing, and interconnected infrastructures. Through empirical case studies spanning manufacturing, healthcare, logistics, energy, and urban governance, the chapter illustrates how IoT fosters capabilities such as sensing, learning, and self-adjustment. It also addresses key implementation challenges, including data security, interoperability, cost, and regulatory compliance. The chapter concludes by identifying future trends, including AIoT, digital twins, and green IoT

1. INTRODUCTION

The digital transformation of businesses has come to an inflexion point with the mainstreaming of the Internet of Things (IoT). IoT has revolutionised business structure dynamics and strategic mindsets in every industry with its hallmark of sensor-embedded, networked physical objects. Success in the modern business world is no longer about operational efficacy or size, but about being agile, adaptive, and anticipatory in uncertain and complex environments. Backed thereby, the convergence of the Internet of Things with advanced analytics, edge computing, artificial intelligence (AI), and on-premises/cloud infrastructures is creating the innovative ecosystems and intelligent enterprises of the future. (El Houari et al., 2025)

Innovative ecosystems are digitally networked environments wherein information streams fluidly between devices, systems, and stakeholders for context-aware decision-making. These ecosystems extend across industrial verticals such as manufacturing, healthcare, transport, retail, energy, and smart cities, combining physical assets with digital smarts. Within the larger innovative ecosystem, the intelligent enterprise is characterised by its ability to take advantage of real-time information and digital technologies to drive optimised decision-making, improve customer experience, and achieve superior operational performance. Interestingly, these enterprises are contemplating a move away from centralised, reactive patterns of deployment towards distributed, proactive, and dynamic structures that facilitate increased operational flexibility.

Operational agility is the capacity of an organisation to speedily detect and react to both internal and external dynamics, whether market change, supply chain breakdown, customer demands, or technological advancements. It involves versatile procedures, responsive systems, and evolutive cultures capable of withstanding unpredictability while maintaining performance. With today's digital economy in which change is the lone constant, the competitive imperative is rapidly becoming agility over strategic choice. Conventional tools and inflexible systems generally fail to meet the responsiveness necessary in such environments. This is where IoT makes its impact.

The capability of IoT to offer real-time visibility of operational parameters, automate routine tasks, and create actionable insights from large sets of data directly aids the pillars of agility: sensing, decision-making, and execution. With the infusion of IoT throughout organisational architectures—supply chains, production lines, logistics, and customer service platforms—businesses are able to move away from static planning towards dynamic responsiveness. As an example, in smart manufacturing, IoT-enabled machinery is able to detect abnormalities, prompting maintenance prior to failure, minimising downtime, and maximising throughput. With shipments having IoT trackers in logistics, routing can be optimised in real-time depending on traffic or weather conditions. These functions are changing the way businesses organise their workflow and manage uncertainties. (Helal, 2025)

Apart from that, integrating IoT with machine learning and AI has unlocked the doors of predictive analytics and autonomous decision-making. These smart features not only aid in reacting to change, but they can also aid in anticipating change, a central component of being agile. Demand forecasting, predictive maintenance, customer sentiment analysis, and power optimisation are some of the applications that IoT and AI use to create smart enterprises. With the acquisition of nearby data (data locality) as well as processing in nearly real-time, enterprises can make localised decision-making, avoid delays, and achieve enhanced accuracy and efficiency.

Significantly, smart ecosystems transcend an individual organisation. They comprise inter-organisational collaboration, platform business models, networked value chains with partners, suppliers, and customers linked through collaborative data infrastructures. Such extended business agility allows enterprises not only to work with stakeholders in real time, react accordingly to shifts in supply and demand, but also to co-create value at scale. The feasibility of such ecosystems is, however, dependent upon interoperability of data, cybersecurity, standards of governance, and scalability of IoT infrastructures.

Despite such advantages, business use in operations is not free of challenges. Challenges such as integration of existing systems, scalability, data protection requirements, initial costs, and a shortage of talent often slow down large-scale adoption. Moreover, as businesses undertake the journey of becoming more data-driven, ethical concerns with regard to algorithmic transparency, autonomous decision-making, and digital inclusion also have to be addressed for innovation to be ethical. These concerns call for balanced adoption of technological innovations in harmony with human-driven design as well as sustainable governance models.

This chapter aims to provide a comprehensive understanding of how IoT is reshaping operational agility within intelligent enterprises embedded in smart ecosystems. The scope spans both conceptual underpinnings and empirical case examples across industries. By examining IoT's architectural layers—devices, connectivity, data processing, and application interfaces—the chapter deconstructs how agility is operationalised through digital infrastructures. It also highlights sector-specific innovations and strategic frameworks that enable scalable transformation. From smart factories powered by industrial IoT (IIoT) to real-time healthcare systems and adaptive urban planning, the chapter investigates how IoT is catalysing a shift from linear to adaptive operational models. (Pelletier et al., 2025)

In doing so, the chapter contributes to the burgeoning body of work on Industry 4.0, cyber-physical systems, and digital transformation strategy. It elaborates existing work further in situating IoT not just as an instrument of technological nature, but also as a socio-technical facilitator of organisational agility as well as ecosystem-level intelligence. Moreover, it integrates systems theory, the dynamic capabilities approach, and digital business models in order to conceive of the IoT-agility nexus in an interdisciplinary manner.

2. CHAPTER OBJECTIVES

The rapid convergence of digital technologies, data-driven intelligence, and real-time automation is redefining the contours of enterprise agility. Among these transformative technologies, the Internet of Things (IoT) plays a pivotal role in enabling adaptive, responsive, and intelligent organisational architectures. This chapter seeks to provide a comprehensive and multidisciplinary exploration of how IoT technologies are structurally and functionally reshaping operational agility in the context of smart ecosystems and intelligent enterprises. The research objectives are carefully designed to integrate conceptual clarity, technological depth, and practical insight, ultimately contributing to both academic discourse and industry practice.

Objective 1: To Investigate the Intellectual Foundations of Intelligent Enterprises, as Well as Novel Ecosystems Within the Umbrella of Digital Transformation

The first aim establishes the foundational model through questioning the changing nature of enterprise ecosystems in the digital age. The change from linear traditional organisations toward coordinated, digital-first ecosystems calls for the redefinition of organisational boundaries, roles, and capabilities. Value is co-created in smart ecosystems through collaborative platforms, digital interfaces, and joint intelligence, facilitated with the help of an Internet of Things infrastructure.

The notion of the intelligent enterprise emerged as a response to the growing demand for agility and responsiveness. It refers to an organisation that strategically leverages digital technologies—especially IoT, AI, and cloud computing—to enable real-time decision-making, process optimisation, and ecosystem collaboration. Drawing from systems theory and digital business model literature, this section conceptualises how the interplay between physical assets and digital intelligence drives innovation and agility within these ecosystems. (Alghamdi, 2024)

This goal also touches upon creating digital ecosystems with an emphasis on platform-based innovation, multi-sided value production, and real-time data exchange. The establishment of cyber-physical systems (CPS) and Industry 4.0 paradigms also enhances the pervasiveness of IoT in orchestrating the decentralisation of intelligence in institutions. Understanding these concepts is key in an effort to bring context about the revolutionary potential of IoT in transcending technological singularity.

Objective 2: To Analyse the Technological Characteristics and Architecture of IoT Systems, Which Render Them Operationally Agile

The second aim is related to an analysis of the architectural elements of IoT and the contribution of these elements towards enterprise agility. The architecture of IoT usually comprises four interlinked elements: sensing/perception, network/ communication, data processing, and application. Each of them enables some capability- data acquisition, conveyance in real time, smart analysis, and actionable usage. (Amalia & Hindarto, 2024)

The perception layer is made of physical hardware as well as sensor devices capturing real-time environmental and operational conditions. The communication layer makes use of protocols such as MQTT, LPWAN, or 5G in order to connect devices with platforms. The processing layer, which is facilitated through the use of edge computing, AI, and cloud platforms, facilitates real-time analytics, pattern identification, and predictive modelling. The application layer then facilitates decision-making interfaces, automation routines, and dashboard visualisations.

This objective investigates how these layers, when effectively orchestrated, underpin key dimensions of agility: speed, accuracy, flexibility, and adaptability. By mapping these components to real-time visibility, predictive analytics, and autonomous operations, the chapter explains how IoT systems act as the digital nervous system of agile enterprises.

It also highlights the necessity of interoperability standards (for example, OPC UA, REST APIs), modular design, and middleware platforms in making sure that IoT implementations are scalable, secure, and integrable with existing IT infrastructures. Additionally, the section puts in perspective the role of edge computing and fog computing in mitigating latency and allowing local decision-making, which is critical for prompt operations.

Objective 3: To Assess how IoT Enables Dynamic Capabilities, Including Sensing, Learning, Adapting, and Responding in Organisational Functions

Operational agility is also linked with developing dynamic capabilities—the capacity of the firm to integrate, create, and reconfigure external, as well as internal, competencies in order to respond favourably to rapidly changing environments. Such an aim harmonises IoT's functional capability with the dynamic capabilities approach, investigating how businesses apply IoT for ongoing sensing, real-time learning, as well as adaptive execution. (Atmakuri et al., 2021)

Sensing is amplified with the pervasive sensing of data from multiple sources of diversity, such as supply chains, customers, equipment, and environments, so that anomalies, trends, and opportunities can be sensed early. Learning is facilitated through inputs of such sensing being put through machine learning algorithms that tune predictions continuously, as well as optimise resource utilizations. Adaptability results from enterprises reconfiguring their operations, repurposing their assets, or adjusting workflows in accordance with context shifts. Responsive capability is brought about through autonomous systems that respond on the receipt of triggers such as schedule adjustments of production, logistics rescheduling, or changing configurations of the product.

This goal underscores how IoT facilitates these dynamic processes not as separate events but as an integrated, continuous operating circuit. Also captured is how human-machine collaboration, digital twins, and simulated environments aid in organisational learning and vision. The chapter connects IoT adoption with dynamic capabilities to close the gap between technological infrastructure and strategic nimbleness.

Objective 4: To Showcase Empirical Examples of the use of IoT in Agile Operations in Industry Sectors

The fourth goal provides practical rigour to the chapter with examples of working cases in various sectors, such as manufacturing, healthcare, logistics, agriculture, energy, and retail. Every case represents how IoT has been deployed to facilitate greater speed, either through predictive maintenance, real-time stock tracking, optimisation of power consumption, or smart grid management.

For instance, in the manufacturing sector, companies like Siemens and GE have adopted industrial IoT platforms (e.g., MindSphere and Predix) to optimise asset utilisation and reduce unplanned downtime. In healthcare, IoT wearables and connected devices enable remote monitoring and personalised treatment, which became especially crucial during the COVID-19 pandemic. Smart irrigation systems use

IoT sensors in agriculture to monitor soil moisture and automate water delivery, improving yield and resource efficiency. (Bouguern, 2024)

These sectoral illustrations highlight best practices and innovation pathways and underscore contextual enablers and constraints, such as regulatory frameworks, data infrastructure maturity, and ecosystem collaboration. This objective reinforces the argument that while IoT technologies are universally applicable, their implementation strategies and impact trajectories are industry-specific.

Objective 5: Determine the Challenges as Well as Provide Recommendations for the Adoption and Scalability of the Internet of Things in Enterprise Settings

Despite its potential, the adoption of IoT is also accompanied by challenges that can postpone scalability and value realisation. This study scrutinizes such obstacles under five comprehensive themes, including technological, organizational, financial, regulatory, and ethical.

The technological challenges include a lack of standardisation, interoperability issues, cybersecurity vulnerabilities, and the intricacies of integrating data. The organisational challenges include resistance, a low supply of quality resources, and IT misalignment with the business. The cost issues involve the cost of a heavy investment initially, the ROI uncertainty, and the cost of infrastructure maintenance. The regulation issues involve personal data protection, borderless flows of data, and compliance with industry standards (i.e., GDPR, HIPAA). The ethical concerns include algorithmic bias, transparency, and job loss due to automation. (Chaudhary et al., 2024)

The chapter also outlines mitigating actions like using modular Internet of Things platforms, investment in reskilling courses of training, public-private partnerships in innovation, and robust governance structures. As an even-handed overview of drivers and inhibitors, the chapter provides policymakers and practitioners with practical insights.

Objective 6: To Present Future Trends and Areas of Renewed Work Relating to IoT-Driven Operational Dexterity

The ultimate goal is future-oriented, highlighting major trends determining the future phase of IoT-based transformation. These are the emergence of autonomous systems, the intersection of IoT with 5G and blockchain, the development of ambient intelligence, and the emergence of green IoT.

Moreover, the future of decision-support functionality with the help of generative AI, predictive scenario planning with digital twins, and the advancement of edge-native, decentralised architecture are areas of enormous potential for both practice and research. The chapter will go on to discuss how quantum computing will impact the future of processing and encryption for IoT.

From a research perspective, the chapter emphasises the necessity of longitudinal ROI studies of IoT, inter-industrial comparison of adoption patterns, and multi-stakeholder assessments of smart ecosystem governance. It promotes an interdisciplinary-based research agenda of technology management, organisational behaviour, and digital ethics in developing an integrative approach to addressing the challenges raised by IoT. (Coro, 2024)

3. THEORETICAL FRAMING AND CONCEPTUAL FOUNDATIONS

Embedding the Internet of Things (IoT) in enterprise architecture requires a solid foundation of theories explaining its systemic implications for agility, intelligence, and responsiveness. The chapter uses a multidisciplinary approach in combining insights from three fundamental theoretical domains: Dynamic Capabilities Theory (DCT), Systems Theory, and Sociotechnical Systems Design (STS). Each offers a supporting perspective on how IoT contributes toward the organisation's transformation, both technically and behaviorally. The section constructs the conceptual bridge to examine IoT's impact on smart ecosystems, smart enterprises, and operational agility, describing in detail these key concepts in modern digital transformation.

3.1 Dynamic Capabilities Theory (DCT

Teece, Pisano, and Shuen's (1997) Dynamic Capabilities Theory is central to explaining how business firms cope with and respond to disruptive environments. Unlike the static-based traditional Resource-Based View (RBV), DCT underscores the firm's capacity for aggregating, constructing, and reassembling internal and external capabilities to respond to turbulent contexts. This frame of thought is immensely useful in deploying IoT, as it explains the strategic mechanisms through which IoT increases firm-level adaptability and resilience. Dynamic capabilities in the context of IoT exist in three fundamental dimensions:

3.1.1 Sensing

IoT systems, through sensors, analytics, and edge computing, can detect external environmental change in real-time (customer behaviour, supply disruptions, machine anomalies). These functions enhance the firm's forecasting and environmental scanning capability.

3.1.2 Capturing

IoT enables the conversion of insights to action. For example, insights from IoT-based logistics platforms enable businesses to redirect deliveries, redistribute stock, or prioritise deliveries in response to current demand patterns. (dos Santos et al., 2024)

3.1.3 Reconfiguring

With IoT-based infrastructure, companies can redesign business flows, automate operations, and redistribute resources in near real-time, thus reshaping their working models in reaction to change.

By linking IoT capabilities with the DCT framework, this chapter contends that IoT is enabling not just operations but strategic agility through embedding adaptability and learning in the core of enterprise systems.

3.2 Systems Theory

Systems Theory, originally developed by Ludwig von Bertalanffy (1968), views organisations as complex, adaptive systems of interrelated and interdependent components. When applied to IoT-driven enterprises, this framework helps conceptualise how different subsystems—people, machines, data, and workflows—interact through feedback loops, control mechanisms, and adaptive behaviours. (Dubey & Yadav, 2024)

IoT devices function as nodes of an enterprise's larger cyber-physical system, constantly collecting and sending back data that represents the current status of operations.

Feedback mechanisms–made possible through real-time analytics–support self-regulation and course correction. For instance, temperature sensors in an intelligent building can auto-regulate HVAC systems to ensure maximum energy efficiency.

Homeostasis and adaptation, which are central concepts in systems theory, are demonstrated in the enterprise's capacity for maintaining functional equilibrium while adapting in reaction to internal as well as external stimuli.

The connectivity provided through IoT turns siloed business units into interoperable modules in which process synchronisation and information symmetry are the rule of the day. From a systems viewpoint, IoT is the glue that allows for both structural integration and functional integration in order to provide distributed yet coordinated decision-making necessary for operational adaptability.

3.3 Sociotechnical Systems Design (STS

The Sociotechnical Systems Design (STS) approach, which emerged from work by Emery and Trist in the 1960s, highlights the significance of co-optimisation of human (social) and machine (technical) subsystems within organisational environments. Understanding STS is essential in order to comprehend how the deployment of IoT technologies influences human jobs, business routines, and areas of decision-making authority.

3.3.1 Smart Ecosystem

Smart ecosystems are networked environments in which physical infrastructure, human actors, and computational systems interact symbiotically to generate adaptive, responsive, and sustainable systems. These ecosystems span multiple organisations, extending throughout value chains, industries, and geographies, linking heterogeneous stakeholders through Internet of Things (IoT), cloud computing, edge analytics, artificial intelligence (AI), and machine learning (ML). Fundamentally, smart ecosystems facilitate context-aware communication between devices, platforms, and users in real-time, enabling ongoing exchange of data, predictive analytics, and automated decision-making.

Practically, smart ecosystems are manifested in use cases like smart cities, smart transport systems, health-oriented connected health, smart agriculture, and smart manufacturing networks. For example, in smart cities, IoT devices placed on traffic lights, public transit, utilities, and environmental sensors work together with the aim of streamlining traffic, mitigating pollution, and enhancing the safety of citizens. These systems are based upon open standards, interoperability platforms, and modular architectures, which facilitate plug-and-play compatibility of devices or services. (Kamijo & Ogasawara, 2023)

The key differentiator for smart ecosystems is their ability to adapt to learning. Physical entities' created data is processed in real-time, allowing the ecosystem to learn, adapt, and continuously improve its performance. The outcome is the elevation from siloed activities to collective intelligence, where the ecosystem is greater than the individual components.

3.3.2 Smart Companies

Smart enterprises are the future of technologically advanced businesses that leverage real-time insights, advanced analytics, and automation in order to drive maximum business outcomes. These companies embed intelligence within their core functions—in domains ranging from production and supply-chain management through customer interactions right down to financial operations—through harnessing technological advancements such as the Internet of Things (IoT), artificial intelligence (AI), digital twins, and robotic process automation (RPA).

In contrast with traditional enterprises relying on backwards-looking reporting and control in the centre, smart enterprises apply predictive analytics and prescriptive analytics to anticipate both internal and external stimuli through proactive response. For example, predictive maintenance for manufacturing removes equipment downtime through anticipating failure, whereas customer service platforms enabled by AI create customised interactions leading towards greater satisfaction as well as loyalty.

A smart enterprise is characterised as being driven by its culture in the context of data, being democratically decision-making, having insights in real-time, and being optimised in actions through automation. The smart enterprise is also agile in nature in order to scale operations, redesign processes, and innovate rapidly as the conditions in the market change. The major characteristics include modular IT infrastructure, systems operating through API, cloud-native platforms, as well as leadership models supporting digital collaboration between functions.

3.3.3 Operational Agility

Operational agility is the capacity of the organisation to sense, translate, and respond to change in its operating environment with speed and effectiveness. The concept of operational agility entails strategic responsiveness (reconfiguring in reaction to change in the long term) as well as tactical adaptability (adjusting in reaction to short-term disruptions). It is particularly critical in today's volatile, uncertain, complex, and ambiguous (VUCA) business world.

Agility is based on the abilities of real-time sensing, rapid decision-making, dynamic resource allocation, and autonomous action. These abilities are radically enhanced with the use of IoT through the availability of the necessary data, connectivity, and processing power. For instance, an IoT-based supply chain system can dynamically reallocate logistics in accordance with weather conditions or delays in supply, curbing disruptions and increasing the delivery of services. (Muntés-Mulero et al., 2019)

By anticipating risks, seizing emerging opportunities, and guaranteeing continuity, operational agility generally enables enterprises to be competitive, resilient, and to continuously grow in digitally driven markets.

4. IOT AS AN OPERATIONAL AGILITY ENABLER

Operational adaptability—the capacity of an organisation to respond swiftly and successfully to change—is no longer an attractive business skill; in an era of technological change, market uncertainty, and shifting customer needs, it is an imperative. The Internet of Things (IoT) is the prime facilitator of operational adaptability, embedding intelligence, interactivity, and automation within enterprise operations. The five key mechanisms whereby IoT enables operational adaptability are discussed in this section: Sensing and Monitoring, Connectivity and Integration, Advanced Analytics and AI, Automation and Control, and Feedback Loops and Learning. The mechanisms in tandem enable enterprises to move from being reactive in nature towards being predictive, adaptive, and resilient systems. (Oproiu et al., 2024)

4.1 Sensing and Monitoring: Greater Visibility and Situational Awareness

The first of the pillars of operational agility is sensing environmental as well as operational change in real-time. IoT facilitates such sensing through sensor networks integrated in physical infrastructure, assets, objects, as well as human-machine interfaces. These devices capture granular details about temperature, pressure, humidity, motion, position, speed, and usage patterns, providing real-time situational awareness for an organisation.

For instance, in production, equipment-mounted IoT sensors can monitor unusual vibrations or overheating, indicating future machine failure. For logistics, GPS-based sensors monitor the movement of the fleet as well as cargo health, enabling businesses to monitor delivery schedules and maximise routing. (Panichakarn et al., 2024)

With continuous monitoring, businesses can move away from infrequent checks toward ongoing real-time decision-making environments. The outcome is a significant decrease in information asymmetry and delays, enabling quick response, as well as sped-up reaction, in the event of deviations, interruptions, or spikes in the demand. The capacity to "sense early and act fast" is directly linked with the responsiveness as well as the accuracy of an agile operation. The interconnection of sensing, network, and analytics components within enterprise systems follows a structured, layered model as illustrated in **Figure 1**, which demonstrates how IoT architecture translates operational data into agility outcomes

4.2. Connectivity and Integration: Overcoming Organizational Silos

As sensing captures raw information, operational responsiveness also calls for frictionless data sharing between departments, systems, and stakeholders. IoT facilitates this through strong connectivity based on wireless communication protocols (5G, Zigbee, LoRaWAN) and integration platforms (REST APIs, middleware platforms).

By connecting disparate systems—ERP, CRM, SCM, and MES—IoT breaks down traditional organisational silos and facilitates horizontal and vertical integration. In a smart factory, IoT links production machines with enterprise-level planning systems, enabling synchronised scheduling, predictive maintenance, and just-in-time inventory management.

Additionally, cloud and edge computing environments guarantee not just that such data is gathered, but also that such data is available, sharable, and actionable throughout the enterprise. This creates collaborative environments within departments, allowing such functions as procurement, operations, and customer service to communicate in real-time, enhancing alignment and eliminating bottlenecks in operations. (Patil, 2024)

The connectivity layer of the Internet of Things therefore serves as an electronic nervous system, supporting fluidity of data as well as systemic coherence—the agile organisation's main characteristics for adapting as a group, not in silos.

4.3 Advanced Analytics and AI: From Data to Foresight

Raw data in itself will not make an organisation agile. The potential of IoT is realised when advanced analytics, machine learning (ML), and artificial intelligence (AI) capabilities are added. These capabilities take voluminous data from IoT sources and turn them into predictive insights as well as actionable intelligence, thereby enabling organisations to take forward-looking, data-driven decisions. (Zimmermann et al., 2020)

A prime example is the adoption of digital twins, virtual copies of physical systems, driven by live IoT data and machine learning algorithms. These twins mimic performance under different conditions, enabling organisations to test reactions to potential disruptions in the absence of impact on actual operations.

By infusing intelligence into the operations, analytics not only make them more accurate and efficient, but also decrease decision delays—a central necessity of agility. Enterprises are empowered to pre-empt instead of respond to change, thus constructing adaptive foresight into planning for operations.

4.4. Automation and Control: Abolishing Latency Through Autonomy

The responsiveness of an organisation also hinges on being capable of making instant decisions and corresponding adjustments. IoT solutions enable automation on multiple fronts, from factory-floor control actions to provisioning of services in virtual environments. With actuators, robotics, and control systems in combination, IoT devices can trigger autonomous actions based on predetermined thresholds or algorithmic measures. (Yammanur & Chowdhury, 2024)

As an example, in smart manufacturing, an IoT-based quality control system can stop production in its tracks when it finds a defect, divert work flows, and alert maintenance teams. For agriculture, smart irrigation systems make use of the moisture in the soil in order to control the supply of water autonomously, maximising the utilisation of resources as well as crop yields. This capacity for autonomous low-level decision-making frees human resources for the resolution of higher-order problems with continuity of operations. Latency is reduced, as is the amount of repetitive work, and therefore, all these contribute towards faster cycles as well as increased agility.

Moreover, automation through IoT facilitates decentralisation, where local devices or units can make independent judgments based on their local knowledge. This decentralisation is useful in large, scattered enterprises where centralised decision-making can be slow or out of touch with local conditions.

4.5 Feedback Loops and Learning

The process of continuous sensing, decision-making, and adaptation can be viewed as a closed-loop system, as represented in **Figure 2**, where IoT data cycles through sensing, deciding, acting, and learning functions. Allowing for Continual Improvement. Finally, operational dexterity is not just about reacting or anticipating – it is about learning continuously and adapting. IoT is about constructing closed feedback cycles wherein operational data is continuously being captured, analysed, and used in the system in order to make future decisions, alter processes, and optimise performance. This continuous feedback allows for the learning of the organisation on a scale. For example, customer feedback collected through IoT-based products (for example, smart homes or wearable devices) can update the R&D teams about the iterative features of the device. Such feedback in logistics can optimise routes, warehouses, and employees through delivery feedback in real-time. IoT-based learning cycles are also central for agile innovation cycles such as DevOps for software development or Lean for manufacturing. The rapid experimentation, short cycles of iteration, and scaling up of what is found to work are enabled through such cycles. The ability for "fail fast, learn fast, improve fast" is enabled through streams of real-time data and performance insights from connected systems. Strategically, such feedback cycles also enable evidence-based optimisation of strategy, whereby businesses are able to realign their goals as well as their allocation of resources based on current market signals, as well as current operational conditions. (Manavalan, 2020)

Figure 1. IoT-to-Agility Reference Architecture

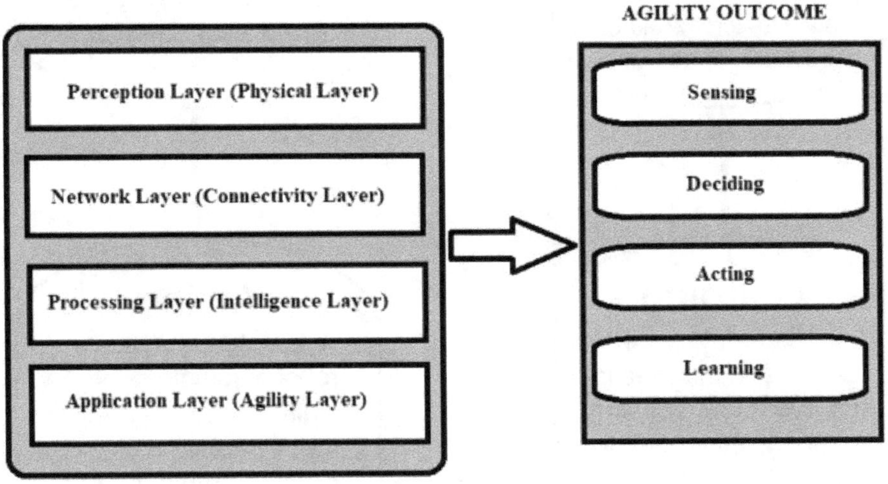

Figure 2. The Sensing–Deciding–Acting–Learning Loop

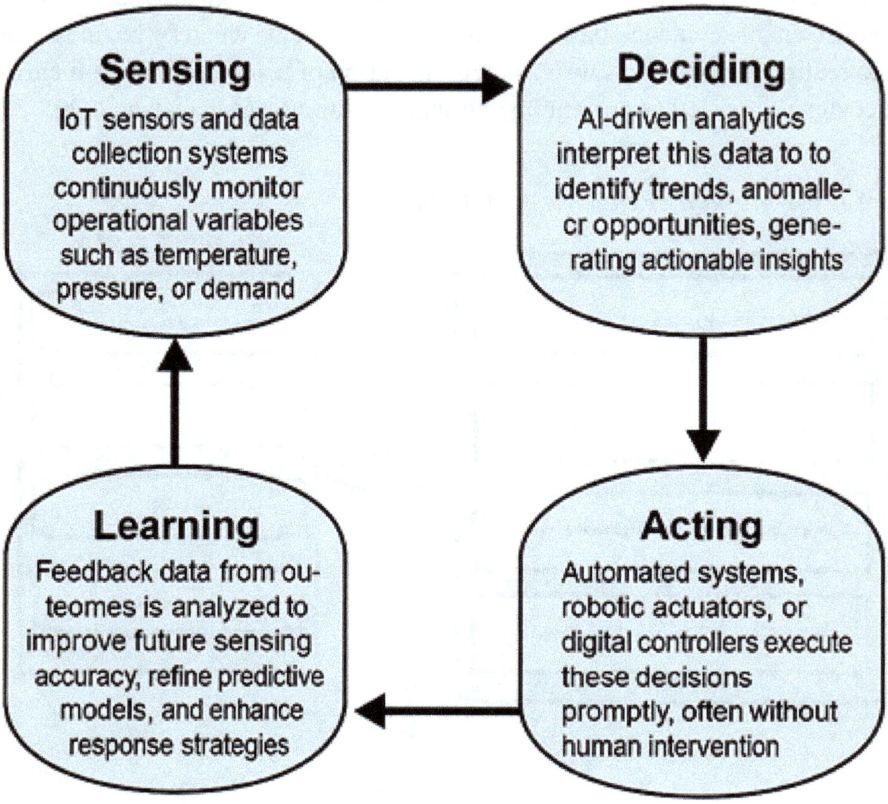

4.6 IoT-Enabled Agility Metrics Framework

Operational agility can be effectively assessed through a coherent set of quantifiable indicators that capture an organisation's responsiveness, adaptability, and decision velocity. To translate the conceptual role of IoT into measurable outcomes, an **IoT-Enabled Agility Metrics Framework** is proposed. This framework aligns technological functions—sensing, data processing, analytics, and automation—with time- and performance-based metrics that reflect agility maturity across enterprise systems.

4.6.1. Time to Detect (TTD)

IoT Influence: IoT sensors, real-time monitoring dashboards, and connected devices significantly reduce TTD by providing instant alerts on deviations in operational parameters.

Agility Impact: Shorter TTD means faster situational awareness, enabling proactive maintenance and incident prevention — a fundamental characteristic of agile enterprises.

4.6.2. Time to Decide

IoT Influence: With embedded AI analytics and edge computing, IoT systems drastically reduce decision latency by processing data close to the source. Predictive and prescriptive analytics help decision-makers act without waiting for manual data consolidation.

Agility Impact: A reduction in decision latency fosters dynamic responsiveness, enabling organisations to move from reactive to predictive operations.

4.6.3. Time to Act

IoT Influence: Automation, robotic systems, and actuator-based controls in IoT networks translate decisions into action instantly. This eliminates manual intervention and accelerates process execution.

Agility Impact: By reducing the decision-to-action gap, IoT transforms static workflows into self-adjusting operational systems.

4.6.4. Mean Time to Repair (MTTR)

IoT Influence: IoT-enabled predictive maintenance tools and digital twins improve diagnosis accuracy and enable remote troubleshooting, thereby reducing downtime.

Agility Impact: A lower MTTR signifies higher resilience and adaptability, as systems recover faster and operations resume without prolonged disruptions.

4.6.5. Overall Equipment Effectiveness (OEE)

IoT Influence: Through continuous equipment monitoring and analytics-driven process optimisation, IoT enhances each OEE component. Data collected from sensors helps identify idle times, bottlenecks, and quality defects in real time.

Agility Impact: High OEE reflects an agile system capable of maintaining performance consistency even under fluctuating operational conditions.

4.6.6. Forecast Accuracy / Order Cycle Time

IoT Influence: Real-time data streams from IoT devices in supply chains enhance forecasting models by incorporating up-to-the-minute insights on inventory, demand, and logistics conditions.

Agility Impact: Higher forecast accuracy and shorter order cycles increase flexibility, reduce waste, and improve customer responsiveness, reinforcing both operational and strategic agility.

4.7 Case Study Methodology Box

Before presenting the empirical cases, the methodological basis for their selection and analysis is summarised below.

To empirically validate the conceptual framework, this chapter adopts a multiple case study approach examining how IoT enhances operational agility across industries. The method enables deep exploration of the sensing–deciding–acting–learning dynamics within real organisational ecosystems. Case selection followed clear criteria: (1) industry leadership in digital transformation, (2) IoT maturity reflecting large-scale deployment beyond pilot stages, (3) data availability and verifiability from credible sources, and (4) demonstrable agility outcomes such as reduced Time to Detect (TTD), improved Mean Time to Repair (MTTR), and increased Overall Equipment Effectiveness (OEE).

Each case represents a digital ecosystem—not a single firm—highlighting networked collaboration among suppliers, partners, and customers. The study draws exclusively from secondary data (peer-reviewed papers, government and industry reports) published between 2020 and 2025, ensuring relevance to the current phase of Industry 4.0 convergence. Analytical emphasis is placed on cross-organisational connectivity, technological integration (IoT, AI, and edge computing), and performance improvements reflecting agility and resilience.

Limitations include dependence on secondary data and ecosystem-level analysis, which prioritises comparative insight over technical detail. Nevertheless, triangulation across multiple sources ensures methodological validity and analytical transparency. The approach provides a robust foundation for interpreting the five selected cases—Siemens, Amazon, GE, Apollo Hospitals, and Smart Cities—as exemplars of IoT-enabled agility in action.

5. EMPIRICAL CASES AND SECTORAL APPLICATIONS

To bring the operational power of the Internet of Things (IoT) into perspective of its operational impact, this section presents an array of empirical cases in key industrial segments. The cases present an example of how real-time sensing, automation, analytics, and machine intelligence are not just concepts of the future but are actually creating tangible results in terms of responsiveness, adaptability, and efficiency. The examples presented here—Siemens (smart manufacturing), Amazon (consumer retail supply chains), GE (energy grid management), Apollo Hospitals (healthcare), and Smart Cities (urban planning)—illustrate how IoT-based solutions are being used strategically in building intelligent enterprises as well as smart ecosystems with embedded agility in their DNA.

5.1 Siemens – Digital Twins and Smart Manufacturing

Table 1. Sector Crosswalk: IoT Applications and Agility Outcomes

Sector	IoT Application	Key Agility Outcome	Example KPI
Manufacturing (Siemens)	Digital Twin and Predictive Maintenance	Reduced downtime, optimised asset utilisation	OEE ↑ (68% → 88%), MTTR ↓ (8h → 2h)
Retail Logistics (Amazon)	Smart fulfilment, robotics, and IoT-enabled routing	Faster delivery, adaptive logistics	Order Cycle Time ↓ (30min → 3min)
Energy (GE)	Industrial IoT for grid monitoring and load balancing	Predictive maintenance and grid resilience	TTD ↓ (2h → 10min), MTTR ↓
Healthcare (Apollo Hospitals)	Remote monitoring and connected health systems	Faster diagnosis and improved continuity of care	Time to Decide ↓ (1h → 5min)

Table 2. Before–After KPI Comparison for IoT Implementation

Metric	Before IoT Implementation	After IoT Implementation	Improvement (%)
Time to Detect (TTD)	2 hours	10 minutes	91.7% faster detection
Time to Decide	1 hour	5 minutes	91.6% faster decision-making
Time to Act	30 minutes	3 minutes	90.0% reduction in latency

continued on following page

Table 2. Continued

Metric	Before IoT Implementation	After IoT Implementation	Improvement (%)
Mean Time to Repair (MTTR)	8 hours	2 hours	75.0% improvement
Overall Equipment Effectiveness (OEE)	68%	88%	+20 percentage points
Forecast Accuracy	70%	95%	+25 percentage points

Siemens AG, a global leader in industrial automation and digitalisation, exemplifies the application of IoT for operational agility in the manufacturing sector. Through its MindSphere IoT platform, Siemens has pioneered the use of digital twins—virtual replicas of physical assets—to enable real-time simulation, monitoring, and predictive analytics.

To provide a comparative view of how IoT applications contribute to operational agility across industries, Table 1 summarises sector-specific use cases, their agility outcomes, and representative key performance indicators (KPIs).

At Siemens' smart factories, machine-embedded IoT sensors continuously stream data about temperature, vibration, pressure, and load. That data is input into digital twin models, which mimic the performance of assets under different conditions. Based on these simulations, operators can predict system failure, determine inefficiencies, and schedule predictive maintenance well in advance of breakdown. The anticipatory strategy cuts downtime radically, increases machine availability, and optimises schedules for production.

Additionally, these insights facilitate adaptive production planning in which manufacturing activities are dynamically adapted in line with machine health, material stock, and demand variability. Digital twin strategy not only enables machine-level agility but also facilitates plant-wide coordination and scalability. With production lines being modular and reconfigurable, Siemens outlines how IoT facilitates an industrial ecosystem shift from reactive to predictive and self-regulating. (Aljarrah et al., 2023)

5.2 Amazon – Retail Logistics and Automation Fulfilment

Amazon, the globe's biggest e-commerce organisation, has revolutionised retail logistics through the large-scale deployment of IoT devices, robotics, and real-time analytics. The key to Amazon's speed is its robot-based fulfilment centres, in which networked devices as well as smart algorithms operate in tandem for quick, precise, and scalable stock management.

Within Amazon warehouses, temperature conditions, package movement, and shelf availability are tracked using IoT sensors. The floors of warehouses are traversed autonomously by Kiva robots, which are integrated with IoT, in order to pick items and deliver them to human pickers. This reduces order cycle time dramatically. Manual effort is minimised, with maximum speed and consistency.

Additionally, RFID-tagged receptacles and GPS-tracked delivery trucks create end-to-end real-time visibility for product locations. This connectivity facilitates dynamic routing, whereby delivery routes are continually optimised in relation to traffic patterns, weather, and order priority, allowing Amazon to ship millions of packages daily with unparalleled accuracy and responsiveness. Essentially, Amazon uses insights from consumer patterns and geographical trends in predictive analytics in order to foresee spikes in demand, allowing for nimble restocking as well as localised warehousing. This way, Amazon demonstrates how the Internet of Things can harmonise front-end demand with back-end supply, creating end-to-end supply chain responsiveness. (Hameed et al., 2020)

5.3 General Electric – Industrial Internet of Things in Energy Infrastructure

General Electric (GE), in its Predix platform, is an industry benchmark for Industrial IoT (IIoT) integration for the energy and utilities industry. Predix's emphasis is on real-time performance monitoring of assets, mainly in generation, transmission, and distribution infrastructure.

GE installs in gas turbines, wind farms, and power grids an extensive sensor network that captures measurements of heat, pressure, speed of the rotors, humidity, and indicators of wear and tear. The collected telemetry is used to recognise subtle trends leading to hardware degradation or system breakdown. For example, a subtle shift in the vibration frequency of the turbine could signal an emerging bearing failure, enabling planned maintenance before it can lead to an outage.

Additionally, GE's remote diagnostics enables operators to compare performance between facilities, benchmark world-class practices, and alter operationally driven parameters in real-time. The cross-facility adaptability is critical in an industry where failure can have downstream repercussions for public services and industrial operations.

A key use is load balancing, with IoT-based power grids dynamically regulating output in line with real-time demand, input from renewable sources (for instance, sun or wind variability), and storage capability. With adaptive power distribution enabled, both cost savings and operational resilience are assured, strengthening the argument for the role of IoT as an infrastructure of future power systems.

5.4 Apollo Hospitals – IoT in Connected Healthcare

Apollo Hospitals, India's leading healthcare network, is an ideal example of how IoT is changing the way patients are treated, as well as medical operations. Confronted with increasing demand, geographical dispersedness, and the necessity of delivering care remotely, Apollo has infused various aspects of its service delivery with IoT.

Through home-monitoring kits, biosensors, and wearable devices, Apollo monitors real-time patient vitals like oxygen saturation, glucose, heart rate, and mobility. The information is transmitted to healthcare providers via secure cloud-based platforms for remotely ordered diagnostics, medication adherence, as well as early complication alerts, especially for chronic disease management. (Gramegna et al., 2020)

Within hospitals, IoT also assists in tracking equipment, determining availability, and optimising the use of critical equipment such as ventilators and wheelchairs. Patient mobility can be monitored with innovative bed systems in order to prevent falls, while environmental sensing provides air quality as well as temperature in operational areas for added safety for the patients.

During the COVID-19 period, Apollo used tele-ICU platforms and linked diagnostic devices, allowing speciality physicians to control critical care units from other cities. This geographically dispersed nimbleness, made possible through IoT, relieved the load from frontline workers while increasing the scale of quality care.

Apollo's experience demonstrates the capability of IoT in revolutionising hospitals as smart systems of care that are responsive, personalised, and scalable in the face of uneven healthcare access and infrastructural challenges. (Ibrahimi & Benchekroun, 2023)

5.5 Smart Cities – Urban Governance and Real-Time Response

Smart city is the large-scale implementation of IoT for enhancing urban management, public safety, and environmental sustainability. Singapore, Barcelona, and Bengaluru are some of the cities that have implemented IoT solutions in an attempt to counteract the challenges of urbanisation, traffic congestion, pollution, and the management of resources.

Traffic management is one of the major applications. Vehicle count as well as pedestrian movement is monitored in real-time through IoT-based traffic signals as well as CCTV cameras. These systems dynamically alter traffic signal timings based on AI-driven algorithms, reducing congestion, boosting traffic speed, and promoting safety on roads. (Alkan, 2020)

Environmental monitoring is performed with the help of air quality, pollution, and water contamination sensing through the use of sensors. Authorities are hence able to identify hotspots of pollution and take the necessary corrective action. For instance, in Delhi, public health alerts are made in real time, and responses in the event of an emergency are facilitated through IoT-based air sensing. Public safety is also heightened through smart surveillance with integrated behavioural sensing as well as facial detection. During emergencies such as fire or flood, networked alarms, as well as evacuation alerts, coupled with assessments through drones, facilitate effective disaster response. For the government, various smart cities have established integrated command and control centres where inputs from utilities, the water supply, transport, and sanitation are consolidated. These centres function as agile centres of decision-making, whereby city administrators can allocate resources, redress citizens' complaints, and integrate multi-agency responses in real time.

The results shown in **Table 2** reinforce that IoT adoption yields quantifiable agility gains—particularly in Time to Detect (TTD), Mean Time to Repair (MTTR), and Forecast Accuracy—across all examined sectors.

6. CHALLENGES AND LIMITATIONS IN IOT DEPLOYMENT

While its transformative potential is vast, the mass-scale deployment of the Internet of Things (IoT) is fraught with some serious issues. These issues span technical, economic, legal, and organisational spheres and can acutely impair the scalability, reliability, and ethical deployment of systems of IoT. This section critiques the most serious constraints with which organisations must cope in order to actualise the complete potential of operational dexterity through IoT.

6.1. Data Security and Privacy Threats

IoT environments significantly enhance the digital presence of businesses through the extensive use of connected devices that collect, relay, and process data in real-time. Although such connectivity facilitates agility, it also creates serious vulnerabilities. The increased attack surface of environments in the IoT makes them prime targets for criminals.

As opposed to mainstream IT infrastructure, the computing capability of the majority of IoT devices is limited, nor do they always feature advanced protection mechanisms like encryption, authentication methods, or intrusion detection. They are, therefore, vulnerable to malware injection, botnets (e.g., Mirai botnet), or unauthorised monitoring. Compromised devices can be used as jumping points for laterally moving within networks, posing not only risks for operational systems but also for customers ' and employees' data. (Nuerk & Dařena, 2023)

Securing these risks calls for an approach of security-by-design, frequent firmware updates, secure communication protocols (TLS, DTLS), as well as strong encryption standards. Such actions, though, need extensive resources as well as knowledge, which in turn are mainly lacking in low-resource environments. (Uchirova et al., 2021)

6.2 Interoperability Issues

Legacy systems introduce an added layer of complexity. Connecting the IoT with existing enterprise software or legacy hardware tends to involve costly middleware, specialised APIs, and ongoing maintenance. (Schianchi, 2023)

To bridge this gap, open standards (e.g., MQTT, CoAP, OPC-UA) and interoperability frameworks supported by governments and industry consortia are in increasing demand. Activities like the Open Connectivity Foundation (OCF) and Industrial Internet Consortium (IIC) are valuable, but their adoption globally is uneven.

Most organisations operate in brownfield environments—legacy systems that were not originally designed for connectivity. Transitioning to IoT-native, agile systems requires a phased migration strategy that maintains continuity while enabling gradual digital transformation.

1. Assessment: Begin by mapping existing brownfield infrastructure, identifying integration bottlenecks, obsolete components, and interoperability gaps.
2. Middleware Integration: Deploy middleware solutions (e.g., IoT gateways, APIs) to connect legacy systems with cloud or edge platforms, allowing partial interoperability without full system replacement.
3. Modular Deployment: Introduce greenfield IoT-native components incrementally—such as smart sensors, edge nodes, and AI-driven controllers—while maintaining operational stability.
4. Standardisation and Compliance: Gradually align all systems with recognised interoperability and security standards (as listed in **Table 3** to ensure seamless data flow and compliance readiness.

To address these challenges, a coordinated standards-based approach is essential. Interoperability ensures that heterogeneous devices and applications can share data in real time, while security standards guarantee the confidentiality, integrity, and availability of that data.

Table 3. Interoperability and Security Standards Map

Category	Representative Standards / Frameworks	Purpose and Function
Interoperability	OPC-UA, MQTT, CoAP, REST API, ISO/IEC 30141	Enables cross-platform data exchange and machine-to-machine (M2M) communication through standardised protocols and messaging formats.
Data Representation	ISO/IEC 20924, IEC 62541	Establishes consistent data schemas, metadata models, and ontologies for IoT devices and platforms.
Connectivity	5G, LPWAN, Zigbee, LoRaWAN	Provides scalable and low-latency communication infrastructures for IoT networks.
Security and Privacy	ISO/IEC 27001, NIST Cybersecurity Framework, GDPR, OWASP IoT Top 10	Ensures data protection, encryption, user privacy, and vulnerability management within connected environments.
Governance and Compliance	ISO/IEC 38500, ENISA Guidelines, IEEE P2413	Provides governance models and compliance frameworks for responsible and ethical IoT system deployment.

6.3 High Capital and Maintenance Costs

IoT deployment involves heavy upfront capital costs for hardware (controllers, gateways, sensors), network infrastructure (5G, LPWAN, Wi-Fi), and data platforms (edge nodes, analytics engines, cloud). Apart from first-time costs, organisations will also have ongoing operational costs in terms of software licenses, system upgrades, power consumption, and technical support.

6.4 Skill Shortfalls and Talent Shortages

The nature of IoT systems demands an interdisciplinary workforce with embedded systems, network engineering, cybersecurity, data science, and cloud infrastructure expertise. Many of these skill sets, though, have glaring shortfalls in most organisations. (Mayorova & Balashova, 2021)

One of the top three adoption impediments is the IoT skills shortage, according to several industry reports. The organisations either lack in-house talent or are unable to onboard competent professionals. With the fast-paced development of the landscape of the IoT, the situation is worsened as the requirements for skills change with the introduction of novel protocols, platforms, and AI adoption.

Tackling this issue requires investment in reskilling programs, cross-training, academia-industry collaborations, and certification. The government, as well as universities, need to play an active role in tapping into the talent pipeline through curriculum development as well as experiential learning. (Souri et al., 2023)

6.5. Governance, Ethics, and Regulatory Compliance

The legal environment for the Internet of Things (IoT) is still underdeveloped in most jurisdictions. The lack of harmonisation of global regulation on data ownership, interoperability, liability, and consumer rights leaves potential adopters uncertain, notably multinational corporations.

There are also concerns about ethical surveillance, profiling, and decision-making through AI systems without human control. Without robust governance structures, IoT can inadvertently exacerbate algorithmic bias, digital inequality, and exclusion. Regulatory agencies should implement value-oriented models that ensure accountability and balance with innovation. Regulatory Sandboxes and Ethics-by-Design principles can provide structured mechanisms for the responsible adoption of IoT. (Mahdad et al., 2022)

Ethical governance in IoT and AIoT systems ensures transparency, accountability, and responsible innovation. A ***Mini AIoT Governance Stack*** provides a structured framework for aligning agility with ethical control.

1. **Data Stewardship:** Defines ownership, consent, and data minimisation to protect privacy and ensure lawful use.
2. **Model Risk Management:** Detects bias, validates models, and monitors drift to maintain fairness and reliability.
3. **Explainable AI (XAI):** Ensures interpretability and transparency in automated decisions through clear documentation and dashboards.
4. **Audit Mechanisms:** Maintain logs, reviews, and compliance dashboards for traceability and regulatory assurance.
5. **Incident Playbooks:** Outline protocols for breaches, ethical violations, and AI errors, ensuring prompt response and remediation.

7. TRENDS OF THE FUTURE AND RESEARCH DIRECTIONS

Despite the challenges above, the IoT landscape is rapidly evolving, driven by technological convergence, innovation ecosystems, and policy shifts. This section outlines the most significant trends shaping the future of IoT-enabled enterprise agility and highlights areas requiring scholarly and strategic attention.

7.1 Edge Computing and 5G for Real-Time Responsiveness

As more large-scale IoT deployments are being made, the amount of generated data can overwhelm centralised clouds with latencies and increased bandwidth requirements. Edge computing is the solution in which computation is brought closer to the source of the data. Organisations can minimise latencies, ensure reliability, and uphold real-time responsiveness with local data processing on devices or gateways. (Zelenkov, 2023)

7.2 AIoT - The Artificial Intelligence of Things

AIoT systems in intelligent retailing customise customer experiences by processing real-time behavioural patterns. In manufacturing, AI optimises production schedules according to machine health and stock availability. AIoT in healthcare facilitates diagnostic support through ongoing patient monitoring. Emerging trends will emphasise explainable AI (XAI), federated learning models, as well as ethically aligned AI design for maintaining transparency, security, and user confidence in AIoT ecosystems. (Issa et al., 2022)

7.3 Blockchain for IoT Security and Traceability

Blockchain can also enable secure device authentication, automated service-level agreements through smart contracts, as well as peer-to-peer transactions directly between IoT devices. For example, in a smart grid for electricity, blockchain can enable decentralised trading of electricity directly between producers and consumers. (Jain et al., 2022)

7.4 Digital Twin Ecosystems for Simulation and Optimisation

As digital twin ecosystems continue to mature, they will enable collaborative planning, ongoing learning, and adaptive innovation, rendering them invaluable assets for agile operations. Studies should look into standard modelling languages, interoperability layers, and techniques of privacy preservation in digital twin platforms. (Kühnel & Au-Yong-Oliveira, 2022)

7.5. Green Internet of Things (G-IoT) and Sustainable

As the deployment of IoT expands, its environmental footprint also increases. Green Internet of Things (G-IoT) is the implementation of low-carbon, energy-efficient IoT solutions that meet worldwide sustainability standards.

G-IoT activities concentrate on:

a. Energy harvesting technologies (e.g., solar, kinetic) and low-power sensors.
b. Biodegradable materials in device design.

c. Smart resource management (e.g., reducing energy or water consumption through IoT-enabled systems).

Electronic waste lifecycle management of outmoded IoT devices. Eco-design standards, circular economy policies, and carbon accountability should be prioritised in future policy blueprints as well as in related research. This will make sure that the digital revolution is not at the expense of planetary health.

7.6 Economic Roadmap for IoT Adoption

The successful deployment of IoT initiatives requires not only technological readiness but also economic feasibility and financial discipline. Many IoT transformations fail due to underestimation of total cost of ownership (TCO), unclear ROI pathways, or premature scaling. To ensure structured, evidence-based adoption, this section proposes a 90-Day Pilot Plan Framework (Table 4) and an ROI/TCO Evaluation Model (Table 5), supported by defined Scale-Up Gates.

Table 4. 90-Day Pilot Plan Framework

Phase	Time Frame	Objective	Key Deliverables
Phase 1: Needs Assessment & Architecture Planning	0–30 days	Define business objectives, select pilot area, establish baseline KPIs.	Architecture blueprint, hardware/software list, initial investment plan.
Phase 2: Prototype Deployment & KPI Baseline	31–60 days	Implement IoT prototype; integrate edge and cloud analytics; start data collection.	Functional pilot system, KPI dashboard, preliminary performance data.
Phase 3: Evaluation, ROI Estimation & Scale-Up Proposal	61–90 days	Evaluate pilot performance; calculate ROI/TCO; prepare scale-up roadmap.	ROI analysis report, risk assessment, management review presentation.

Table 5. ROI and TCO Worksheet Framework

Cost Category	Description	Measurement Approach
Hardware & Sensors	IoT devices, gateways, and controllers	CapEx depreciation over project lifespan
Software & Connectivity	Licenses, APIs, data storage, and network usage	Subscription and usage-based costs
Integration & Training	System integration, user training, and change management	One-time or annualised investment

continued on following page

Table 5. Continued

Cost Category	Description	Measurement Approach
Maintenance & Security	Upgrades, monitoring, cybersecurity tools	Ongoing OpEx
Total Benefits	Efficiency gain, downtime reduction, agility improvement	ROI = (Benefits − Costs) / Costs

7.7 Scale-Up Gates

Before large-scale expansion, enterprises must meet three key evaluation checkpoints:

Gate 1: KPI Validation: Confirm measurable improvement in key agility indicators (e.g., OEE ↑, MTTR ↓, Forecast Accuracy ↑).

Gate 2: Integration Maturity: Ensure interoperability, cybersecurity compliance, and stable system performance across connected assets.

Gate 3: Financial Breakeven: Validate ROI ≥ 1.5× baseline cost before allocating additional investment.

By following this structured roadmap, organisations can minimise financial risk, ensure accountability, and scale IoT deployments sustainably. The model also facilitates communication between technical teams and financial stakeholders by quantifying agility benefits in economic terms.

8. CONCLUSION

The Internet of Things (IoT) is no longer an emerging concept of the future—it is an omnipresent force fundamentally reshaping the structure of contemporary enterprise activities. As described in detail in this chapter, IoT breaks free from being an enabler of technology to position itself as an asset that infuses adaptability, intelligence, and quickness of thought in the fabric of an organisation. The power of transformation of IoT not only comes in the ability to capture and transport data, but also in its capacity for creating smart ecosystems as well as intelligent businesses that learn, react, and improve in real time. (Rajbhar, 2022)

A rigorous examination of industrial cases in manufacturing (Siemens), logistics (Amazon), energy (GE), healthcare (Apollo Hospitals), and public governance (Smart Cities) showed how IoT is being applied pragmatically with the aim of achieving scale-based agility. The examples showed the move from reactive to proactive as well as even predictive operations, to enable early intervention, dynamic resource allocation, as well as ongoing service optimisation. (Liu et al., 2021)

Nonetheless, the journey of achieving operational excellence through IoT is anything but linear. The chapter has also critically analysed an array of issues and constraints hindering the seamless adoption of IoT. Cybersecurity and data privacy threats are more serious owing to the increased attack surface within IoT ecosystems. Interoperability issues stemming from the failure of standard protocols as well as from vendor lock-ins pose system integration challenges. Scalability is undermined through the concomitant high capital costs as well as technical support, significantly for small and medium-sized enterprises (SMEs). Simultaneously, skill shortage in the fields of data science, embedded systems, and cybersecurity impedes effective deployment. Finally, matters of governance, compliance, and ethical issues remain unresolved in many jurisdictions, additionally deterring adoption. (Schlömer, 2022)

Despite the issues, the future of the Internet of Things (IoT) is marked by emerging technological trends that will continue to enhance both resilience and agility. Edge computing, as well as 5G, will significantly reduce latency and enable hyper-responsive decision-making within the network's edge. The integration of artificial intelligence with the Internet of Things (AIoT) will energise autonomous systems with self-healing, self-optimisation, and contextual adaptability. Blockchain will provide transparency, trust, as well as traceability in complex systems of the Internet of Things, particularly in supply chain, health, and energy. Digital twin ecosystems will enable simulation as well as stress testing of multiple business cases prior to physical deployment. Green Internet of Things (G-IoT) initiatives will ensure that the green profile of connected devices is aligned with overall sustainability goals, for example, the United Nations Sustainable Development Goals (SDGs).In summary, the convergence of IoT technologies with changing enterprise requirements is creating an environment of rich opportunity for smart ecosystems as well as nimble operations. Companies that welcome convergence and smartly integrate IoT into their operational DNA will be in a position to navigate disruptive change, capture nascent opportunities, and maintain competitive advantage in uncertain environments. (Yan, 2022)

The results of the present work have implications for several stakeholders:

a. Enterprise leaders must align IoT strategies with long-term organisational goals, invest in skill development, and champion a data-driven culture.
b. Policymakers need to supply regulatory certainty, encourage interoperability standards, and facilitate SME financing as well as capacity development.
c. Developers and technologists should ensure user-centricity, secure data, and ethical innovation when developing IoT systems.

Ultimately, as businesses aim to be smarter, nimbler, and more capable of withstanding challenges, IoT will not just be an array of associated technological capabilities but an evolutionary force that remodels the way value is created, delivered, and maintained. That said, such an evolution must be sought under full awareness of its constraints, alignment with corporate values, and wise management of the associated technology and data. (Chirumalla, 2021)

IoT Adoption Pathways for SMEs

For small and medium enterprises (SMEs), IoT adoption can drive competitiveness, yet financial and technical constraints often limit transformation. A structured, phased approach can bridge this gap. **IoT-as-a-Service (IaaS)** offers subscription-based access to IoT platforms, enabling SMEs to deploy devices, analytics, and cloud services without heavy upfront investment. **Cluster Data Hubs** promote shared infrastructure and knowledge exchange among regional or sectoral SME groups, lowering costs and fostering interoperability. In parallel, **government incentives** such as tax credits, innovation grants, and co-financing programs reduce entry barriers.

A three-step adoption framework supports progressive integration:

Step 1 – pilot IoT within a specific business function;
Step 2 – collaborate through regional or industry data hubs to scale capability;
Step 3 – evolve into full digital ecosystem participation. This pathway enables SMEs to build digital maturity incrementally, achieving agility, resilience, and sustainable innovation in the connected economy.

REFERENCES

Alghamdi, H. (2024). Assessing the impact of enterprise architecture on digital transformation success: A global perspective. *Sustainability (Basel)*, *16*(20), 8865. Advance online publication. DOI: 10.3390/su16208865

Aljarrah, M. M., Zawaideh, F. H., Magableh, M., Al Wahshat, H., & Mohamed, R. R., & K V, A. (2023). Internet of Things and data analytics: Challenges and future applications. *2023 International Conference on Computer Science and Emerging Technologies (CSET)*. DOI: 10.1109/CSET58993.2023.10346664

Alkan, D. (2020). Re-shaping business strategy in the era of digitisation. In *Digital Transformation and Innovative Services for Business and Learning* (pp. 76–97). DOI: 10.4018/978-1-7998-1125-1.ch004

Amalia, N., & Hindarto, D. (2024). Enterprise architecture for efficient integration of IoT lighting systems in smart city frameworks. *Sinkron*, *8*(2), 1091–1099. Advance online publication. DOI: 10.33395/sinkron.v8i2.13591

Atmakuri, V. V., Lari, M. S. N., & Thangaraj, A. (2021). Design for sustainable smart cities. DOI: 10.1007/978-981-16-0041-8_79

Bouguern, S. (2024). Designing the future: Exploring the smart manufacturing ecosystem and future landscape. *Journal of Novel Engineering Science and Technology*. DOI: 10.56741/jnest.v3i03.603

Chaudhary, J., Jain, U., Sudarshan, N., Pai, V., & Sutaria, K. & N. L. (2024). AI-driven digital mirror technology for securing IoT-enabled smart infrastructures. *2024 International Conference on Integrated Intelligence and Communication Systems (ICIICS)*. DOI: 10.1109/ICIICS63763.2024.10859436

Chirumalla, K. (2021). Building digitalisation capabilities for innovation in manufacturing firms. *Technovation*. Advance online publication. DOI: 10.1016/j.technovation.2021.102215

Coro, M. B. (2024). *Navigating digital transformation: Insights from recent studies on process automation and innovation*. International Seven Journal of Multidisciplinary., DOI: 10.56238/isevmjv2n1-011

dos Santos, M. R. P., Callado, A. C., & Laurindo, L. E. C. (2024). Enhancing IoT conceptual, practical, and programming learning skills. *Anais do XXXII Workshop sobre Educação em Computação (WEI 2024)*. DOI: 10.5753/wei.2024.1944

Dubey, A., & Yadav, S. K. (2024). Basics of Internet of Things. *International Journal of Scientific Research in Engineering and Management*. DOI: 10.55041/IJSREM37970

El Houari, M., El Haloui, M., & Ettaki, B. (2025). A new enterprise architecture-based approach for smart city value co-creation. [IJECE]. *International Journal of Electrical and Computer Engineering, 15*(1), 767. Advance online publication. DOI: 10.11591/ijece.v15i1.pp767-782

Gramegna, N., Greggio, F., & Bonollo, F. (2020). Smart factory competitiveness based on real-time monitoring and a quality predictive model. DOI: 10.1007/978-3-030-57997-5_22

Hameed, M., Jervis, M., & Ikushima, T. (2020). Intel® FPGAs in smart factory – A short case study. https://consensus.app/papers/intel-®-fpgas-in-smart-factor-y---a-short-case-study-hameed-al-doori/22cc4881be6e50d7aedf3393000a7c3d Ibrahimi, G., & Benchekroun, B. (2023). The contribution of agility to an organisation's digital transformation. *TEM Journal*. DOI: 10.18421/tem124-48

Helal, M. (2025). Current developments, applications, challenges and future trends in internet of things: A survey. *International Journal of Data and Network Science*. DOI: 10.5267/j.ijdns.2024.9.008

Issa, W., Moustafa, N., Turnbull, B., Sohrabi, N., & Tari, Z. (2022). Blockchain-based federated learning for securing IoT. *ACM Computing Surveys, 55*(8). Advance online publication. DOI: 10.1145/3560816

Jain, S., Yadav, N., Husain, M., Aggarwal, M., Arya, P., & Aggarwal, S. (2022). Internet of Underwater Things. *Internet of Things : Engineering Cyber Physical Human Systems*, 107–120. Advance online publication. DOI: 10.1201/9781003181613-9

Kamijo, H., & Ogasawara, H. (2023). Efforts to improve business agility in enterprise agile methodology. *IIAI-AAI, 2023*, 627–632. Advance online publication. DOI: 10.1109/IIAI-AAI59060.2023.00124

Kühnel, K., & Au-Yong-Oliveira, M. (2022). Optimal distribution of current resources in a production environment. DOI: 10.1007/978-3-031-04829-6_55

Liu, X., Li, A., Fu, X., Luo, B., Du, X., & Guizani, M. (2021). Understanding digital forensic characteristics of smart speaker ecosystems. *IEEE Globecom Workshops*, 1–6. Advance online publication. DOI: 10.1109/GLOBECOM46510.2021.9685816

Mahdad, M., Hasanov, M., Isakhanyan, G., & Dolfsma, W. (2022). A smart web of firms, farms and IoT. *British Food Journal*. Advance online publication. DOI: 10.1108/BFJ-07-2021-0756

Manavalan, M. (2020). *Intersection of AI, ML, and IoT: An economic overview.* Global Disclosure of Economics and Business., DOI: 10.18034/gdeb.v9i2.584

Mayorova, K. S., & Balashova, E. (2021). Digital transition of industrial enterprises into the "smart" ecosystem. *Russian Journal of Industrial Economics*. DOI: 10.17073/2072-1633-2021-4-433-444

Muntés-Mulero, V., Ripolles, O., Gupta, S., Dominiak, J., Willeke, E. R., Matthews, P., & Somoskoi, B. (2019). Agile risk management for multi-cloud software development. *IET Software*, *13*(3), 172–181. Advance online publication. DOI: 10.1049/iet-sen.2018.5295

Nuerk, J., & Dařena, F. (2023). Activating supply chain business models' value potentials through systems engineering. *Systems Engineering*, *26*(5), 660–674. DOI: 10.1002/sys.21676

Oproiu, M. I., Ileana, M., & Marian, C.-V. (2024). Architectural framework for IoT ecosystem. *2024 IEEE ECAI*. DOI: 10.1109/ECAI61503.2024.10607423

Panichakarn, B., Pochan, J., Shafiq, M., Saleem, I., Wang, Y., & Nazeer, S. (2024). Interplay of digital transformation, agility, and innovation. *Journal of Open Innovation*. Advance online publication. DOI: 10.1016/j.joitmc.2024.100408

Patil, B. S. (2024). *The role of the Internet of Things in the telecom sector*. IJRASET., DOI: 10.22214/ijraset.2024.66194

Pelletier, C., L'Écuyer, F., & Raymond, L. (2025). Building organisational agility through digital transformation. *Industrial Management & Data Systems*. Advance online publication. DOI: 10.1108/IMDS-05-2024-0488

Rajbhar, R. (2022). *World of IoT and its challenges*. Data Analytics and Artificial Intelligence., DOI: 10.46632/daai/2/6/6

Schianchi, M. (2023). IoT-based framework for agile supply chains. *International Journal of Innovation in Engineering*. DOI: 10.59615/ijie.3.1.63

Schlömer, I. (2022). Agility as a driver of digital transformation – A literature review. DOI: 10.1007/978-3-031-15342-6_19

Souri, A., Al-Masri, E., & Kumari, S. (2023). Blockchain architecture and methodologies for IoT. *Security and Privacy*, *6*. Advance online publication. DOI: 10.1002/spy2.299

Uchirova, M., Baurina, S., & Khudyakov, S. (2021). *Industrial technologies in digital transformation*. Modern Global Economic System., DOI: 10.1007/978-3-030-69415-9_114

Yammanur, V., & Chowdhury, R. H. (2024). *Leveraging enterprise architecture for digital transformation.* AJSTEME., DOI: 10.69593/ajsteme.v4i04.135

Yan, D. (2022). *Innovative talent ecosystem under digital transformation.* Lecture Notes in Electrical Engineering., DOI: 10.1007/978-981-16-4258-6_98

Zelenkov, Y. (2023). Enterprise agility in the era of smart IoT systems. *Business Informatics*. DOI: 10.17323/1998-0663.2023.3.52.69

Zimmermann, A., Schmidt, R., Jugel, D., & Möhring, M. (2020). Evolution of enterprise architecture for intelligent digital systems. DOI: 10.1007/978-3-030-50316-1_9

Chapter 4
Integrating AIoT Data Streams:
Challenges and Solutions in Healthcare

Zokir Mamadiyarov
Termez University of Economics and Service, Uzbekistan

Anorgul Ashirova
Mamun University, Uzbekistan

Temur Eshchanov
Urgench State University, Uzbekistan

Munir Ahmad
http://orcid.org/0000-0003-4836-6151
Survey of Pakistan, Pakistan

ABSTRACT

This chapter explores how the integration of Artificial Intelligence and the Internet of Things (AIoT) is transforming healthcare by enabling personalized, predictive, and continuous care. It examines cutting-edge innovations such as neuromorphic computing, digital twin models, and real-time biosignal analytics, which collectively push the boundaries of intelligent health monitoring and decision-making. The chapter also addresses key challenges such as data governance, ethics, and interoperability, and proposes a strategic, collaborative roadmap to responsibly scale AIoT in healthcare while prioritizing human-centered values.

DOI: 10.4018/979-8-2600-1263-5.ch004

INTRODUCTION

Artificial Intelligence (AI) and the Internet of Things (IoT) bring another paradigm, the Artificial Intelligence of Things (AIoT), rapidly re-transforming the global healthcare systems. AIoT integrates the sensor and data-generating potential of IoT devices with the cognitive and decision-making power of AI and leads to intelligent and autonomous, and real-time healthcare solutions. In healthcare, AIoT is a wide world of interconnected smart tools and devices, including wearable fitness trackers, implantable biosensors, and AI-based diagnostic systems, which can gather, analyze, and interpret high quantities of physiological and clinical data to assist in monitoring, diagnosis, and customized treatment (Qureshi & Newe, 2024; Seng et al., 2022; Thamik et al., 2024).

AIoT in healthcare is already proving to be contextually transformative in the real world. Smart patient monitoring Systems, consisting of remote patient monitoring paired with smart sensors, enable constant monitoring of vital signs and timely alert caregivers to critical anomalies, intervene earlier, and cut the number of hospital readmissions. Non-invasive wearable diagnostics, including smartwatches and biosensing patches, are useful during chronic disease management because they provide real-time information on the heart rate, blood glucose, and exercise. The use of AI-enhanced sensor networks in smart ICUs can help clinicians monitor trends of patient deterioration and generate the most efficient resource allocation. These applications are associated with a move towards a proactive rather than reactive care, where patients and providers have the power to make decisions (Baker & Xiang, 2023; Hemalatha et al., 2025; A. Pise et al., 2023; A. A. Pise et al., 2022; Talukder & Haas, 2021).

The blistering pace with which the AIoT is gaining traction in the healthcare sector also reveals a two-sided nature of the same. On the one hand, the deployment of smart technology improves the quality of care, efficiency, and health. Conversely, it also presents its complex complications, especially when it comes to data management. Heterogeneity, volume, and real-time characteristics of data produced by AIoT systems represent critical issues of scalability and interoperability of storage capabilities, latency, and data security. Moreover, it is important to avoid the fact that such data is not just collected, but significantly used, which can be considered a considerable challenge.

This chapter intends to focus on investigating the data-driven aspects of AIoT adoption in healthcare. It is structured in the following way: Section 2 talks about the nature of AIoT-generated data and the underlying issues of its management. Section 3 discusses scalable data systems and frameworks in the care contexts. In Section 4, further sophisticated data processing methods are explored, such as edge and fog computing. The working and application of AI and machine learning to extract clinical value out of raw data streams are highlighted in section 5. The Last Section provides a strategic perspective of future changes, ethical grounds, and opportunities towards the practice of sustainable AIoT in healthcare ecosystems.

SOURCES AND CHARACTERISTICS, AND THE CHALLENGES

The spread of AIoT technology in health centers has accelerated an explosion of data previously unseen- a continuous state of data deluge, which is plentiful in its potential to revolutionize clinical decision-making, patient care, and precision medicine.

Types of Healthcare AIoT Devices and Data

The idea of healthcare AIoT systems involves a rapidly increasing number of smart and connected devices that can capture, analyze, and transfer biomedical and environmental information. These devices are very different in functionality, deployment setting, shape factor, and data modalities- but in combination, they enable a novel paradigm of real-time, individualized, predictive medicine. Table 1 presents a comparative view of how key AIoT device categories differ in terms of data volume, granularity, clinical relevance, and processing requirements.

Table 1. Comparative Analysis of Data Characteristics Across AIoT Devices

Device Type	Data Volume	Data Granularity	Clinical Use Case	Processing Urgency
Wearables	Medium	Continuous	Fitness tracking, early alerts	Low to medium
Implantable	High	High-frequency	Chronic disease monitoring	High
Smart Facilities	Very High	Multi-modal	ICU monitoring, emergency triage	High
Ingestible	Episodic	Internal sensors	GI diagnostics, med adherence	Medium

Wearable Devices

Wearables are one of the most popular types of healthcare AIoT. Smartwatch and fitness band, biosensing patch, and wearable ECG monitors measure such parameters as heart rate variability (HRV), blood oxygen levels (SpO 2), body temperature, sleep, and step count. Higher-end models are also able to read an electrocardiogram (ECG) waveform, blood pressure, and electrodermal activity, and are able to provide early cardiac arrhythmia or stress illness warnings. Wearable data is usually time-series in nature and high-frequency data supporting user metadata like age, gender, activity tags, etc (Beniczky et al., 2021; Hughes et al., 2023; Iqbal et al., 2021; Poongodi et al., 2020).

Implantable and Insertable Devices

Examples of implantable devices are smart pacemakers, cardioverter-defibrillators (ICDs), and glucose sensors (e.g., CGMs, Continuous Glucose Monitors) in the management of diabetes. They are implanted in the body and may automatically adjust the therapeutic settings (such as pacing rates or insulin delivery) in response to feedback provided in real-time. Insertable loop recorders and neurological stimulators to treat epilepsy or Parkinson's are included in this category, too. These devices produce high-resolution physiologic measures, sometimes more clinically relevant and ongoing than wearables, and send them through secured, usually proprietary, communications protocols to physician dashboards (Barbone et al., 2019; Chimene et al., 2024; Heffernan et al., 2021; Kim, 2021).

In-Hospital AIoT Systems

In the case of critical care settings, the integration of AIoT results in the expansion of precision and safety. Smart Beds, patient monitors, connected ventilators, and infusion pumps enable Smart ICU to monitor the patient continuously and trace vital signs, medication flow, oxygen levels, and patient movement in real-time. Patterns that indicate deterioration of the patient, onset of sepsis, or ventilator misconfiguration can be identified by the AI algorithms that were installed in these systems. These devices include a lot of multisensory high-frequency data streams that need low-latency edge processing and incorporation into Electronic Health Records (EHRs) (Jayachitra et al., 2023; Kavitha et al., 2025).

Ingestible Sensors and Smart Pills

Smart pills are one of the frontiers of diagnostic AIoT; these devices are ingestible and have miniature sensors and transmitters that present themselves in the gastrointestinal tract. These aids check the pH factor, temperature, and gastrointestinal motility, or confirm the intake of medicines. Others come with micro-cameras and are used to transfer images and video data to carry out internal diagnostics. Besides facilitating the detection of a disease, smart pills enhance the monitoring of medication compliance, especially in the psychiatric or geriatric setting (Chai et al., 2022; Litvinova et al., 2022; Mukherjee et al., 2022).

Ambient and Environmental AIoT Devices

Physiological data are accompanied by the environmental data provided by such environmental sensors as air quality monitors and motion sensors, and infrared thermal scanners, with the aim to buttress the context under which a patient lives/is treated. They are especially applicable in geriatric care or in dealing with infectious diseases to monitor exposure-related issues or falls in a care facility where someone needs assistance (A. Pise et al., 2023).

Imaging and Audio-Based AIoT Tools

Some of the AIoT items have been equipped with image sensors or sound analysis devices/applications. As an example, digital stethoscopes, dermatological imagers, and intelligent ultrasound probes collect unstructured data (e.g., high-resolution pictures, periodic sounds) and send them to cloud services where they are analyzed by AI models on an anomaly (e.g., lung cracks, skin lesions). This kind of data needs high bandwidth and sophisticated machine learning algorithms to classify and interpret data (Emvoliadis et al., 2024; Pervez et al., 2024).

Data Format Diversity Across the AIoT Ecosystem

The diversity of AIoT devices implemented in healthcare generates a large spectrum of data, which selects their definitive peculiarities and processing needs. The backbone of most AIoT applications is structured data, and comprises time-stamped vital signs, laboratory results, and system-generated logs, which are easy to store, query, and analyze using traditional database systems. Device configuration files, alert events, and the log data of the user interactions live in a gray area because they are not very clearly tabular, but do contain some schema or tagging that can partially order and allow parsing. On the more complicated extreme is the unstructured data, which includes audio signals, such as cough or breath sound recordings, image or video images produced with diagnostic tools, e.g., smart endoscopes or digital stethoscopes, and ad-hoc text notes that are typed in by the medical staff. To illustrate the diversity of AIoT sources and their corresponding data formats, Figure 1 maps common healthcare AIoT devices across three care settings, wearable, implantable, and facility-based, and shows the nature of data they generate (e.g., real-time vitals, logs, images). To synthesize the discussion, Figure 2 illustrates the typical data journey in an AIoT healthcare system, from sensor collection through transmission, storage, processing, and finally, to actionable clinical insight.

Figure 1. Overview of AIoT Devices and Data Types in Healthcare

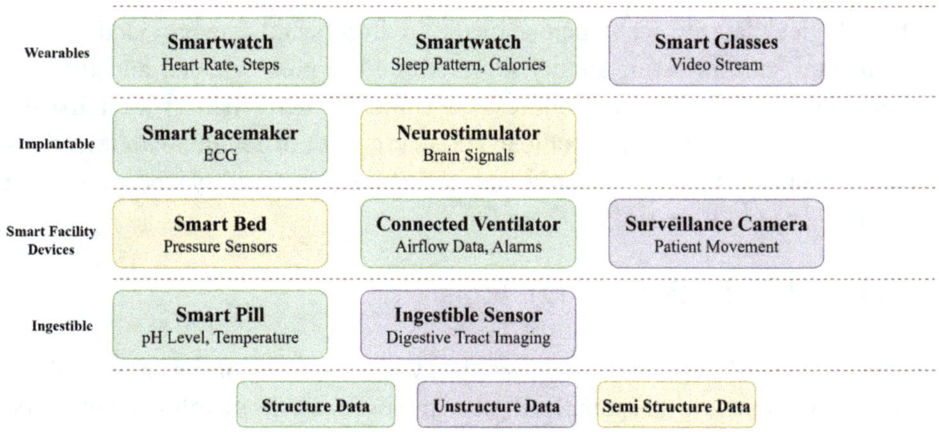

Figure 2. Data Journey from Device to Insight

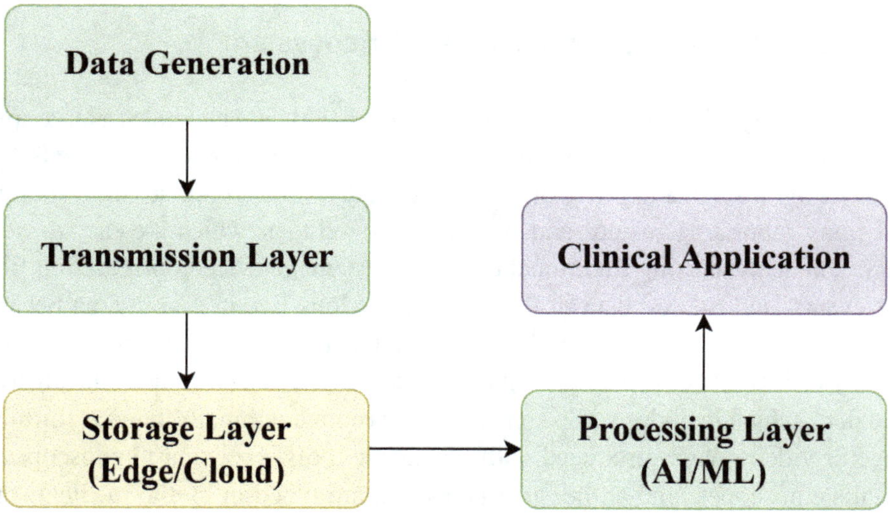

Data Characteristics

The spectrum of data produced by health-related AIoT systems is huge and complex, which can be successfully explained with the 5Vs architecture: volume, velocity, variety, veracity, and value. All these dimensions represent different features of the behavior of data within the ecosystem of smart healthcare and provide different opportunities and challenges to data processing and its clinical application.

- The term volume indicates the massive size of data generated by AIoT systems. The ubiquity of embedded sensors in wearables, medical equipment, and hospital infrastructure can be especially overwhelming in the healthcare field. For example, an ICU bed that has vital sign monitors, infusion pumps, and ventilators can generate more than 100,000 pieces of data per day. If this is rolled up by tens or hundreds of beds, the data inflow can grow rapidly to terabytes. To effectively store all this huge amount of data, there are strong data storage systems are needed, a scalable cloud infrastructure, and even data compression analytics that will efficiently make the collection and retrieval process a breeze.
- Velocity brings the speed of data creation, transmission, and processing into perspective. Within healthcare AIoT, data transmission is real-time or near real-time and, in many cases, running at millisecond levels. Such speed is more urgently needed in time-conditional medical disorders. As an example, ultra-low latency data pipelines are required in detecting and responding to an abnormal rhythmic heartbeat or a dramatic decrease in blood glucose level. In order to facilitate ongoing monitoring and autonomous responses, systems should be developed to consume, digest, and intervene on this data without time delay.
- Variety means different kinds and forms of data processed by AIoT systems. Not all healthcare AIoT data is the same; we can find structured numeric values such as pulse rate or blood pressure; categorical data such as alarms, device settings, etc.; multimedia data such as radiology images, video clips of movement, audio of respiratory sounds, etc.; and unstructured data like the clinical notes, system logs, and so on. Such a broad range creates integration problems and demands standards of interoperability and adaptable models of data to harmonize heterogeneous sources to analyze.
- Veracity covers the reliability, quality, and validity of the data. Healthcare decisions that are made with inaccurate or defective data are hazardous. But an AIoT system has a likelihood of sensor failure, signal drift, noise in the environment, and human error when inputting the data. To ensure truthfulness, sensor calibration procedures, redundancy procedures, data validation procedures, and data anomaly identification mechanisms need to be applied to identify inconsistencies or data gaps in the data stream.
- Value addresses the end objective of healthcare AIoT systems, to generate insights with raw data that benefit patients. Not every bit of data works the

same. Oxygen saturation or ECG waveforms are examples of some that can be used directly to diagnose and intervene, whereas others bandwidths or the angular frequency of recording with ECG frequencies post post-processing with machine learning AI algorithms, are only valuable when processed and the patterns or predicted clinical events identified. Value extraction involves more advanced analytics, clinical context, and loop feedback, moving information to decisions and activity.

All five features support the complexity of healthcare AIoT data. To achieve the greatest value possible, healthcare systems will have to implement smarter architectures and governance systems that can handle the amount, respond to the speed, support the variety, ensure the accuracy, and embrace the worth of information, and thus deliver smarter, safer, and more responsive care.

Core Challenges in Managing AIoT Healthcare Data

Although the application of AIoT technologies in the medical field can bring a breakthrough, there exists a range of challenges that severely complicate the efficient control and use of large data flows produced by these systems. These are not skin-deep technical challenges but are interlaced with regulation, ethics, and the organizational challenges that need to be sorted out to achieve the potential of AIoT in clinical practice.

- One of the greatest technical challenges is called heterogeneity. The AIoT landscape in healthcare represents the environment of a multifarious range of devices manufactured by a variety of vendors and sharing a variety of data formats, encoding patterns, communication protocols, and specifications of the corresponding hardware (Awaisi et al., 2024; Xu et al., 2024). This heterogeneity contributes to disaggregation and establishes challenges to data harmonization and aggregation. In the absence of a universal means of data depiction and trade, it is much too difficult to establish integrated systems that are able to present a unified picture of patient wellbeing at several points of contact.
- There are the Real-Time Requirements that create additional complexity. Sometimes, in critical care units, split-second decision-making could make a difference between life and death. Examples of apps that require real-time or ultra-low-latency data processing are apps to detect arrhythmia, automated insulin adjustment, or ventilator control. But most legacy systems incorporated in the health care sector are based on batch processing and the later analysis of data, but are not appropriate in cases where there has been an emergency,

whereby the data needs to be analyzed and given certain action immediately. Developing AIoT infrastructure that will process high-frequency real-time data flow is important to enable the delivery of time-sensitive interventions.

- Interoperability can be understood as the capacity of heterogeneous systems and equipment to communicate and work cooperatively (Awaisi et al., 2024; Xu et al., 2024). A veritable interoperability should enable the AIoT sensor data to interface with the hospital information systems, electronic health records (EHRs), and cloud and analytics systems. Alas, this smooth exchange is hampered by a lack of standard APIs, messaging systems, and standards of data schema design. Consequently, data can become so fragmented, sequestered in individual silos, that they become minimally useful and capable of hindering the development of complete patient profiles or making coordinated care feasible.
- The concepts of privacy and security are especially demanding in terms of healthcare AIoT, as the data of patients is very sensitive and proliferates (Awaisi et al., 2024; Xu et al., 2024). The presence of AIoT systems proliferates the endpoints, wearable devices, and remote monitoring systems, each may present a target of a cyberattack, illegal access, or data loss. The attack surface is also increased with the use of cloud computing and wireless communication. Minimizing theft and loss or leakage of data, having the ability to control availability, encryption, enforcement of legal frameworks, HIPAA, GDPR, or local data protection regulations are some of the most sophisticated yet important requirements.
- Issues of data governance and ownership arise, as data is transferred in a complicated ecosystem of stakeholders those are patients, clinicians, medical device manufacturers, insurers, and technology vendors. It becomes debatable as to who the owner of the data is and who is allowed to access the data, and in what conditions. Also, issues about informed consent, monetization of data, possible surveillance, and abuse of personal health data exist. Such issues stipulate the necessity of developing efficient governance structures, taking care of the balance among innovation, transparency, accountability, and patient empowerment.

Table 2 summarizes the core challenges faced in managing healthcare AIoT data, along with brief implications and possible solution pathways. In order to handle these issues comprehensively, healthcare facilities should not search only for technical solutions. The remedies should be composed of regulatory change, the development of industry-standard rules, public-private association, and a human-oriented design approach where the requirements, privileges, and prosperity of patients should become the primary focus of AIoT building and implementation. It is only in such a multi-dimensional way that the potential of AIoT in healthcare can be adequately and appropriately actualized.

Table 2. Key Challenges in AIoT Healthcare Data Management

Challenge	Implications	Example Scenario	Potential Mitigation
Heterogeneity	Integration bottlenecks	Multi-vendor device networks	Common data models, standard protocols
Real-Time Requirements	Risk of delayed care	Arrhythmia detection	Edge/fog computing, event-driven AI
Interoperability	Data silos, fragmented records	Cross-hospital referrals	FHIR/HL7 APIs, middleware
Privacy & Security	Data breach risks, compliance burden	Remote monitoring via mobile apps	Encryption, federated learning
Governance & Ownership	Ethical ambiguity, liability issues	AI diagnosis by cloud platforms	Consent mechanisms, legal frameworks

ARCHITECTURES AND FRAMEWORKS FOR SCALABLE DATA MANAGEMENT

Real-time data storage, organization, and retrieval envisioned by the use of AIoT systems in the healthcare setting not only requires the ability to gather and perform analytics on data transversely in real time, but also sturdy and extensible data storage and retrieval structures. Given the ongoing accelerating volume and diversity of data that wearable devices, implantable, smart diagnostics, and remote monitors are producing, the healthcare system needs to be able to deploy more flexible and interoperable architectures that enable both short-term clinical use and long-term analytic application.

Data Lakes and Data Warehouses in Healthcare

The major components of the healthcare data architecture are two storage paradigms: data warehouses and data lakes. Although both continue to perform the same functions of focusing data to analyze and report, they have great differences in their structure and usability (Gentner et al., 2023; Idowu et al., 2023; Lamer et al., 2024). The data warehouses are the central data stores that are optimized for structured data and are in in-line with predefined schema. They can be used when data purity, data integrity, and high-speed SQL-based querying are important, like those systems found in transactional applications of healthcare, like billing, laboratory result reporting, or structured electronic health records (EHRs). But they are not agile, well-equipped to handle the high-impact, chaotic, and unstructured data created by AIoT devices.

In comparison, data lakes make it possible to store heterogeneous data in raw format, both structured (vital signs), semi-structured (device logs), and unstructured (medical imaging, audio, video). They are very re-scorable, schema-adaptable, and more supportive of the emerging turbulent and multimodal AIoT data specialty. The data lakes allow healthcare organizations to consume massive amounts of sensor data and perform big data analytics and machine learning workflows on these datasets without the necessity of hardware-based preprocessing. A common model is a blended strategy: data lakes are applied where raw data is ingested and transformed, and data warehouses are used to host curated, cleaned, and query-enabled data needed to report and to comply.

On-Premise, Cloud-Based, and Hybrid Storage Solutions

The architecture should be selected as the data storage system, which is of critical importance in healthcare systems with AIoT applications, since it influences the possibilities of scale, security, local and remote access, and compliance. These three different models of which are cloud-based, on-premise, and hybrid, come into play, and they all have unique advantages as well as disadvantages. The model that is chosen all depends on the particular needs of the healthcare provider in terms of operation and regulatory requirements, as well as the technical needs of the healthcare provider (Ali et al., 2024; Deb & Choudhury, 2021; Gorantla et al., 2024).

AWS HealthLake (Dubey et al., 2025) and Microsoft Azure Health Data Services are examples of cloud-based storage, which are highly scalable so that they can be virtually limitless in terms of capacity and elastic computing resources. Artificial intelligence and machine learning services are also integrated into those platforms, so it is simpler to use advanced analytics and predictive models on healthcare data. The cloud model has many advantages to require in distributed care networks or even those of the telemedical approach, since it enables remote access, management, and regular attainments. But there is a price to pay when you have this convenience- a dependency on third-party providers leaves the question of data sovereignty (particularly with cross-border situations), possible vendor lock-in, and the threats of latency and internet outages.

Controlled management of data is more thorough in on-premise storage, which is managed within the premises of a data center of a hospital or a healthcare organization. The model is particularly useful for institutions that are in a tight regulatory environment or have very delicate and sensitive health-related data that cannot be left in foreign hands. On-premise system also gives more reasonable performance in cases when access to the internet is inconsistent or limited. These benefits, however, have severe trade-offs: ensuring that the infrastructure can attract the growing amount of data may not come cheap, and the responsibility of maintaining the hardware, guaranteeing cybersecurity, and overseeing that the system is falls fully on the organization.

Hybrid storage models are introduced to combine the best characteristics of the cloud and an in-house approach. In the method, sensitive or important data, like that which is identifiable by a person, including health records, are stored and distributed locally to allow certain privacy and low-latency decision-making. In the meantime, less sensitive anonymized or historical data may be moved into the cloud, where it may be stored or used to perform longer-term analytics or train machine learning models. Such division can enable healthcare systems to have data ownership and responsiveness in real-time, as well as use the scale and computing power of the cloud. In edge-to-cloud architecture, Hybrid models are more appropriate, as the edge devices conduct an instant analysis, as close to the exploited data source as possible, and the cloud is used as a universal centralized point towards aggregation and expanded intelligence. Table 3 summarizes the key characteristics, advantages, and limitations of cloud-based, on-premise, and hybrid storage models in healthcare AIoT environments, enabling stakeholders to choose the most appropriate architecture for their operational and regulatory needs. To illustrate how data flows and is managed across AIoT-enabled healthcare infrastructures, Figure 3 shows a layered architecture that integrates edge devices, fog nodes, on-premise systems, and cloud platforms. This hybrid design ensures real-time responsiveness, secure local control, and scalable analytics.

Table 3. Comparative Overview of Healthcare AIoT Storage Architectures and Integration Models

Model	Key Features	Advantages	Challenges	Best Use Cases
Cloud-Based	Remote, elastic infrastructure; supports big data & AI services	High scalability, low upfront cost, integrated analytics	Latency, data sovereignty concerns, and dependence on connectivity	Telehealth, mobile health apps, and large hospital networks
On-Premise	Locally hosted servers and systems	Full control, high security, compliance-ready	High setup/maintenance costs, limited scalability	Critical care units, regulatory-sensitive institutions
Hybrid	Combines local and cloud systems	Flexible, balances control and scalability	Complexity in integration and synchronization	Smart hospitals, phased modernization, edge-to-cloud setups

Figure 3. Hybrid AIoT Data Architecture for Intelligent Healthcare

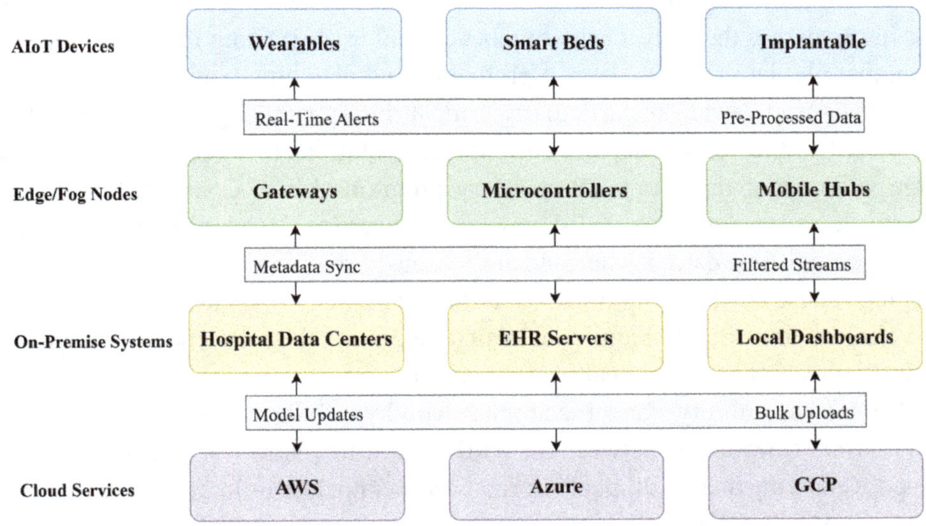

APIs, Middleware, and Interoperability Standards

Scalable AIoT data ecosystems are built on the idea of interoperability. With the spreading of devices, platforms, and systems, it is essential to ensure unhindered communication in terms of data exchange and integration.

Application Programming Interfaces (APIs) are the critical digital glue in AIoT healthcare solutions, and they are essential in enabling interconnection among the range of components of the system, including wearable devices, such as hospital information systems (HIS), and cloud platforms, among other systems. These interfaces outline the standards and guidelines that allow various programs to harmonize information conveniently without going through the tiresome process of coordination. APIs enable the rapid development and growth of healthcare ecosystems via the support of the modular system design that provides low-friction integration of new devices, services, and systems within the ecosystem. The most popular RESTful APIs are extremely simple and compatible with web technologies, although GraphQL is already popular as it allows streamlining data queries in a mobile and real-time context. The interoperability and flexibility of the suite in the open APIs help unlock the ability of various systems to integrate without being subjected to proprietary barriers, whereas closed APIs or proprietary APIs may hamper scalability and create vendor lock-in, restraining the responsiveness of the healthcare system in the future.

The middleware platforms act as the essential data translators in this architecture, as they can allow communication between disparate systems by translating, routing, and harmonizing the data. They are most crucial in abstracting the redundancy of incompatible data formats, legacy protocols, and changing communication standards. The middleware is particularly critical during challenges of incorporating the older healthcare systems into current AIoT solutions that generate diverse and large volumes of data flows. Proprietary programs Mirth Connect, Redox, and InterSystems Ensemble are well-known middleware tools that provide such capabilities as real-time data transfer, semantics transformations, message auditing, and logging. These attributes optimize data transfer between systems, preserve context and clinical context, and requirements that determine the efficiency of operations and patient safety in smart healthcare systems.

The interoperability standards are the shared vocabulary that enables a similar and relevant flow of data between the AIoT healthcare platforms. The standards are aimed at ensuring that the clinical information does not lose its integrity and usability along the way as it passes through devices, databases, and analytical systems. There are several most popular standards of messaging and sharing clinical documents with electronic health record (EHR) systems, such as HL7 v2 and HL7 CDA. A more modern solution, web-native, is FHIR (Fast Healthcare Interoperability Resources), which enables access to data in fine-grained, e.g., grabbing an individual lab result or vital sign, which makes it an ideal candidate to become the backbone of cloud services and mobile AIoT applications. The adoption process also relies on domain-specific ones, which are fundamental to the management of medical image data, such as DICOM, and on the interoperability with personal health monitoring services, such as glucose meters or ECG development ones, such as IEEE 11073. The combination of the standards provides the foundation of scalability, reliability, and intelligence of AIoT-driven healthcare by ensuring that the data is available, well-organized, and clinically useful through the care continuum.

INTELLIGENT DATA PROCESSING

With the spread of AIoT devices in the healthcare setting, the amount of constantly ongoing, real-time information is huge, and immediate analysis and reaction are necessary. Without an external on-demand edge-located data processing service, such as a centralized cloud setup, the processing of this data may experience unacceptable latency and bandwidth issues with additional sensitivity to drops or attacks. In order to overcome these constraints, contemporary health system data architectures are rapidly incorporating multi-layer processing models that extend across networks toward the centralized cloud models. In this section, the capabilities of intelligent data processing on the edge, fog, and cloud levels are discussed and studied to understand how they can optimize healthcare performance, responsiveness, and scalability.

Edge and Fog Computing

Edge Computing is the act of local data processing of data, either at or close to the source of the data production, such as in or above an AIoT device, like wearable monitors, biosensors, or portable medical devices etc (Chang et al., 2021). Rather than transmission of enormous flows of raw data back to central servers, edge computing supports real-time analytics, filtering, and initial decision making locally on the device or proximate to it. As an illustration, an intelligent ECG patch could be equipped with on-device AI that will identify arrhythmia immediately and deliver only life-threatening notifications/abnormalities to a physician. This method helps keep delays in transmission to a minimum and makes immediate life-saving insights to be produced without using remote servers.

Fog Computing, in turn, is the intermediate level between centralized cloud infrastructure and edge devices that is distributed. Fog nodes, i.e., local servers, gateways, or edge clusters deployed in hospitals, provide edge-to-edge analytics and operational insight and can collect, aggregate, and process a combination of edge device outputs. This model lessens numerical pressure on the cloud systems, as activities such as information pre-processing, encryption, and rule-based event manipulation can be performed at the local level. Fog computing solves edge-to-cloud data management capabilities that are scalable, resilient, and context-aware in healthcare environments like mobile clinics, emergency response units, and hospital subnets, among others.

Edge and fog computing have great benefits in healthcare settings with AIoT. They can support low-latency responses critical to time-sensitive tasks such as the detection of seizures or the control of a ventilator, enhance the bandwidth efficiency by sending only high-value/preprocessed data to the cloud, and strengthen patient privacy by letting anonymized or secure data be treated at the local level. There are, however, trade-offs to these benefits. These edge devices usually possess low processing capacities and memory, so they need to be optimized and resource management. Also, operating a decentralized system of edge and fog nodes brings about operational complexity in terms of data consistency, software upgrades, and a distributed security system. Nonetheless, a combination of both edge and fog computing offers the foundation on which real-time intelligent healthcare delivery operates within AIoT ecosystems.

Distributed Systems for Latency-Sensitive Applications

Distributed systems are vital in the support of latency-sensitive healthcare applications by providing a guarantee of high availability, resilience, and responsiveness opportunities. Centralized processing by itself is usually insufficient in situations where every millisecond is vital, i.e., in intensive care units, emergency departments, or remote monitoring. Distributed architectures address this through the use of a network representing the interconnection of devices, fog nodes, and edge processors, by being their computation, data sharing, and decision-making collaborators.

Take, as an example, an intelligent hospital that implements AIoT: With several fog nodes distributed at the boundaries of the facility, in the ICUs, and in the wards or diagnostic units, several patient vitals could be monitored concurrently; anomaly detection could be performed, and signal preprocessing could be carried out locally. Such distributed nodes distribute their workloads and cross-check their data, such that patterns of critical deterioration are identified in as near real-time as possible. Such a system can even be integrated with the electronic health records in real-time and may even tell a clinician by sending out alerts without relying wholeheartedly on cloud connectivity. In addition to enhancing fault tolerance, this form of architecture also ensures that the services are continuous in the event of network breakdown or peak-time traffic.

Scaling the AIoT infrastructure should not compromise performance, but the distributed nature of its system permits the healthcare institution to divide the computational resources, such as signal normalization, predictive modeling, or multi-source data fusion, and distribute them across a distributed system. Distributing this intelligence is key in the provision of reliable, contextual care, particularly in resource- or time-limited situations.

Real-Time vs. Batch Processing Frameworks

When referring to healthcare data processing frameworks, one can make a rough generalization between such processing models as real-time processing and batch-based processing, which have different sets of requirements in an AIoT-enabled healthcare setting. Real-time processing is meant to analyze and make decisions based on data as soon (or as close to it) as possible. It is essential in those applications where responses are to be quick, e.g., seizure predictions, insulin pump control, or elderly care, where falls may be predicted or detected. In such a case, milliseconds count, and data should be processed near the source. Stream processing like Apache

Kafka Streams, Apache Flink, as well as TensorFlow Lite, enables light computation on edge or fog devices, and is used when there is a need to have real-time analytics.

On the other hand, batching is optimized when analyzing huge data whose time requirement is not critical. It is appropriate to use in a retrospective or cumulative scenario like population health research, identification of chronic disease patterns, or training a complicated machine learning model. Such tasks are commonly performed in cloud-based environments using a higher level of scaling tools like Apache Spark, Google Cloud Dataflow, or AWS Lambda, where latency is less vital but the processing power and storage are foundational.

Frequently, the hybrid architecture can provide an ideal compromise. Streams of real-time data are filtered and acted on at the edge or fog layer in an attempt to resolve time-sensitive clinical needs, whereas flows of raw or semi-processed data are transported to the cloud, where further longitudinal analysis can be performed on it, and colonial processing. This provides the healthcare systems the capacity to remain responsive in real-time and insightful over time, which is dynamic as per the current needs of patients. To clarify the trade-offs and strengths of each computational layer, Table 4 provides a comparative summary of edge, fog, and cloud processing in healthcare AIoT systems.

Table 4. Comparative Analysis of Edge, Fog, and Cloud Computing in AIoT-Enabled Healthcare Systems.

Feature	Edge Computing	Fog Computing	Cloud Computing
Location	On or near an AIoT device	Local network (hospital routers/gateways)	Remote data centers
Latency	Ultra-low (milliseconds)	Low	High (seconds to minutes)
Processing Power	Limited	Moderate	High
Bandwidth Usage	Minimal	Moderate	High
Use Cases	Real-time alerts, local anomaly detection	Data aggregation, local dashboards	Model training, population health analytics
Privacy and Security	High (data stays local)	Moderate	Lower (requires encryption, policies)
Scalability	Limited	Moderate	Very high
Maintenance	Device-specific updates	Network management	Centralized cloud management

AI AND MACHINE LEARNING FOR HEALTHCARE DATA UTILIZATION

The amount and intricacy of data produced by AIoT devices in healthcare are enormous in comparison to the scope of conventional analytics procedures. Artificial Intelligence (AI) and Machine Learning (ML) are being used increasingly with the objective of leveraging this data to realize meaningful clinical utility by deriving insights and automatic decision-making to facilitate personalized care.

AI/ML Solutions to AIoT Healthcare Systems

Artificial intelligence and machine learning in combination with AIoT healthcare infrastructures represent a paradigm change in healthcare delivery systems between the past reactive healthcare environment and the present data-driven and proactive healthcare action. AI/ML models interpolate streams of data captured by wearables, sensors, and clinical systems and provide ad hoc insights in real-time that can assist in the management of individual patients as well as leading population health strategies.

- Among the most effective applications, one can distinguish predictive analytics. With the help of historic and real-time data, AI models can predict the course of the disease, arrange patients who may have a readmission, or foresee negative clinical outcomes before they arise. As an example, machine learning algorithms that analyze data captured by continuous glucose monitors (CGMs) can be used to forecast hypoglycemic events with ample time in advance so that patients and providers can take early intervention, thereby avoiding complications.
- Another critical application is anomaly detection, during which the edge devices equipped with AI can examine and recognize specific physiological signals that are deviations in behavioural patterns. They can detect evidence of arrhythmias, sleep apnea, or early sepsis in unsupervised learning systems or through time-series analysis without any operator input. Edge computing with embedded intelligence allows real-time, decidedly local decision-making, which is essential in times of emergency.
- Patient stratification can also improve clinical workflows, as people can be divided into subgroups between individuals on different risks, subtypes of the disease, or who are likely to respond to treatment. Within high-pressure settings like an intensive care unit or emergency department, this type of grouping aids in efficient distribution of resources and prioritization of the sickest.

- In addition, context-sensitive alerting systems merge multifarious data transmissions, such as vital signs, activity levels, and medication adherence records, to provide clinically significant warning signs. In contrast to the common non-AI-based alarm systems, which are based on a fixed threshold, these AI-based notifications are customized to the whole clinical picture of the patient, and therefore, they are less likely to produce ineffective alarms and lead to caregiver alert overload.

When combined, all of these applications of AI/ML allow the full potential of AIoT in healthcare analytics to be realized by turning high-dimensional data with complex formulations into actionable insights in time. Not only can this improve clinical decision-making but also give rise to a more proactive and personalized manner of delivering care.

Challenges

Despite these opportunities, AI/ML in healthcare has several severe limitations that restrict its scalability and reliability.

- It is demonstrated that technical complexity is not the only factor determining the successful implementation of AIoT systems in healthcare: their efficiency depends on the ethical soundness of the AI models, as well. Among the first challenges is the quality of training data. The very nature of AI models means that they are also reliant on the data used to train, which in a healthcare domain may be imperfect, noisy, or unbalanced. To illustrate, electronic health records can possess missing responses, and datasets might disproportionately reflect some people according to their demographic group and underrepresent the rest. Moreover, sensor drift in real-world operation or defective hardware, or patient non-compliance (e.g., inconsistency with the use of devices) may result in data influenced by real-world issues (generated by AIoT). Left unaddressed, these issues can jeopardize the validity of AI predictions and decisions when it is not adequately addressed using preprocessing, imputation, and strict validation.
- The other important issue is that of model bias and fairness. When AI is trained using unrepresentative data, there is a risk of simply reinforcing the current disparities in the health field. An example of such a system could be a fall detection system that would be initially trained using the data in young, healthy persons and would therefore not accurately diagnose falls in older persons or low mobility persons. This may be applied to other diagnostic algorithms or treatment recommendation systems and may increase dispari-

ties in care provision. Fairness must be achieved by purposely not excluding diverse groups in the development of models and subsequent performance audits based on subsets of the demographic groups.

- Interpretability and trust are very important, particularly in clinical applications where a decision can change someone's life. Healthcare professionals, as well as regulators, tend to be skeptical of black-box models, i.e., those whose inner logic is a black box. Clinicians should be capable of deciphering, substantiating, and believing in the logic of the AI-produced outputs, especially when those are used in making diagnoses or therapeutic plans. This has motivated the development of explainable AI (XAI) methods that provide more readable and understandable behavior of models. XAI helps clinical integration by assuring ethical compliance and regulatory clearance through its capacity to improve interpretability, establishing the foundation of responsible and trustworthy AIoT healthcare systems.

It is necessary to develop a multidisciplinary approach bringing data scientists, clinicians, ethicists, and policymakers to agree on core themes and focus on the ethical, safety, and fairness of AI systems that are safe, fair, and clinically meaningful. Table 5 provides an overview of AI/ML use cases in AIoT-driven healthcare and associated data challenges.

Table 5. AI/ML Use Cases in AIoT-Driven Healthcare and Associated Data Challenges

Use Case	Data Source	AI/ML Method	Challenge(s)	Processing Urgency
Predictive Analytics	EHRs, wearable sensors	Time-series forecasting, regression	Data incompleteness, imbalanced datasets	Early detection of disease or deterioration
Anomaly Detection	ECG, glucose monitors, smart beds	Unsupervised learning, autoencoders	Noisy signals, false positives	Rapid intervention for critical events
Patient Stratification	Historical EHR + real-time IoT feeds	Clustering, classification	Model generalization, bias	Resource optimization and risk grouping
Federated Learning	Decentralized hospital/device data	Federated averaging, differential privacy	Non-IID data, communication overhead	Privacy-preserving collaborative learning
Feedback-Driven Optimization	Smart pills, monitoring apps, EMRs	Reinforcement learning	Feedback loop delay, system integration	Continuous care adaptation and personalization
Explainable Decision Support	AIoT + clinical guidelines	XAI (e.g., SHAP, LIME)	Lack of transparency, clinician skepticism	Trust, adoption, and regulatory compliance

Federated Learning for Privacy-Aware ML

Among the main challenges to the implementation of AI in healthcare, we can outline the sensitivity of patient information and the strict policies of data privacy. The alternative paradigm that has been proposed to solve this problem is federated learning (FL).

Machine learning models in federated learning run locally and analyze decentralized data on the edge (e.g., at hospitals, medical devices). It only shares and aggregates model parameters (not raw data), making sure that no patient data will ever leave its source. This solution lowers the privacy risk considerably and is in line with the legal regulations like HIPAA, GDPR, and other health data management regulations.

To illustrate, different hospitals can train a model to predict early strokes using sensor data and hospital EHR without data exchange between them, with identifiable data about patients. FL is especially applicable to AIoT environments in which data are collected at the edge and may be used to facilitate lifelong learning in a privacy-respectful way in multiple clinical settings.

Nevertheless, the process of federated learning also brings about a number of technical complexities that should be resolved to make it successful. Another serious problem is that devices and data distributions are heterogeneous; in real-life applications of healthcare, institutions or the devices of patients generate data that is not always independent and identically distributed (is not IID), causing model training to fail. Also, communication latency and synchronization cost may become an obstacle to efficiency, especially in cases when constant updates need to be communicated between the nodes, which are far apart and have no high bandwidth. Achieving fairness and consistency among the nodes involved is also a challenge, because differences in data quality, quantity, and available computational capacity may lead to biased contributions to any model. In spite of these issues, the potential and need for federated learning is the next major step in the practical deployment of scalable and collaborative AI in healthcare without loss of data privacy.

CONCLUSION

The use of AIoT technologies in healthcare is opening a new paradigm shift in collecting data, processing it, and using it to enhance the outcomes of patients. The combination of artificial intelligence and sensor-rich IoT systems opens completely new frontiers, as discussed throughout this chapter, on personalized medicine, continuous monitoring, and predictive care. Whether edge-based anomaly detection,

AI-driven decision-making systems, or any other application of the combination of data and intelligence facets, synergies are at the core of the change.

Neuromorphic computing and digital twin models, real-time biosignal analytics are new technologies that are extending the limits of intelligent healthcare. Neuromorphic chips hold the promise of AI calculations on the actual medical device, with power consumption in the millions of times lower than current medical hardware; digital twins will allow a truly individualized simulation of human physiology; the next generation of biosignal AI will allow analyzing health status on a second-to-second level. All these innovations are a pointer to the future where care is not only predictive, but also proactive.

But this does not come to the future without friction. Such remaining issues as data control, responsible AI deployment, and an absence of shared interoperability guidelines remain the barriers to the broad use of AIoT. With issues of patient privacy, algorithm biases, and whether decisions were made transparently, it is important that these concerns are met with open frameworks and governance strategies that are participatory.

In order to overcome these challenges, a strategic plan is imperative, particularly focusing on facilitating policies, inter-sector cooperation, and national capacity development. Both healthcare institutions and governments need to act in unison to establish regulations and policies that do not endanger patients but encourage innovation. Another aspect that can be essential to grow these technologies responsibly is investing in AI literacy, as well as regulatory sandboxes and digital infrastructure.

AIoT in healthcare is in the future of multidisciplinary cooperation, the collaboration between clinicians, engineers, data scientists, ethicists, and the patients themselves to code solutions collaboratively, scalable, ethical, and human-centered. The possibilities of using AIoT to transform healthcare across the board can only be achieved when the technological changes are in line with societal values.

REFERENCES

Ali, A., Laghari, A. A., Kandhro, I. A., Kumar, K., & Younus, S. (2024). Systematic analysis of on-premise and cloud services. *International Journal of Cloud Computing, 13*(3), 214–242. DOI: 10.1504/IJCC.2024.139604

Awaisi, K. S., Ye, Q., & Sampalli, S. (2024). A Survey of Industrial AIoT: Opportunities, Challenges, and Directions. *IEEE Access : Practical Innovations, Open Solutions, 12*, 96946–96996. DOI: 10.1109/ACCESS.2024.3426279

Baker, S., & Xiang, W. (2023). Artificial Intelligence of Things for Smarter Healthcare: A Survey of Advancements, Challenges, and Opportunities. *IEEE Communications Surveys and Tutorials, 25*(2), 1261–1293. DOI: 10.1109/COMST.2023.3256323

Barbone, A. S., Meftah, M., Markiewicz, K., & Dellimore, K. (2019). Beyond wearables and implantables: A scoping review of insertable medical devices. *Biomedical Physics & Engineering Express, 5*(6), 062002. DOI: 10.1088/2057-1976/ab4b32

Beniczky, S., Karoly, P., Nurse, E., Ryvlin, P., & Cook, M. (2021). Machine learning and wearable devices of the future. *Epilepsia, 62*(S2), S116–S124. DOI: 10.1111/epi.16555 PMID: 32712958

Chai, P. R., Vaz, C., Goodman, G. R., Albrechta, H., Huang, H., Rosen, R. K., Boyer, E. W., Mayer, K. H., & O'Cleirigh, C. (2022). Ingestible electronic sensors to measure instantaneous medication adherence: A narrative review. *Digital Health, 8*. Advance online publication. DOI: 10.1177/20552076221083119 PMID: 35251683

Chang, Z., Liu, S., Xiong, X., Cai, Z., & Tu, G. (2021). A Survey of Recent Advances in Edge-Computing-Powered Artificial Intelligence of Things. *IEEE Internet of Things Journal, 8*(18), 13849–13875. DOI: 10.1109/JIOT.2021.3088875

Chimene, D., Queener, K. M. K., Ko, B. S., McShane, M., & Daniele, M. (2024). Insertable Biosensors: Combining Implanted Sensing Materials with Wearable Monitors. *Annual Review of Biomedical Engineering, 26*(1), 197–221. DOI: 10.1146/annurev-bioeng-110222-101045 PMID: 38346276

Deb, M., & Choudhury, A. (2021). Hybrid cloud: A new paradigm in cloud computing. *Machine Learning Techniques and Analytics for Cloud Security*, 3–23. DOI: 10.1002/9781119764113.ch1

Dubey, P., Thinakaran, A., & Rewatkar, R. M. (2025). Digitizing Wellness: A Deep Dive Into EHR/EMR Systems. *The Impact of Algorithmic Technologies on Healthcare*, 375–396. DOI: 10.1002/9781394305490.ch17

Emvoliadis, A., Vryzas, N., Stamatiadou, M. E., Vrysis, L., & Dimoulas, C. (2024). Multimodal Environmental Sensing Using AI & IoT Solutions: A Cognitive Sound Analysis Perspective. *Sensors 2024, Vol. 24, Page 2755, 24*(9), 2755. DOI: 10.3390/s24092755

Gentner, T., Neitzel, T., Schulze, J., Gerschner, F., & Theissler, A. (2023). Data Lakes in Healthcare: Applications and Benefits from the Perspective of Data Sources and Players. *Procedia Computer Science, 225*, 1302–1311. DOI: 10.1016/j.procs.2023.10.118

Gorantla, V. A. K., Gude, V., Sriramulugari, S. K., Yuvaraj, N., & Yadav, P. (2024). Utilizing Hybrid Cloud Strategies to Enhance Data Storage and Security in E-Commerce Applications. *2024 2nd International Conference on Disruptive Technologies, ICDT 2024*, 494–499. DOI: 10.1109/ICDT61202.2024.10489749

Heffernan, K. J., Vetere, F., & Chang, S. (2021). *Insertables: Beyond Cyborgs and Augmentation to Convenience and Amenity*. 185–227. DOI: 10.1007/978-3-030-30457-7_6

Hemalatha, J., Balasubramanian, C., Sekar, M., Senthil Pandian, P., & Rajeswari, S. (2025). AIoT-powered proactive elderly healthcare: Wearable monitoring. *Rehabilitation Engineering, Assistive Technologies and the Future of Healthcare Using Robotics*, 165–182. DOI: 10.1016/B978-0-443-31624-1.00009-5

Hughes, A., Shandhi, M. M. H., Master, H., Dunn, J., & Brittain, E. (2023). Wearable Devices in Cardiovascular Medicine. *Circulation Research, 132*(5), 652–670. DOI: 10.1161/CIRCRESAHA.122.322389 PMID: 36862812

Idowu, E. A. A., Teo, J., Salih, S., Valverde, J., & Yeung, J. A. (2023). Streams, rivers, and data lakes: An introduction to understanding modern electronic healthcare records. *Clinical Medicine, 23*(4), 409–413. DOI: 10.7861/clinmed.2022-0325 PMID: 37524426

Iqbal, S. M. A., Mahgoub, I., Du, E., Leavitt, M. A., & Asghar, W. (2021). Advances in healthcare wearable devices. *Npj Flexible Electronics 2021 5:1, 5*(1), 1–14. DOI: 10.1038/s41528-021-00107-x

Jayachitra, S., Prasanth, A., Hariprasath, S., Benazir Begam, R., & Madiajagan, M. (2023). *AI Enabled Internet of Medical Things in Smart Healthcare*. 141–161. DOI: 10.1007/978-3-031-31952-5_7

Kavitha, N., Nivethitha, T., Deebanchakkarawarthi, G., & Shakthipriya, P. (2025). Transforming Healthcare : Unleashing the Power of Artificial Intelligence of Things (AIoT). *AIoT*, 99–129. DOI: 10.1201/9781003482338-5

Kim, C. (2021). Evolution of Advanced Miniaturization for Active Implantable Medical Devices. *Nano-Bio- Electronic, Photonic and MEMS Packaging*, 407–415. DOI: 10.1007/978-3-030-49991-4_17

Lamer, A., Saint-Dizier, C., Paris, N., & Chazard, E. (2024). Data Lake, Data Warehouse, Datamart, and Feature Store: Their Contributions to the Complete Data Reuse Pipeline. *JMIR Medical Informatics, 12*(1), e54590. DOI: 10.2196/54590 PMID: 39037339

Litvinova, O., Klager, E., Tzvetkov, N. T., Kimberger, O., Kletecka-Pulker, M., Willschke, H., & Atanasov, A. G. (2022). Digital Pills with Ingestible Sensors: Patent Landscape Analysis. *Pharmaceuticals 2022, Vol. 15, Page 1025, 15*(8), 1025. DOI: 10.3390/ph15081025

Mukherjee, S., Suleman, S., Pilloton, R., Narang, J., & Rani, K. (2022). State of the Art in Smart Portable, Wearable, Ingestible and Implantable Devices for Health Status Monitoring and Disease Management. *Sensors 2022, Vol. 22, Page 4228, 22*(11), 4228. DOI: 10.3390/s22114228

Pervez, F., Shoukat, M., Suresh, V., Farooq, M. U., Sandhu, M., Qayyum, A., Usama, M., Girardi, A., Latif, S., & Qadir, J. (2024). Medicine's New Rhythm: Harnessing Acoustic Sensing via the Internet of Audio Things for Healthcare. *IEEE Open Journal of the Computer Society, 5*, 491–510. DOI: 10.1109/OJCS.2024.3462812

Pise, A., Yoon, B., & Singh, S. (2023). Enabling Ambient Intelligence of Things (AIoT) healthcare system architectures. *Computer Communications, 198*, 186–194. DOI: 10.1016/j.comcom.2022.10.029

Pise, A. A., Almuzaini, K. K., Ahanger, T. A., Farouk, A., pant, K., Pareek, P. K., & Nuagah, S. J. (2022). Enabling Artificial Intelligence of Things (AIoT) Healthcare Architectures and Listing Security Issues. *Computational Intelligence and Neuroscience, 8421434*(1), 1–14. DOI: 10.1155/2022/8421434 PMID: 36911247

Poongodi, T., Krishnamurthi, R., Indrakumari, R., Suresh, P., & Balusamy, B. (2020). Wearable Devices and IoT. *Intelligent Systems Reference Library, 165*, 245–273. DOI: 10.1007/978-3-030-23983-1_10

Qureshi, K. N., & Newe, T. (2024). Artificial Internet of Things : A New Paradigm of Connected Networks. *Artificial Intelligence of Things (AIoT)*, 3–20. DOI: 10.1201/9781003430018-2

Seng, K. P., Ang, L. M., & Ngharamike, E. (2022). Artificial intelligence Internet of Things: A new paradigm of distributed sensor networks. *International Journal of Distributed Sensor Networks, 18*(3). Advance online publication. DOI: 10.1177/15501477211062835

Talukder, A., & Haas, R. (2021). AIoT: AI meets IoT and Web in Smart Healthcare. *ACM International Conference Proceeding Series*, 92–98. DOI: 10.1145/3462741.3466650

Thamik, H., Cabrera, J. D. F., & Wu, J. (2024). The Digital Paradigm: Unraveling the Impact of Artificial Intelligence and Internet of Things on Achieving Sustainable Development Goals. *Lecture Notes on Data Engineering and Communications Technologies*, *192*, 21–40. DOI: 10.1007/978-3-031-53433-1_2

Xu, H., Seng, K. P., Ang, L. M., & Smith, J. (2024). Decentralized and Distributed Learning for AIoT: A Comprehensive Review, Emerging Challenges, and Opportunities. *IEEE Access : Practical Innovations, Open Solutions*, *12*, 101016–101052. DOI: 10.1109/ACCESS.2024.3422211

Chapter 5

CGM IoT-Based Systems as a Biometric Data Input for Real-Time Marketing: A New Frontier to Consumer Decision-Making

Tatiana Tolusso
http://orcid.org/0009-0002-8154-9603
IULM, Italy

ABSTRACT

This chapter deals with the integration of Continuous Glucose Monitoring (CGM) IoT-based systems into real-time and automation marketing strategies. In response to the increasing complexity of digital context, the study introduces glucose as a novel biometric indicator that provides insights into consumer decision-making. Through the use of CGM IoT-based systems, the real-time collection of biometric data supports the personalisation and optimisation of marketing strategies aligned with consumers' real-time physiological states and decision-making process. The study proposes a new conceptual framework for biometric marketing, by introducing glucose as a dynamic variable that complements existing behavioural and contextual signals. The interdisciplinary approach adopted opens new avenues for the development of real-time and automation marketing strategies grounded in biometric inputs and consumers' psychophysiological responses.

DOI: 10.4018/979-8-2600-1263-5.ch005

INTRODUCTION

The development of Internet of Things (IoT) technologies is transforming business and marketing practices by enabling timely, context-aware, and data-driven customer engagement (Tariq et al., 2020). IoT systems now play a central role in the integration of real-time data across omnichannel ecosystems and facilitate the personalisation of interactions and dynamic adaptation to consumer needs (Tariq et al., 2020; Amosu et al., 2024). The integration of wearable and sensor-based IoT devices has further expanded the possibilities data collection capabilities and is increasingly recognised as a strategic advantage in the context of real time analytics and automation marketing strategies (Dian et al., 2020; Tariq et al., 2020).

A particularly promising development in this area is the convergence of IoT and biometric technologies, with wearable biosensors supporting continuous monitoring of physiological parameters and providing new insights into consumer behaviour (Dian et al., 2020).

In particular, Continuous Glucose Monitoring (CGM) technology — originally developed for clinical use to measure blood glucose levels – is emerging as a valuable source of biometric data with broader applicability (Rodríguez-Rodríguez et al., 2024). When integrated into IoT-based systems, CGM provides meaningful indicators not only of blood glucose, but also of cognitive states and decision-making processes. This is supported by a growing body of research showing that glucose regulation is closely linked to key psychological functions — such as cognitive performance, self-regulation, attention, self-control, and decision making — all of which significantly influence marketing effectiveness (Donohoe & Benton, 1999; Wang, 2018; McElroy et al., 2020).

Although real-time and automation marketing have significantly enhanced the capacity for personalisation and optimising within consumer engagement, prevailing approaches remain largely anchored in observable behavioural patterns and contextual variables — such as temporal dynamics, geolocation, and stated preferences (Amosu et al., 2024). Yet, within the contemporary digital ecosystem, consumers are increasingly exposed to a relentless and growing stream of stimuli, interactions, and notifications across multiple channels (Gurtner et al., 2024). This intensification of exposure contributes to a state of attentional saturation, ultimately impairing focus and reducing decision-making efficacy (Broniarczyk & Griffin, 2014).

In such a digital context, characterised by a progressive saturation of attention and choice, traditional real time marketing models are no longer sufficient. Instead, there is a growing need for new indicators and adaptive systems capable of detecting and responding to the consumer's psychophysiological state and to identifying the most suitable moment in which individuals are cognitively and physiologically prepared to make decisions, thereby enhancing the effectiveness of marketing strategies.

To address these challenges, this chapter introduces a novel conceptual framework for biometric marketing, positioning blood glucose levels, as measured through CGM technologies integrated with IoT systems, as an innovative source of biometric data for use in real-time analytics and marketing automation. Accordingly, the objective of this conceptual position paper is twofold: (1) to develop a theoretical framework in which real-time glucose data are conceptualised as a proxy for cognitive and behavioural states, thereby enhancing the responsiveness, timing, and personalisation of marketing strategies; and (2) to propose the integration of CGM-based technological infrastructures as a means of acquiring and operationalising glucose data within adaptive marketing systems.

To explore this theoretical proposition, the chapter addresses the following research question (RQ): *Given the established link between blood glucose levels and decision-making processes, can CGM IoT-based systems be effectively employed as biometric data sources to inform and optimise real-time and automation marketing strategies?*

Indeed, the central argument is that blood glucose levels, as a dynamic and measurable indicator of cognitive performance and behaviour, can play a critical role in shaping consumer's decision-making processes. By repositioning CGM technologies beyond their conventional clinical application and categorising them as proxies for decision-making processes, the study aims to contribute to the emerging field of continuous biometric marketing. In this context, the integration of physiological data into real-time analytics and automation marketing will be advanced by introducing glucose as a novel parameter for personalisation and optimisation of marketing automation strategies.

This line of inquiry is grounded in the theoretical premise that real-time fluctuations in blood glucose levels function as physiological correlates of cognitive and behavioural states implicated in consumer decision-making. On this basis, the hypothesis (H) is that *biometric data derived from IoT-based CGM systems may be meaningfully integrated into real time and automation marketing to enhance marketing strategies.*

The proposed conceptual framework addresses three interconnected thematic pillars. First, it explores the development and the evolution of IoT-based CGM systems, particularly non-invasive systems, and explores their emerging role as biometric inputs and data within consumer analytics. Second, the link between glucose availability and decision-making is highlighted, considering glucose levels as a dynamic physiological modulator of cognitive and behavioural processes. Third, a theoretical integration of biometric data into real-time marketing is presented by proposing glucose as a decision aid in modelling systems derived from IoT-based CGM systems. From an interdisciplinary perspective, continuous biometric marketing is advanced by introducing glucose-based physiological signals as novel inputs for consumer decision-making modelling. In this way, the chapter proposed a theoretical framework, referred to as Glucose-Informed Real-Time Marketing (GIRTM), that supports a shift towards real-time adaptive marketing strategies that dynamically respond to consumers' psychophysiological state.

BACKGROUND

To develop the proposed conceptual framework, it is necessary to provide an interdisciplinary overview underpinning the integration of three domains of the study: (1) the technological evolution of CGM systems within the healthcare sector; (2) the psychophysiological relevance of glucose in shaping cognitive, emotional, and decision-making processes; and (3) the emerging challenges faced by marketers in the contemporary digital ecosystem. For improved conceptual clarity and to support the integration of emerging technologies, these foundational elements of background collectively support the incorporation of glucose-informed biometric data CGM IoT-based system into real-time marketing strategies.

THE EVOLUTION OF IOT-BASED CONTINUOUS GLUCOSE MONITORING SYSTEMS IN HEALTHCARE

In recent years, advances in information and communication technology – such as Big Data, Artificial Intelligence (AI), IoT, Cloud Computing, and Machine Learning (ML) algorithms – have fundamentally changed in several sectors, particularly in the healthcare (Rodríguez-Rodríguez et al., 2024; Guleria, 2022). Within the healthcare sector, the evolution of the Internet of Medical Things (IoMT) represents a significant technological shift, characterised by the deployment of interconnected medical devices and systems that communicate and share data, enabling remote monitoring of patients' health conditions (Ahmed et al., 2024; Alalhareth & Hong, 2024).

These infrastructures integrate automated interface sensors with machine learning algorithms, facilitating the continuous collection, processing, and transmission of biometric and clinical data (Rodríguez-Rodríguez et al., 2024). The incorporation of 5G wireless technologies and cloud computing-based infrastructures has significantly enhanced the capacity of CGM systems to respond quickly and handle large-scale data transmissions efficiently (Rodríguez-Rodríguez et al., 2018; Ahmed et al., 2024).

From diabetes patient monitoring and neurological nursing care to real-time elderly health tracking, cardiac monitoring, and infectious disease management, IoMT technologies have become increasingly embedded in contemporary healthcare systems (Ahmed et al., 2024). But among the most significant IoMT-based technologies is CGM, which has proven essential for the technological advancement and for enhancing disease management in individuals with diabetes (Janapati et al., 2024; Murugan et al., 2024; Rothenbühler et al., 2025).

Characterised by chronic hyperglycaemia, diabetes mellitus (Cappon et al., 2017) – often referred to as the epidemic of the century (Kharroubi & Darwish, 2015) – encompasses a spectrum of metabolic disorders resulting from impairments in insulin secretion, insulin action, or a combination of both (Rodríguez-Rodríguez et al., 2018; 2024; Prasad et al. 2025).

The condition is broadly categorised into two principal types: 1) Type 1 diabetes (T1DM) is an autoimmune disorder that leads to the destruction of pancreatic beta cells, resulting in a complete deficiency of endogenous insulin production and the management typically requires lifelong administration of exogenous insulin (Kharroubi & Darwish, 2015); 2) Type 2 diabetes (T2DM) is predominantly associated with modifiable lifestyle factors, such as sedentary behaviour and poor dietary habits and it is defined by insulin resistance, whereby the body's cells fail to respond appropriately to insulin signalling (Cappon et al., 2017).

In diabetes mellitus, the blood glucose levels are chronically dysregulated and necessitates continuous and highly accurate monitoring to support insulin therapy and maintain effective glycaemic control (Janapati et al., 2024; Kharroubi & Darwish, 2015, Rodríguez-Rodríguez et al., 2018). This, in turn, requires uninterrupted disease management on a 24/7 basis and therapy is generally self-administered by the patient or managed by a caregiver (Cappon et al., 2017).

Given the inherent complexity of maintaining glucose homeostasis, individuals living with T1DM typically depend on multifaceted therapeutic approaches. These include subcutaneous insulin administration — either through multiple daily injections or continuous infusion via insulin pumps—alongside frequent capillary glucose measurements performed with portable glucometers (Rodríguez-Rodríguez et al., 2024). Home-based glucose tracking became a practical reality in the late 1970s, when Self-Monitoring of Blood Glucose (SMBG) devices were first introduced for individual use (Cappon et al., 2017; Kharroubi & Darwish, 2015). These handheld instruments, still essential today for calibrating IoT-integrated CGM systems, allowed patients to assess glucose levels using a small drop of capillary blood, with the analysis relying on enzymatic oxidation—typically via glucose oxidase—to estimate glucose concentration (Cappon et al., 2017). But the effective management of DM necessitates continuous and real-time monitoring of blood glucose levels. Moreover, effective therapy management also requires the ability to identify glycemic patterns and to cognitively anticipate future fluctuations through the use of glucometers (Rodríguez-Rodríguez et al., 2024; Rothenbühler et al., 2025).

Indeed, these processes of monitoring and prediction of the glucose level are a key part of the therapy too and they are essential for calculating appropriate dosages of exogenous insulin. In recent years, driven by the need to develop devices capable of more frequent blood glucose monitoring, glucose tracking itself has undergone a significant transformation with the advent of CGM sensors, which are always more minimally invasive or wearable (Cappon et al., 2017; Rodríguez-Rodríguez et al., 2018; 2024; Rothenbühler et al., 2025).

For this reason, key developments are focused on IoT-based CGM technologies, that play a central role in real-time glucose measurement and prediction of glucose value (Goel et al., 2024). The first prototypes of CGM systems were introduced in the late 1990s but only became commercially available in 2005 (Cappon et al., 2017). To this day, the most well-known CGM and IoT-based systems include: the Dexcom G7 (Dexcom, San Diego, CA, USA), Medtronic Guardian Sensor 3 (Medtronic Minimed, Northridge, CA, USA), and Abbott Freestyle Libre 3 (Abbott Diabetes Care, Alameda, CA, USA) (Cappon et al., 2017; Prasad et al., 2025).

IoT-based CGM systems use a minimally invasive needle sensor, typically inserted into the subcutaneous tissue and placed on the abdomen or arm (Cappon et al., 2017; Rothenbühler et al., 2025). The sensor measures an electrical current signal generated by the glucose-oxidase reaction — a signal that is proportional to the glucose concentration present in the interstitial fluid.

These systems monitor glucose levels at short sampling intervals, usually every 1 to 5 minutes, significantly increasing both the volume and resolution of real-time data on glycaemic fluctuations (Rodríguez-Rodríguez et al., 2018; 2024). As shown in **Figure 1**, the biosignals captured by the sensor are transmitted to the next layer through established protocols such as Bluetooth or Mobile and an intermediate processing layer consolidates and pre-processes the data, which are then analysed using AI within the computational layer to extract clinically relevant insights to storage (Rodríguez-Rodríguez et al., 2018; 2024). The resulting information is subsequently presented to patients or caregivers via display interfaces and/or dedicated smartphone applications (Rodríguez-Rodríguez et al., 2018).

Figure 1. Functional architecture of an IoT-based CGM system for diabetes management

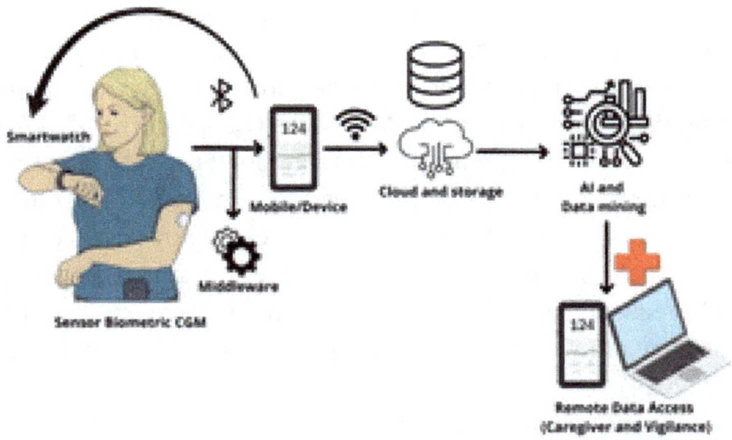

Such devices typically have a wear-time of approximately 10-14 days and incorporate a range of functionalities that can significantly improve the patient's ability to make informed decisions regarding self-administered therapeutic interventions (Cappon et al., 2017; Rodríguez-Rodríguez et al., 2018; 2024). In this context, mobile devices have increasingly established themselves as a critical component of the system, enhancing monitoring capabilities by enabling CGM software management, data transmission to the cloud, and integration with insulin pumps — devices that allow real-time monitoring of glucose levels and insulin delivery based on algorithmic model (Rodríguez-Rodríguez et al., 2018; 2024).

Since their introduction to the market, CGM devices have steadily improved in accuracy and longevity, while becoming more compact and expanding their connectivity to include smartphones, smartwatches, and insulin pumps (Rothenbühler et al., 2025).

In summary, recent developments in CGM–IoT based systems have predominantly addressed three main aspects. First, considerable attention has been devoted to improving the accuracy of glucose measurement, in order to ensure more reliable and clinically meaningful data (Cappon et al., 2017; Rodríguez-Rodríguez et al., 2018; 2024). Second, efforts have focused on reducing the invasiveness of sensor technologies, with the aim of enhancing user comfort and adherence by transitioning towards non-invasive solutions (Guntha, 2019; Murugan et al., 2024; Prasad et al., 2025). Third, increasing emphasis has been placed on enhancing computational power and predictive capabilities, allowing the systems to analyse real-time data and anticipate glycaemic fluctuations through the application of advanced AI and ML techniques (Cappon et al., 2017; Rodríguez-Rodríguez et al., 2018; 2024).

One of the main areas of focus for improving measurement accuracy concerns the reduction of the Mean Absolute Relative Difference (MARD), which is currently regarded as the most widely adopted accuracy metric in recent scientific literature for assessing the performance of CGM devices (Cappon et al., 2017; Rodríguez-Rodríguez et al., 2018; 2024). The MARD values for the latest generation of devices range, for example, from 7.9% in the Freestyle Libre 3 (Abbott) to 9.2% in the Freestyle Libre 2 (Abbott). Although these devices employ advanced algorithms to mitigate signal delays and noise, several challenges remain unresolved, particularly regarding the reduction of signal noise, the minimisation of rectification latency, and the enhancement of raw data accuracy (Cappon et al., 2017; Rodríguez-Rodríguez et al., 2018; 2024).

The second aspect concerns the fact that many CGM IoT-based systems remain either invasive or minimally invasive – as they require the subcutaneous implantation of the device – and relatively costly, limiting their widespread use (Murugan et al., 2024). In response to these critical issues, recent innovations in engineering and medical biotechnology have focused on the development of non-invasive measurement devices, to deliver smart healthcare services using wearable IoT-based technologies (Guntha, 2019; Murugan et al., 2024; Prasad et al., 2025).

These devices use biometric signals – including heart rate, body temperature (Murugan et al., 2024), sweat, and spectroscopy (Prasad et al., 2025) – and are mainly integrated into wearables and fitness trackers to enable continuous glucose monitoring in real-time.

According to the studies conducted by Rothenbühler (2025) and colleagues, non-invasive glucose monitoring is feasible, and their findings confirm that optical systems combined with advanced computational models are highly promising, with performance comparable to that of first-generation CGM devices. Through advanced computational methods, these devices enable continuous and non-invasive blood glucose measurement without the need for invasive calibration (Dasari, 2020).

IoT-enabled wearable CGM technologies are rapidly gaining traction due to their ability to provide accurate and uninterrupted blood glucose data (Guntha, 2019) and are increasingly expanding their applicability beyond the medical context (Rothenbühler et al., 2025). Indeed, although invasive CGM systems have significantly improved the quality of care for individuals with insulin-dependent diabetes mellitus, non-invasive CGM technology has the potential to eliminate the discomfort and risks associated with invasive monitoring, thereby removing a major barrier to adoption. Furthermore, its applications need not be confined to medical settings, non-invasive CGM holds promising potential for broader use, including in preventive health measures, wellness monitoring, sports performance, and even nutritional tracking, extending its utility well beyond traditional clinical systems.

Within this evolving landscape, both invasive and non-invasive next-generation IoT-based CGM systems are capable of capturing and processing biometric data in real time (Janapati et al., 2024; Goel et al., 2024). This enables not only continuous monitoring but also the development of advanced predictive capabilities, through the integration of ML algorithms, that can accurately predict glucose levels up to 45 minutes in advance (Rodríguez-Rodríguez et al., 2024). The integration of IoT technologies with the capabilities of cloud computing opens up new perspectives for advanced data analysis and the development of reliable predictive models, by enabling the processing of large datasets generated by connected sensors of various type.

Real-time glucose forecasting represents a crucial element in the prevention and management of glycaemic fluctuations, particularly in individuals with type 1 diabetes (Rodríguez-Rodríguez et al., 2018; 2024). Although deep learning algorithms have achieved significant advances in glucose level prediction, their integration into T1DM management systems remains challenging due to the high computational demands involved, which entail considerable energy and financial costs.

Biometric glucose data gathered via IoT-based CGM systems play a central role in the management of diabetes, underpinning both real-time monitoring and therapeutic decision-making. Recent technological advancements have broadened the applicability of these systems beyond traditional clinical settings, with increasing emphasis on non-invasive, wearable solutions that facilitate continuous glucose tracking across a variety of contexts.

As CGM technologies continue to improve in terms of accuracy, invasiveness, and connectivity, they are paving the way for new applications in preventive healthcare, athletic performance optimisation, and everyday wellness monitoring. These developments point towards a future in which glucose data may constitute a key biometric input not only for clinical management, but also for real-time, personalised health and behavioural analytics across multiple domains. Indeed, beyond its clinical applications, glucose also functions as a key regulator of brain and behavioural processes, with significant implications for decision-making. The following section examines the broader psychophysiological role of glucose in shaping cognition, emotion, and decision-making behaviour.

THE ROLE OF GLUCOSE IN DECISION-MAKING BEHAVIOUR

The emergence of minimally or non-invasive CGM technologies, integrated into IoT-based systems, also offers unprecedented opportunities to collect of glucose-related biometric data and provide novel insights of individuals' physiological states.

Indeed, glucose itself plays a central role not only in the clinical management of DM, but also in the physiological functioning of the general population.

Glucose is a critical physiological factor in cognitive performance and behavioural regulation, and it is the brain's primary source of energy (Donohoe & Benton, 1999). Although the brain accounts for only 2% of total body weight, it consumes 20–30% of the body's energy, mainly in the form of glucose (Benton, 1990; Rao, 2013). Glucose constitutes the primary form of sugar circulating in the bloodstream and plays a vital role in supporting optimal brain function. However, the brain has a limited capacity to store glucose over extended periods, rendering it highly dependent on a continuous supply to maintain its cognitive operations (Benton, 1990; Gonder-Frederick et al., 1987).

Following the intake of food or beverages containing sugar, blood glucose levels typically rise markedly within 12–15 minutes, gradually returning to baseline over the course of approximately two hours (McElroy et al., 2020). Several studies (Donohoe & Benton, 1999) have confirmed a strong relationship between glucose availability and cognitive performance, suggesting that glucose demand and utilisation are closely linked to cognitive activity. Indeed, in the event of glucose depletion, cognitive efficiency may be impaired, as the brain lacks the necessary energy to function effectively.

Glucose – particularly its fluctuations in relation to high or low availability in the bloodstream – is essential for sustaining core cognitive functions such as memory, attention, and learning (Donohoe & Benton, 1999; Schöpf et al., 2013).

The conceptual scoping review of studies focusing on the effect of glucose identified four key functional domains in which fluctuations in glucose levels appear to play a particularly salient role: (1) cognitive, (2) behavioural, (3) emotional, and (4) decision-making processes.

First. In the cognitive domain, glucose has been found to exert a modulatory influence on several key mental processes, with particularly notable effects on working memory performance and task completion accuracy (Messier et al., 1998; Sunram-Lea et al., 2001). In addition, there is substantial evidence that complex cognitive tasks, such as mental arithmetic, are especially sensitive to fluctuations in glucose levels. Performance on these tasks tends to decline under conditions of glucose depletion, suggesting a strong dependence on metabolic support for higher-order cognitive functioning (Kennedy & Scholey, 2000; Scholey et al., 2001; Schächinger et al., 2003; Schöpf et al., 2013). Second. In the behavioural domain, glucose appears to play a critical role in self-regulation and impulse control. Following cognitively effortful tasks, individuals exhibit reduced capacity for self-regulation, a pattern associated with declining glucose availability (Gailliot et al., 2007). Additionally, glucose levels are linked to temporal discounting behaviours, with lower availability correlating with increased impatience and a preference for immediate over delayed rewards (Orquin & Kurzban, 2016). These metabolic influences also manifest in variability in inhibitory control and risk-taking tendencies, underscoring the behavioural consequences of glucose-dependent energy states. Third. Regarding the emotional domain, glucose has been found to contribute to affective arousal in response to emotionally salient or stressful stimuli (Verago et al., 2001). Furthermore, glucose participates in the dynamic interplay between homeostatic and affective systems, influencing emotional reactivity, mood fluctuations, and cravings, particularly under conditions of energy imbalance (Schöpf et al., 2013). Fourth. In the domain of decision-making, glucose availability appears to influence both the style and efficacy of choice behaviour. Empirical studies indicate that higher glucose levels may support a more deliberative mode of processing, while lower levels are associated with a shift towards intuitive or heuristic-based decision strategies (Orquin & Kurzban, 2016; McElroy et al., 2020). Performance in complex decision tasks, including accuracy and response times, also varies as a function of glucose levels (Dickinson et al., 2014). Moreover, glucose may modulate susceptibility to cognitive biases such as the decoy effect (Masicampo & Baumeister, 2008), and influence intertemporal choice, with higher levels promoting greater preference for delayed, future-oriented outcomes (Wang & Huangfu, 2017).

Table 1. Overview of the effects of glucose across key functional domains.

Functional domains	Effect of glucose
Cognitive	• Modulates facial recognition accuracy (Metzger, 2000); • Influences verbal working memory performance (Messier et al., 1998; Sunram-Lea et al., 2001); • Affects spatial ability performance (Sunram-Lea et al., 2001); • Impacts the efficiency of complex cognitive task execution (Kennedy & Scholey, 2000; Scholey et al., 2001) • Alters performance in mental arithmetic and other demanding tasks (Schächinger et al., 2003).
Behavioural	• Associated with fluctuations in self-regulation behaviour following effortful cognitive tasks (Gailliot et al., 2007); • Linked to impatience and a stronger tendency to favour immediate over delayed outcomes, reflecting shifts in temporal preferences under metabolic influences (Orquin & Kurzban, 2016); • Linked to variability in performance on tasks requiring behavioural inhibition and self-control (Gailliot et al., 2007); • Modulations in risk-taking tendencies (Orquin & Kurzban, 2016).
Emotional	• Modulates amygdala functioning and enhances emotional memory processes (Schroeder & Packard, 2003); • Linked to affective arousal in response to emotional or stressful stimuli (Verago et al., 2001); • Involved in the interaction between homeostatic and affective systems, influencing irritability, mood shifts, and craving under energy imbalance (Schöpf et al., 2013).
Decision-making	• Affects the balance between intuitive and deliberative processing in choice contexts (Orquin & Kurzban, 2016; McElroy et al., 2020); • Associated with variation in accuracy and response times in complex decision tasks (Dickinson et al., 2014) • Influences susceptibility to decoy effects and heuristic strategies (Masicampo & Baumeister, 2008); • Influences intertemporal decision-making and the tendency to favour future-oriented over immediate outcomes (Wang & Huangfu, 2017); • Appears to modulate key aspects of decision-making, including temporal discounting, effort-related motivation, and decision style. Evidence suggests that metabolic signals may influence how individuals prioritise immediate versus delayed rewards and adapt their strategies according to the type and context of the reward (Orquin & Kurzban, 2016).

In line with decision-making exploration, Orquin and Kurzban (2016) conducted a meta-analysis of 42 studies examining the role of blood glucose in shaping four key dimensions of human decision-making: delay discounting, willingness to pay, willingness to work, and decision style. To account for interpreting the effect of glucose in cognition and on the behaviour, Orquin and Kurzban (2016) proposed a theoretical distinction between two explanatory frameworks: constraint models and signal models. Constraint models, rooted primarily in psychology, posit that glucose functions as a limited energetic resource. According to this view, reduced glucose availability impairs the functioning of metabolically demanding brain regions—particularly the prefrontal cortex—thereby compromising executive functions such as working memory, sustained attention, and self-regulation (Gailliot et al., 2007;

Messier, 2004). From this perspective, cognitive impairments emerge as a consequence of energetic insufficiency. By contrast, signal models—emerging from disciplines such as behavioural economics and evolutionary biology—conceptualise glucose not merely as fuel but as an informational molecule, capable of initiating adaptive behavioural responses. In particular, glucose is proposed to act as a metabolic signal that informs the organism of its internal resource status, thereby modulating foraging behaviour and the prioritisation of energy acquisition strategies. For example, reductions in blood glucose levels are thought to trigger the release of orexigenic peptides, which stimulate goal-directed behaviours oriented toward food seeking.

These models suggest that glucose fluctuations not only limit cognitive resources, but also guide behaviour in response to internal metabolic needs. As stated by Orquin and Kurzban (2016, p. 559), "glucose acts as an input that guides adaptive behaviour" that trigger an emotion.

While early investigations predominantly addressed the cognitive, emotional, and behavioural effects of glucose availability, more recent contributions have placed increasing emphasis on its implications for decision-making processes. This shift reflects a growing recognition of glucose not exclusively as a metabolic resource, but as a dynamic physiological signal capable of modulating higher-order executive functions and regulatory capacities (McElroy et al., 2020; Orquin & Kurzban, 2016). Within this emerging line of inquiry, several studies have drawn upon dual-process theories of Daniel Kahneman (2011), which conceptualise cognition as the interaction of two distinct systems: the first, commonly referred to as System 1, is fast, automatic, intuitive, and relatively effortless; the second, System 2, is slower, deliberate, analytically driven, and dependent upon greater cognitive effort and executive control. These frameworks suggest that the degree to which individuals rely on one system over the other is contingent upon the availability of cognitive and physiological resources, including glucose (Kahneman, 2011; Masicampo & Baumeister, 2008). In this regard, glucose has been shown to play a crucial role in supporting the cognitive functions. Lower levels of blood glucose are associated with diminished attentional capacity, compromised behavioural regulation, and a reduced inclination to engage in effortful cognitive tasks (McElroy et al., 2020). In contrast, elevated glucose availability appears to facilitate more reflective and deliberative forms of thinking, enabling individuals to exert greater self-control and to adopt goal-directed strategies in decision contexts (Masicampo & Baumeister, 2008; Orquin & Kurzban, 2016; Wang, 2018). The literature suggests that fluctuations in glucose levels shape not only the efficiency of cognitive performance but also the underlying strategic orientation in decision-making. In states of glucose deprivation, individuals tend to exhibit an increased reliance on intuitive, heuristic-based reasoning styles, which, while efficient under conditions of energetic constraint, may compromise accuracy and foresight (McElroy et al., 2020). Conversely, sufficient glucose availability is associated with an increased propensity for deliberative and future-oriented decision-making (McElroy et al., 2020).

Glucose acts as a dynamic physiological indicator that extends its influence beyond cognition, affecting behavioural control, emotional regulation, and decision-making. Lower glucose levels impair attention and self-regulation, fostering intuitive, heuristic-based strategies, while higher levels support reflective and deliberate thinking (McElroy et al., 2020; Orquin & Kurzban, 2016). As such, glucose availability not only constrains cognitive resources but also modulates the style and quality of decision-making, with important implications for understanding behaviour in real-time and decision context. Complementary evidence from narrative neuroscience further supports the notion that physiological and affective states jointly shape decision-making. Zak (2015) demonstrates that emotionally engaging narratives can elicit the release of oxytocin — a neurochemical that enhances empathy, trust, and prosocial motivation. This finding reinforces the view that decision-making is not merely a cognitive or metabolic act but an embodied process in which biochemical signals, such as glucose or oxytocin, interact with emotional and contextual stimuli to guide attention, evaluation, and choice. For this reason, and in order to gain a deeper understanding of decision-making processes, it is essential to enable continuous measurement of blood glucose levels through the use of available CGM IoT-based systems, but also to consider the broader contextual challenges that characterise the contemporary digital landscape, particularly those that hinder consumers' capacity to process information and make effective decisions. Understanding these constraints is crucial for positioning glucose-informed data as a valuable resource within real-time marketing environments.

CHALLENGES IN REAL-TIME MARKETING AND IN DIGITAL CONTEXT

Decision-making processes, as previously discussed, are not solely determined by internal physiological factors such as glucose availability but are continuously shaped by the external cognitive and environmental pressures of the phygital ecosystem. The interaction between biological readiness and digital overstimulation defines the contemporary landscape in which consumers make decisions — a space where attention, motivation, and self-regulation are persistently taxed by the velocity and density of information flows.

The contemporary digital environment is markedly characterised by an overwhelming abundance of content and the accompanying informational noise generated through its production, interaction, and monitoring, what Eichhorn (2022) identifies as the new millennium's form of social capital: content itself. The widespread diffusion of digital platforms – ranging from social media and mobile technologies to cloud-based systems – has significantly expanded consumers' access to information (Gurtner et al., 2024). Individuals are confronted every day with thousands of content items and data inputs, following a trajectory that is expected to grow exponentially in the years ahead (Eichhorn, 2022). Within this context, consumers are increasingly exposed to a relentless and intensifying stream of stimuli, interactions, and notifications distributed across multiple digital channels (Gurtner et al., 2024). While this shift has undeniably transformed how consumers discover products, communicate, and make purchase decisions (Darley et al., 2010), it has also posed new challenges for marketers, who must develop innovative strategies to identify, anticipate, and respond to consumers' evolving needs and desires (Amosu et al., 2024).

In response to these growing demands, real-time data analytics and marketing automation – now commonly encompassed under the umbrella term "MarTech" (Bilro, 2024) – have represented a significant turning point in the evolution of business models within the digital paradigm, and more broadly in the development of digital marketing strategies. The capacity of firms to process and interpret data with precision in real time has notably improved their responsiveness to consumer needs, enhanced the accuracy of advertising efforts, and contributed to a more efficient and adaptive marketing performance (Amosu et al., 2024). Within the current phygital context, real-time marketing has undoubtedly opened new avenues for understanding consumer behaviour, as well as for monitoring performance and campaign effectiveness (Amosu et al., 2024).

The real-time availability of data enables firms to implement timely and highly targeted interventions, with significant implications for the dynamic adaptation to both consumer needs and market conditions (Gurtner et al., 2024). At the same time, the use of predictive models based on AI and ML has contributed to increasing levels of hyper-personalisation and hyper-segmentation, thereby transforming brand–consumer interactions and enhancing the competitive positioning of promotional strategies (Prasad et al., 2023). Real-time insights play a crucial role in improving the tailoring of consumer experiences – an increasingly critical factor for securing and sustaining a competitive edge in today's saturated digital marketplace (Ramachandran, 2018). The capacity to deliver personalised and timely offerings not only enhances consumer satisfaction and strengthens brand loyalty, but also contributes to long-term business success. In this regard, real-time marketing emerges as a strategic resource, offering firms a means to align marketing initiatives more closely with evolving consumer expectations and contextual dynamics (Amosu et al., 2024). According with the extant literature, the implementation of real-time and automation marketing offers a wide range of strategic advantages, including: (i) dynamic personalisation, (ii) real-time automation, (iii) campaign optimisation, and (iv) enhanced segmentation accuracy.

From this perspective, the integration of real-time data analytics within marketing strategies provides several key benefits. First. It enables the level of flexibility required for marketing operations to adapt swiftly and dynamically to changes in consumer behaviour and market conditions, thus ensuring responsiveness and competitiveness (Ramachandran, 2018). Second. It facilitates more precise audience segmentation based on real-time behavioural patterns, preferences, and purchasing data. This allows for the creation of dynamic customer segments, which not only improve the targeting of personalised campaigns and tailored offers (Rahaman et al., 2021), but also enhance the capacity to respond promptly to shifts in consumption trends (Amosu et al., 2024). Third. Real-time feedback contributes to the optimisation of marketing performance and resource allocation. By enabling continuous monitoring and agile management of campaigns, firms can reduce marketing costs and improve Return On Investment (ROI) through more effective campaigns based on data monitoring (Saksena, 2024). Fourth. The combined effect of personalisation and real-time automation serves as a key competitive advantage. The ability to analyse customer interactions as they occur allows for the timely delivery of tailored recommendations, content, and promotions (Amosu et al., 2024). Immediate feedback also supports the rapid identification and resolution of critical issues, ensuring the ongoing relevance and impact of communication efforts. Real-time analytics enables marketers to test multiple strategies and assess their performance instantly, supporting a data-informed, iterative approach to campaign optimisation. The integration of real-time analytics with marketing automation platforms further amplifies these effects. Automated systems can trigger personalised actions based on real-time consumer behaviour, ensuring timely and contextually relevant communication. This level of automation not only enhances operational efficiency but also significantly improves customer experience by delivering coherent and customised interactions across all digital touchpoints (Amosu et al., 2024).

The contemporary phygital context has profoundly reshaped the modalities through which consumers interact with brands and construct their decision-making processes. Within this transformation, real-time data analytics and marketing automation have emerged as central enablers, significantly enhancing firms' capacity for personalisation, campaign optimisation, and precision targeting (Amosu et al., 2024). Nevertheless, prevailing approaches remain predominantly grounded in observable behavioural indicators and contextual parameters, such as temporal patterns, geolocation, and declared consumer preferences. Yet, as digital environments become increasingly saturated, the limitations of these models are brought into sharper relief. Consumers are now subject to a relentless and escalating influx of content, notifications, and interactions, often dispersed across multiple platforms (Gregori & Holzmann, 2024). Although the expansion of informational access and choice ostensibly promises greater consumer empowerment, it simultaneously engenders a set of critical cognitive challenges and disempowerment — most notably, information overload, attentional fatigue, and decision paralysis (Broniarczyk & Griffin, 2014; Gregori & Holzmann, 2024). Paradoxically, the very abundance of choice and content may undermine, rather than enhance, the consumer's decision-making (Gregori & Holzmann, 2024). This phenomenon bears significant implications for marketing practice. As attentional resources are progressively depleted, individuals' ability to engage in reflective processing and make deliberate choices is diminished. Despite their technological sophistication, existing real-time marketing frameworks often fall short in capturing the cognitive and physiological states that shape consumers' readiness to engage with decision tasks. Such limitations become particularly acute in overstimulated, hyper-competitive digital environments, where cognitive bandwidth is persistently taxed.

Accordingly, a critical research and operational gap emerges: to what extent can marketers identify and operationalise indicators that reflect consumers' real-time cognitive readiness to make decisions? Moreover, are there technology that could be integrated into contemporary marketing systems to enhance their responsiveness and contextual sensitivity? In light of these challenges, the development of adaptive, psychophysiologically informed marketing systems appears increasingly essential. These systems must transcend conventional behavioural segmentation and instead incorporate real-time physiological and cognitive markers, improving the timely detection of optimal moments for engagement – when individuals are receptive to marketing stimuli.

Understanding consumer decision-making as it unfolds in real time is thus not only a matter of strategic optimisation, but a fundamental requirement for delivering more effective and meaningful customer experiences. Personalisation – particularly when driven by real-time analytics – has been shown to improve the contextual relevance of communications, increase customer satisfaction, foster engagement, and reinforce loyalty (Amosu et al., 2024). Such personalised interactions convey a sense of recognition and appreciation, thereby encouraging repeated transactions and the formation of enduring brand relationships. Furthermore, the dynamic refinement of personalisation strategies based on real-time feedback allows firms to proactively address consumer needs, mitigate churn, and sustain competitive advantage. The integration of real-time responsiveness into marketing systems supports long-term growth and resilience in increasingly volatile and cognitively saturated markets.

GLUCOSE-INFORMED REAL-TIME MARKETING (GIRTM): A NEW FRONTIER IN CONSUMER DECISION-MAKING THROUGH CGM IOT-BASED SYSTEMS

As highlighted in the literature review, the critical dimension that must not be overlooked within the contemporary digital context is the proliferation of stimuli, which has the potential to disrupt — and in some cases inhibit — with consumers' decision-making processes, particularly in relation to information search, cognitive processing, and evaluative judgement. As consumers are continuously exposed to a relentless and intensifying stream of content across multiple platforms, the ability to accurately interpret and anticipate decision-making behaviour in real time emerges as a defining challenge for current marketing strategies.

To address this complexity, the study introduces a new conceptual framework: Glucose-Informed Real-Time Marketing (GIRTM). This framework proposes for the first time a theoretical model that integrates biometric data – specifically, blood glucose levels – into real time and automation marketing strategies. At the core of the GIRTM framework there is the assumption that glucose plays a central role in regulating decision-making process. Indeed, as noted by the literature (McElroy et al., 2020; Orquin & Kurzban, 2016), glucose is fundamental in cognitive performance, behavioural regulation and moreover in shaping decision-making processes. In general, as previously shown, lower glucose levels impair attention and self-regulation, whereas higher levels promote reflective and deliberate thinking. These fluctuations also have broader implications for consumer decision-making (McElroy et al., 2020).

Accordingly, within the GIRTM framework, blood glucose is reconceptualised not only as a clinical indicator, but as a reliable physiological proxy and a dynamic psychophysiological signal capable of modulating attention, self-regulation, emotion, behaviour and, most crucially, decision-making. Within the context of today's overstimulated and content-saturated digital environment, the ability to modulate decision-making process gains increasing theoretical relevance and offers unprecedented opportunities for marketing strategy development.

In this regard, real-time fluctuations in blood glucose levels data are introduced as a novel biometric variable fundamental in the digital environments. These physiological dynamics may be continuously monitored and translated into actionable insights, with the specific aim to informing and adapting real-time and automated marketing strategies, for optimising experience and behavioural outcomes of users.

By incorporating glucose data into the marketing analytics pipeline, the GIRTM model introduces a new dimension to traditional data-driven approaches, which have thus far relied predominantly on behavioural, contextual, or preference-based indicators. The model makes it possible to identify "micro-windows", that represent brief, time-specific intervals of heightened cognitive and emotional receptivity, during which consumers are more likely to engage with, elaborate, and respond to marketing stimuli. Their identification enables the temporal synchronisation of content delivery with consumers' psychophysiological state, thereby enhancing message relevance, reducing resistance, and increasing the likelihood of conversion. As a result, GIRTM overcomes the limitations of existing marketing models that rely predominantly on behavioural, contextual, or preference-based indicators.

Glucose is positioned as a dynamic signal, enabling for the first time a form of biometric personalisation that aligns deeply with the consumer's real-time psychophysiological state.

Biometric insights are now technically feasible due to the emergence of CGM IoT-based systems, which enable minimally or non-invasive and continuous measurement of glucose levels data. These systems offer a dynamic and contextualised representation of physiological fluctuations data, which can be mapped onto cognitive and behavioural patterns across population segments. As a result, and drawing on studies that illustrate the effects of glucose on decision-making, marketers can gain insights not only into what consumers do or prefer, but also into when they are most predisposed to respond to specific stimuli, and which types of stimuli are most likely to lead to conversion.

As illustrated in Figure 2, the conceptual flow of the GIRTM framework involves that a biometric CGM device collects continuous glucose data from the user, which are processed through mobile-connected systems and transmitted as biometric input. These data inform real-time assessments of blood glucose levels, which are analysed via AI and ML to extract glucose-informed insights. These insights feed into adaptive marketing systems, supporting the personalisation, timing, and strategic delivery of content and offers. The model enables marketing interventions to align dynamically with the consumer's psychophysiological state, thereby enhancing decision-making readiness and overall marketing effectiveness.

Figure 2. Glucose-Informed Real-Time Marketing (GIRTM) System

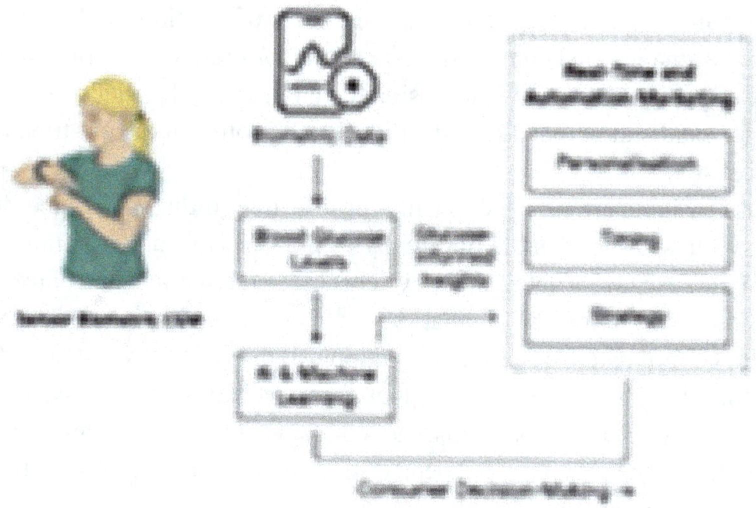

Naturally, operationalising the GIRTM model requires the development of an integrated and interoperable technological infrastructure capable of capturing, processing, and responding to biometric data in real time. Figure 3 proposes a technological architecture based on the integration of non-invasive or minimally invasive CGM device and IoT-based systems – currently available commercially and originally developed for T1DM – that enable the continuous collection of glucose-related biometric data real time. Indeed, the CGM sensor continuously measures glucose levels and transmits data via Bluetooth to a mobile device. This device functions as a gateway to cloud-based environments where data are pre-processed through middleware systems. The cloud infrastructure enables seamless connection with AI modules and data analytics platforms, which extract relevant patterns and indicators from glucose streams.

These insights can then be integrated (optionally) with other datasets already used in strategic marketing to increase precision and optimization of marketing strategies. Advanced analytics platforms provide real-time modelling and feedback, enabling the system to issue targeted alerts or deliver marketing stimuli based on physiological readiness. In this way, consumers receive content only when their cognitive state is most receptive, as inferred from ongoing glucose fluctuations.

Figure 3. Data flow architecture of IoT-based CGM systems for real-time biometric monitoring and marketing

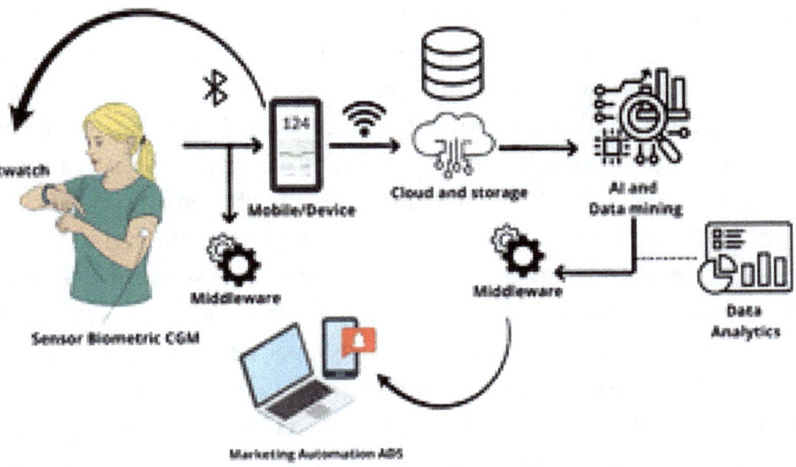

Grounded in interdisciplinary evidence and supported by advances in CGM IoT-based systems, the GIRTM framework delineates a novel theoretical pathway by positioning blood glucose as a strategic biometric input within real-time marketing processes. And it establishes the conceptual development for a new generation of marketing strategies.

While the GIRTM framework provides a theoretically robust foundation for integrating physiological data into marketing analytics, its application must also be critically examined through the lenses of data governance and ethical accountability. The same glucose-informed insights that enable unprecedented personalisation also introduce new tensions between efficiency and transparency, automation and human oversight.

DISCUSSION

The findings presented throughout this chapter substantiate the theoretical relevance and strategic potential of incorporating glucose level data into real-time marketing frameworks. Building on the evidence previously discussed, this contribution introduces a novel conceptual framework – so called GIRTM – which offers an integrative reflection on how glucose levels, as dynamic psychophysiological signals, may inform and guide marketing strategies in digital contexts.

As highlighted, in response to the increasing volume of stimuli and the growing competitiveness of the digital environment, consumers are now confronted with ever more complex decision-making tasks. These conditions expose individuals to heightened cognitive workloads and an overload of information, which in turn influence both their implicit and explicit choices. In such a scenario, the core challenge for marketers is no longer merely to optimise for being seen or for receiving attention by consumers, but fundamentally for being chosen.

Within this context, the role of marketing is no longer limited to reaching the right segment, person, or target at the right moment, as suggested by the theory of "micro-moments", nor is it exclusively about the right place, as in geofencing strategies, or the most suitable message, as in hyper-personalisation. Instead, in a digital environment marked by increasing complexity, it becomes essential to identify new variables capable of enabling real-time marketing and marketing automation strategies that can be optimised based on novel indicators. These new indicators must align with emerging pull strategies – less invasive yet more attractive – by capturing the most appropriate moment with the most relevant message.

As Todd McElroy (2020, p. 538) aptly notes: "Every decision-making event can be thought of as consisting of two players: the person and the tasks." In the current landscape, there is undoubtedly a wealth of knowledge available regarding tasks, thanks to increasingly precise measurements of actions, events, and behaviours, particularly in digital environments. Similarly, it is possible to collect considerable insight into people, including their preferences, status, and location. Yet what remains largely unknown is the relationship between the person and the task.

Indeed, at the heart of the GIRTM framework lies the recognition that decision-making is not a static or purely rational process, but rather a dynamic interplay between the individual's cognitive state and the demands of the task. Undoubtedly, individuals vary not only in their cognitive dispositions but also in the degree of effort they devote to decision-making – at times engaging in deliberate and reflective processing, while at other times relying on fast, intuitive judgements (Kahneman, 2011).

Blood glucose and its fluctuations constitutes one of the main indicators of this relationship and play a central role in shaping decision-making processes (McElroy et al., 2020). As numerous studies confirm (Orquin & Kurzban, 2016; Wang, 2018) there is a positive correlation between blood glucose levels and decision-making, suggesting that lower glucose availability increases the tendency to rely on intuitive strategies. Overall, the available evidence suggests that glucose deprivation tends to promote automatic, less reflective decision strategies, whereas higher glucose availability is associated with more deliberate, conscious, and rational decision-making (McElroy et al., 2020; Masicampo & Baumeister, 2008).

In this regard, CGM technologies offer a previously unexplored capability: the ability to continuously measure an individual's physiological decision-readiness in real time. The literature suggests that fluctuations in glucose levels can serve as reliable indicators of attention span, cognitive load, and motivational orientation. All of which are critical determinants in consumer decision-making processes (Donohoe & Benton, 1999; McElroy et al., 2020).

When integrated with IoT infrastructures, CGM systems can thus generate a stream of biometric data capable of identifying so-called "micro-windows" of heightened receptivity: brief temporal intervals in which individuals are more predisposed to elaborate and respond to marketing stimuli, that will naturally vary depending on the consumer's current psychophysiological state.

The correlation between glucose levels and decision-making processes opens up also unexplored opportunities in the field of biometric marketing and real-time automation marketing strategies. The integration of these biometric insights addresses a fundamental limitation of current real-time marketing systems, which remain largely constrained by observable behaviour, location data, or declared preferences. In overstimulated digital environments, where informational noise impairs cognitive focus and contributes to decision fatigue (Broniarczyk & Griffin, 2014; Gregori & Holzmann, 2024), the ability to personalise communication based on internal psychophysiological states represents a significant advance in marketing theory and practice.

Importantly, the GIRTM framework does not propose to replace existing behavioural or contextual marketing indicators but to enrich them through the addition of biometric data streams. By doing so, it enables an adaptive marketing logic that is not only responsive to external triggers but also attuned to the consumer's internal readiness for engagement. From this perspective, glucose represents a strategic proxy an indicator that signals the moment in which a decision is more likely to be made with attention, effort, and cognitive commitment (Orquin & Kurzban, 2016).

Establishing a conceptual interconnection between glucose activity and decision-making processes represents a key challenge within the phygital marketing environment in which contemporary marketing operates. This connection was necessary to explore the potential for technological and business implementation within current marketing strategies.

This contribution, therefore, offers a novel perspective by considering not only the integration of glucose data into marketing strategies, but also by introducing a new dimension grounded in individual physiology and real-time monitoring of the consumer's psychophysiological state. As previously discussed, the conceptual flow of the GIRTM framework involves the continuous collection of glucose data via biometric CGM devices, which are transmitted through mobile-connected systems and processed as biometric input. These data inform real-time glucose level assessments, which are analysed using AI and ML to extract glucose-informed insights. These insights subsequently feed into adaptive marketing systems, enabling the dynamic alignment of marketing interventions with the consumer's current condition and enhancing both decision-making readiness and overall marketing effectiveness.

The development of real-time marketing strategies within the GIRTM conceptual model has been facilitated by recent technological advances in IoT-enabled CGM systems, which allow for continuous glucose measurement. Building on technologies already available for individuals with diabetes and integrating them with dedicated software solutions, it becomes possible to interconnect middleware infrastructures. These systems may operate independently or in conjunction with existing analytics to deliver the most appropriate communication at the right moment, based on the user's glucose state.

This approach is particularly relevant in a communication environment characterised by high information pressure, and where consumers are often exposed to cognitive overload and constant distraction (Gregori & Holzmann, 2024). In such a context, the ability to target consumers in a physiologically optimal state, or deliver messages tailored to increased receptivity, represents a competitive advantage to improve engagement, conversion rates, and overall marketing effectiveness (Roy et al., 2015).

In this context, the potential applications of glucose-informed data in real-time analytics and marketing automation are extensive, encompassing benefits such as dynamic personalisation, real-time automation, campaign optimisation, and more accurate segmentation.

As a novel biometric indicator, glucose not only supports real-time marketing strategies on its own but also complements existing behavioural and location-based data stream. Notably, glucose signals enable the temporal synchronisation of marketing and support the continuous and personalised adaptation of campaigns to the evolving physiological state.

In this scenario, characterised by increasingly complex and non-linear customer journey models, the availability of a biometric indicator to support decision-making is becoming as a strategic resource, aimed at improving the resonance and effectiveness of information search and processing activities (Amosu et al., 2024). Real-time personalisation and message automation not only improve consumer engagement and increase the effectiveness of brand communications but also have the potential to influence consumers' decision throughout the decision-making process (Gregori & Holzmann, 2024). In light of the literature review and the interdisciplinary correlations and interconnections identified at both theoretical and technological levels, the potential impact of the GIRTM framework within the current landscape becomes evident. It not only reconceptualises glucose as a meaningful biometric input for real-time marketing strategies, but also creates concrete opportunities for strategically optimising messages and campaigns according to consumers' blood glucose levels and their corresponding decision-making predispositions. As such, GIRTM represents a significant step forward in aligning data-driven innovation with the psychophysiological dynamics that underpin consumer behaviour and neuroscience.

SOLUTIONS AND RECOMMENDATIONS

Building upon the theoretical insights and implications derived from the proposed conceptual framework, the development of marketing strategies – grounded in the integration of glucose data as an input for real-time personalisation – emerges as a critical advancement. These strategies should capitalise on the potential of CGM IoT-based systems to identify moments in which consumers are in a psychophysiologically receptive state to receive specific stimuli and, consequently, are more inclined to engage in decision-making. In this context, glucose functions as a dynamic indicator of decision readiness, enabling the synchronised delivery of content, advertising and promotional stimuli. The incorporation of glucose data into real-time marketing and automation practices facilitates novel segmentation approaches, shifting from static criteria – such as demographic data, location, temporal windows, behavioural triggers, or expressed preferences – to adaptive and biometric segmentation, grounded in physiological patterns detected in real time. In particular, the use of micro-structured temporal windows, identified through glycaemic levels, allows for precision targeting based on consumers' internal states.

Biometric input serves as an additional layer to the already employed analytical variables, with the aim of enhancing the relevance and timeliness of marketing communication. In doing so, the proposed model overcomes the limitations of conventional frameworks by enabling a more advanced form of personalisation through the convergence of biometric and analytical data streams. The inclusion of glucose data collected via CGM technologies further enhances the key benefits already associated with real-time marketing previously expressed. Moreover, this approach is made feasible through the development of an interoperable infrastructure that connects CGM sensors (invasive or non-invasive) with software systems capable of integrating glucose data with existing analytical inputs. By employing ML and AI techniques, it becomes possible to interpret glucose levels in real time, thereby identifying not only the optimal timing for communication, but also the most appropriate type of content or offer to maximise conversion rates. The practical implementation of the GIRTM model requires the establishment of several enabling conditions, including:

a) the widespread adoption of CGM devices among consumers, b) the availability of interoperable IoT infrastructures, c) an application system for the model d) and the development of scalable technological architectures, such as edge computing systems, capable of processing real-time data with minimal latency.

ETHICS AND LIMITATIONS

The integration of IoT-based CGM sensors into real-time marketing strategies raises a number of critical challenges. These issues, unsurprisingly, stem from and overlap with those associated with CGM technologies and the system architectures into which they are embedded. In particular, they concern data acquisition, data quality and the CGM invasive technology. A primary concern commonly raised with CGM IoT-based systems is technical in nature, specifically relating to the accuracy and precision of the collected data. Despite technological advancements, sensors remain susceptible to noise, artefacts, and other forms of interference, which may result in the transmission of misleading or distorted data (Rodríguez-Rodríguez et al., 2024). Furthermore, the continuous influx of biometric data and its integration into broader analytical systems can lead to information overload, complicating real-time data processing. Real-time analytics also necessitate robust and computational infrastructure, particularly when artificial intelligence techniques are deployed, introducing potential issues of latency and system responsiveness. It becomes essential to implement efficient algorithms and scalable processing solutions to ensure timely responses (Klonoff & Kerr, 2016). Equally important are user-centred technical challenges, including sensor wearability, battery life, and overall comfort, even in the case of minimally invasive designs. These factors cannot be overlooked, as they directly influence user compliance and the overall reliability of real-time data acquisition (Koydemir & Ozcan, 2018). Indeed, the level of invasiveness undoubtedly represents a significant limitation to the widespread adoption of CGM devices among the general population. Secondly, data security emerges as a pressing issue. The growing connectivity and real-time data sharing across sensors and systems substantially increase the risk of data breaches and unauthorised access (Alalhareth & Hong, 2024). In response, more closed and decentralised architectures such as blockchain are increasingly considered as viable solutions to safeguard data integrity and confidentiality (Ahmed et al., 2024; Alalhareth & Hong, 2024). Beyond these considerations, the ethical and legal governance of biometric data represents a crucial dimension that cannot be overlooked. The use of glucose-derived information for marketing purposes intersects with existing data protection frameworks such as the General Data Protection Regulation (GDPR) in the European Union and the Health Insurance Portability and Accountability Act (HIPAA) in the United States.

Both frameworks categorise health and biometric data as special categories of personal data, thus demanding explicit, informed consent, purpose limitation, and proportionality in data processing. Yet, while these regulations provide essential safeguards, they were primarily designed for medical and administrative contexts rather than for marketing environments, creating a grey area where interpretation and accountability remain contested. This regulatory gap highlights the need for proactive ethical design and internal governance mechanisms that extend beyond mere legal compliance. In parallel, emerging AI ethics guidelines – such as the European Commission's (2021) Ethics Guidelines for Trustworthy AI – advocate a more holistic approach grounded in fairness and transparency, whereby any algorithm translating physiological signals into marketing actions should be auditable, non-discriminatory, and subject to human oversight in sensitive cases. A critical challenge lies in balancing the pursuit of predictive accuracy with the preservation of individual autonomy: the same data that enables hyper-personalisation can also, if misused, constrain freedom of choice. Thus, responsible innovation in biometric marketing must be guided not only by the letter of data protection law but also by the spirit of ethical accountability and user trust. Insights from narrative neuroscience further illuminate this tension. As Zak (2015) shows, emotionally charged or morally salient stories can induce neurochemical synchronisation between message and recipient, enhancing trust and persuasive impact. When such narrative mechanisms intersect with glucose-informed data streams, they have the potential to intensify both engagement and ethical vulnerability. The convergence of metabolic readiness and emotional storytelling may therefore represent not only a powerful tool for meaningful connection, but also a critical boundary requiring transparent governance and conscious restraint. Thirdly, privacy concerns are particularly salient in both IoT-based CGM systems and the broader domain of digital marketing (Amosu et al., 2024). Privacy and security become especially critical in real-time data environments, where the rapid processing of large volumes of personal data heightens the potential for violations and misuse (Ahmed et al., 2024). Robust data protection measures, fully compliant with relevant data protection regulations, must be implemented to secure consumer information. Additionally, organisations must ensure clear communication of their data policies to consumers, thereby fostering trust in their data governance practices. This includes obtaining explicit informed consent from users prior to data collection and usage, and providing transparent explanations of what data is being collected, for what purposes, and how it is protected (Rodríguez-Rodríguez et al., 2024). Such transparency is particularly crucial in real-time analytics, where personal data is continuously monitored and analysed (Amosu et al., 2024). Indeed, ethical and transparent data practices not only reduce privacy-related risks but also serve to build consumer trust and loyalty.

FUTURE RESEARCH DIRECTIONS

The conceptual mapping proposed in this chapter creates an innovative framework for the emerging field of real-time biometric marketing. Future research should empirically investigate the relationship between glucose fluctuations and consumer decision-making in a marketing context. Interdisciplinary approaches that combine biometric data, behavioural analytics, and marketing strategies using IoT-based CGM systems will be essential for validating and refining the conceptual framework presented for future automation development.

CONCLUSION

This chapter explored the potential of CGM systems as non-invasive, real time biometric inputs for analytics in marketing. By repositioning blood glucose levels as a physiological proxy for decision-making, the study introduces an innovative theoretical frontier – GIRTM – in biometric analytics for IoT-enabled marketing strategies. For the first time, glucose is introduced as a strategic variable in marketing, through the integration of real-time and biometric techniques. What sets this approach apart is the use of glucose levels as the first decision-oriented biometric indicator with predictive power, enabling precisely timed strategic interventions throughout the customer's decision-making process.

By including blood glucose levels as a key physiological variable, this perspective goes beyond the traditional goal of reaching the right consumer, at the right time, through the right channel. Instead, it identifies the psychophysiological optimal window for message reception and processing, as well as behavioural response making blood glucose levels a critical parameter for marketing strategies.

Glucose based analytics could herald the next stage of real-time biometric marketing in consumer neuroscience.

ACKNOWLEDGMENT

The author declares that the technological system proposed in this chapter is the subject of a patent application filed with the Italian Patent and Trademark Office (UIBM) on 31 December 2025, with the right to extend protection internationally under the Paris Convention.

REFERENCES

Ahmed, S. F., Sharmin, S., Kuldeep, D. A., Lameesa, A., Bin Alam, M. S., Liu, G., & Gandomi, A. H. (2024). Internet of Medical Things (IoMT)-based healthcare technologies: Recent advances, taxonomy, and future outlook. *Results in Engineering*, *22*, 103787. DOI: 10.1016/j.rineng.2024.103787

Alalhareth, M., & Hong, S.-C. (2024). Enhancing the Internet of Medical Things (IoMT) security with meta-learning: A performance-driven approach for ensemble intrusion detection systems. *Sensors (Basel)*, *24*(11), 3519. DOI: 10.3390/s24113519 PMID: 38894310

Amosu, O. R., Kumar, P., Fadina, A., Ogunsuji, Y. M., Oni, S., & Adetula, K. (2024). Harnessing real-time data analytics for strategic customer insights in e-commerce and retail. *World Journal of Advanced Research and Reviews*, *23*(2), 880–889. Advance online publication. DOI: 10.30574/wjarr.2024.23.2.2407

Benton, D. (1990). The impact of increasing blood glucose on psychological functioning. *Biological Psychology*, *30*(1), 13–19. DOI: 10.1016/0301-0511(90)90087-D PMID: 2223932

Broniarczyk, S. M., & Griffin, J. G. (2014). Decision difficulty in the age of consumer empowerment. *Journal of Consumer Psychology*, *24*(4), 608–625. DOI: 10.1016/j.jcps.2014.05.003

Cappon, G., Acciaroli, G., Vettoretti, M., Facchinetti, A., & Sparacino, G. (2017). Wearable continuous glucose monitoring sensors: A revolution in diabetes treatment. *Electronics (Basel)*, *6*(3), 65. DOI: 10.3390/electronics6030065

Darley, W. K., Blankson, C., & Luethge, D. J. (2010). Toward an integrated framework for online consumer behavior and decision making process: A review. *Psychology and Marketing*, *27*(2), 94–116. DOI: 10.1002/mar.20322

Dasari, S. (2020). Ichor - An IoT, cloud, and mobile technologies based noninvasive glucose monitoring system. In *IEMTRONICS 2020 - International IOT, Electronics and Mechatronics Conference, Proceedings*. https://doi.org/DOI: 10.1109/IEMTRONICS51293.2020.9216345

Dian, F. J., Vahidnia, R., & Rahmati, A. (2020). Wearables and the Internet of Things (IoT), applications, opportunities, and challenges: A survey. *IEEE Access : Practical Innovations, Open Solutions*, *8*, 69200–69211. Advance online publication. DOI: 10.1109/ACCESS.2020.2986329

Dickinson, D. L., McElroy, T., & Stroh, N. (2014). Impact of glucose on Bayesian versus heuristic-based decision making. *Journal of Neuroscience, Psychology, and Economics*, *7*(4), 237–247. DOI: 10.1037/npe0000030

Donohoe, R. T., & Benton, D. (1999). Cognitive functioning is susceptible to the level of blood glucose. *Psychopharmacology*, *145*(4), 378–385. DOI: 10.1007/s002130051071 PMID: 10460314

Eichhorn, K. (2022). *Content.* MIT Press. DOI: 10.7551/mitpress/13809.001.0001

European Commission. (2021). Ethics guidelines for trustworthy AI. High-Level Expert Group on Artificial Intelligence. Brussels: European Commission.

Gailliot, M. T., Baumeister, R. F., DeWall, C. N., Maner, J. K., Plant, E. A., Tice, D. M., Brewer, L. E., & Schmeichel, B. J. (2007). Self-control relies on glucose as a limited energy source: Willpower is more than a metaphor. *Journal of Personality and Social Psychology*, *92*(2), 325–336. DOI: 10.1037/0022-3514.92.2.325 PMID: 17279852

Goel, A., Tamrakar, P., Lal, M., Bhende, M., Wani, M., & Saoji, S. (2024). Real-time medical IoT for continuous glucose monitoring. In *2024 International Conference on Intelligent Systems and Advanced Applications (ICISAA)*. IEEE. https://doi.org/DOI: 10.1109/ICISAA62385.2024.10828888

Gregori, N., & Holzmann, P. (2024). Same same, but different: Consumers' decision–making process and the role of digital context. *Journal of Interactive Marketing*, *66*, 24–37. DOI: 10.1080/10696679.2024.2361431

Guleria, P. (2022). Predictions on diabetic patient datasets using big data analytics and machine learning techniques. In *Big Data Analytics for Intelligent Healthcare Management*. IEE., DOI: 10.1016/B978-0-323-91907-4.00018-2

Guntha, R. (2019). IoT architectures for noninvasive blood glucose and blood pressure monitoring. In *Proceedings of the 2019 International Symposium on Embedded Computing and System Design (ISED)* (pp. 120–124). https://doi.org/DOI: 10.1109/ISED48680.2019.9096233

Gurtner, N., Gurtner, S., Laub, L., Zuber, A., & von Däniken, T. (2024). Same same, but different: Consumers' decision-making process and psychological disempowerment in the digital society. *Journal of Marketing Theory and Practice*, *68*(3), 470–500. DOI: 10.1080/10696679.2024.2361431

Janapati, K. C., Vemula, Y. S., Chindam, V., & Bajjuri, A., & Koushik. (2024). IoT-based continuous glucose monitoring system. In *Proceedings of the 2024 International Conference on Expert Clouds and Applications (ICOECA)* (pp. 488–493). https://doi.org/DOI: 10.1109/ICOECA62351.2024.00091

Kahneman, D. (2011). *Thinking, fast and slow*. Farrar, Straus and Giroux.

Kennedy, D. O., & Scholey, A. B. (2000). Glucose administration, heart rate and cognitive performance: Effects of increasing mental effort. *Psychopharmacology*, *149*(1), 63–71. DOI: 10.1007/s002139900335 PMID: 10789884

Kharroubi, A. T., & Darwish, H. M. (2015). Diabetes mellitus: The epidemic of the century. *World Journal of Diabetes*, *6*(6), 850–867. DOI: 10.4239/wjd.v6.i6.850 PMID: 26131326

Klonoff, D. C., & Kerr, D. (2016). Digital diabetes communication: There's an app for that. *Journal of Diabetes Science and Technology*, *10*(5), 1003–1005. DOI: 10.1177/1932296816660210 PMID: 27464752

Koydemir, H. C., & Ozcan, A. (2018). Wearable and implantable sensors for biomedical applications. *Annual Review of Analytical Chemistry (Palo Alto, Calif.)*, *11*(1), 127–146. DOI: 10.1146/annurev-anchem-061417-125956 PMID: 29490190

Masicampo, E. J., & Baumeister, R. F. (2008). Toward a physiology of dual-process reasoning and judgment: Lemonade, willpower, and expensive rule-based analysis. *Psychological Science*, *19*(3), 255–260. https://www.jstor.org/stable/40064920. DOI: 10.1111/j.1467-9280.2008.02077.x PMID: 18315798

McElroy, T., Dickinson, D. L., & Levin, I. P. (2020). Thinking about decisions: An integrative approach of person and task factors. *Journal of Behavioral Decision Making*, *33*(5), 538–555. DOI: 10.1002/bdm.2175

Messier, C., Pierre, J., Desrochers, A., & Gravel, M. (1998). Dosedependent action of glucose on memory processes in women: Effect on serial position and recall priority. *Brain Research. Cognitive Brain Research*, *7*(2), 221–233. DOI: 10.1016/S0926-6410(98)00041-X PMID: 9774737

Metzger, M. M. (2000). Glucose enhancement of a facial recognition task in young adults. *Physiology & Behavior*, *68*(4), 549–553. DOI: 10.1016/S0031-9384(99)00215-2 PMID: 10713296

Murugan, K., Shaheen, N., Kumar, P. S., Homera, D. S., Saketh, M., & Sivaji, P. (2024). Development of an IoT based sugar tracker diabetic monitoring system. In *Proceedings of the 5th International Conference on IoT Based Control Networks and Intelligent Systems (ICICNIS)* IEEE (pp. 481–486). https://doi.org/DOI: 10.1109/ICICNIS64247.2024.10823123

Orquin, J. L., & Kurzban, R. (2016). A meta-analysis of blood glucose effects on human decision making. *Psychological Bulletin*, *142*(5), 546–567. DOI: 10.1037/bul0000035 PMID: 26653865

Prasad, A., Rastogi, T., Paolo, T., Tyagi, U., & Benedetto, F. (2023). Optimization of outcomes: Professional perspectives on mastering data-driven marketing. In Smith, E., & Doe, J. (Eds.), *Data engineering for data-driven marketing* (pp. 217–234). Springer.

Prasad, P. N. S. B. S. V., Hussain, S. A., Singha, A. K., Jana, B., Mandal, P., & Sanki, P. K. (2025). An advanced IoT-based non-invasive in vivo blood glucose estimation exploiting photoacoustic spectroscopy with SDNN architecture. *Sensors and Actuators. A, Physical*, *162*, 116391. Advance online publication. DOI: 10.1016/j.sna.2025.116391

Rahaman, S. U., Kumar, S., & Puchakayala, P. R. A. (2021). Data-driven customer segmentation: Advancing precision marketing through analytics and machine learning techniques. *Journal of Artificial Intelligence. Machine Learning and Data Science*, *1*(1), 1–7. DOI: 10.51219/JAIMLD/shafeeq-ur-rahaman/309

Ramachandran, K. K. (2018). Enhancing customer experience with real-time marketing analytics. *Eurasian Journal of Analytical Chemistry*, *13*(6), 406–413.

Rao, A., Hu, H., & Nobre, A. C. (2013). The effects of combined caffeine and glucose drinks on attention in the human brain. *Psychopharmacology*, *227*(1), 141–153. DOI: 10.1080/10284150500096994 PMID: 16117181

Rodríguez-Rodríguez, I., Campo-Valera, M., Rodríguez, J.-V., & Lok Woo, W. (2024). IoMT innovations in diabetes management: Predictive models using wearable data. *Expert Systems with Applications*, *238*, 121994. DOI: 10.1016/j.eswa.2023.121994

Rodríguez-Rodríguez, I., Zamora-Izquierdo, M.-A., & Rodríguez, J.-V. (2018). Towards an ICT-based platform for type 1 diabetes mellitus management. *Applied Sciences (Basel, Switzerland)*, *8*(4), 511. Advance online publication. DOI: 10.3390/app8040511

Rothenbühler, M., Lizoain, A., Rebeaud, F., Perotte, A., Stoffel, M., & DeVries, J. H. (2025). A prospective pilot study demonstrating noninvasive calibration-free glucose measurement. *medRxiv*. https://doi.org/DOI: 10.1101/2024.08.17.24312052

Roy, S., Padmakumar, R., Jeganathan, S., & Kumaraguru, K. (2015). Personalization and consumer engagement in digital marketing. *Journal of Interactive Advertising*, *15*(1), 35–46.

Saksena, N. (2024). Hyper-personalization in retail: Leveraging data science and real-time streaming. *International Journal of Scientific Research in Computer Science Engineering and Information Technology*, *10*(6), 1382–1392. DOI: 10.32628/CSEIT241061179

Schächinger, H., Cox, D., Linder, L., Brody, S., & Keller, U. (2003). Cognitive and psychomotor function in hypoglycemia: Response error patterns and retest reliability. *Pharmacology, Biochemistry, and Behavior*, *75*(4), 915–920. DOI: 10.1016/S0091-3057(03)00167-9 PMID: 12957236

Scholey, A. B., Harper, S., & Kennedy, D. O. (2001). Cognitive demand and blood glucose. *Physiology & Behavior*, *73*(4), 585–592. DOI: 10.1016/S0031-9384(01)00476-0 PMID: 11495663

Schöpf, V., Fischmeister, F. P. S., Windischberger, C., Gerstl, F., Wolzt, M., Karlsson, K. Æ., & Moser, E. (2013). Effects of individual glucose levels on the neuronal correlates of emotions. *Frontiers in Human Neuroscience*, *7*, 212. Advance online publication. DOI: 10.3389/fnhum.2013.00212 PMID: 23734117

Schroeder, J. P., & Packard, M. G. (2003). Systemic or intra-amygdala injections of glucose facilitate memory consolidation for extinction of drug-induced conditioned reward. *The European Journal of Neuroscience*, *17*(7), 1482–1488. DOI: 10.1046/j.1460-9568.2003.02578.x PMID: 12713651

Sunram-Lea, S. I., Foster, J. K., Durlach, P., & Perez, C. (2001). Glucose facilitation of cognitive performance in healthy young adults: Examination of the influence of fast-duration, time of day and preconsumption plasma glucose levels. *Psychopharmacology, 157*(1), 46–54. DOI: 10.1007/s002130100771 PMID: 11512042

Tariq, B., Taimoor, S., Najam, H., Law, R., Hassan, W., & Han, H. (2020). Generating marketing outcomes through Internet of Things (IoT) technologies. *Sustainability (Basel), 12*(22), 9670. DOI: 10.3390/su12229670

U.S. Department of Health and Human Services (HHS). (1996). *Health Insurance Portability and Accountability Act of 1996 (HIPAA), Public Law 104–191*. U.S. Government Publishing Office.

Verago, J. L., Grassi-Kassisse, D. M., & Spadari-Bratfisch, R. C. (2001). Metabolic markers following beta-adrenoceptor agonist infusion in footshock-stressed rats. *Brazilian Journal of Medical and Biological Research = Revista Brasileira de Pesquisas Médicas e Biológicas, 34*(9), 1197–1207. DOI: 10.1590/S0100-879X2001000900014 PMID: 11514845

Wang, X.-T. (2018). Resource signaling via blood glucose in embodied decision making. *Frontiers in Psychology, 9*, 1965. DOI: 10.3389/fpsyg.2018.01965 PMID: 30374322

Wang, X. T., & Huangfu, G. (2017). Glucose-specific signaling effects on delay discounting in intertemporal choice. *Physiology & Behavior, 169*, 195–201. DOI: 10.1016/j.physbeh.2016.12.001 PMID: 27940144

Zak, P. J. (2015). Why Inspiring Stories Make Us React: The Neuroscience of Narrative. *Cerebrum : the Dana Forum on Brain Science, 2015*(2). PMID: 26034526

Chapter 6
IoT-Driven Smart Configurations and Systemic Restructuring at the Convergence of Digital Economies and Adaptive Industries

Jose De Jesus Reyes-Sánchez
http://orcid.org/0000-0002-3866-2363
TECNM Instituto Tecnologico Superior De Fresnillo, Mexico

Jannet Maricela Barrientos Luján
http://orcid.org/0009-0009-3244-5016
TECNM Instituto Tecnologico Superior De Fresnillo, Mexico

Mario Alberto García-Camacho
http://orcid.org/0000-0002-9645-3199
Tecnológico Nacional de México, ITS Fresnillo, Mexico

Hugo Jimenez Alvarez
http://orcid.org/0009-0002-4497-0327
Tecnológico Nacional de México, ITS Fresnillo, Mexico

ABSTRACT

This study examines how intelligent configurations based on the Internet of Things (IoT) are driving a profound systemic restructuring in various industries, favoring the convergence between digital economies and adaptive sectors. A theoretical-practical

DOI: 10.4018/979-8-2600-1263-5.ch006

review shows that the digitalization generated by IoT optimizes operational efficiency, improves predictive capacity and fosters sustainable business models. However, important challenges such as interoperability, data security, and organizational resilience remain, critical aspects that must be addressed for effective integration.

INTRODUCTION

The digital revolution that has characterized the last decade is based on an unprecedented convergence between information technologies, global connectivity and the integration of physical devices through intelligent systems. In this scenario, the Internet of Things (IoT) has emerged as the central element that makes possible the massive interconnection of objects and devices, with the collection, processing and analysis of large volumes of data in real time. This transformative capacity has enabled the digitalization of processes in domestic and industrial environments, opening the door to new forms of ownership and management (Atzori et al., 2010; Gubbi et al., 2013; Sicari et al., 2015).

In this environment, it can be said that the case of IoT integration is an indispensable agent for the systemic restructuring of industries. Companies have modified their business models through digitization and process automation. Previously based on traditional and hierarchical structures, now each of these processes has become an interconnected and decentralized system in which it is not so clear who makes the decision since all the information comes in real time, from the work area to a predictive analysis or simulation area. This change not only facilitates the reduction of downtime, but also has a positive effect on operational efficiency by making processes harder and more flexible to perform better or withstand the market's sharply changing load.

The IoT is creating cyber-physical environments in which physical machinery, movers, and engineers communicate seamlessly. This is possible because there are advanced sensors, actuators, and communication protocols. For example, in car manufacturing, the automotive industry has followed the example of companies such as IBM or BMW. Ford Motor Company has installed monitoring devices that allow the entire production chain to be controlled in real time and is based on predictive analysis systems. That is why we can now see where things are going wrong before they happen, and another advantage is that this way a high level of quality in the products is always guaranteed. Similarly, in energy companies, thanks to the integration of smart grids with IoT devices, we can modify the amount of energy supply dynamically. The way energy is sent is optimized and renewable methods of obtaining energy are encouraged, thus reinforcing the durability of the system (Atzori et al., 2010; Gubbi et al., 2013; Sicari et al., 2015).

In fact, the integration of IoT in the logistics sector has led to the optimization of supply chains on a global scale. Some international organizations, such as DHL, have made use of the ability of IoT devices to know the location of their vehicles in real time, the environmental circumstances of the warehouse and track shipments. This has meant that efficiency has been significantly enhanced, expenses have decreased substantially and higher levels of customer satisfaction. The advent of this phase is the result of the fusion between analysis technologies and communication systems that provide the entire value chain with a complete vision.

The use of these technologies not only increases the level of safety and quality of care, but also helps to ease the workload in hospitals, with the resulting advantages for both those suffering from illnesses and for the staff themselves in medical facilities

One of the main problems lies in this lack of standardization for devices and protocols that makes the interoperability of heterogeneous systems complicated. In addition, concerns about information security and privacy protection further exacerbate the problem. The persistence of the organizational structures of the same companies is also another obstacle to organizational change that tempts towards economical methods aimed at quickly analyzing data in real time

In terms of quantitative metrics, the use of KPIs (Key Performance Indicators) has allowed comparisons of different international standards for which productivity has been improved, as well as greater operational flexibility and maintenance forecasting capacity. Through these parameters, it has been shown that IoT-driven digitalization not only leads to greater efficiency, but at the same time strengthens the resilience of production processes and allows companies to ultimately respond more effectively to changes in the global market

In addition, the integration of the digital economy with industry stands as one of the pillars on which to reward business models in an increasingly connected and interconnected environment. Digital platforms and huge data analysis have enabled companies to strategize based on co-creation of value. They were able to optimize coordination in their supply chains, resulting in unprecedented 100% personalized products and services. While the technological perspectives of the 1960s opposed a guttural and uncompromising approach to these and other lines of research, their data seem to have been misinterpreted.

A collaborative and flexible approach, which is based on this paradigm shift, is essential for companies to adapt to the dynamics of an ever-changing global market. Another significant aspect of IoT integration is its impact on sustainability, as it facilitates the optimization of the use of resources and reduces the environmental impact of industrial operations. Theoretical models based on the Triple Bottom Line approach have shown that this type of initiative not only brings economic benefits, but also contributes to environmental protection and social well-being (Atzori et al., 2010; Gubbi et al., 2013; Sicari et al., 2015).

A global view like this is crucial for sustainable business models to become a reality, based on environmental and social responsibility plus operational efficiency. This guarantees a true equitable and lasting digital transformation. From these observations it is easy to infer that, although the role of IoT in intelligent configuration in efficiency, competition and adaptation has changed a lot, there is a need to continue exploring research sectors that address these challenges.

Likewise, the convergence of IoT with other AR technologies, such as blockchain, edge computing and quantum computing, must be investigated, since the integration of these technologies considerably increases the power of analysis, real-time response time and the obscuring mechanism of customization of processes. A new horizon is contemplated for innovation in sustainable smart business models. This disciplinary approach will have to be jointly led by specialists, entrepreneurs and regulatory agencies to find an overall solution that is at the same time technical, economic, ethical and legal (Le et al., 2024).

Future research should focus on how to establish regulatory frameworks that allow ethical monitoring and safeguarding of personal rights in highly digitized environments, fostering social justice and responsible decision-making regarding the use of these new technologies. Internalizing ethical aspects in transformation processes is vital to avoid gaps in this regard and to ensure that technical progress benefits everyone equally.

The benefits of operational efficiency, adaptability, efficient use of resources and sustainability are clear, but innovative solutions in interoperability, security, privacy and internal cultural change still need to be applied. Future research should focus on developing unified standards, exploring the confluence of emerging technologies, and creating robust regulatory and ethical frameworks to ensure downstream influence results.

STATEMENT OF THE PROBLEM

The promise of IoT-based smart configurations is to articulate interconnected value chains where data flows with consistent semantics from the edge to the cloud to support adaptive decisions in near real-time. The manuscript advances this ambition, but in practice structural gaps persist: lack of semantic and messaging interoperability between disparate systems, weakness of data governance frameworks for secondary use and machine learning, increasing exposure to attack vectors due to IT and OT convergence, and asymmetries of capabilities that prevent SMEs from capitalizing on network economies. These tensions block the leap from isolated pilots to systemic reconfigurations that integrate platforms, standards, and business models into truly adaptive digital economies. Consequently, the central problem addressed by this study is the distance between an ideal state of reliable, traceable, and secure integration and a current state characterized by technological islands, cyber risks, and uneven organizational maturity that erode the performance and resilience of data-intensive industries (Kannisto et al., 2022; Mekala et al., 2023).

The ideal state assumes interoperable information flows at the vertical and horizontal levels, with ontologies and exchange models that reduce friction in distributed plants and extended chains. Recent evidence shows that, even when there are message bus-based architectures and integration approaches that decouple control and data, protocol heterogeneity, poor metadata quality, and lack of alignment between standards prevent truly orchestrable configurations on an industrial scale. This semantic inconsistency leads to integration costs, engineering delays, and suboptimal decisions in operations, logistics, and maintenance, confirming a technical gap whose resolution is a condition for any IoT-based systemic restructuring (Kannisto et al., 2022; Senna et al., 2022).

Beyond the technical, data governance and organizational culture appear as bottlenecks. Without clear policies on ownership, lineage, access, and reuse, data assets do not reach maturity to support advanced analytics and continuous learning, while resistance to change reduces the adoption of connected and collaborative practices. The literature identifies strategic tensions between products and platforms, between firm and ecosystem, and between people and tools, which translate into political and operational frictions when looking for network effects and scaling of use cases. Without governance mechanisms that articulate value, risk, and compliance, the convergence of digital economies and adaptive sectors is anchored in tactical initiatives, without translating into sustainable advantages (Koohang et al., 2022; Furr et al., 2022).

The security plane intensifies the problem. The attack surface grows with device densification, critical latency at the edge, and exposure of industrial services, which demands specific and continuous controls. Empirical evidence in industrial environments documents vulnerabilities derived from the convergence between operational and information technologies, with direct impacts on continuity, process integrity and data reliability. Without a security posture designed for distributed architectures and cyber-physical services, any attempt at systemic reconfiguration risks amplifying the potential damage and weakening the interorganizational trust that underpins data exchanges (Mekala et al., 2023; Torre et al., 2023).

Finally, a gap in results persists. Even with investments in technologies of the so-called fourth industrial revolution, the systemic benefits do not materialize homogeneously. Recent studies show that technology adoption only impacts resilience and performance when it translates into dynamic capabilities at the chain level, with visibility and real collaboration. Where capabilities, standardization, and out-of-the-box solutions are lacking, adoption stagnates and returns are diluted.

This combination of organizational and technical barriers configures a design and governance problem that prevents IoT-based smart configurations from converting heterogeneous data into effective ecosystem-scale coordination (Huang et al., 2023; Senna et al., 2022).

In summary, the problem under investigation is twofold: on the one hand, the lack of interoperability, data governance and security adequate for intelligent configurations to function as living decision systems; on the other, the adoption and capability gaps that limit value capture in interdependent digital economies. Addressing these fronts in an integrated manner is essential to close the gap between the declared vision and the observable results in adaptive industries (Koohang et al., 2022; Shao et al., 2023).

With this dissertation, the following guiding questions arise that guide the analysis: How and to what extent do IoT-based smart configurations enable the systemic restructuring of operations and value chains in adaptive industries considering efficiency, flexibility and sustainability? What are the main technical and organizational obstacles to implementing IoT effectively, and how to overcome them without compromising operational stability or data privacy? How does the convergence of IoT with 5G, edge computing, blockchain, and advanced analytics, along with regulatory and ethical frameworks, enable the interoperability and security needed to scale ecosystem-level use cases?

BACKGROUND

The evolution of technology for the IIoT The Internet of Things (IoT) has radically changed industrial dynamics, both by changing the operational structures and business models of different sectors: Originally conceived as a network of connected devices to optimize processes and increase efficiency, it has now left behind its pioneering applications in logic and manufacturing to become a powerful engine for digital industrialization (Palmaccio et al., 2021; Mu et al., 2024).

The shape change made possible by the Internet of Things in industry refers to the creation of cyber environments, in which devices, systems, and people are connected through an intelligent network, enabling real-time data collection, automation, and information-based decision-making (Pivoto et al., 2021; Soori et al., 2023).

Over the past ten years, IoT has been increasingly integrating with other emerging technologies such as Big Data, artificial intelligence (AI), and predictive analytics. This allows companies to have a total view of their operations and make decisions based on real-time data.

IoT as a Catalyst for Industrial Digitalization

The Internet of Things (IoT) has also become a key catalyst for this new phase of digitalization. This digitalization is not only the automation of processes, but a transformation of value chains and a real-time optimization of resources. According to Westerman et al. (2014), companies that have taken IoT into their manufacturing strategies would experience greater agility in production and lower cost of a fundamental part of the raw material, electricity, allowing these companies to compete in a more rigorous global market (Wang et al., 2021; Qi et al., 2023).

This digital transition has had a particularly strong impact on the manufacture of smart factories 4.0, devices that allow for fully automated and connected management for entire production. These cyber-physical systems can make machines talk to each other; share data and adjust automatically, which improves efficiency and reduces human error in factories. The fusion of IoT with Big Data has greatly improved the ability of companies to perform predictive analysis of their operations. IoT data collected by large sensors allows companies to anticipate problems in their machinery, such as wear and tear, fluctuation in demand or logistical problems. The end result of this anticipation is that the company can save resources and costs (Mallioris et al., 2024; Wang et al., 2021).

5G Connectivity and the Industrial Internet of Things

They have made a qualitative leap. 5G provides high speed and low latency online, allowing IoT devices to work more efficiently, especially in applications that require real-time responses, such as remote monitoring of machinery or smart grid management. 5G has broadened the It Our IoT reference beyond companies, thanks to it we can also enjoy smart cities, where energy interference and distribution is being controlled. Even more importantly, communications infrastructure has led companies to adopt more advanced modernization techniques, increasing service quality and operational efficiency (Haque et al., 2023).

The integration of digital economies with adaptive industries The integration of digital economies with adaptive industries is now a significant phenomenon, and the key lies in the following: all these manufacturing industries have begun to adopt advanced digital technologies and have thus radically changed their business models to make them more flexible and more resilient. The digital economy, focused on creating value through the collection, analysis, and distribution of data, has profoundly altered production patterns and consumption structures, bringing traditional industries to a more interconnected state in the digital world (Aldehim et al., 2025).

Digital Economies and Their Integration With Agriculture

Digital economies are characterized by being dependent on information and communication technology, in which data and connectivity are the two main drivers. In this context, adaptive industries refer to those that are able to adjust quickly to new market demands. This is possible thanks to the IoT, which allows real-time monitoring of measurements and automation of processes. This flexible model is necessary if companies are to adapt to a dynamic and volatile economic environment. Without the ability to respond quickly, they will not compete (Duan et al., 2024).

In addition to improving operational efficiency, digital economies also transform industrial business models by orienting them towards the shared technology platform (Lee et al., 2020). These platforms improve interoperability between sectors and thus optimize resources. Integrating shared data platforms allows companies to work more closely together as a team. Improve your supply chain management and opex trading through artificial intelligence and data analytics (Shahab et al., 2024).

Transforming Traditional Industries Using IoT

Another visible consequence of the progressive convergence between digital economies and industries appropriate to change is the transformation of traditional ones. In the manufacturing sector, the IoT has facilitated the transformation of smart factories: the autonomous management of each and every production process by interacting tools, devices, and other means reduces costs and improves product quality. In the energy sector, smart grids have enabled a more complete integration of renewable energy sources and more efficient control of energy consumption, resulting in sustainable development (Powell et al., 2024).

Transportation, on the other hand, has once again been improved in its logistics through IoT; following both the vehicle and the cargo in real time from the perspective of business control provides economic benefits and greater efficiency in operations (Helo & Thai, 2024).

Impact of Digital Globalization and E-Commerce on Adaptive Industries

The increase in digital content and e-commerce has also had a major influence on the transformation of the industry. The digitalization of business has allowed the global company to access new markets that is increasing global competition and has led to the adoption of digital technologies to stay competitive (Le et al., 2024).

Smart configurations as part of the systemic restructuring of intelligent configuration systems are changing the way companies work, no longer merely increasing process efficiency but also providing greater flexibility to changing market conditions. In an Industry 4.0 environment, organizations can use IoT technologies to build interconnected systems that not only enable automation, but also self-manage industrial processes. These smart configurations will mean the integration of IoT devices, smart management software, and data platforms to achieve more efficient resource management and autonomous decision-making.

Defining and Featuring Smart Settings

A complex socio-technical system consited in intelligent configurations with connected devices, sensors, software platforms and communication networks designed concomitantly.

Professional Systemic Restructuring Through the Internet of Things

The IoT has played a central role in the systemic restructuring of industries, by allowing the creation of more flexible business models oriented towards the mass customization of products, with real-time monitoring of production processes. IoT has allowed industries to adapt to changes more quickly, reducing the response time to market demands and improving competitiveness. Intelligent systems are reorganizing the organizational structures of organizations, fostering a more decentralized rurality in which decisions are made autonomously based on the data generated by connected devices (Powell et al., 2024).

Semantic Interoperability and the Role of Asset Administration Shell (AAS)

At the heart of industrial digitalization remains a familiar obstacle: the difficulty of making equipment, applications, and platforms understandable without costly ad-hoc integrations. Your own manuscript explicitly identifies the lack of interoperability as a systemic barrier for intelligent configurations to function as true living systems of decision-making, and links it to data governance and security deficits, as well as organizational adoption gaps. In recent years, the AAS has matured as a proposal to describe industrial assets through standardized submodels and shared vocabularies; this semantic layer allows digital twins to dialogue with MES/ERP, edge and cloud, without reinventing models by project. We are even beginning to see approaches that combine AAS with foundational models to enrich the description of process quality and close the loop from detection to action, without losing traceability or operational context (Shi et al., 2024). In parallel, architectural decisions as earthly as the interoperability bus influence the latency and bandwidth available for that semantics: recent comparisons between OPC UA and MQTT, typical in IIoT, show distinct trade-offs between robustness, overhead, and efficiency in scenarios with thousands of data points per second (Ladegourdie et al., 2022).

Real-Time Convergence: Edge Computing, Private 5G and TSN

The enhanced connectivity that your text outlines for real-time response applications is supported today by a converged fabric that bridges TSN in the wired domain with 5G in the radio domain, reinforced by near-machine edge processing. The technical literature accurately maps this union: systematic reviews show that 70% of the studies focus on sub-microsecond time synchronization and end-to-end coordination, necessary conditions to control mobile robots, AMRs or reconfigurable lines without losing determinism (Satka et al., 2023). Moreover, there are integrated 5G-TSN prototypes that validate in the plant replication/frame deletion mechanisms (FRER) and schedules based on 802.1Qbv, achieving adequate reliability and latency for critical traffic (Kehl et al., 2025). In parallel, scheduling configured grant proposals adjust the radio assignment in 5G to TSN windows, reducing conflicts between flows with different periodicities and bringing closer the deterministic behavior demanded by hybrid cells (Larrañaga-Zumeta et al., 2024; Satka et al., 2023; Kehl et al., 2025; Larrañaga-Zumeta et al., 2024).

Industrial Data Quality and Governance

As intelligent configurations expand in scope, the challenge is no longer to capture data and to govern it reproducibly across areas, plants, and partners. The text itself stresses that, without management policies and processes, organizations run into limits in analytics and privacy, which slows down value capture at scale. Recent evidence proposes frameworks that integrate domains of quality (accuracy, timeliness, completeness), lineage, and stewardship with catalogs that operate on AAS-like semantic assets and purpose-based access policies; in addition, it links this governance with business results in innovation and transversal efficiency (Bernardo et al., 2024). For IIoT environments, reference frameworks have been specified that adapt governance to IT/OT convergence, contemplating edge and cloud, and aligning international standards with practical artifacts (roles, processes, building blocks) that allow governance to be implemented without paralyzing the operation (Zorrilla & Yébenes, 2022; Bernardo et al., 2024).

Cybersecurity and Resilience in IIoT Ecosystems

Your manuscript already warns that security is as critical an axis as interoperability, especially in contexts where a failure can impact physical security and business continuity. Recent literature converges on three operational lines: defense-in-depth with risk-based segmentation, protection of data from the sensor to the service with object-centric encryption and device identity management; and, finally, detection and response supported by network telemetry and behavior. A holistic view updates layered attack surfaces (device, network, application, platform) and emphasizes lightweight controls suitable for limited resources, as well as integration with digital forensics for industrial environments (Hossain et al., 2024). For 5G-TSN and edge deployments, these practices must be accompanied by 5G-TSN bridge hardening, isolation of critical flows, and continuous monitoring of jitter and loss to detect malicious degradations before compromising deterministic processes. The premise is clear: without security by design, any gains in flexibility and autonomy described by your background will be compromised by a larger exhibition area (Wang et al., 2023; Hossain et al., 2024).

Digital Maturity and Dynamic Capabilities to Scale Value Capture

Beyond technology, the bottleneck translates to the ability to change, something your paper acknowledges by mentioning adoption and governance gaps that prevent the value promise from materializing. Empirical evidence suggests that dynamic digital capabilities mediate the relationship between digitalization initiatives and operational resilience; when they exist and are exercised, supply chains better absorb disruptions and capture sustainable efficiencies (Dubey et al., 2023). In addition, new maturity assessment frameworks offer operational taxonomies to prioritize investments (people, processes, technology, governance) and align metrics with business results, avoiding transforming for the sake of transforming (Kao et al., 2024). That's why lighthouse use cases need to be inserted into a maturity roadmap: first secure data foundations and governance; then pilot in representative cells; finally, scaling with interoperability standards and a continuous improvement system that internalizes organizational learning (Dubey et al., 2023; Kao et al., 2024).

THEORETICAL FRAMEWORK

Conceptual Foundations of the Internet of Things (IoT)

The Internet of Things (IoT) can be defined as the massive interconnection of physical devices and objects that, through the use of sensors, actuators, and communication protocols, enables the capture, processing, and transmission of data in real time. This technology has transformed the way both domestic and industrial environments are conceived. In the field of IoT, on the one hand, consumer applications are distinguished, which integrate smart equipment into the home and into their day-to-day lives; on the other hand, we reserve the industrial (IIoT) that focuses on the automation, monitoring and optimization of production processes in factories and production plants (Atzori et al., 2010; Gubbi et al., 2013; Sicari et al., 2015).

The integration of these elements: environmental and operational sensors; actors who act according to the result received; and protocols expressly designed for the transmission of information with high speed, security and efficiency. Thanks to this, it starts from a traditional isolation between devices and we manage to link heterogeneous systems with each other. These ties not only drive the automatic process, but also open up new business opportunities and innovative model operations replacing the outdated, where efficiency and flexibility become key drivers for a company's success (Trifonov & Heffernan, 2023).

In addition, there are fundamental differences between consumer and industrial IoT. while the former focuses on the personal experience through wearables, smart assistants and home automation building; the IIoT to the integration of technology into industrial environments to improve productivity, redundancy in downtime and the management of energy and material resources. Likewise, this fork implies different challenges: The IIoT needs a solid infrastructure, high levels of security and scalability; in contrast, consumer IoT is primarily faced with interoperability and usability issues in common home devices (Domínguez-Bolaño et al., 2022; Ahmed et al., 2023).

Theories and Technology Models Applicable to IoT

The adoption and diffusion of IoT has been based on various contexts based on theoretical frameworks that explain how technological innovations spread in organizations and society. Roger's theory of Diffusion of Innovations illustrates that the adoption of a technology depends on factors such as competitive advantage, complementarity, complexity and observability of the results, these elements allow us to identify various pearls of adoption and rhythms of integration in the digital society

Another basic model, the Technology Acceptance Model (TAM) has been adapted to investigate IoT acceptance at the organizational level, with an emphasis on perceived usefulness and ease of use. This model is an empirical explanation of how user attitudes and conditions in the workplace contribute to success in carrying out new technologies. Its integration into organizational innovation analysis allows us to foresee the barriers and enablers of digital transformation in several areas (Domínguez-Bolaño et al., 2022; Ahmed et al., 2023).

These approaches frame the application of service-oriented architectures (SOA) and emerging technologies such as edge computing, which allows the distribution of processed data between the parties generates latencies when analyzed there very close to their origin. This allows the system to enter real-time and respond smoothly to critical events, which is essential in cutting-edge industrial and urban environments (Lu, 2017; Xu et al., 2018; Dalenogare et al., 2018).

IoT as the Structuring Axis of Industry 4.0

Industry 4.0 is characterised by the integration of digital technologies into industrial products through the digitalisation of processes and the application of cyber-physical systems. However, in this new era, the IoT assumes a central role in the intelligent interconnection of machines, systems and human beings. The ability of these devices to switch and exchange information in real time allows for an automated factory optimized to customer measurements, the optimal supply chain that adjusts to different situations or production environments and a drastic reduction in downtime (Lasi et al., 2014).

Studies point to the importance of models such as Industry 4.0 in the transformation of production operations, which incorporate advanced artificial vision (V) systems, predictive analysis or robotic cooperation. And we are also faced with a range of technologies that are highly efficient in connection: for example, intelligent automation not only increases productivity but also facilitates the customization of production and gives way to a new class of factories, in which each component can act individually according to the needs of the market (Zhong et al., 2017; Kusiak, 2018; Villani et al., 2018).

In addition, the integration of IoT into Industry 4.0 is at a very advanced stage of development. This means that it will require very powerful cyber-physical systems so that machines can communicate with each other and organize themselves autonomously according to operational processes. This intercommunication promotes resilience and adaptability in the production environment, auguring trends that will become the future Industry 5.0, where human-machine collaboration will be even closer. Another parallel contribution in this axis is represented by recent research that shows how the integration of breakdown technologies favors the adaptability and efficiency of industrial processes (Nahavandi, 2019).

The concept of intelligent configurations encompasses the combination of hardware and software or communication protocols necessary to create adaptive environments, which fit into the real world and can be directed by freelancers. In addition, in these systems, of marked individualism, their most important characteristics are their autonomy in decision-making, self-learning based on histories that they analyze, scalability to add new devices and resilience to failures or cyberattacks (Monostori, 2014; Lee et al., 2015).

It is interesting to consider a wide range of taxonomies, which filter these models into three categories: centralized in which all processing is concentrated in a single core; distributed in which a workload is distributed among many nodes or hybrids trying to combine the best of both approaches. For example, in centralized configurations, you can achieve unitary control, but suffer from latency issues. On the other hand, distributed networks improve processing efficiency at the edge, although at the cost of developing more complex synchronization mechanisms (Shi et al., 2016; Bonomi et al., 2012).

The ability to integrate and coordinate these components is crucial in digital transformation since it allows any organization to create highly automated and adaptive operations. In this sense, the implementation of intelligent configurations not only optimizes operability, but also encourages business model innovation and inter-organizational collaboration, which is essential when working in competitive industrial environments (Xu et al., 2018; Lu, 2017; Dalenogare et al., 2018).

Systemic Restructuring From an Organizational Approach

IoT adoption and process digitization require a fundamental transformation of organizations. The model of the technological corporation that drives change is enough to discard a hierarchical structure in which all decisions are made from above and adopt a decentralized network in decision-making that is subject to real-time and updated information. Under this change, it also implies the development of digital skills at all levels. and a redefinition of the roles and responsibilities of those involved.

Strength in digital governance emerges as a key strategy to ensure that digital transformation is carried out safely and equitablyThese policies shape a context for the collection of devices and systems that fosters a collaboration that not only contributes to other perspectives, but also fosters innovation In the words of IDG, the ability to handle large data clusters and respond proactively to the evolution of the environment becomes a competitive advantage for organizations that are able to complete this transition (Tambare et al., 2022).

Interoperability, Security, and Ethics in IoT Ecosystems

The heterogeneity of devices and systems in the IoT ecosystem brings substantial challenges in interoperability: it is absolutely necessary that hardware and software from different backgrounds can understand and work seamlessly. At the same time, data security is decisive, especially in critical environments where the vulnerability of the digital infrastructure can have serious consequences. The implementation of advanced cryptography protocols, robust authentication methods and means for permanent maintenance is absolutely necessary to mitigate the dangers posed by digitalization (Zorrilla & Yébenes, 2022).

On the other hand, very relevant ethical questions arise. They address issues such as the treatment of algorithmic surveillance, the protection of the privacy of personal data available to you with strong prior consent, or your ability to make independent decisions. The mix of solutions that bring together both those computer security techniques and also have a legal framework from multiple disciplines is essential to ensure that fundamental rights are respected in IoT practice and progress is made towards digital justice.

Convergence Between Digital Economy and Adaptive Industries

The integration of IoT technologies has generated a convergence between the digital economy and adaptive industries. In this sense, there is the creation of value networks and platforms that can configure orientations for businesses towards collaboration and co-creation of value. Digital platforms provide an environment for coordination throughout the entire supply chain cycle between different participants and co-producers. The concentration of information between peers allows for instant exchange and, this mobility of information, drives the personalization of products and services in an increasingly competitive environment (Mishra et al., 2024).

Massive data analysis, supported by artificial intelligence and machine learning techniques, allows companies to anticipate market trends and optimize processes. In this way, they are able to develop strategies for innovation that combine operational efficiency and sustainability. On the other hand, the IoT is key to promoting the circular economy, as it allows the control of the use of natural resources and the adoption of environmentally and socially responsible practices

Deepening this convergence requires examining the impact of integrating digital technology on the rethinking of global value chains. This is enabling the formation of collaborative ecosystems and the creation of business models focused on open innovation. Thus, we are seeing a profound change in the way value is generated and distributed in the digital age (Jacobides et al., 2018).

Theoretical Models on Technological Sustainability and Digital Transformation

In this context of IoT and digital transformation, we frame sustainability from theoretical perspectives that consider economic, environmental and social aspects. This approach is known as the Three Dimensions of Performance approach. This model helps companies to evaluate the profitability of their digital initiatives from a triple bottom line approach, in terms of reducing environmental impacts and their positive effect on social life. This is especially important for these industries, which seek operational excellence without fatally harming the environment (Senna et al., 2023; Hortovanyi et al., 2023).

In addition, digital maturity models have emerged as a tool to measure the degree of transformation and the state of business readiness to the demands of the digital world. These models can serve as a guide for companies to pursue advancements in their digital quality and, at the same time, provide a framework for them to pursue this goal systematically as intermediate steps

Evaluation and Performance Indicators in Smart Industrial Environments

The integration of IoT into industrial environments is bound to become a reality. Key performance indicators (KPIs) must be able to measure, for example, production efficiency, predictive maintenance capacity, cutting energy consumption. Among other things, they also measure how much power is left in your organization to adapt to change or even to move forward. By using these indicators systematically, companies can locate areas for improvement and compare their performance with international standards, which is a condition for strategic decision-making. Likewise, applying flexible cross-industry benchmarking techniques identifies best practices and employs successful models in different contexts based on this, thereby raising global competition levels (Tambare et al., 2022).

Future Perspectives and Strategic Challenges

Looking to the future, the IoT sector's outlook is that this technology will be increasingly deeply integrated with other cutting-edge innovations, such as blockchain, industrial metaverse, and quantum computing. It is predicted that by 2030 it will deploy the backbone of complex and collaborative technological ecosystems with the ability to radically transform entire productions to business models on a global scale (Al-Dulaimy et al., 2024).

Regarding its fundamental strategic challenges, one of them will be the need to create an internationally harmonized regulatory framework that ensures the interoperability and security of devices, as well as the protection of information, personal data and fundamental rights. On the other hand, the scalability of IoT infrastructures poses a crucial challenge, especially in relation to maintaining, updating, and managing increasingly complex networks that are shaped as the number of interconnected devices increases (Mathur et al., 2023).

In addition, it is necessary to assess the impact that the crossing of these technologies will have on the transformation of production processes. For example, the combination of big data analysis and deep learning solutions, supported by placement at the edge of computing, will allow for increasingly elaborate predictive models. This will enable companies not only to respond to market demands, but also to anticipate trends and actively adjust their work systems. It is also important, therefore, to equip the workforce with digital skills so that they can move forward with new technological challenges. It is therefore important that the digital transformation is carried out in a global way, not only dealing with technical or operational factors but also with social and ethical issues, so that the future industry can be sustainable and equitable (Li et al., 2024).

Some works in this regard have advanced in studying how the Internet of Things is connected to other technologies that are bursting onto the scene. Recent research advances have indicated that the convergence of these innovations will open up new opportunities in terms of value generation, but will also pose significant challenges for areas such as investment, regulation and the importance of embracing certain cultural changes (Al-Dulaimy et al., 2024).

The theoretical journey outlined in this framework allows us to glimpse the magnitude of the transformation that the inclusion of the Internet of Things entails in the organization of productive environments and companies. From basic theorization and application of models that explain how technologies are disseminated and accepted, to the incorporation of IoT as a central axis in Industry 4.0, the consolidation of intelligent configurations and systemic restructuring, together with challenges such as interoperability, security and ethics, each of these aspects is intertwined to create a paradigm where digitalization acts as a driver of innovation and performance (Javeed et al., 2024).

The convergence of thought between the digital economy and the cognitive industries, the construction of technological performance criteria and survival models reflect the idea that new industrial structures will be based on cooperation, adjustment and social responsibility. Ultimately, the success of digital transformation will depend to a large extent on whether organisations and society as a whole are able to integrate technologies in a safe and harmonious way, in line with what the Charter of Fundamental Rights promotes, while also fostering sustainable and equitable promotion (Van 't Schip, 2025).

The challenge is to overcome obstacles of magnitude. A comprehensive approach is required that combines investment in technology, training for the digital age, strong legal frameworks and, above all, collaboration between all those involved. Only in this way can we guarantee that the digital revolution, the result of the IoT, will in fact reconfigure the way we do business and those intelligent ecosystems that are formed promote the emergence of new types of value in a globalized world and build a prosperous and sustainable future for all (Rikala et al., 2024).

METHODOLOGY

The systematic review of the literature allows us to # This methodology allowed us to approach research on IoT-driven smart configurations in digital economies and adaptive industries. This approach allows for an in-depth synthesis of what is available in both academic and empirical material on related topics, helping to also identify the main trends, theories, models and practices relevant to this field. Below, we complement the literature review with an analysis of case studies in different industries that have adopted IoT, to see both the obstacles they have had to overcome and the benefits they have seen.

The collection of articles was carried out in academic databases using several composite platforms, with a focus on research published in the last ten years. The selection criteria included the relevance of each article to the topics of systemic restructuring and IoT adoption in an industrial context, while seeking methodological quality and practical empirical application of the studies.

An in-depth analysis of the articles identified as potential for the agenda was analyzed, with theoretical and empirical research being listed equally, as well as cases at the meso (digital economies) and micro (adaptive industry) levels. In addition, case studies were added in different specialized fields that explore specific IoT implementation situations in areas such as manufacturing, logistics, and energy. The results of this review provide a comprehensive look at what motivates IoT adoption in the industry and what problems companies face in integrating these systems into their way of doing things (Powell et al., 2024).

Examples of Implementation in Companies or Organizations

In the automotive field, large manufacturers have adopted IoT solutions for the development of smart factories. Ford Motor Company, for example, has pioneered this area by implementing sensors and real-time monitoring systems along with predictive analytics systems. This adoption of smart configurations has resulted in a substantial improvement in production line efficiency, reduced downtime, and significant optimization in assembly quality, placing the company in a position of greater competitiveness. Siemens devises the strategy for smart grids rather than merely following others, but also takes the lead in new Internet of Things technologies (Shahab et al., 2024).

As an example that can be taken in logistics, DHL's supply chain clearly takes advantage of IoT. Indeed, the company has a solid network of IoT devices; Carrying sensors in transport vans or containers, in the long run, it allows real-time monitoring of the fast progress of the shipment and parameters such as temperature or environmental conditions. With this visibility into operational work, route control has become much more rational and with optimized distributions; with the disappearance of chaos, the cities near the provinces are still very happy for it (Duan et al., 2024).

In the area of health, several establishments have begun to implement solutions aimed at continuous care and IoT for the control of hospital resources. For example, some hospitals are using smart devices to record, in real time, patients' vital signs. This allows for early detection of critical situations and knowing what to do at such a time. The indexing of technologies not only contributes to the quality of care but also patient safety, as well as an issue of automating tasks that avoids overload. This results in greater processing of clinical information and the information itself becomes self-provided, which reduces the workload of the assisting staff (Mallioris et al., 2024; Wang et al., 2021).

From agriculture, to the medical field or school education, using the application of IoT-based smart configuration generates a noticeable effect on the structure of different fields. If an organization is given the power to change its processes, reduce costs and adapt in a short time to the changing needs of the market; It will then be able to both survive and adapt to changing market demands (Wang et al., 2021; Qi et al., 2023).

RESULTS

Various organizations report that the adoption of IoT technologies has ensured a notable improvement in their operational efficiency. Today, the realization of these forecasts is beginning to be a reality and faces minor technological challenges. It is based on multiple studies that, through comparisons abroad, have shown that it is precisely the IoT that transforms production processes and structures more agile and resilient operating facilities (Haque et al., 2023).

In addition, the results show that the application of IoT leads to an optimization of the use of both energy and material resources, which saves operating costs and allows the use of predictive analysis technologies to predict failures in the value chain such as production or logistics. From this perspective, the company is also very adept at acquiring a large amount of information in real time, which has driven the digitalization of industries as diverse as manufacturing, energy and logistics.

Thus, when examining the results obtained by leading companies in the adoption of these technologies, the case of the automotive sector stands out, where companies such as Ford Motor Company have implemented smart configurations that combine IoT devices and real-time analysis systems. In this context, the implementation of advanced sensors and the use of machine learning algorithms have made it possible to continuously monitor assembly lines, which led to a significant reduction in the frequency of failures in production and to a consistency of better finished product quality. Similarly, companies such as Siemens in the energy sector have adopted IoT solutions that integrate networks of smart sensors with autonomous control systems, which has greatly facilitated the dynamic adjustment of energy distribution according to demand and has greatly reduced power transmission, which increasingly consolidates more stable and sustainable systems (Pivoto et al., 2021; Soori et al., 2023).

In the logistics industry, it has been documented that international organizations such as DHL have leveraged the power of IoT devices for shipment tracking, real-time environmental condition monitoring, and distribution route optimization. In addition, through the use of sensors in vehicles and containers, these results are entirely satisfactory: they reduce transit times, make cargo safer, and optimize customer satisfaction through unprecedented traceability and transparency (Huang et al., 2023; Senna et al., 2022).

These improvements represent a radical change in the way of managing logistics chains for production in a globalized world. Another field where particularly good results have emerged is in the health sector. Let's take the case of medical institutions that have integrated real-time monitoring sensors for patients within their hospital system, since here you can find immediate economic results.

In addition, exemplary case solutions were identified to a number of difficulties encountered in the implementation of the Internet of Things (IoT). One of these challenges is the absence of a standard set of devices and protocols, which in turn hinders interoperability between systems belonging to different manufacturers in any country (Mekala et al., 2023; Torre et al., 2023).

Resistance to change in organizations has also been pointed out, as many companies still maintain traditional hierarchical structures that prevent the adoption of new technologies and the transition to decentralized and collaborative models. In terms of quantitative analysis, the results obtained through the application of key performance indicators (KPIs) have revealed significant improvements in production efficiency and the ability to anticipate operational problems(Koohang et al., 2022; Furr et al., 2022).

In this regard, study the future prospects that the convergence between IoT and other emerging technologies such as blockchain, industrial metaverses, and quantum computing promises a number of possibilities to disrupt business models and production systems. Recent studies suggest that by 2030, the IoT will consolidate itself as the basic infrastructure invoked for collaboration between technological ecosystems, with which it will integrate disruptive innovations and thus enhance the adaptability and mass customization of production (Kannisto et al., 2022; Mekala et al., 2023).

Digital transformation, triggered by the IOT, is therefore a crucial factor in the competitiveness of today's global economy, not only when it comes to improving operational performance but also by affecting the very structure of the organization itself (Le et al., 2024).

CONCLUSIONS

This methodological proposal makes it clear that the adoption of intelligent configurations based on the Internet of Things has produced a real transformation in the way companies operate, thus marking a turning point in terms of operational efficiency, ability to respond and ability to personalize processes. Leading companies in both the automotive and energy sectors can significantly reduce downtime and improve resource utilization today. In the same way, it also increases the quality of products and services they offer, thanks to the integration of real-time monitoring, predictive analysis technologies (Atzori et al., 2010; Gubbi et al., 2013; Sicari et al., 2015).

However, it certainly tends to identify critical challenges that limit the potential for fullness of this digital revolution. Unfar from the lack of standardization and interoperability between heterogeneous devices are major barriers to complete system integration. In addition, data security and the protection of privacy are urgent problems in an environment where the manipulation of large volumes of information almost live is increasingly widespread (Mathur et al., 2023).

Resistance to organisational change has also been highlighted as an obstacle to be overcome, as many companies continue to operate under traditional hierarchical models that make it difficult to move to collaborative and decentralised structures.

Performance indicators elaborated from meticulous measurements and comparative strategies, show that IoT (Internet of Things) as well as significantly improved efficiency, operational flexibility and predictability of maintenance. This translates into the reduction of operating expenses and also the consolidation of the company's global competitiveness, since comparative data allows the identification of areas for improvement and successful replication of best practices in dissimilar production environments (Zorrilla & Yébenes, 2022).

In the context of the convergence between the digital economy and adaptive industries, the IoT is being used as a new hub that changes old traditional business models. Similarly, digital platforms and big data analytics have allowed organizations to reinvent their strategies, enabling the personalization of products and services as well as supply chain optimization. But this shift, based on a collaborative approach and the co-creation of value, ushers in a dynamic economy; where connectivity and interoperability are fundamental (Tambare et al., 2022).

On another note, the convergence of IoT with emerging technologies – such as edge computing, blockchain and the industrial metaverse – allows the development of intelligent systems that can respond in real time to changes in the environment. This phenomenon opens up new opportunities for the development of predictive models in analytical data, which improves decision-making and will allow proactively adapting to market dynamics. On the other hand, it is noted that this technological image is the future basis from which collaborations and systems of resistance will be built in 2030. Security, privacy, and adaptability will ultimately be fundamental in these ecosystems.

In Chouinard's opinion, in the sustainable aspect, models based on Triple Bottom Line (3BL) ideas can be taken as a global take that allows the organization to evaluate its attempts at digitization not only in an economic field, but also in an environmental and social one. The results indicate that the application of intelligent configurations integrated with predictive analytics results in lower environmental impact. That in turn optimizes the use of natural resources, elevates a company's social responsibility(Jacobides et al., 2018).

Integrating the Internet of Things into intelligent configurations has ultimately become an important transformative engine of the industrial and organizational aspects with drastic improvements for performance, adaptability and competitiveness. But to make them realize their full potential, they need to face challenges in the future such as interoperability, security of private information, privacy protection, and planning against change.

In addition, together with emerging convergence technologies and the establishment of models for sustainability, they are essential fields to be investigated in an interdisciplinary and joint manner.

RECOMMENDATIONS FOR FUTURE RESEARCH

Recommendations for future research focus on developing theoretical and methodological frameworks that allow the creation of unified standards and protocols for the interoperability of IoT devices, as well as defining advanced strategies in cybersecurity and data protection. It will be crucial for new research to take into consideration the integration of IoT with technologies such as blockchain, edge computing, and big data, in order to provide a rapid response and eventually increase the degree of individualization in factories in real time. In addition, it is recommended that the training and retraining of digital skills of staff should be given special attention, so that the transition to smart production environments can be sustainable and cooperative.

At the same time, it is imperative to consider the ethical and societal implications that arise from a broad application of IoT, especially with regard to digital surveillance and autonomous decision-making. Future research should be involved in the development of regulatory frameworks that ensure fairness, privacy, and protection of fundamental rights in an increasingly digital world, so that social justice and an ethical transformation in the digital age are promoted.

REFERENCES

Al-Dulaimy, A., Jansen, M., Johansson, B., Trivedi, A., Iosup, A., Ashjaei, M., Galletta, A., Kimovski, D., Prodan, R., Tserpes, K., Kousiouris, G., Giannakos, C., Brandic, I., Ali, N., Bondi, A. B., & Papadopoulos, A. (2024). The computing continuum: From IoT to the cloud. *Internet of Things : Engineering Cyber Physical Human Systems*, *27*, 101272. DOI: 10.1016/j.iot.2024.101272

Aldehim, G., Khan, S., Shahzad, T., Khan, M. A., Ghadi, Y. Y., Jiang, W., Mazhar, T., & Hamam, H. (2025). Balancing sustainability and security: A review of 5G and IoT in smart cities. *Digital Communications and Networks*, *11*(6), 1722–1737. Advance online publication. DOI: 10.1016/j.dcan.2025.06.007

Atzori, L., Iera, A., Morabito, G., & Perrone, M. (2010). The Internet of Things: A survey. *Computer Networks*, *54*(15), 2787–2805. DOI: 10.1016/j.comnet.2010.05.010

Bernardo, B. M. V., de Sousa, M. C., Silva, M. M., & Azevedo, A. I. (2024). Data governance & quality management—Innovation and breakthroughs across different fields. *Journal of Innovation & Knowledge*, *9*(4), 100598. DOI: 10.1016/j.jik.2024.100598

Bonomi, F., Milito, R., Zhu, J., & Addepalli, S. (2012). Fog computing and its role in the Internet of Things. *Proceedings of the First MCC Workshop on Mobile Cloud Computing*, 13–16. https://doi.org/DOI: 10.1145/2342509.2342513

Dalenogare, L. S., Benitez, G. B., Ayala, N. F., & Frank, A. G. (2018). The expected contribution of Industry 4.0 technologies for industrial performance. *International Journal of Production Economics*, *204*, 383–394. DOI: 10.1016/j.ijpe.2018.08.019

Domínguez-Bolaño, T., Campos, O., Barral, V., Escudero, C. J., & García-Naya, J. A. (2022). An overview of IoT architectures, technologies, and existing open-source projects. *Internet of Things : Engineering Cyber Physical Human Systems*, *20*, 100626. DOI: 10.1016/j.iot.2022.100626

Duan, W., Eva, A., Andrews, L., & Liu, Y. (2024). The role of platform ecosystem configuration toward performance bifurcation. *Journal of Innovation & Knowledge*, *9*(2), 100490. DOI: 10.1016/j.jik.2024.100490

Dubey, R., Bryde, D., Ali, S. M., & Papadopoulos, T. (2023). Dynamic digital capabilities and supply chain resilience. *International Journal of Production Economics*, *259*, 108790. DOI: 10.1016/j.ijpe.2023.108790

Furr, N., Shipilov, A., & Hagiu, A. (2022). What is digital transformation Core tensions facing established companies. *Global Strategy Journal, 12*(3), 517–544. DOI: 10.1002/gsj.1442

Gubbi, J., Buyya, R., Marusic, S., & Palaniswami, M. (2013). Internet of Things (IoT): A vision, architectural elements, and future directions. *Future Generation Computer Systems, 29*(7), 1645–1660. DOI: 10.1016/j.future.2013.01.010

Haque, M. E., Tariq, F., Khandaker, M. R. A., & Wong, K.-K. (2023). *A survey of scheduling in 5G URLLC and outlook for emerging 6G systems*. IEEE., DOI: 10.1109/ACCESS.2023.3264592

Helo, P., & Thai, V. V. (2024). Logistics 4.0 – Digital transformation with smart connected tracking and tracing devices. *International Journal of Production Economics, 275*, 109336. DOI: 10.1016/j.ijpe.2024.109336

Hossain, M., Islam, M. R., & Rahman, M. M. (2024). A holistic analysis of Internet of Things (IoT) security. *Future Internet, 16*(2), 40. DOI: 10.3390/fi16020040

Huang, K., Wang, K., Lee, P. K. C., & Yeung, A. C. L. (2023). The impact of industry 4.0 on supply chain capability and supply chain resilience A dynamic resource based view. *International Journal of Production Economics, 262*, 108913. DOI: 10.1016/j.ijpe.2023.108913

Jacobides, M. G., Cennamo, C., & Gawer, A. (2018). Towards a theory of ecosystems. *Strategic Management Journal, 39*(8), 2255–2276. DOI: 10.1002/smj.2904

Javeed, D., Almusaylim, Z. A., Cuomo, S., Postolache, O., & Roman, R. (2024). Quantum-empowered federated learning and 6G wireless networks: Challenges, opportunities, and future directions. *Future Generation Computer Systems*. Advance online publication. DOI: 10.1016/j.future.2024.06.023

Kannisto, P., Hästbacka, D., Gutiérrez, T., Suominen, O., Vilkko, M., & Craamer, P. (2022). Plant wide interoperability and decoupled data driven process control with message bus communication. *Journal of Industrial Information Integration, 26*, 100253. DOI: 10.1016/j.jii.2021.100253

Kao, L.-J., Chiu, C.-C., Lin, H.-T., Hung, Y.-W., & Lu, C.-C. (2024). Unveiling the dimensions of digital transformation: A comprehensive taxonomy and assessment model for business. *Journal of Business Research, 176*, 114595. DOI: 10.1016/j.jbusres.2024.114595

Kehl, P. E., Kramarz, T., Münch, F., Witt, L., Giebe, C., Peitz, C., & Cimdins, M. (2025). 5G-TSN integrated prototype for reliable industrial communication. *Electronics (Basel), 14*(4), 758. DOI: 10.3390/electronics14040758

Koohang, A., Paliszkiewicz, J., Nord, J. H., & Goluchowski, J. (2022). Internet of Things from awareness to continued use. *International Journal of Information Management*, *61*, 102442. DOI: 10.1016/j.ijinfomgt.2021.102442

Ladegourdie, G., Boydens, J., & Hennebert, J. (2022). OPC UA vs. MQTT: A performance evaluation for Industrial IoT applications. *IoT*, *3*(4), 465–484. DOI: 10.3390/iot3040027

Larrañaga-Zumeta, A., Lucas-Estañ, M. C., Gozálvez, J., & Arriola, A. (2024). 5G configured grant scheduling for seamless integration with TSN industrial networks. *Computer Communications*, *226–227*, 107930. DOI: 10.1016/j.comcom.2024.107930

Lasi, H., Fettke, P., Kemper, H.-G., Feld, T., & Hoffmann, M. (2014). Industry 4.0. *Business & Information Systems Engineering*, *6*(4), 239–242. DOI: 10.1007/s12599-014-0334-4

Le, T., & Fan, R. (2024). Digital twins for logistics and supply chain systems. *Computers & Industrial Engineering*, *187*, 109768. Advance online publication. DOI: 10.1016/j.cie.2023.109768

Lee, J., Bagheri, B., & Kao, H.-A. (2015). A cyber-physical systems architecture for Industry 4.0-based manufacturing systems. *Manufacturing Letters*, *3*, 18–23. DOI: 10.1016/j.mfglet.2014.12.001

Lee, J., Bagheri, B., Kao, H.-A., & Lin, C. (2015). A cyber-physical systems architecture for Industry 4.0-based manufacturing systems. *Manufacturing Letters*, *3*, 18–23. DOI: 10.1016/j.mfglet.2014.12.001

Li, S., Xie, H.-L., Zheng, P., & Wang, L. (2024). Industrial metaverse: A proactive human-robot collaboration perspective. *Journal of Manufacturing Systems*, *76*, 314–319. DOI: 10.1016/j.jmsy.2024.08.003

Lu, Y. (2017). Industry 4.0: A survey on technologies, applications and open research issues. *Journal of Industrial Information Integration*, *6*, 1–10. DOI: 10.1016/j.jii.2017.04.005

Mallioris, P., Aivazidou, E., & Bechtsis, D. (2024). Predictive maintenance in Industry 4.0: A systematic multi-sector mapping. *CIRP Journal of Manufacturing Science and Technology*, *50*, 80–103. DOI: 10.1016/j.cirpj.2024.02.003

Mathur, S., Kalla, A., Gür, G., Bohra, M. K., & Liyanage, M. (2023). A survey on role of blockchain for IoT: Applications and technical aspects. *Computer Networks*, *227*, 109726. DOI: 10.1016/j.comnet.2023.109726

Mekala, S. H., Bandara Ekanayake, T. N., & Jayaraman, P. P. (2023). Cybersecurity for industrial IoT threats, countermeasures, challenges and future directions. *Computer Communications*, *208*, 44–69. DOI: 10.1016/j.comcom.2023.06.020

Mishra, S.. (2024). A survey on security and cryptographic perspective of IIoT. *Internet of Things : Engineering Cyber Physical Human Systems*, *26*, 101037. DOI: 10.1016/j.iot.2023.101037

Monostori, L. (2014). Cyber-physical production systems: Roots, expectations and R&D challenges. *Procedia CIRP*, *17*, 9–13. DOI: 10.1016/j.procir.2014.03.115

Mu, X., & Antwi-Afari, M. F. (2024). The applications of Internet of Things (IoT) in industrial management: A science mapping review. *International Journal of Production Research*, *62*(5), 1928–1952. Advance online publication. DOI: 10.1080/00207543.2023.2290229

Nahavandi, S. (2019). Industry 5.0: A human-centric solution. *Sustainability (Basel)*, *11*(16), 4371. DOI: 10.3390/su11164371

Palmaccio, M., Dicuonzo, G., & Belyaeva, Z. S. (2021). The internet of things and corporate business models: A systematic literature review. *Journal of Business Research*, *131*, 610–618. DOI: 10.1016/j.jbusres.2020.09.069

Pivoto, D. G. S., de Almeida, L. F. F., da Rosa Righi, R., Rodrigues, J. J. P. C., Lugli, A. B., & Alberti, A. M. (2021). Cyber-physical systems architectures for industrial internet of things applications in Industry 4.0: A literature review. *Journal of Manufacturing Systems*, *58*, 176–192. DOI: 10.1016/j.jmsy.2020.11.017

Powell, J., McCafferty-Leroux, A., Hilal, W., & Gadsden, S. A. (2024). Smart grids: A comprehensive survey of challenges, industry applications, and future trends. *Energy Reports*, *11*, 5760–5785. Advance online publication. DOI: 10.1016/j.egyr.2024.05.051

Qi, Q., Xu, Z., & Rani, P. (2023). Big data analytics challenges to implementing intelligent IIoT systems in sustainable manufacturing operations. *Technological Forecasting and Social Change*, *190*, 122401. DOI: 10.1016/j.techfore.2023.122401

Rikala, P., Braun, G., Järvinen, M., Stahre, J., & Hämäläinen, R. (2024). Understanding and measuring skill gaps in Industry 4.0 — A review. *Technological Forecasting and Social Change*, *201*, 123206. DOI: 10.1016/j.techfore.2024.123206

Satka, Z., Ashjaei, M., Fotouhi, H., Daneshtalab, M., Sjödin, M., & Mubeen, S. (2023). A comprehensive systematic review of integration of time sensitive networking and 5G communication. *Journal of Systems Architecture*, *138*, 102852. DOI: 10.1016/j.sysarc.2023.102852

Senna, P. P., Barros, A. C., & Bonnin Roca, J.. (2023). Development of a digital maturity model for Industry 4.0 based on the technology-organization-environment framework. *Computers & Industrial Engineering*, *185*, 109645. DOI: 10.1016/j.cie.2023.109645

Senna, P. P., Ferreira, L. M. D. F., Barros, A. C., Bonnin Roca, J., & Magalhães, V. (2022). Prioritizing barriers for the adoption of industry 4.0 technologies. *Computers & Industrial Engineering*, *171*, 108428. DOI: 10.1016/j.cie.2022.108428

Shahab, H., Iqbal, M., Sohaib, A., Ullah Khan, F., & Waqas, M. (2024). IoT-based agriculture management techniques for sustainable farming: A comprehensive review. *Computers and Electronics in Agriculture*, *220*, 108851. DOI: 10.1016/j.compag.2024.108851

Shao, D., Calo, F., & Bryan-Kinns, N. (2023). Integration of IoT into e government. *Foresight*, *25*(6), 495–514. DOI: 10.1108/FS-04-2022-0048

Shi, D., Meyer, O., Oberle, M., & Bauernhansl, T. (2024). Interoperable information modelling leveraging asset administration shell and large language model for quality control toward zero defect manufacturing. *Journal of Manufacturing Systems*, *77*, 678–696. DOI: 10.1016/j.jmsy.2024.10.011

Shi, W., Cao, J., Zhang, Q., Li, Y., & Xu, L. (2016). Edge computing: Vision and challenges. *IEEE Internet of Things Journal*, *3*(5), 637–646. DOI: 10.1109/JIOT.2016.2579198

Sicari, S., Rizzardi, A., Grieco, L. A., & Coen-Porisini, A. (2015). Security, privacy and trust in Internet of Things: The road ahead. *Computer Networks*, *76*, 146–164. DOI: 10.1016/j.comnet.2014.11.008

Soori, M., Arezoo, B., & Dastres, R. (2023). Internet of things for smart factories in Industry 4.0: A review. *Internet of Things and Cyber-Physical Systems*, *3*, 192–204. DOI: 10.1016/j.iotcps.2023.04.006

Tambare, P., Meshram, C., Lee, C.-C., Ramteke, R. J., & Imoize, A. L. (2022). Performance measurement system and quality management in data-driven Industry 4.0: A review. *Sensors (Basel)*, *22*(1), 224. DOI: 10.3390/s22010224 PMID: 35009767

Torre, D., Chennamaneni, A., & Rodriguez, A. (2023). Privacy preservation techniques for IoT devices A systematic mapping study. *IEEE Access : Practical Innovations, Open Solutions*, *11*, 26429–26453. DOI: 10.1109/ACCESS.2023.3245524

Trifonov, H., & Heffernan, D. (2023). OPC UA TSN: A next-generation network for Industry 4.0 and IIoT. *International Journal of Pervasive Computing and Communications*, *19*(3), 386–411. DOI: 10.1108/IJPCC-07-2021-0160

Van 't Schip, M. (2025). The Internet of Forgotten Things: European cybersecurity regulation and the cessation of Internet-connected consumer devices. *Computer Law & Security Review*, *57*, 106152. DOI: 10.1016/j.clsr.2025.106152

Villani, V., Pini, F., Leali, F., & Secchi, C. (2018). Survey on human–robot collaboration in industrial settings: Safety, intuitive interfaces and applications. *Mechatronics*, *55*, 248–266. DOI: 10.1016/j.mechatronics.2018.02.009

Wang, J., Xu, C., Zhang, J., & Zhong, R. Y. (2021). Big data analytics for intelligent manufacturing systems: A review. *Journal of Manufacturing Systems*, *62*, 738–752. DOI: 10.1016/j.jmsy.2021.03.005

Wang, M., Sun, Y., Sun, H., & Zhang, B. (2023). Security Issues on Industrial Internet of Things: Overview and Challenges. *Computers*, *12*(12), 256. DOI: 10.3390/computers12120256

Xu, L. D., Xu, E. L., & Li, L. (2018). Industry 4.0: State of the art and future trends. *International Journal of Production Research*, *56*(8), 2941–2962. DOI: 10.1080/00207543.2018.1444806

Zhong, R. Y., Xu, X., Klotz, E., & Newman, S. T. (2017). Intelligent manufacturing in the context of Industry 4.0: A review. *Engineering (Beijing)*, *3*(5), 616–630. DOI: 10.1016/J.ENG.2017.05.015

Zorrilla, M. E., & Yébenes, J. (2022). A reference framework for the implementation of data governance systems for Industry 4.0. *Computer Standards & Interfaces*, *81*, 103595. DOI: 10.1016/j.csi.2021.103595

Chapter 7
Exploring the Role of Digital Twins in Enhancing Smart City IoT Applications: A Critical Review

Noble Pete-I Gotolph Eiaseb
http://orcid.org/0009-0002-0318-9761
University of Namibia, Namibia

Nathalie Goagoses
University of Namibia, Namibia

Simeon Shiweda Hamukoshi
NCRST, Namibia

Rejoyce Hatago Sara Eiases
University of Namibia, Namibia

ABSTRACT

The rational of this chapter is to explore the role of Digital Twins (DTs) in enhancing smart city Internet of Things (IoT) applications. Furthermore, the chapter investigates how Digital Twin (DT) technologies might improve the sustainability, functionality, and efficiency of IoT applications within the framework of smart cities. Moreover, the incorporation of DTs presents the opportunity to model, track, and optimize intricate urban systems in real time as cities grow more networked and data-driven. Additionally, in order to evaluate the creation, implementation, and effects of DTs across international smart city projects, the research conducts a thorough literature

DOI: 10.4018/979-8-2600-1263-5.ch007

review of scholarly and empirical studies published between 2015 and 2025, relying on more than 120 peer-reviewed articles, technical reports, and policy documents. Subsequently, the chapter focuses on five prominent smart cities, namely: Helsinki, Amsterdam, London, Singapore, and Barcelona which have led the way in implementing DTs in urban infrastructure, mobility, energy, and public services.

1. INTRODUCTION

Globalisation and digitalisation have become major trends in recent years. Furthermore, a spike in rural-urban migration have forces relevant stakeholders and policy makers to search for creative and innovative ways to ensure that towns and cities have the capacity and capability to host an ever-increasing population (Mohammadi & Taylor, 2017; Farsi et al., 2020). Deren et al. (2021) further maintains that the notion of smart cities is derived from the need to utilise solution driven technologies to enable a city or town to be able to host the population in a dignified manner. Moreover, the Internet of Things (IoT) ensure interconnectivity of systems, processes, and policies, thereby enhancing urban planning and management.

Additionally, Mohammadi and Taylor (2020) maintain that IoT helps with monitoring and managing complex transportation systems, electrification efforts and infrastructural development in real time. However, to achieve full potential usage of IoT, dynamic, creative, and innovative models must be used to revolutionise industries. This can be done by implementing Digital Twin Technology (DTT). Mazzetto (2024) propounds that DTT is a model of IoT used in major industries such as manufacturing, transportation and logistics and the aerospace sphere. DTT is used to simulate and predict behaviour of systems and processes, thereby allowing for effective and efficient solution implementation for energy projects, traffic management, water resource utilisation and public health (Deren et al., 2021).

In addition, the integration of DTT and IoT in smart cities could possibly enhance strategic decision-making and planning, ensure sustainability and economic development. Ultimately, making sure that residents of are provided with adequate and prompt service is the rationale (Mazzetto, 2024). The chapter will comprehensively cover the following key aspects, namely: the context and relevance of the study, key objectives of the study, followed by the background and problem statement. Thereafter, the role of the DTT in smart cities IoT applications will be provided, followed by technical architecture and integration of DTT with IoT. A holistic empirical literature will ensue to demonstrate current global DTT smart cities. Challenges and limitations will be provided followed by the future trends and research directions. Ultimately, strategic recommendations and a comprehensive conclusion will close the chapter.

1.1 Context and Relevance of the Study

1.1.1 Definition of Digital Twins (DTs) and Their Emerging Role in Urban Development

DTs are the virtual representation of physical assets in real time. Furthermore, DTs were developed as a solution for resolving complex problems in critical sectors such as aerospace and manufacturing industries (Ketzler et al., 2020). Moreover, Batty (2018) argue that the technological advancement of DTs has enhanced productivity and effectiveness for service delivery in the public sector. Ferré-Bigorra et al. (2022) agrees and postulates that the simulation, monitoring and optimization of urban ecosystems has been drastically improved by DTs. According to Giaveno (2021), DTs synchronises data received from internal sensor by integrating IoT to ensure seamless communication between DTs and their physical counterparts.

Therefore, the real time relay of critical information from the physical infrastructure to their digital model counterpart enables forecasting and strategic decision-making (Giaveno, 2021). DTs is critical to urban planning and development. Waste management, water distribution, transportation networks and infrastructural are part of the significant areas' DTs integrate with IoT to ensure relevant planning officials and stakeholders make informed decisions (Austin et al., 2020). DTs plays a critical role in urban development in instances such as natural disasters. For instance, urban planners could utilise synchronised data of affected areas and create resilient solutions to alleviate and prevent further damage in future (Ketzler et al., 2020).

In addition to providing solutions with an infrastructural aspect, DTs can also be used in global sustainability efforts. Furthermore, DTs can be used for environmental monitoring, creation of sustainable supply chains, remote-work, and collaboration. This could ensure data-driven decision-making (Austin et al., 2020). An inference can be made that DTs makes cities human centric by integrating adoptive and smarter data (Saeed et al., 2022). Subsequently, DTs helps to identify ineffective and inefficient procedures in processes and systems, thereby ensure timely and informed responses are taken.

1.1.2 Overview of Smart Cities and their Reliance on IoT Technologies

Smart cities utilise advanced technology derived from real time data to improve the quality of life of its inhabitants (Mazzetto, 2024). This is done by ensuring comprehensive and strategic interconnectivity throughout the urban development value chain. Moreover, the reliance of smart cities on IoT, enables the collection, transmission, analysing and distribution of data in real time (Deng et al., 2021). IoT ensures optimisation of automated urban systems to minimise human interventions. Thereby creating prompt response measures and protocols to ensure efficiency and transparency.

According to Mazzetto (2024), IoT utilisation in traffic management systems, utility meters and waste bin connections provide for the collection of granular data. These aspects could be used to control and prevent pollution, congestions and service inefficiencies urban centres might face (Deren et al., 2021). A critical benefit of IoT has been experienced most particularly in the transportation sector. IoT thus helps urban planners to schedule transit, and plan remedies for key congestion centres (Mohammadi & Taylor, 2020). IoT implementation in smart cities transportation systems and infrastructure has thus contributed to lower accidents, improve the experience of commuters and possibly lower emissions. (Austin et al., 2020).

Furthermore, Mohammadi and Taylor (2020) explicate that energy demand and production can be monitored through the smart grid enabled by IoT. Consequently, this could allow for strategic energy demand forecasting to avoid power shortages and inadequate provision of energy to certain parts of the urban area (Austin et al., 2020). Subsequently, this could ensure resilient energy supply and its associated infrastructure function optimally without undue strain (Saeed et al., 2022). Therefore, IoT enabled smart grids can be inferred to decrease customer dissatisfaction, and ultimately ensure longevity in the optimal function of energy infrastructure (Ketzler et al., 2020).

A surprising innovative intervention by way of waste management digitalisation has become apparent through smart bins installations throughout urban centres. Furthermore, Petrova-Antonova and Ilieva (2020) asserts that smart bins have sensors installed to inform relevant waste management teams on the fill-levels of bins. This ensures that dust bin overflows and subsequent waste spillage are avoided (Saeed et al., 2022). Consequently, smart bins safe municipal waste management teams from unnecessary routes, thereby also safe money on unnecessary overtime payments (Petrova-Antonova & Ilieva, 2020).

IoT help ensure critical care in the health sector through the installation of remote health monitoring devices (Abdulmalek et al., 2022). This is particularly important for chronic disease monitoring and care. Valsalan et al. (2020) maintains that machinery installed with sensor, provide health professionals with real time data to ensure prompt response in case of worsening health of patients. Furthermore, smart health devices can be of significance in palliative care as IoT in health devices could provide for early health deterioration data to prompt for emergency intervention (Valsalan et al., 2020).

According to Lulla et al. (2021), IoT-enabled security devices such as surveillance cameras, gunshot detection, window and door sensors, asset trackers, alarm systems and motion sensors can be utilised to curtail crime. Moreover, Sanjay et al. (2020)

contend that IoT-enabled security devices ensure for prompt real-time emergency attendance and possible resolutions thereof. Furthermore, public safety is drastically improved through situational awareness creation, and adequate resource allocation to crime prone areas (Kumar & Kushwaha, 2019). Ultimately, Sanjay et al. (2020) argues that for smart cities to comprehensively integrate IoT, they have created major data storage sites. This helps to compartmentalise and deal with relevant problems at the relevant level and response rate. An inference can be made that IoT transforms urban centres into intelligence environments that improve the livelihoods of their inhabitants (Lee et al., 2024).

1.1.3 Relevance of the Chapter

This chapter is significant as it bridges the knowledge gap between IoT and DTTs in the context of smart cities. The integration of DTTs and IoT can contribute to the transformation of urban governance and ensure effective service delivery in urban areas. Moreover, this chapter could assist urban planners to revolutionise how they plan, monitor, and manage for better outcomes. Furthermore, this chapter elucidates the challenges and limitations faced by smart cities. The area of smart cities, IoT and DTTs has not been researched so widely, more so in the emerging economies. Therefore, by exploring the role of DTs in enhancing smart city IoT applications this chapter contributes to the body of knowledge which can be further utilised to inform emerging policy development and implementation. This chapter also deals with ethical considerations as IoT integration with DTs in smart cities.

1.14 Aim of the Chapter

The aim of this chapter is to explore the role of DTs in enhancing IoT applications within smart cities, through a comprehensive review of current technologies, methodologies, and potential impacts.

1.2 Research Objectives

1.2.1 Main Research Objective

- To comprehensively review the application of DTs in enhancing IoT systems for smart cities, analysing current methodologies, technologies, and their integration in urban infrastructures.

1.2.2 Secondary Research Objectives

- To examine the existing research and case studies that highlight the role of DTs in improving IoT applications by identifying key benefits and challenges associated with their implementation in smart cities;
- To explore future trends and innovations in the use of DTs for smart cities, identifying potential opportunities for integration with emerging technologies; and
- To provide recommendations for policymakers, urban planners, and technologists, based on the findings of the review, to support the successful implementation and scaling of DTs within smart city IoT ecosystems.

1.3 Background of the Study

Global urban development effort has necessitated the integration of IoT and DTs to create smart cities. Smart cities utilise sensor-based elements in infrastructure to improve service delivery and enable a sustainable urban ecosystem (Su & Fan, 2023). Moreover, the rationale of smart cities is to ultimately the reduction of operational costs, stimulate public service delivery, and for the optimisation of resources (Cai et al., 2023). Furthermore, data analytics and network integration ensure the collection of real time data than can be used to support strategic decision-making to support urban management (Addas, 2023).

According to Gokhale et al. (2018), IoT is made up of sensors, actuator, communication networks and data processing infrastructure. These critical components of the IoT are deployed throughout urban areas to improve transportation systems, health sector lifesaving equipment, and community safety infrastructure (Gokhale et al., 2018). Sharma et al. (2018) agrees and asserts that the seamless flow of real-time data enhances the capacity and efficiency for urban planners to deal with any eventualities that may arise promptly and effectively. DTT are data-based replications of physical systems, objects, and probable processes (Berte, 2018; Dudhe et al., 2017).

Furthermore, the DTs imitative nature started out primarily for mechanical systems but has since been expanded to cover key areas such as industrial processes, whole cities and building complexes (Hämäläinen, 2021). Moreover, Hämäläinen (2021) asserts that DTs utilise simulation techniques for monitoring, inspection and optimisation of urban infrastructural development and service delivery. The incorporation of real-time data and predictive analytics can make it possible to forecast and improve systems and processes before any negative eventuality occurs (Tzachor et al., 2022). Moreover, DTs integration with IoT can assist in making informed decisions and system optimisation.

Ultimately, the benefits emulating from DTs integration with IoT for urban development and improvement are quite evident (Gokhale et al., 2018). However, Tzachor et al. (2022) maintains that challenges such as diverse technologies, incompatible systems synchronisation, privacy and data ethical concerns, cyber threats, and the requirement for massive storage infrastructure to back up data prevent its implementation especially in emerging economies. To curb these ramifications, there needs to be collaborative professional relationship between local authorities and relevant stakeholders. The world is moving into an AI era with exciting and innovative IoT elements such as rapid advancement of 5G networks and DTs integration to ensure seamless smart city creation (Hämäläinen, 2021; Tzachor et al., 2022).

1.4 Problem Statement

The rapid increase in urbanisation has placed major strain on urban centres. Furthermore, these urban centres struggle with major issues incorporating and integrating DTs with diverse IoT. Moreover, lack of seamless integration puts further strain on traffic management, waste management, infrastructure development, energy consumption and public safety (Nzimakwe, 2020). Ideally, smart cities which are powered by IoT could enhance interoperability, scalability and ultimate real-time responsiveness to ensure inhabitants receive effective and efficient service delivery. Furthermore, massive data and fragmented systems hinder the seamless integration of DTs with IoT (Pee & Pan, 2022).

In addition, lack of training and development of city planners could possibly be inferred as a major hindrance. Subsequently, this could lead to uninformed hap hazardous decision making without proper know-how (Cook & Karvonen, 2024).). Another key challenge could be lack of data analytical specialist in city planning and governance. Consequently, decision making slows down and ultimately leads to delays in service delivery and stagnated city development (Pettit et al., 2018). Lack of proper know-how of DTs integration with IoT can lead to operational inefficiencies and slowed real-time feedback. This can result in increase in traffic congestion, underdevelopment, and underutilisation of the full potential of what DTs have to offer.

Furthermore, lack of empirical evidence on DTs integration with IoT has hampered efforts to increase awareness of the benefits for smart cities (Kandt & Batty, 2021). Smart city ecosystems are further hampered by lack of data synchronisation, limited data analytics and the multidisciplinary nature of smart city development. Data governance and ethical DTs integration with IoT could be deemed as another challenge (Sapienza et al., 2024). However, DTs integration with IoT can create self-sustaining smart cities which could promote higher social equity, increase development of suburbs, and ensure long term urban resilience (Alcaraz et al., 2025).

This chapter is therefore significant as it aims to provide a comprehensive review of the role DTs play in urban development and improvement.

2. COMPREHENSIVE LITERATURE REVIEW

2.1 The Role of Digital Twins in Smart City IoT Applications

2.1.1 Urban Planning and Infrustructure

2.1.1.1 Data-Driven Urban Planning

The significant increase in urbanisation has forced city planners and relevant authorities in urban areas to turn to DTs in order to transform urban planning efforts. Furthermore, this has been necessitated by the integration of DTs with IoT for dynamic digitalisation of urban ecosystems (Engin et al., 2020). Moreover, the utilisation of satellite imagery which collects real time data through sensors of IoT provides and opportunity to visualise urban spaces thereby allowing for data-driven urban planning. Bokolo (2023) agree and state that DTs allows for modelling urban infrastructure to improve transportation systems, waste management infrastructure and to plan updated security infrastructure (Charitonidou, 2022). Ultimately, Engin et al. (2020), Bokolo (2023) aver that DTs integration with IoT helps city planners and architects create modern solutions by making informed data-driven decisions. When locations have to be expanded or major improvements must align with climate change associated risk, DTs can play a major role (MacLachlan et al., 2021).

2.1.1.2 Optimizing Construction and Maintenance

Constructing and maintaining vast urban environments has been very costly and takes a lot of time without DTs. Furthermore, DTs could enhance the optimisation of construction and maintenance by utilising sensors in IoT to identify wear and tear or other structural weaknesses (Kamal et al., 2025). Subsequently, this could enable city planners and urban architects to implement robust predictive maintenance schedules in order to have continuous maintenance of infrastructure before they break down completely (Mahmoodian et al., 2022). Therefore, DTs could help expand the lifespan of infrastructure and ensure structural integrity of infrastructure (Hu, 2024). An inference can be made that DTs could potentially improve the efficiency and reduce exorbitant cost in urban development projects. Ultimately, the city's infrastructure might possibly remain in an optimal condition for a longer period of time (Omrany et al., 2023).

2.1.1.3 Virtual City Models for Simulating Urban Systems

DTs use advanced modelling to create virtual replicas of cities. According to Ghorbanian (2025), these virtual representations can be used by city planners to introspect various problem areas such as major traffic congestion areas, high air pollution zones and also identify security risk areas. Subsequently, equipped with this knowledge, city planners can make informed decisions to improve traffic flows, energy consumption and distribution, manage water distribution and waste (Del Campo et al., 2024). In agreement, Nechesov et al. (2025) state that virtual city models simulate urban environments which helps with prediction and informed data-driven solutions. Furthermore, virtual city models could enable city planners to adjust to sustainable energy for certain zones by assessing energy consumption needs (Ghorbanian, 2025).

2.1.1.4 Enhancing Sustainability With Digital Twins

DTs play a major role in enhancing sustainability in urban environments (Maksimovic, 2017). Furthermore, the utilisation of advanced data-driven analytics, DTs monitor and analyse scarce resource utilisation, pollution prone zones and identify high carbon footprint areas effectively and efficiently. Supported by this, Kabir et al. (2024) aver that DTs enable city planners to create green spaces to investigate the impact of weather changes or urban development on the environment. Furthermore, DTs optimises the implementation of robust renewable energy infrastructure by identifying potential zones and also predicting potential hazards based on informed data driven IoT integrated results (Ishola, 2024; Kabir et al., 2024).

2.1.1.5 Urban Resilience and Future-Proofing Infrastructure

DTs enables city planners to retrofit and upgrade infrastructure to withstand adverse unpredictable natural disasters. Furthermore, DTs provide urban resilience enhancing tools which could help mitigate the impact of economic crisis and climate change (Srivastava & Ghazala, 2025). Moreover, Cheng et al. (2023) found that DTs could possibly help in future-proofing infrastructure by allowing city planners to use state of the art data driven analytics to predict and better prepare. As a result, city could suffer less damage thereby reducing injuries and fatalities in future (Pillai et al., 2023). For instance, flood prone areas could utilise DTs to better plan water drainage and stormwater systems. Thereby reducing loss of life and damage to property in future (Cheng et al., 2023).

2.1.2 Smart Mobility and Transportation

2.1.2.1 Optimising Traffic Flow and Congestion Management

Urban mobility and transportation have faced major challenges due to extreme congestion and lack of development (Huang et al., 2017). Furthermore, Ali et al., (2021) asserts that this is made more difficult by lack of proper road and/or rail infrastructure. However, DTs utilise sensor integrated IoT to optimise traffic flow and manage congestion crisis (Huang et al., 2017). Moreover, by utilising GPS devices, DTs can provide more optimal routes for inhabitants, thereby decrease traffic bottlenecks (Chaudhary et al., 2025). Another benefit of DTs could be the utilisation of adjustable traffic light management systems to decrease travel time and ease possible congestions thereby accidents and road rage incidents (Hui et al., 2024).

2.1.2.2 Predictive Maintenance for Transportation Networks

DTs help identify structural damage and use predictive maintenance software to provide real time monitoring of damage to infrastructure. Furthermore, roads, railways and runways can be monitored with DTs (Ammar, 2024). Moreover, DTs can be used to ascertain damage or repairs needed for public transportation, thereby allowing timely response which ultimately increase the life span of public transportation. In addition, Eddy et al. (2024), Lu et al. (2025) propound that the predictive nature of DTs makes it an invaluable part of transportation network upkeep. This is done by proactively identifying cracks, major wear and tears, potholes and assign repair job orders to city maintenance departments (Dirnfeld et al., 2024).

2.1.2.3 Dynamic, Real-Time Transportation Models

DTs can help city planners holistically plan for major events such as world cup or major concerts by providing real time data which can be used to plan alternative routes to decrease congestion (Kušić et al., 2023). Alternatively, DTs could provide adjustment recommendations to ensure there is ample public parking space in case of large-scale events (Suh et al., 2017). Furthermore, the fact the IoT sensor update in real time can enable city planners to create prompt responsive models for urban transportation systems (Irfan et al., 2024). Ultimately, this could lead to less road closures, increased parking space, and decreased congestion. Finally, dynamic real time transportation utilising DTs which integrate with IoT can possibly improve the effectiveness and efficiency of urban transportation. This can result in better living standards and convenience for residents (Wu et al., 2025).

2.1.1.4 Enhancing Public Transportation Systems

DTs enhance public transportation systems by representing visualised routes, travel schedules and public transport performance (Feng et al., 2023). According to Li et al. (2025), this could help city planners to effectively and efficiently improve urban mobility, thereby decrease accidents, delays and congestion. Furthermore, real time data from buses, trains, metro lines and trams could be integrated with the IoT to provide accurate information (Nag et al., 2025). Moreover, armed with this new vast trove of information, city planners and private sector could collaborate to find strategies to enhance public transportation systems in urban areas (Xiao et al., 2024).

2.1.1.5 Autonomous Transportation and Smart Mobility

The advent of autonomous vehicles (AVS) has made it a necessity to enhance safety mechanism and thorough planning. Furthermore, DTs play a pivotal role by utilising sensor data to stimulate and deploy AVs more efficiently, effectively, and safely. Hassan et al. (2024) proffer that this could be achieved improving transportation modelling integration and interaction between AVs and inhabitants by mirroring the most used routes, cycling lanes and overall traffic flows. Consequently, this could possibly lead to city planners making more informed choices when planning transportation development and improvement (Bachechi, 2022). Ultimately, Dureja et al. (2024) maintains that smart mobility can be enhanced by DTs by enabling the creation of smart lanes and autonomous data-driven traffic signal systems that communicate directly with AVs. As a result, the overall experience of commuters might improve due to reduction in overcrowding, punctuality and less accidents or road rage incidents (Babu et al., 2025).

2.1.3 Energy Management and Sustainability

2.1.3.1 Energy Consumption Optimization

DTs help cities use real time data to tract and analyse energy consumption in various sectors. Thereby allowing for a thorough assessment of where energy consumption patterns are erratic to implement energy conservation strategies (Arsecularatne et al., 2024). Moreover, DTs can provide data on peak energy periods in order to sustainably distribute energy efficiently. Therefore, Bortolini et al. (2022) argue that DTs can provide city planners with invaluable information to plan energy demand and supply matrices. Ultimately, DTs could help save energy more efficiently by enabling informed decision making (Fathy et al., 2021).

2.1.3.2 Renewable Energy Integration

DTs can manage the complex transition of incorporating renewable energy systems in urban ecosystems (Galopoulou & Varga, 2023). Subsequently, Belik and Rubanenko (2023) found this could be achieved through utilising virtual energy infrastructure models to simulate renewable energy systems with traditional energy systems. Furthermore, DTs could perhaps predict adverse weather conditions better and enhance energy output efforts (Fan & Li, 2023). Moreover, the interlink between renewable energy and traditional power generation methods could be enhanced by integrating DTs and IoT (Zhao & Zhang, 2024). As a result, this could potentially ensure energy reliability and also decrease the carbon footprint of cities (Al-Shetwi et al., 2025).

2.1.3.3 Smart Grids and Energy-efficient Buildings

DTs can enable virtual smart grid representations and be significant in developing energy efficient buildings. Moreover, Cioara et al. (2021) propound that DTs could monitor and provide real time data on how transformers, cables and energy meters perform. This could help city planners to create energy consumption and saving mechanisms (Jiang et al., 2022; Cioara et al., 2021). Furthermore, the utilisation of IoT integrated DTs might detect major energy equipment failures and potential faults which could be repaired in advance before major blackouts (Mchirgui et al., 2024). Finally, sensor based IoT which are integrated with DTs could enable informed retrofitting of buildings to make them energy efficient, thereby reducing consumption and improving efficiency Jafari (2023).

2.1.3.4 Eco-Friendly Urban Solutions

DTs could be used to propel sustainability in urban environments. Furthermore, DTs can help city planners to model water consumption management and waste management strategies by identifying key strategies to reduce water wastage, pollution or improving waste recycling (Yang et al., 2022). Moreover, Sahu and Upadhyay (2024) maintains that DTs can help cities to enhance green spaces that could possibly reduce the adverse effects of climate change and improve the quality of air. DTs could be inferred to promote environmental sustainability by implementing effective solutions that reduce pollution congestion and liveability of inhabitants of the city (Filippova et al., 2025).

2.1.4 Public Health and Safety

2.1.4.1 Monitoring Environmental Factors and Pollution Levels

Zhivkov (2025) asserts that the rate of pollution has increased drastically due to globalisation and urbanisation. This places greater strain on cities efforts to curb their carbon footprint. Moreover, public health is put on higher risk due to higher pollution, lower air quality and accidents caused by industrial activities (Topping et al., 2021). In addition, DTs could simulate emissions which are spread by higher levels of carbon monoxide from factories. Therefore, DTs could monitor and model the possible spread of pollutants and help city planners divert inhabitants away from affected zones (Cowell et al., 2025).

2.1.4.2 Health Risk Prediction and Response

DTs utilises real time data to manage disease outbreaks. Furthermore, Katsoulakis et al. (2024) states that by assessing and evaluating social data, environmental patterns and demographic movements, DTs could provide pertinent information on the movement of inhabitants and spread of diseases. This could help to create cordoned off danger zones and safe zones (Ahmadi-Assalemi et al., 2020). Furthermore, Vallée (2024) contend this might lead to creating predictive health risk models which could be used by public health officials to curb disease spread. Ultimately, DTs could also track infection rates and effectiveness of interventions to improve health risk predictions (Katsoulakis et al., 2024).

2.1.4.3 Disaster Management and Emergency Response

When natural disaster strikes, if all systems are not readily in place, one can infer that the damage and loss of life could be higher. However, when city planners utilise DTs and predictive disaster and emergency analytics many lives could be saved (Korada, 2022). Furthermore, Razavi et al. (2024), Ford and Wolf (2020) maintains that DTs utilise real data from satellites to evaluate weather patterns which could capacitate city planners to use historical data to plan for possible future disasters and emergency response. Timely conveyance of critical information from DTs to city planners could thus allow emergency response teams to be ready promptly and provide needed assistance to inhabitants (Fan et al., 2021).

2.2 Challenges in Integration

According to Mazzetto (2024), Hemdan et al. (2023), Adreani et al. (2024) integration between DTs and IoT for smart cities face several key challenges which might hamper its seamless implementation as illustrated below, namely:

- Heterogeneous IoT Device Integration's Complexity;
- Accuracy and Quality of Data;
- Problems with Data Synchronisation;
- Limitations of the Network and Data Latency;
- Internet of Things System Scalability;
- Expensive System Upkeep;
- Insufficient Standardisation;
- Privacy and Security Issues;
- IoT Systems' Limited Interoperability;
- Data Overload and IoT Device Energy Consumption Management;
- Integration of Real-Time Data Processing with Legacy Systems;
- Issues with Regulation and Compliance and a Skilled Workforce;
- Unreliable Data Formats;
- Calibration Drift and Sensor Calibration;
- Complexity of Real-World System Modelling;
- Expensive initial setup fees;
- Uptime and Network Reliability;
- Issues with Data Governance and Ownership;
- Difficulty Connecting with Outside Data Sources;
- Resistance to Technology Adoption;
- ROI (Return on Investment) is uncertain;
- Maintaining Adaptability and Flexibility in the System;
- Ethical Issues with Data Use;
- Disjointed Data Environment; and
- Maintaining Sustainability Over Time.

2.3 Sector-Specific Applications

2.3.1 Transportation: Real-time Traffic Simulation and Predictive Maintenance of Transport Systems

Real-time traffic simulation and better infrastructure management are made possible by DT technology, which is completely changing the transportation industry. According to Jafari et al. (2023), in order to test and apply traffic control measures in virtual environments prior to real-world implementation, cities are using DTs to duplicate traffic flow, congestion patterns, and public transportation dynamics. Furthermore, in agreeing Shen et al. (2024) maintain that in order to simulate real-time road behaviour and minimize bottlenecks and improve traffic light synchronization, these simulations can integrate data from IoT sensors, GPS units, and linked automobiles.

Digital twins help in predictive maintenance of transportation systems, such as roads, bridges, railroads, and automobiles, in addition to traffic flow (Ertürk, 2023). Consequently, based on usage patterns, environmental factors, and sensor data, DTs can forecast wear and tear, structural stress, or possible breakdowns through ongoing monitoring and analytics (Jafari et al., 2023). Proactive maintenance prolongs the life of vital transportation and infrastructure assets and minimizes unplanned downtime. Ertürk (2023) further maintains that DTs can be used to replicate entire fleets of buses, trains, or aircraft in public transportation systems. Llagostera-Brugarola et al. (2025) proffer that operators can lower expenses and improve service quality by optimizing scheduling, fuel efficiency, and route planning.

Additionally, this technology simulates alternative routes or interventions in real-time, facilitating improved response techniques during emergencies, accidents, or natural disasters. The potential of DTs is further increased by integrating them with platforms for autonomous vehicles (Shen et al., 2024; Llagostera-Brugarola et al., 2025). Subsequently, before being used on public roads, autonomous navigation algorithms can be developed and tested in simulated environments with the help of real-time data from DT models, significantly increasing safety and efficiency. The combination of AI and DT technologies represents a major step forward for more intelligent, secure, and flexible transportation systems (Werbińska-Wojciechowska et al., 2024).

2.3.2 Energy: Smart Grids and Energy-efficient Buildings Using Digital Twin Models

Omar (2025) propounds that through the creation of smart grids, DT technology is essential to the energy sector's efforts to optimize electricity generation, delivery, and consumption. Furthermore, these systems replicate and monitor energy flow using real-time data from sensors placed across the power grid, giving utilities the ability to identify outages, predict demand spikes, and react more efficiently (Elnour et al., 2024). Furthermore, Bortolini et al. (2022) found that in order to increase resilience and dependability, utilities can use DTs to forecast grid performance, model various load situations, and make data-driven choices. Ultimately, DTs greatly improve energy efficiency and sustainability in smart buildings and infrastructure.

According to Yang et al. (2022), in order to replicate patterns of energy use and climatic conditions, DT models of buildings use information from occupancy sensors, HVAC systems, lighting, and weather forecasts. This knowledge may be used by facility managers to automate processes, change settings, and cut down on energy waste, which will ultimately lessen operating expenses and their impact on the environment (Omar, 2025). DTs can be used to model the energy consumption patterns of homes and businesses at the grid-to-consumer interface, allowing consumers and utilities to optimize usage.

Furthermore, for example, better planning, performance prediction, and smooth grid integration are made possible by combining digital twins with renewable energy systems like wind turbines or solar panels. Therefore, this increases the stability and dependability of renewable energy sources (Francisco et al., 2020). Additionally, DTs also make it easier to build and run energy infrastructure projects, including power plants or substations. In addition, engineers can use accurate digital copies to train staff, simulate equipment failures, and test the effects of design changes. In the energy sector, this not only improves safety and dependability but also drastically cuts down on project schedules and development expenses (Bortolini et al., 2022).

2.3.3 Healthcare: Monitoring and Optimizing Health Services and Infrastructure Using IoT and Digital Twins

Adibi et al. (2024) asserts that by facilitating real-time monitoring, predictive diagnostics, and individualized treatment planning, DT technology is revolutionizing the way healthcare is delivered. Additionally, clinicians can monitor vital signs, identify abnormalities early, and model treatment results by generating virtual versions of patients utilizing IoT-enabled devices like wearables and medical sensors (Alazab et al., 2022).

Alazab et al. (2022) further argue that these patient-specific digital twins have enormous potential for preventive treatment, post-operative rehabilitation, and managing chronic diseases. In addition, Faisal et al. (2025) maintain that DTs help hospitals and healthcare facilities manage resources and optimize operations. Digital representations of hospital settings can replicate equipment use, patient flow, and ER traffic. Consequently, this enhances overall effectiveness and patient experience by assisting administrators in making well-informed decisions about scheduling, staffing, and resource allocation (Alazab et al., 2022).

Furthermore, Yang et al. (2022) maintain that DTs can be used to simulate the transmission of infectious diseases, assess intervention tactics, and maximize vaccine distribution in the larger public health setting. These models can be used by authorities to forecast the demand on healthcare systems during pandemics or major health emergencies and make appropriate plans to prevent hospital overcrowding or the depletion of vital supplies (Abd Elaziz et al., 2024). DTs also support healthcare workers' education and training. Virtual models of human anatomy and physiological systems can be used by surgeons and medical students to provide immersive, risk-free instruction. Finally, by bridging the gap between theoretical learning and actual application, this improves patient outcomes, increases procedure accuracy, and fosters competency (Awasthi et al., 2025).

2.3.4 Data Privacy and Security: Concerns about Privacy, Data Sovereignty, and the Security of IoT-connected Devices in Digital Twin Applications

Yadav (2025) elucidates that the merging of DTs and IoT devices poses substantial data privacy and security risks that must be addressed to ensure safe and ethical implementation. Furthermore, large amounts of sensitive operational, infrastructure, and personal data are frequently processed by DT systems (Nativi et al., 2020). In areas like healthcare and transportation, breaches can lead to not only financial and reputational loss but potentially bodily danger or legal penalties (Pandita et al., 2023). Furthermore, another urgent concern is data sovereignty, particularly in multinational implementations where data produced by DTs may be handled or kept in other countries.

Consequently, Nativi et al. (2020) further maintain that this raises problems about compliance with local data protection requirements such as GDPR, HIPAA, or other region-specific rules. In order to retain and define data ownership and management, organizations must carefully traverse different legal environments. According to Pandita et al. (2023) DTs rely on IoT-connected devices as their data backbone, yet these devices are frequently weak points in the network. Cyberattacks on these devices can take many forms, from ransomware or fabricated sensor data to more complex threats like data theft and denial-of-service attacks (Goyal, 2025).

Moreover, strong encryption procedures, ongoing monitoring, and frequent security updates are necessary for protecting these devices. In addition, there are ethical issues with data disclosure, permission, and surveillance. Additionally, it is important to notify users and stakeholders about the collection, use, and sharing of their data Stergiou et al. (2023). Furthermore, Goyal (2025) state that establishing confidence in DT systems requires openness, transparent data governance procedures, and the application of privacy-by-design principles. Regulators, businesses, and the general public may oppose the broad use of digital twins if these important concerns are not resolved (Pandita et al., 2023).

2.4 Empirical Case Studies of Smart Cities

2.4.1 Barcelona's Smart City Infrastructure

Barcelona's transition to a smart city started with a vast network of fibre-optic and Internet of Things infrastructure. In order to provide citywide Wi-Fi, sensor networks, smart lighting, parking systems, and irrigation controls, the city made use of 500 kilometers of fibre that was first put in place for municipal connectivity (Gascó-Hernandez, 2018). Sentilo, an open-source sensor-actuator platform introduced in 2014, lies at the heart of this ecosystem. Sentilo was created to offer interoperable urban services and uniform data collecting by integrating older systems and diverse sensors across agencies. CityOS, a semantic data middleware that combines sensor inputs and facilitates the creation of public apps, visualization, and predictive modelling, is layered on top of Sentilo (March & Ribera-Fumaz, 2018).

For instance, CityOS can predict pollution surges and use Sentilo pollution data to advise government interventions or citizen-facing apps. One of the smart mobility innovations is a revamped orthogonal bus network that covers 95% of routes with a single transfer, which reduces emissions and wait times (Bolici & Mora, 2016). Wi-Fi and air-quality sensing are now integrated into smart lighting, which dims when streets are empty. As a result of the city's IoT interventions, 47,000 jobs were created in Barcelona's growing tech center, $58 million was saved on water, $37 million was saved on energy, and $50 million was contributed to parking revenues (Tomàs, 2024). Barcelona also transitioned from surveillance-driven smart cities to democratic data sovereignty by introducing technologies like Decidim for participatory policymaking and DECODE for privacy-centric, citizen-owned data platforms (Calzada, 2018).

2.4.2 Singapore's Smart Nation Initiative

Launched in 2014 by the Government Technology Agency, Singapore Land Authority, and National Research Foundation, Virtual Singapore is acclaimed as the first national-scale DT in the world. This incredibly realistic 3D model was created with Dassault Systèmes' 3DEXPERIENCity platform, which combines population, transit, infrastructure, environmental, and topography data (Chang & Das, 2020). Urban stakeholders can use it to analyze energy, health, and environmental trends, predict traffic consequences, simulate disaster responses, and visualize developments (Chan & Chye, 2023). Additional developments occurred such as VIZZIO Technologies produced a full-scale 3D clone of Singapore with real-time data streaming, consisting of 728 million 1 × 1 m tiles, while Bentley Systems and GPS Lands built a dynamically updateable national digital twin using lidar and aerial data (Cavada et al., 2019).

As part of the 2GW peak solar objective by 2030, planners utilize building models to optimize rooftop panel positions, which is one way the twin helps environmental goals like solar PV deployment (Soon & Khoo, 2017). Furthermore, by providing a shared high-fidelity visualization foundation, Virtual Singapore also facilitates cross-agency urban planning, transportation optimization, and flood and climate-risk modelling (Ignatius et al., 2019). Researchers, start-ups, the government, and individuals are empowered for sustainability, smart design, and disaster preparedness through the centralization of data and models. The example of Singapore's DT shows how high-resolution, nationally scaled 3D models can promote cross-sector convergence in planning, data, and sustainable development (Gobeawan et al., 2018).

2.4.3 London's "Smart London" Infrastructure

A DT of London's transit system powered by graphs is being pioneered by Transport for London (TfL). Through the use of a knowledge graph, TfL is now able to model the complete physical transport network by combining disparate datasets that were previously isolated in different systems (Tekin & Dikmen, 2024). Real-time traffic event simulation and pre-emptive mitigation are made possible by this, as demonstrated by a proof of concept that expedited deployment because of its impressive outcomes (Brown et al., 2020). Moreover, by superimposing transportation logic and incident modelling on top of physical infrastructure, this digital twin enables TfL to predict traffic, assess the effects of various scenarios, and optimize responses for example, during significant events or regular disruptions (Bibri & Krogstie, 2020). Given that London's yearly congestion costs are estimated to be £5.1 billion, the tool encourages desire to reduce congestion by 10% annually, a target with substantial economic advantages.

An accompanying project is the Queen Elizabeth Olympic Park Smart Mobility Living Lab (SMLL), a closed-environment DT for autonomous and networked vehicle testing (Peng et al., 2017). The SMLL, which spans 24 km of instrumented roads and is controlled from control rooms, enables businesses to virtually test transportation prototypes in real-world circumstances, accelerating development and guaranteeing safety (Cowley et al., 2018; Contreras & Platania, 2019). These initiatives collectively demonstrate London's dual focus which encompasses an experimental, controlled digital twin infrastructure to promote mobility technology innovation and an integrated, data-driven urban mobility DT for governance (Kadiri et al., 2023).

2.4.4 Amsterdam's Smart City IoT Integration

The goal of Amsterdam's Smart City strategy is to promote sustainability and citizen-centric urbanism by integrating energy, mobility, connectivity, and governance. In terms of energy management, the city reduces CO_2 emissions by creating virtual power plants, supporting local renewable energy sources, and constructing eco-efficient structures (Capra, 2019). In order to lessen traffic and pollution, smart mobility initiatives include increasing EV charging, adaptive traffic controls, and shared transportation including car and bike sharing. Openness promotes smart governance in Amsterdam such as resource optimization and service innovation are fuelled by open data policies, predictive analytics, and citizen participation (Putra et al., 2018).

Furthermore, in terms of smart connection, the city expands high-speed broadband and uses LoRaWAN for IoT, enabling a thriving start-up sector and empowering sensor networks in infrastructure like trash monitoring (Noori et al., 2020; Almuhaya et al., 2022). However, in 2025, the Dutch Data Protection Authority voiced privacy concerns over extensive vehicle tracking, leading to the abandonment of a significant smart mobility pilot project: GPS-enabled smart traffic lights that prioritize bicycles and emergency vehicles (Alkemade & Toet, 2020). This demonstrates how important data privacy and public trust are despite innovation. The story of Amsterdam highlights how crucial it is to integrate energy, transportation, governance, and connectivity in a comprehensive smart city while upholding privacy and transparency protections (Mancebo, 2020).

2.4.5 Helsinki's Smart Mobility Program

A dynamic digital doppelganger of Helsinki's transportation system has been produced by the city's Mobility Lab (Tenkanen & Toivonen, 2020). Street layout, traffic signage, real-time car, bicycle, and pedestrian counts, infrastructure condition, interruptions, and environmental metrics are just a few of the available data sources that this model compiles into a composite digital picture (Hämäläinen, 2019). The use cases are diverse and include logistics, infrastructure maintenance, accessibility, urban planning, and traffic forecasts (Anttiroiko et al., 2020).

To facilitate adaptive routing, maintenance notifications, and city-service planning, the pair maps sidewalk networks, construction zones, and foot traffic in real time for pedestrians (Hämäläinen, 2021). Furthermore, it facilitates the creation of new mobility services and real-time decision-making because it is an updated system. Therefore, in order to better understand commuter patterns and facilitate better planning for infrastructure and public transportation, Helsinki also uses mobility data from Bluetooth beacons, GPS, and smartphone apps like TravelSense (Ylipulli & Luusua, 2020). In conclusion, Helsinki's initiative is a prime example of a contemporary digital twin: it is data-driven, multimodal, real-time, and integrated to enhance city operations and the mobility user experience.

3. RECOMMENDATIONS

- **Adopt Interoperability Protocols and Open Standards**

To guarantee smooth integration between DTs and other IoT systems across city departments and service providers, promote the use of open data standards and interoperability frameworks.

- **Invest in Digital Twin Architectures That Are Scalable and Modular**

Create DT systems that are modular, scalable, and responsive to changing urban needs so that cities may progressively increase their capacities without having to completely rebuild their infrastructure.

- **Create Strong Frameworks for Data Governance**

Establish unambiguous data ownership, privacy, and security policies to foster public confidence and guarantee adherence to national and international laws like the GDPR.

- **Encourage Public-commercial Partnerships (PPPs)**

Make use of partnerships between the public and commercial sectors to pool resources, collaborate on technology, and spur innovation in IoT services enabled by DT.

- **Boost Your Ability to Make Decisions in Real Time**

Incorporate AI-powered simulations and real-time analytics into DT platforms to facilitate prompt solutions to changing urban concerns and proactive governance.

- **Create Training and Capacity-Building Initiatives for Digital Twins**

To enhance digital literacy and guarantee the efficient implementation and administration of DT systems, provide training to public administrators, engineers, and city planners.

- **Utilize Participatory Platforms to Involve Citizens**

Enhance public participation in urban governance, increase transparency, and improve service delivery by integrating citizen feedback mechanisms into DT platforms.

- **Give cybersecurity first priority while integrating DT with IoT**

Create cybersecurity plans at the municipal level that are specific to IoT and digital twins to reduce the risk of service interruptions, system manipulation, and data breaches.

4. CONCLUSION

DTs are becoming a game-changing paradigm in the field of smart city development, with its ability to analyse, monitor, and control complex urban systems through real-time, data-driven simulations. In addition, this thorough analysis has looked at the development and real-world uses of DTs in five of the world's most successful smart cities, namely: Helsinki, Amsterdam, London, Singapore, and Barcelona. Therefore, emphasizing how they integrate with IoT infrastructures to improve sustainability, urban services, and citizen participation. According to research findings and actual investigations, DTs greatly improve the responsiveness and effectiveness of urban systems by facilitating cross-sectoral coordination, real-time decision-making, and predictive modelling. These skills are especially useful in fields like environmental monitoring, infrastructure repair, transportation, and energy management.

Nevertheless, there are a number of drawbacks to DT adoption, such as high costs, data silos, privacy issues, and the requirement for technical know-how. However, to overcome these barriers, governance and policy could possibly play a crucial role. Furthermore, the full benefits of DT technologies are more likely to be realized in cities with robust institutional backing, open data policies, and collaborative innovation ecosystems. Furthermore, preserving public confidence and guaranteeing fair access to smart services depend heavily on citizen participation and ethical data use. Ultimately, DTs provide a strategic tool for managing complexity and uncertainty as cities throughout the world deal with mounting demands from population, climate change, and resource shortages.

Urban leaders may use DTs to create smarter, more resilient, and more inclusive cities by adopting a set of well-founded recommendations that cover everything from cybersecurity to open standards to participatory governance. This chapter lays the groundwork for future studies on the co-evolution of DTs, IoT, and sustainable urban development while also adding to the expanding corpus of scholarly and applied knowledge about smart city innovation. In the upcoming years, the ongoing convergence of these technologies is expected to transform service delivery and urban governance.

REFERENCES

Abd Elaziz, M., Al-qaness, M. A., Dahou, A., Al-Betar, M. A., Mohamed, M. M., El-Shinawi, M., Ali, A., & Ewees, A. A. (2024). Digital twins in healthcare: Applications, technologies, simulations, and future trends. *Wiley Interdisciplinary Reviews. Data Mining and Knowledge Discovery*, *14*(6), e1559. DOI: 10.1002/widm.1559

Abdulmalek, S., Nasir, A., Jabbar, W. A., Almuhaya, M. A., Bairagi, A. K., Khan, M. A. M., & Kee, S. H. (2022, October). IoT-based healthcare-monitoring system towards improving quality of life: A review. []. MDPI.]. *Health Care*, *10*(10), 1993. PMID: 36292441

Addas, A. (2023). The concept of smart cities: A sustainability aspect for future urban development based on different cities. *Frontiers in Environmental Science*, *11*, 1241593. DOI: 10.3389/fenvs.2023.1241593

Adibi, S., Rajabifard, A., Shojaei, D., & Wickramasinghe, N. (2024). Enhancing healthcare through sensor-enabled digital twins in smart environments: A comprehensive analysis. *Sensors (Basel)*, *24*(9), 2793. DOI: 10.3390/s24092793 PMID: 38732899

Adreani, L., Bellini, P., Fanfani, M., Nesi, P., & Pantaleo, G. (2024). Smart city digital twin framework for real-time multi-data integration and wide public distribution. *IEEE Access : Practical Innovations, Open Solutions*, *12*, 76277–76303. DOI: 10.1109/ACCESS.2024.3406795

Ahmadi-Assalemi, G., Al-Khateeb, H., Maple, C., Epiphaniou, G., Alhaboby, Z. A., Alkaabi, S., & Alhaboby, D. (2020). Digital twins for precision healthcare. In *Cyber defence in the age of AI, Smart societies and augmented humanity* (pp. 133–158). Springer International Publishing. DOI: 10.1007/978-3-030-35746-7_8

Al-Shetwi, A. Q., Atawi, I. E., El-Hameed, M. A., & Abuelrub, A. (2025). Digital Twin Technology for Renewable Energy, Smart Grids, Energy Storage and Vehicle-to-Grid Integration: Advancements, Applications, Key Players, Challenges and Future Perspectives in Modernising Sustainable Grids. *IET Smart Grid*, *8*(1), e70026. DOI: 10.1049/stg2.70026

Alazab, M., Khan, L. U., Koppu, S., Ramu, S. P., Boobalan, P., Baker, T., Maddikunta, P. K. R., Gadekallu, T. R., & Aljuhani, A. (2022). Digital twins for healthcare 4.0—Recent advances, architecture, and open challenges. *IEEE Consumer Electronics Magazine*, *12*(6), 29–37. DOI: 10.1109/MCE.2022.3208986

Alcaraz, C., Meskini, I. H., & Lopez, J. (2025). Digital twin communities: An approach for secure DT data sharing. *International Journal of Information Security, 24*(1), 17. DOI: 10.1007/s10207-024-00912-1

Ali, A., Qureshi, M. A., Shiraz, M., & Shamim, A. (2021). Mobile crowd sensing based dynamic traffic efficiency framework for urban traffic congestion control. *Sustainable Computing : Informatics and Systems, 32*, 100608. DOI: 10.1016/j.suscom.2021.100608

Alkemade, G., & Toet, J. (2020). Data protection regulation in the Netherlands. In *Data Protection Around the World: Privacy Laws in Action* (pp. 165–188). TMC Asser Press.

Almuhaya, M. A., Jabbar, W. A., Sulaiman, N., & Abdulmalek, S. (2022). A survey on Lorawan technology: Recent trends, opportunities, simulation tools and future directions. *Electronics (Basel), 11*(1), 164. DOI: 10.3390/electronics11010164

Ammar, M. (2024). *Advanced Digital Twins for Current Real Time Condition Monitoring*. Diagnosis and Predictive Remaining Lifecycles.

Anttiroiko, A. V., Laine, M., & Lönnqvist, H. (2020). City as a growth platform: Responses of the cities of Helsinki metropolitan area to global digital economy. *Urban Science (Basel, Switzerland), 4*(4), 67. DOI: 10.3390/urbansci4040067

Arsecularatne, B., Rodrigo, N., & Chang, R. (2024). Digital Twins for Reducing Energy Consumption in Buildings: A Review. *Sustainability (Basel), 16*(21), 9275. DOI: 10.3390/su16219275

Austin, M., Delgoshaei, P., Coelho, M., & Heidarinejad, M. (2020). Architecting smart city digital twins: Combined semantic model and machine learning approach. *Journal of Management Engineering, 36*(4), 04020026. DOI: 10.1061/(ASCE)ME.1943-5479.0000774

Awasthi, M., Raghuvanshi, C. S., Dudhagara, C., & Awasthi, A. (2025). Exploring virtual smart healthcare trends using digital twins. In *Digital twins for smart cities and villages* (pp. 377–406). Elsevier. DOI: 10.1016/B978-0-443-28884-5.00017-8

Babu, C. S., Anniyappa, C. A., & Raut, A. (2025). Toward seamless mobility: Integrating connected and autonomous vehicles in smart cities through digital twins. In *Digital Twins for Smart Cities and Villages* (pp. 169–187). Elsevier. DOI: 10.1016/B978-0-443-28884-5.00008-7

Bachechi, C. (2022, August). Digital twins for urban mobility. In *European Conference on Advances in Databases and Information Systems* (pp. 657-665). Cham: Springer International Publishing.

Batty, M. (2018). Digital twins. *Environment and Planning. B, Urban Analytics and City Science*, *45*(5), 817–820. DOI: 10.1177/2399808318796416

Belik, M., & Rubanenko, O. (2023). Implementation of digital twin for increasing efficiency of renewable energy sources. *Energies*, *16*(12), 4787. DOI: 10.3390/en16124787

Berte, D. R. (2018, May). Defining the iot. In *Proceedings of the international conference on business excellence* (Vol. 12, No. 1, pp. 118-128). Pearson Educational. DOI: 10.2478/picbe-2018-0013

Bibri, S. E., & Krogstie, J. (2020). The emerging data–driven Smart City and its innovative applied solutions for sustainability: The cases of London and Barcelona. *Energy Informatics*, *3*(1), 5. DOI: 10.1186/s42162-020-00108-6

Bokolo, A. J. (2023). Data driven approaches for smart city planning and design: A case scenario on urban data management. *Digital Policy. Regulation & Governance*, *25*(4), 351–367.

Bolici, R., & Mora, L. (2016). The development process of smart city strategies: the case of Barcelona. In *RE-CITY Future City-Combining Disciplines* (pp. 155-181). Juvenes print.

Bortolini, R., Rodrigues, R., Alavi, H., Vecchia, L. F. D., & Forcada, N. (2022). Digital twins' applications for building energy efficiency: A review. *Energies*, *15*(19), 7002. DOI: 10.3390/en15197002

Cai, M., Kassens-Noor, E., Zhao, Z., & Colbry, D. (2023). Are smart cities more sustainable? An exploratory study of 103 US cities. *Journal of Cleaner Production*, *416*, 137986. DOI: 10.1016/j.jclepro.2023.137986

Calzada, I. (2018). (Smart) citizens from data providers to decision-makers? The case study of Barcelona. *Sustainability (Basel)*, *10*(9), 3252. DOI: 10.3390/su10093252

Capra, C. F. (2019). The Smart City and its citizens: Governance and citizen participation in Amsterdam Smart City. In *Smart Cities and Smart Spaces: Concepts, Methodologies, Tools, and Applications* (pp. 1407-1427). IGI Global Scientific Publishing.

Cavada, M., Tight, M. R., & Rogers, C. D. (2019). A smart city case study of Singapore—Is Singapore truly smart? In *Smart city emergence* (pp. 295–314). Elsevier. DOI: 10.1016/B978-0-12-816169-2.00014-6

Chan, J. J., & Chye, S. W. C. (2023). Impact of Smart City Initiatives on urban planning strategies in Singapore: An in-depth analysis of technology-driven solutions and their influence on sustainable development and quality of life. *Journal of Strategy and Management*, *7*(7), 11–21.

Chang, F., & Das, D. (2020). Smart nation Singapore: Developing policies for a citizen-oriented smart city initiative. In *Developing national urban policies: Ways forward to green and smart cities* (pp. 425–440). Springer Nature Singapore. DOI: 10.1007/978-981-15-3738-7_18

Charitonidou, M. (2022). Urban scale digital twins in data-driven society: Challenging digital universalism in urban planning decision-making. *International Journal of Architectural Computing*, *20*(2), 238–253. DOI: 10.1177/14780771211070005

Chaudhary, A., Meenakshi, M., Sharma, S., Rahman, M., & Srinivasan, S. (2025). Enhancing urban mobility: Machine learning-powered fusion approach for intelligent traffic congestion control in smart cities. *International Journal of System Assurance Engineering and Management*, •••, 1–8. DOI: 10.1007/s13198-024-02672-6

Cheng, R., Hou, L., & Xu, S. (2023). A review of digital twin applications in civil and infrastructure emergency management. *Buildings (Basel, Switzerland)*, *13*(5), 1143. DOI: 10.3390/buildings13051143

Cioara, T., Anghel, I., Antal, M., Salomie, I., Antal, C., & Ioan, A. G. (2021). An overview of digital twins application domains in smart energy grid. *arXiv preprint arXiv:2104.07904*.

Contreras, G., & Platania, F. (2019). Economic and policy uncertainty in climate change mitigation: The London Smart City case scenario. *Technological Forecasting and Social Change*, *142*, 384–393. DOI: 10.1016/j.techfore.2018.07.018

Cook, M., & Karvonen, A. (2024). Urban planning and the knowledge politics of the smart city. *Urban Studies (Edinburgh, Scotland)*, *61*(2), 370–382. DOI: 10.1177/00420980231177688

Cowell, N. H., Chapman, L., Topping, D., James, P., Bell, D., Bannan, T., Murabito, E., Evans, J., & Birkin, M. (2025). Moving from monitoring to real-time interventions for air quality: Are low-cost sensor networks ready to support urban digital twins? *Frontiers in Sustainable Cities*, *6*, 1500516. DOI: 10.3389/frsc.2024.1500516

Cowley, R., Joss, S., & Dayot, Y. (2018). The smart city and its publics: Insights from across six UK cities. *Urban Research & Practice*, *11*(1), 53–77. DOI: 10.1080/17535069.2017.1293150

Del Campo, G., Saavedra, E., Piovano, L., Luque, F., & Santamaria, A. (2024). Virtual reality and internet of things based digital twin for smart city cross-domain interoperability. *Applied Sciences (Basel, Switzerland)*, *14*(7), 2747. DOI: 10.3390/app14072747

Deng, T., Zhang, K., & Shen, Z. J. M. (2021). A systematic review of a digital twin city: A new pattern of urban governance toward smart cities. *Journal of Management Science and Engineering*, *6*(2), 125–134. DOI: 10.1016/j.jmse.2021.03.003

Deren, L., Wenbo, Y., & Zhenfeng, S. (2021). Smart city based on digital twins. *Computational Urban Science*, *1*(1), 4. DOI: 10.1007/s43762-021-00005-y

Dirnfeld, R., De Donato, L., Somma, A., Azari, M. S., Marrone, S., Flammini, F., & Vittorini, V. (2024). Integrating AI and DTs: Challenges and opportunities in railway maintenance application and beyond. *Simulation*, *100*(9), 903–917. DOI: 10.1177/00375497241229756

Dudhe, P. V., Kadam, N. V., Hushangabade, R. M., & Deshmukh, M. S. (2017, August). Internet of Things (IOT): An overview and its applications. In *2017 International conference on energy, communication, data analytics and soft computing (ICECDS)* (pp. 2650-2653). IEEE. DOI: 10.1109/ICECDS.2017.8389935

Dureja, A., Dureja, A., Kumar, V., & Sabharwal, S. (2024). Combining digital twin technology and intelligent transportation systems for smart mobility. In *Transforming Industry using Digital Twin Technology* (pp. 281–296). Springer Nature Switzerland. DOI: 10.1007/978-3-031-58523-4_14

Eddy, C. W., Castanier, M. P., & Wagner, J. R. (2024). Predictive Maintenance of a Ground Vehicle Using Digital Twin Technology. *SAE International Journal of Advances and Current Practices in Mobility, 7*(2024-01-2867), 865-876.

Elnour, M., Ahmad, A. M., Abdelkarim, S., Fadli, F., & Naji, K. (2024). Empowering smart cities with digital twins of buildings: Applications and implementation considerations of data-driven energy modelling in building management. *Building Services Engineering Research and Technology*, *45*(4), 475–498. DOI: 10.1177/01436244241239290

Engin, Z., van Dijk, J., Lan, T., Longley, P. A., Treleaven, P., Batty, M., & Penn, A. (2020). Data-driven urban management: Mapping the landscape. *Journal of Urban Management*, *9*(2), 140–150. DOI: 10.1016/j.jum.2019.12.001

Ertürk, M. A. (2023). Time Series Prediction with Digital Twins in Public Transportation Systems. *Alphanumeric Journal*, *11*(2), 183–192. DOI: 10.17093/alphanumeric.1402897

Faisal, S. M., Ishrat, M., & Khan, W. (2025). Digital Twins in Healthcare: Revolutionizing Patient Care and Medical Operations. In *Digital Twins for Smart Cities and Urban Planning* (pp. 69-89). CRC Press.

Fan, C., Zhang, C., Yahja, A., & Mostafavi, A. (2021). Disaster City Digital Twin: A vision for integrating artificial and human intelligence for disaster management. *International Journal of Information Management*, *56*, 102049. DOI: 10.1016/j.ijinfomgt.2019.102049

Fan, X., & Li, Y. (2023). Energy management of renewable based power grids using artificial intelligence: Digital twin of renewables. *Solar Energy*, *262*, 111867. DOI: 10.1016/j.solener.2023.111867

Farsi, M., Daneshkhah, A., Hosseinian-Far, A., & Jahankhani, H. (Eds.). (2020). *Digital twin technologies and smart cities* (Vol. 32). Springer. DOI: 10.1007/978-3-030-18732-3

Fathy, Y., Jaber, M., & Nadeem, Z. (2021). Digital twin-driven decision making and planning for energy consumption. *Journal of Sensor and Actuator Networks*, *10*(2), 37. DOI: 10.3390/jsan10020037

Feng, H., Lv, H., & Lv, Z. (2023). Resilience towarded digital twins to improve the adaptability of transportation systems. *Transportation Research Part A, Policy and Practice*, *173*, 103686. DOI: 10.1016/j.tra.2023.103686

Ferré-Bigorra, J., Casals, M., & Gangolells, M. (2022). The adoption of urban digital twins. *Cities (London, England)*, *131*, 103905. DOI: 10.1016/j.cities.2022.103905

Filippova, E., Hedayat, S., Ziarati, T., & Manganelli, M. (2025). Artificial Intelligence and Digital Twins for Bioclimatic Building Design: Innovations in Sustainability and Efficiency.

Ford, D. N., & Wolf, C. M. (2020). Smart cities with digital twin systems for disaster management. *Journal of Management Engineering*, *36*(4), 04020027. DOI: 10.1061/(ASCE)ME.1943-5479.0000779

Francisco, A., Mohammadi, N., & Taylor, J. E. (2020). Smart city digital twin–enabled energy management: Toward real-time urban building energy benchmarking. *Journal of Management Engineering*, *36*(2), 04019045. DOI: 10.1061/(ASCE)ME.1943-5479.0000741

Galopoulou, K., & Varga, L. (2023). The role of digital twins in energy transition. *Energy Procedia*, *37*, 1–7.

Gascó-Hernandez, M. (2018). Building a smart city: Lessons from Barcelona. *Communications of the ACM*, *61*(4), 50–57. DOI: 10.1145/3117800

Ghorbanian, M. (2025). From Simulation to Reality: Using Digital Twin Technology (DT) to Design Sustainable Smart Cities. *International Journal of Architectural Engineering & Urban Planning*, *35*(1).

Giaveno, S. (2021). Smart City and Digital Twins: Definitions, Methodologies, and Applications. In *Handbook of Research on Developing Smart Cities Based on Digital Twins* (pp. 243-264). IGI Global.

Gobeawan, L., Lin, E. S., Tandon, A., Yee, A. T. K., Khoo, V. H. S., Teo, S. N., Yi, S., Lim, C. W., Wong, S. T., Wise, D. J., Cheng, P., Liew, S. C., Huang, X., Li, Q. H., Teo, L. S., Fekete, G. S., & Poto, M. T. (2018). Modeling trees for virtual singapore: From data acquisition to citygml models. *The International Archives of the Photogrammetry, Remote Sensing and Spatial Information Sciences*, *42*(W10), 55–62. DOI: 10.5194/isprs-archives-XLII-4-W10-55-2018

Gokhale, P., Bhat, O., & Bhat, S. (2018). Introduction to IOT. *International Advanced Research Journal in Science. Engineering and Technology*, *5*(1), 41–44.

Goyal, N. K. (2025). Security and Privacy in IoT, Fog, and Blockchain Networks. In *Energy-Efficient Deep Learning Approaches in IoT, Fog, and Green Blockchain Revolution* (pp. 371-398). IGI Global Scientific Publishing.

Hämäläinen, M. (2019). A framework for a smart city design: digital transformation in the Helsinki smart city. In *Entrepreneurship and the community: a multidisciplinary perspective on creativity, social challenges, and business* (pp. 63–86). Springer International Publishing.

Hämäläinen, M. (2021). Urban development with dynamic digital twins in Helsinki city. *IET Smart Cities*, *3*(4), 201–210. DOI: 10.1049/smc2.12015

Hämäläinen, M. (2021). Urban development with dynamic digital twins in Helsinki city. *IET Smart Cities*, *3*(4), 201–210. DOI: 10.1049/smc2.12015

Hassan, M. U., Alaliyat, S., & Hameed, I. A. (2024). Towards the creation of a digital twin authoring tool: A smart mobility perspective in smart cities. *IEEE Access : Practical Innovations, Open Solutions*.

Hemdan, E. E. D., El-Shafai, W., & Sayed, A. (2023). Integrating digital twins with IoT-based blockchain: Concept, architecture, challenges, and future scope. *Wireless Personal Communications*, *131*(3), 2193–2216. DOI: 10.1007/s11277-023-10538-6 PMID: 37360142

Hu, W. (2024). Digital twin and AI enabled predictive maintenance in building industry.

Huang, S., Wu, Q., Zhao, H., & Li, C. (2017). Distributed optimization-based dynamic tariff for congestion management in distribution networks. *IEEE Transactions on Smart Grid, 10*(1), 184–192. DOI: 10.1109/TSG.2017.2735998

Hui, Y., Wang, Q., Su, Z., Cheng, N., Chen, R., & Luan, T. H. (2024). Joint optimization of personalized route planning and global traffic scheduling: A dt-enabled integrated framework. *IEEE Transactions on Vehicular Technology, 73*(10), 14474–14485. DOI: 10.1109/TVT.2024.3408756

Ignatius, M., Wong, N. H., Martin, M., & Chen, S. (2019, July). Virtual Singapore integration with energy simulation and canopy modelling for climate assessment. [). IOP Publishing.]. *IOP Conference Series. Earth and Environmental Science, 294*(1), 012018. DOI: 10.1088/1755-1315/294/1/012018

Irfan, M. S., Dasgupta, S., & Rahman, M. (2024). Toward transportation digital twin systems for traffic safety and mobility: A review. *IEEE Internet of Things Journal, 11*(14), 24581–24603. DOI: 10.1109/JIOT.2024.3395186

Ishola, A. (2024). IoT applications in sustainability and sustainable community development. *World Journal of Advanced Research and Reviews _ Awaiting DOI.*

Jafari, M., Kavousi-Fard, A., Chen, T., & Karimi, M. (2023). A review on digital twin technology in smart grid, transportation system and smart city: Challenges and future. *IEEE Access : Practical Innovations, Open Solutions, 11*, 17471–17484. DOI: 10.1109/ACCESS.2023.3241588

Jiang, Z., Lv, H., Li, Y., & Guo, Y. (2022). A novel application architecture of digital twin in smart grid. *Journal of Ambient Intelligence and Humanized Computing, 13*(8), 3819–3835. DOI: 10.1007/s12652-021-03329-z

Kabir, M. R., Halder, D., & Ray, S. (2024). Digital twins for iot-driven energy systems: A survey. *IEEE Access : Practical Innovations, Open Solutions, 12*, 177123–177143. DOI: 10.1109/ACCESS.2024.3506660

Kadiri, D., Pap, M., & Baletić, B. (2023). Smart Cities: London, Paris, Barcelona, Milan; Definitions and Strategies. *Prostor: znanstveni časopis za arhitekturu i urbanizam, 31*(2 (66)), 236-247.

Kamal, M. F. M., Yin, I., Muthuveeran, A. A. S., Affandi, H. M., & Nasir, N. M. (2025). Barriers in The Integration of Digital Twins (DTs) And Building Information Modelling (BIM) For Predictive Maintenance in Facility Management. *Journal of Design and Built Environment*, 112-125.

Kandt, J., & Batty, M. (2021). Smart cities, big data and urban policy: Towards urban analytics for the long run. *Cities (London, England)*, *109*, 102992. DOI: 10.1016/j.cities.2020.102992

Katsoulakis, E., Wang, Q., Wu, H., Shahriyari, L., Fletcher, R., Liu, J., Achenie, L., Liu, H., Jackson, P., Xiao, Y., & Deng, J. (2024). Digital twins for health: A scoping review. *NPJ Digital Medicine*, *7*(1), 77. DOI: 10.1038/s41746-024-01073-0 PMID: 38519626

Ketzler, B., Naserentin, V., Latino, F., Zangelidis, C., Thuvander, L., & Logg, A. (2020). Digital twins for cities: A state of the art review. *Built Environment*, *46*(4), 547–573. DOI: 10.2148/benv.46.4.547

Korada, L. (2022). Using Digital Twins of a Smart City for Disaster Management. *Journal of Computational Analysis and Applications*, *30*(1).

Kumar, T., & Kushwaha, D. S. (2019). An intelligent surveillance system based on IoT for internal security of a nation. [IJISP]. *International Journal of Information Security and Privacy*, *13*(3), 1–30. DOI: 10.4018/IJISP.201907010101

Kušić, K., Schumann, R., & Ivanjko, E. (2023). A digital twin in transportation: Real-time synergy of traffic data streams and simulation for virtualizing motorway dynamics. *Advanced Engineering Informatics*, *55*, 101858. DOI: 10.1016/j.aei.2022.101858

Lee, C., Kim, J., Ko, H., & Yoo, B. (2024). Addressing IoT storage constraints: A hybrid architecture for decentralized data storage and centralized management. *Internet of Things : Engineering Cyber Physical Human Systems*, *25*, 101014. DOI: 10.1016/j.iot.2023.101014

Li, W., Wang, B., Sun, R., Ai, L., & Lin, Z. (2025). Energy-efficient multimodal mobility networks in transportation digital twins: Strategies and optimization. *Energy*, *318*, 134587. DOI: 10.1016/j.energy.2025.134587

Llagostera-Brugarola, E., Corpas-Marco, E., Victorio-Vergel, C., Lopez-Aguilera, E., Vázquez-Gallego, F., & Alonso-Zarate, J. (2025). A Digital Twin for Intelligent Transportation Systems in Interurban Scenarios. *Applied Sciences (Basel, Switzerland)*, *15*(13), 7454. DOI: 10.3390/app15137454

Lu, L., Yin, M., Xie, Y., Pan, Y., Wang, M., & Brilakis, I. (2025). Development of A Trustworthy AI-supported Digital Twin Framework for Road Operation and Maintenance.

Lulla, G., Kumar, A., Pole, G., & Deshmukh, G. (2021, March). IoT based smart security and surveillance system. In *2021 international conference on emerging smart computing and informatics (ESCI)* (pp. 385-390). IEEE. DOI: 10.1109/ESCI50559.2021.9396843

MacLachlan, A., Biggs, E., Roberts, G., & Boruff, B. (2021). Sustainable city planning: A data-driven approach for mitigating urban heat. *Frontiers in Built Environment, 6*, 519599. DOI: 10.3389/fbuil.2020.519599

Mahmoodian, M., Shahrivar, F., Setunge, S., & Mazaheri, S. (2022). Development of digital twin for intelligent maintenance of civil infrastructure. *Sustainability (Basel), 14*(14), 8664. DOI: 10.3390/su14148664

Maksimovic, M. (2017). Greening the future: Green Internet of Things (G-IoT) as a key technological enabler of sustainable development. In *Internet of things and big data analytics toward next-generation intelligence* (pp. 283–313). Springer International Publishing.

Mancebo, F. (2020). Smart city strategies: Time to involve people. Comparing Amsterdam, Barcelona and Paris. *Journal of Urbanism, 13*(2), 133–152. DOI: 10.1080/17549175.2019.1649711

March, H., & Ribera-Fumaz, R. (2018). Barcelona: From corporate smart city to technological sovereignty. In *Inside smart cities* (pp. 227-242). Routledge.

Mazzetto, S. (2024). A review of urban digital twins integration, challenges, and future directions in smart city development. *Sustainability (Basel), 16*(19), 8337. DOI: 10.3390/su16198337

Mchirgui, N., Quadar, N., Kraiem, H., & Lakhssassi, A. (2024). The applications and challenges of digital twin technology in smart grids: A comprehensive review. *Applied Sciences (Basel, Switzerland), 14*(23), 10933. DOI: 10.3390/app142310933

Mohammadi, N., & Taylor, J. E. (2017, November). Smart city digital twins. In *2017 IEEE symposium series on computational intelligence (SSCI)* (pp. 1-5). IEEE. DOI: 10.1109/SSCI.2017.8285439

Nag, D., Brandel-Tanis, F., Pramestri, Z. A., Pitera, K., & Frøyen, Y. K. (2025). Exploring digital twins for transport planning: A review. *European Transport Research Review, 17*(1), 15. DOI: 10.1186/s12544-025-00713-0

Nativi, S., Kotsev, A., Scudo, P., Pogorzelska, K., Vakalis, I., Dalla, B. A., & Perego, A. (2020). IoT 2.0 And The Internet Of Transformation (Web of Things and Digital Twins).

Nechesov, A., Dorokhov, I., & Ruponen, J. (2025). Virtual cities: From digital twins to autonomous ai societies. *IEEE Access : Practical Innovations, Open Solutions, 13*, 13866–13903. DOI: 10.1109/ACCESS.2025.3531222

Noori, N., Hoppe, T., & de Jong, M. (2020). Classifying pathways for smart city development: Comparing design, governance and implementation in Amsterdam, Barcelona, Dubai, and Abu Dhabi. *Sustainability (Basel), 12*(10), 4030. DOI: 10.3390/su12104030

Nzimakwe, T. I. (2020). Urbanisation and future smart cities: challenges of water and sanitation services. In *Reflections on African Cities in Transition: Selected Continental Experiences* (pp. 231–246). Springer International Publishing. DOI: 10.1007/978-3-030-46115-7_11

Omar, O. (2025). Digital Twins for Climate-Responsive Urban Development: Integrating Zero-Energy Buildings into Smart City Strategies. *Sustainability (Basel), 17*(15), 6670. DOI: 10.3390/su17156670

Omrany, H., Al-Obaidi, K. M., Husain, A., & Ghaffarianhoseini, A. (2023). Digital twins in the construction industry: A comprehensive review of current implementations, enabling technologies, and future directions. *Sustainability (Basel), 15*(14), 10908. DOI: 10.3390/su151410908

Pandita, N., Nand, S., Pathak, P., & Bhatt, V. (2023, October). Safeguarding Business Intelligence in Industrial IoT Using Blockchain-Enhanced Security. In *2023 4th International Conference on Data Analytics for Business and Industry (ICDABI)* (pp. 309-314). IEEE. DOI: 10.1109/ICDABI60145.2023.10629300

Pee, L. G., & Pan, S. L. (2022). Climate-intelligent cities and resilient urbanisation: Challenges and opportunities for information research. *International Journal of Information Management, 63*, 102446. DOI: 10.1016/j.ijinfomgt.2021.102446

Peng, G. C. A., Nunes, M. B., & Zheng, L. (2017). Impacts of low citizen awareness and usage in smart city services: The case of London's smart parking system. *Information Systems and e-Business Management, 15*(4), 845–876. DOI: 10.1007/s10257-016-0333-8

Petrova-Antonova, D., & Ilieva, S. (2020, August). Digital twin modeling of smart cities. In *International Conference on Human Interaction and Emerging Technologies* (pp. 384-390). Cham: Springer International Publishing.

Pettit, C., Bakelmun, A., Lieske, S. N., Glackin, S., Thomson, G., Shearer, H., & Newman, P. (2018). Planning support systems for smart cities. *City, Culture and Society, 12*, 13–24. DOI: 10.1016/j.ccs.2017.10.002

Pillai, S. V., Purandare, P., & Jain, R. (2023). Digital Twin-Enabled Solutions for Smart City Applications. In *Handbook of Research on Network-Enabled IoT Applications for Smart City Services* (pp. 19–37). IGI Global. DOI: 10.4018/979-8-3693-0744-1.ch002

Putra, Z. D. W., & Van der Knaap, W. G. (2018). Urban innovation system and the role of an open web-based platform: The case of Amsterdam smart city. *Journal of Regional and City planning, 29*(3), 234-249.

Razavi, H., Titidezh, O., Asgary, A., & Bonakdari, H. (2024). Building resilient smart cities: The role of digital twins and generative AI in disaster management strategy. In *Digital Twin Computing for Urban Intelligence* (pp. 95–118). Springer Nature Singapore. DOI: 10.1007/978-981-97-8483-7_5

Saeed, Z. O., Mancini, F., Glusac, T., & Izadpanahi, P. (2022). Future city, digital twinning and the urban realm: A systematic literature review. *Buildings (Basel, Switzerland), 12*(5), 685. DOI: 10.3390/buildings12050685

Sahu, Y., & Upadhyay, V. K. (2024). Environmental application of digital twins: A review. *Environmental Risk and Resilience in the Changing World: Integrated Geospatial AI and Multidimensional Approach*, 287-295.

Sanjay, A., Vijarania, M., & Jaglan, V. (2020). Security surveillance and home automation system using IoT. *EAI Endorsed Transactions on Smart Cities*, *5*(15), e1.

Sapienza, S., Palmirani, M., & Greco, S. (2024, August). Data Sharing Governance in Digital Twins and Smart Cities: The European Data Strategy. In *International Conference on Electronic Government and the Information Systems Perspective* (pp. 184-197). Cham: Springer Nature Switzerland. DOI: 10.1007/978-3-031-68211-7_15

Sharma, N., Shamkuwar, M., & Singh, I. (2018). The history, present and future with IoT. In *Internet of things and big data analytics for smart generation* (pp. 27–51). Springer International Publishing.

Shen, S., Xiao, J., He, Y., He, Z., & Yahya, K. (2024). Construction of Smart Transportation City System Based on Digital Twins.

Soon, K. H., & Khoo, V. H. S. (2017). CityGML modelling for Singapore 3D national mapping. *The International Archives of the Photogrammetry, Remote Sensing and Spatial Information Sciences*, *42*(W7), 37–42. DOI: 10.5194/isprs-archives-XLII-4-W7-37-2017

Srivastava, M., & Ghazala, S. (2025). Future-Proofing Sustainable Urban Development: Harnessing Fuzzy Logic for Smart Cities. In *Fuzzy Logic in Smart Sustainable Cities* (pp. 215-257). Jenny Stanford Publishing.

Stergiou, C. L., Bompoli, E., & Psannis, K. E. (2023). Security and privacy issues in IoT-based big data cloud systems in a digital twin scenario. *Applied Sciences (Basel, Switzerland), 13*(2), 758. DOI: 10.3390/app13020758

Su, Y., & Fan, D. (2023). Smart cities and sustainable development. *Regional Studies, 57*(4), 722–738. DOI: 10.1080/00343404.2022.2106360

Suh, W., Henclewood, D., Guin, A., Guensler, R., Hunter, M., & Fujimoto, R. (2017). Dynamic data driven transportation systems. *Multimedia Tools and Applications, 76*(23), 25253–25269. DOI: 10.1007/s11042-016-4318-x

Tekin, H., & Dikmen, I. (2024). Inclusive smart cities: An exploratory study on the London smart city strategy. *Buildings (Basel, Switzerland), 14*(2), 485. DOI: 10.3390/buildings14020485

Tenkanen, H., & Toivonen, T. (2020). Longitudinal spatial dataset on travel times and distances by different travel modes in Helsinki Region. *Scientific Data, 7*(1), 77. DOI: 10.1038/s41597-020-0413-y PMID: 32132539

Tomàs, M. (2024). The smart city and urban governance: The urban transformation of Barcelona, 2011–2023. *Urban Research & Practice, 17*(4), 588–605. DOI: 10.1080/17535069.2023.2277205

Topping, D., Bannan, T. J., Coe, H., Evans, J., Jay, C., Murabito, E., & Robinson, N. (2021). Digital twins of urban air quality: Opportunities and challenges. *Frontiers in Sustainable Cities, 3*, 786563. DOI: 10.3389/frsc.2021.786563

Tzachor, A., Sabri, S., Richards, C. E., Rajabifard, A., & Acuto, M. (2022). Potential and limitations of digital twins to achieve the sustainable development goals. *Nature Sustainability, 5*(10), 822–829. DOI: 10.1038/s41893-022-00923-7

Vallée, A. (2024). Envisioning the future of personalized medicine: Role and realities of digital twins. *Journal of Medical Internet Research, 26*, e50204. DOI: 10.2196/50204 PMID: 38739913

Valsalan, P., Baomar, T. A. B., & Baabood, A. H. O. (2020). IoT based health monitoring system. *Journal of critical reviews, 7*(4), 739-743.

Werbińska-Wojciechowska, S., Giel, R., & Winiarska, K. (2024). Digital twin approach for operation and maintenance of transportation system—Systematic review. *Sensors (Basel), 24*(18), 6069. DOI: 10.3390/s24186069 PMID: 39338814

Wu, D., Zheng, A., Yu, W., Cao, H., Ling, Q., Liu, J., & Zhou, D. (2025). Digital twin technology in transportation infrastructure: A comprehensive survey of current applications, challenges, and future directions. *Applied Sciences (Basel, Switzerland)*, *15*(4), 1911. DOI: 10.3390/app15041911

Xiao, M., Chen, L., Feng, H., Peng, Z., & Long, Q. (2024). Sustainable and robust route planning scheme for smart city public transport based on multi-objective optimization: Digital twin model. *Sustainable Energy Technologies and Assessments*, *65*, 103787. DOI: 10.1016/j.seta.2024.103787

Yadav, J. (2025). The Role of Edge Computing in Enhancing IoT Efficiency and Security. *Technology Perception*, *1*(1), 14–18.

Yang, B., Lv, Z., & Wang, F. (2022). Digital twins for intelligent green buildings. *Buildings (Basel, Switzerland)*, *12*(6), 856. DOI: 10.3390/buildings12060856

Ylipulli, J., & Luusua, A. (2020). Smart cities with a Nordic twist? Public sector digitalization in Finnish data-rich cities. *Telematics and Informatics*, *55*, 101457. DOI: 10.1016/j.tele.2020.101457

Zhao, X., & Zhang, Y. (2024). Integrated management of urban resources toward Net-Zero smart cities considering renewable energies uncertainty and modeling in Digital Twin. *Sustainable Energy Technologies and Assessments*, *64*, 103656. DOI: 10.1016/j.seta.2024.103656

Zhivkov, P., Fidanova, S., & Dimov, I. (2025). Digital Twin-Based Framework for Real-Time Monitoring and Analysis of Urban Mobile-Source Emissions. *Atmosphere (Basel)*, *16*(6), 731. DOI: 10.3390/atmos16060731

Chapter 8

Building Trust and Brand Loyalty in the Age of Smart Devices With Security, Transparency, and User Experience as Positioning Pillars in IoT

D. V. Jayanth
http://orcid.org/0009-0000-4608-819X
Dayananda Sagar College of Engineering, India

K. S. Ganesha
http://orcid.org/0000-0001-8181-2411
Dayananda Sagar College of Engineering, India

ABSTRACT

The growing popularity of Internet of Things (IoT) enabled devices has transformed the relationship between technology and consumers, and positioned the technological experience with consumers as a source of unparalleled opportunity and, at the same time, crucial pressure to the brands that hope to build consumer affinity and trust through its use. Chapter examines how trust and brand loyalty are being restructured in the era of connected technology with a validated argument that security, transparency, and user experience are no longer just functional matters but competitive sources that empower the successful brands in a hyper-connected market space. Chapter use examples of interdisciplinary studies and real-life cases in the industry to study how re-engineering customer experience models works to

DOI: 10.4018/979-8-2600-1263-5.ch008

meet the increasing levels of privacy and the pressures of compliance as well as provide emotionally resonating experiences. Chapter propose a multidimensional approach to building digital trust and loyalty that can become a guide to actions that brands to navigate the IoT ecosystem.

INTRODUCTION

Internet of Things (IoT) is actually transforming the technology and brand-interaction people have. This smart trend has filtered into the life of people, in the form of wearing smart devices and home automation/voice-assisted smart devices, providing real-time, context-aware experience, which is allegedly convenient and efficient. Nevertheless, this interrelated ecosystem also brings out increased issues of data privacy, system safety, and ethical utilization of user data, as it shifts brands to be repositioned around digital confidence, openness, and user-centric designing.

Consumers are no longer passive consumers of technology amenities, they are people who are active users and require transparency on the usage, collection, and sharing of their data. According to the increasing number of studies, today brand trust in the world of IoT is less and less based on the perception of a company as a trustworthy entity and more and more on its perception as a more or less responsible user of the data provided by users and conductor of security procedures (Hakiki et al., 2024). The consequences of not acting in regard to the ethics of data are the acquirement of regulatory consequences; customer vengeance and corporate brand harm (Velasco et al., 2024).

Consumers in the modern era deal with what has been referred to as a personalization-privacy paradox: people love highly personalized experiences and at the same time distrust privacy-invading conducts of data (Vishwakarma et al., 2025). Personalization has become an ethical priority, in the form of transparency of algorithmic decision-making, consent-based profiling, user control. Studies affirm that companies that have the capability of dealing with such a trade-off in an ethical way create more customer loyalty and buying behaviour in companies (Iftikhar, S. M. 2024)

Nowadays, security breaches and masked activities are the deal-killers in the digital world. Not only data leaks will cause financial loss, but brand equity will also be harmed significantly. Devices that implement the IoT-based technologies allow consumers to seek closer control over privacy regulations of the IoT-enabled sites and will not tolerate a brand that cannot clarify or justify the use of their information (Magrizos et al., 2025).

The recent literature indicates that trust is reinterpreted in the ecosystem of smart devices. Instead of measuring the performance, consumers also measure whether the brand is responsive on matters of displaying transparency, fair play, and goodwill (El-Annan, S. H., & Hassoun, R. 2025). It is even more so in the case of automatized services or automated decision-making like AI-based recommendation systems or voice assistants (John, B. 2025).

Trust is becoming a key to the comprehensiveness of going digital due to transparency. Privacy controls adjusted with visualizations, real-time access to data, and easier processes related to consent are identified as the best privacy practices available to brands interested in being trusted (Morales Sharp, T. 2023; Ogawara, M. 2025). Customers end up attaching their positive emotions with the brand of technology when they are allowed to feel intelligent and empowered (Owen, A., & Moore, J. 2023)

According to the author, the user experience (UX), which was traditionally regarded through a design and usability lens, must now encompass ethical UX wherein the comfort, control, and informed choice of the user become part and parcel of the interface and the process (Boni, E. K. 2024). Ethical UX can be utilized to create a feeling of trust by not using dark patterns and misleading practices. The fact that it leads to a high level of emotional satisfaction can contribute a lot to brand loyalty, especially among young digital natives Haris, A. (2025).

Other researchers point to the interrelationship of ethical branding and cybersecurity as one that holds the key to customer loyalty in the future. By publicly stating their ethical principles and taking effort to mitigate vulnerabilities, the IoT platforms will find that customers will as well be long-term customers and brand ambassadors (Sadiq, S. & Devi, A. 2024; Al-Mutawa et al. 2025).

The aspect that only brings revenge is making digital marketing extremely personalized without taking the ethical consideration of what it creates i.e., one will feel followed and controlled. However, in a scenario whereby the elements pertaining to personalization are taken into consideration alongside transparency and fairness, it can not only drive conversion through the roof but also helps to build more trust (Prem, R. 2025). Such future innovation as blockchain-driven transparency and data control processes at the user level will help to address the situation in this regard (Kwan et al., 2021).

The labels that will break down personalization and ethical design as well as privacy protection and user-centered communications are the brands that will emerge as the successful ones in this new setting. Customer loyalty, increased activity and customer advocacy will be accrued to ethical transparency, security and control on the part of smart device users (Haris, A. 2025; Ogawara, M. 2025).

Existing literature covers IoT ethics, brand trust, and UX design as separate domains, so their integrated effect on brand trust are largely unexplored. The earlier studies focus on cross-functional teams balancing technical optimization, compliance, and user experience simultaneously. Trust in IoT remains understudied in emerging markets where regulatory enforcement is not consistent and consumer data literacy is a construct. Also, previous studies treats trust as constant, whereas this chapter reconceptualises this concept as dynamic construct across the customer lifecycle. This chapter bridges these gaps by proposing an integrated framework wherein ethical UX serves as the enabler through which IoT platforms rebuild consumer trust, while transforming theory into actionable insights for practitioners in emerging market contexts.

CONCEPTUAL BACKGROUND

The constant growth of Internet of Things (IoT) devices has transformed the consumer-brand relationship, altering the basis of trust, allegiance, and user experience, all of which can no longer be defined by the transactional performance, but on the basis of digital ethics, data transparency, and ambient personalization. With the user being a part of an ongoing feedback loop on these ambient systems that are usually invisible, the interaction is considered to go beyond the use of a product and rather engaging in a loop where data crunching will inform the personalization engine, the brand strategies and predictive analytics. In this kind of landscape, the old paradigms of branding are not enough, but the trust and the loyalty in their brands are created through a lively interplay of technological ability and ethical design thinking.

1. Trust as the Foundation of Brand-User Relationships in IoT

Trust that used to be a passive effect on brand-consumer relationships is now treated as brand strategic asset in digital settings. The systems with IoT ecosystems, where the connected devices exchange the information autonomously, are trusted not on the level of performance but on the level of feeling when the signal transfer is ethical: when users feel conversant with their transparency, security, and accountability. According to (Amil, Y. 2024), a lack of any visibility on the type of data gathered and the interpretation of the data may result in the user experiencing a lot of anxiety. This has the effect of creating what has been dubbed the black box effect of algorithmic processes, where they feel like they feature unexplainable and disempowering processes.

The consumer trust in such environment stands on four pillars that are technical reliability, data stewardship, regulatory alignment, and ethical transparency (Caven, P. J. 2025). As an example, the smart health devices sending their real-time metrics to third-party applications need not only be accurate but also allow the user to easily access data sharing settings and consent history. Failure to do so at whatever level of technical merit may worsen the probability that the consumer may not be keen to interact with the brand ecosystem.

In addition, trust is weak and asymmetrically affected: one flawed data release or non-transparent advice can reverse decades of fruitful relations with the customer. This is supported by empirical data presented by (Saeed, S. 2023) which evinces that going forward, customers find it easier to leave e-commerce sites following a single security breach and failure to communicate post-incident experience, either in a timely or even transparent way.

2. The New Meaning of Loyalty in Hyper connected Spaces

In the world of IoT, loyalty will need to be redefined in new ways that do not correlate with commonly known notions of satisfaction or habit. It is contextual, behavioral and emotional and is created with the help of accumulative micro-interactions via smart touchpoints. The article by (Banerjee, S. & Parisa, S. K. 2024) indicates that loyalty does not depend on repetitive transactions anymore but on the continuity based on data that gives people an impression that the brand is aware of them in a non-invasive, yet useful way.

(Tamrakar et al. 2025) introduce a multilevel structure of brand experience during the digital age, and the emotional connection is mediated through ethical treatment, personalization of data, and the way in which privacy is managed. In this perspective, loyalty does not necessarily come after repeat purchases but after a prolonged sense that the brand is still doing what is best in the interest of the consumer- even when automation or the guide of algorithms is involved.

This can be well demonstrated through some examples in the telecom industry. (Moshed, A., & Al-Jabaly, S. 2024) document an increment in loyalty as a result of strategic integration of the IoT in the **Jordanian telecoms** (e.g., use the location-based offers, bill optimization through automated technology), introduced along with transparent opt-in mechanisms and education of users in addition to making technical upgrades.

3. The Personalization–Privacy Trade-Off: Balancing Intelligence with Consent

The conflict that ensues in the Core of IoT brand engagement is how to achieve hyper-personalization of experiences and to withhold individual data. The concept of privacy-personalization paradox is not simply psychological but requires redesigning the interfaces based on adaptive consent and providing contextual transparency and offering granularity on controls of data exchange (Chan-Olmsted, S., & Kim, H. J. 2024).

The users should also be provided with recommendations that would resonate without them feeling monitored. (Amil, Y. 2024) demonstrates that even reasonably inaccurate recommendations gain the confidence of the crowd once the consumers realize why such an offering was suggested to them. Personalization (e.g. behavior-based price discrimination) is on the other hand, counterproductive to brand affinity and it enhances (or escalates) churn; it is opaque.

A good example of best practice is the Spotify feature, which explains "why a particular song is being played" feature and is an example of contextual awareness of the AI decision. In comparison, most intelligent e-commerce engines fail to elaborate suggestions of products hence causing suspicion. Like (Sharma, S. 2023), I believe there must be transparency in algorithmic logic, in the sense of outcome as well.

4. User-Centricity: From Design Efficiency to Digital Empowerment

The usability of the Modern IoT device should be based on the ethical design, not effectiveness. User-centricity in the present day does not only mean that the interface should be easy to use but that the interface should speak to agency, control, and dignity. As pointed out by (Singh, V. 2024), ethical UX adheres to consent visibility, behavioral predictability, and privacy literacy as the main design objectives rather than the side ones.

(Russell, J., & Ajeigbe, K. 2022) believe that designing experience is essentially facilitating a user in understanding, adapting, and exiting; the latter is something even now most IoT interface designs do not allow. As an example, though Amazon Alexa can be used to make voice commands and integrates its services, the data managed by the assistant is often hidden in non-intuitive menus which discourages users to make use of privacy options.

That is where the concept of ethical nudges would come to play the role of graduating the users into decision-wise users by providing them subtle interface cues that nudge them into making a decision without being controlled. (Yellanki, S. K. 2025) applies the same reasoning to the enterprise settings and promotes the idea of sustainable digital infrastructures that support autonomy of the user on all levels of a system, including network privileges, sensor responsiveness.

5. Cybersecurity: From Infrastructure to Perceived Brand Value

Security vulnerability are not just technical risks but they are reputationally explosive objects. Security seems to be an implicit deal that consumers have with a brand and breaches indicate that the loyalty was betrayed. What (Dobre, J. 2025) proposes is the so-called Secure UX paradigm meaning that everything about security is not hidden but perceptually pronounced and signalled in the interface to create security assurance.

According to (Gujar, P. 2025), the data minimization principle along with the encryption-via-design should be supplemented with the feedback mechanism in software systems embedded in IoT to inform the user about the recent access occurred and/or any change in authorization or system malfunctions. (Saeed, S. 2023) affirms this and acknowledges that transparency systems glean more user trust after breach occurred as compared to systems where silence or the response mode is the standard.

An instance T-Mobile recently published a dashboard facing the user explaining the breach, what to do next, and how to remediate paints a very clear picture of the market power of security literacy. When brands treat their users as knowledgeable parties in the effort to protect data, they will be viewed as allies and not masters.

6. Algorithmic Transparency and Data Governance

Algorithmic decision-making being used in such realms as product suggestions, credit limits and more, the users are demanding accountability on their part. (Manoj et al. 2025) have shown that the brands who make the contents of the black box of their algorithm more accessible to users through easy-to-understand descriptions receive an increasing level of trust that is quantifiable, even among laypeople.

In addition to this, the governance structures should change to proactive management. (Nafees, M., & Kumar, M. 2023) advocate a solution in which the data ownership, lifecycle traceability and the autonomy of deletion form the core of system design. This might in the real situation take the form of dashboards that show real-time data use and provide real-time revocation and guidance as to who has access and why.

This can be conceptually approached similarly to the Fair Information Practice Principles (FIPPs), making strides towards much needed change on a societal level towards a data dignity-oriented world, that of treating digital subjects as a legally conscious citizen.

7. Ethical Communication and Co-Creation of Trust

Trust becomes more and more co-created and not being delivered. In other words, brands do not own the full story anymore- there are expectations of bilateral, open communication that is cognizant of contexts. The work by (Caven, P. J. 2025) emphasizes the importance of user-oriented communication strategies, which should answer not only the questions, but the risks and emotional stimuli.

As an example, in case of data outage or algorithmic error, proactive messaging and recognition of the same would help avoid a backlash. It is not that users are merely tolerating automation, but they are also weighing it on ethical congruence and reliability of relationships. Digital trust so has to be managed both at the backend using robustness as well as front-end using storytelling and design honesty.

(Bakator et al. 2024) frame this within the broader scope of Market 5.0 and Society 5.0 transition, where efficiency or profit are not the only outputs that technology is supposed to bring and where developments are to be inclusive and humanistic to a great extent.

Table 1. Theoretical Framework

Theoretical Framework	Key Constructs	Application to IoT Trust	Limitations
Social Capital Theory (Putnam, 2000)	Trust, reciprocity, networks	Explains trust formation in digital communities; IoT creates new trust networks	Doesn't account for algorithmic intermediation
Technology Acceptance Model (Davis, 1989)	Perceived usefulness, ease of use	Foundational for UX acceptance	Insufficient for ethical considerations
Stakeholder Theory (Freeman, 1984)	Stakeholder interests, value creation	Legitimizes multi-stakeholder approach (users, platforms, regulators)	Doesn't resolve conflicts between stakeholders
Privacy Calculus (Dinev & Hart, 2006)	Privacy concerns vs. benefits	Users weigh privacy loss against personalization value	Assumes rational decision-making; ignores dark patterns
Ethical Framework for Technology Ethics (Shannon & Vallor, 2022)	Character, virtues, care	Grounds ethical UX in philosophical principles	Implementation challenges; harder to operationalize

MODEL FOR TRUST AND LOYALTY IN IOT-DRIVEN BRAND ECOSYSTEMS

Figure 1. Model for Trust and Loyalty in IoT-Driven Brand Ecosystems

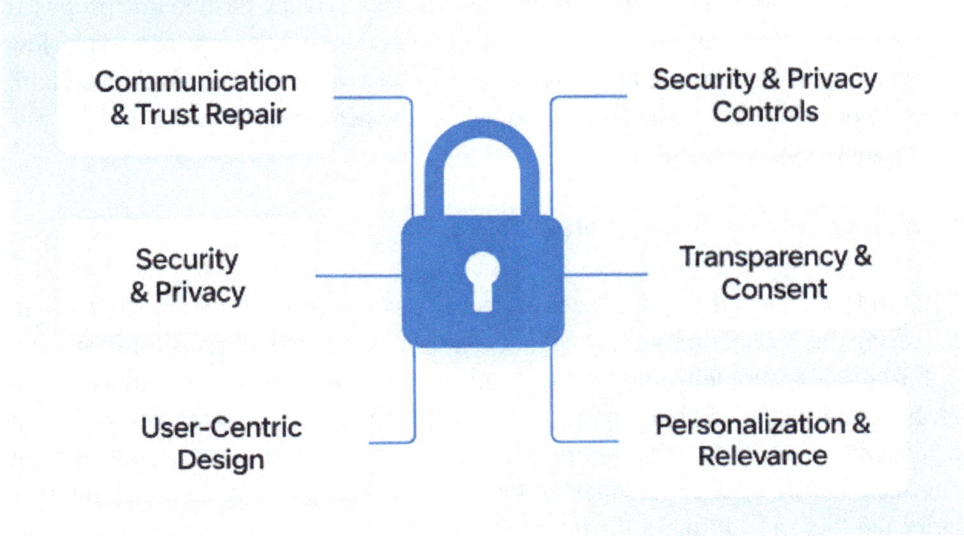

In the digital landscape that is continuously evolving, IoT has transformed itself both as an operational tool as well as a strategic tool of differentiation of brand personality and consumer communication. The recent trend of the occurrence of smart devices both in various industries including the healthcare supportive wearable, voice assistants, and smart home devices as well as in digital entertainment and games domains has brought forward not only the benefits of their functionality usability but also alarming concerns of security, openness, personalization, and ethical application. This paradigm not only requires businesses to put an end to conventional digital strategies and convert into the human-centered such architecture of trust which is mentioned in figure 1.

a. Security & Privacy Controls

With the digital trust environment, data security and privacy are in the spotlight and have become brand guarantees instead of a technical concern. The more accessible the given brand is to the community, the more likely are the users to feel safe after sharing some sensitive data with the associated systems: their personal health information, their movement history, or their preferences. According to (Gujar, P. 2025), data privacy and software usability have to co-exist in a fashion that neither deprives the customers of their strengths nor hinders protection. The infrastructure makes use of secure encryption, access governance, permission trails, and alerts in a timely manner, but what makes the difference is the visibility and the understanding by the user.

As an illustration, the responses of consumers to privacy dashboards proposed by Apple and Fitbit indicate the increased requests to have clear opt-in or data flow control. Brands that do not have visibility or proactive privacy controls lose faith in all the populations of consumers even where the performance of the devices was satisfactory (Dobre, J. 2025).

b. Transparency & Consent

Closely connected to the aspect of security is the concept of transparency in delivering data collection services, AI decision-making, and release of information to third parties. People would like to be informed not only that their data is secure but how and why it is being applied so that, based on this determination, certain results can be achieved. (Chan-Olmsted et al., 2024) stress that individuals are not comfortable with opacity personalization as it provokes a sense of distrust but rather understanding and willingness to trust are achieved through contextual explanations.

Control systems such as GDPR and CCPA have captured the necessity of the consent in the regulation setting, yet genuine transparency entails more than just conformity. Prominent brands even offer real-time views of the flow of data and the explainers of why one is seeing it. These characteristics contribute to closing the algorithmic black box so, that consumers can have rational confidence instead of blind trust.

c. User-Centric Design

The essential component is security, followed by transparency, and hardcoded is the layer of user-centric design that actualizes the meaning of trust. According to (Singh, V. 2024), ethical UX requires instilling the principles of privacy into the structure of the design work that will allow ensuring that users can make informed decisions about consent, their movement will be automatic and users would feel in control. An interface that is greased wouldn't t do the trick; it has to speak of intent, limits, and respect.

(Russell, J., & Ajeigbe, K. 2022) extend this to the concept of designing trusting, and autonomy comes to the capacity to personalize the environment, to be alerted in a way that allows consuming information and wanted behavior reversal when it becomes necessary to automation. A good example of the following is that the smart thermostats or home assistants with options to manually override or delete voice history are empowering, in their design, to drive brand closeness because of a perception of ethical alignment.

d. Personalization & Relevance

User satisfaction and brand loyalty are some of the aspects of personalization that Basic founds on a high-level basis of mutuality and permission. According to (Banerjee et al. 2024), excessive personalization can go terribly awry and result in privacy fatigue and a lack of user engagement at best, or antagonism and a lack of revenue at worst.

(Amil, Y. 2024) discovered that, as valuable as AI-driven customization is in terms of increased satisfaction, it heightens the level of privacy unless there is meaningful customization of such algorithms done by the users. Such adaptive level personalization approach with the user having ability to tune her experience or manage data sensitivity level is becoming an established best practice among platforms as diverse as Spotify to personalized banking apps.

The dignity should not be applied to overcome the relevance. Brands should know that there is a line between help and espionage. (Tamrakar et al.2025) have argued that an ethical balance should be made where relevance should be sought ethically, and user agency should also be treated as a perennial design variable, instead of a design variable.

e. Communication & Trust Repair

Security as well as UX are strong, but the trust can never be stagnant, and thus in times of crisis, it should be maintained by speaking with customers. According to (Caven, P. J. 2025), consumers have changed how they judge brands as they now consider how quickly brands respond to the breakdowns: How fast did they recognize a problem? Was the explanation clear? Were the proposed solutions adequate and feasible?

Such post-breach messages, as the ones made by companies like Zoom and T-Mobile, reveal that honesty and humility can help regain trust that is lost during an incident, provided that there already are visible efforts and user training. This matches the model of trust-co creation where organizations engage the users as more knowledgeable partners in the decision-making process rather than recipients of technical choices.

In addition, according to the idea of (Bakator, M., & Nikolić, M. 2024) in the context of Marketing 5.0, consumer needs are shifting towards humanistic orientations, sympathy and involvement in governing the digital environment. Communication has now stopped being about announcements but is about creating a digital rapport as time goes by.

f. Integrating the Pillars: A Lock Mechanism for Trust

The form of the lock of the model conveys the closed-loop digital trust system in artistic form. Through the given pillars, the core is also protected, brand loyalty in IoT ecosystems. The moment a single support shakes, one of the above-mentioned (and the list is long) security neglect or inadequate transparency in personalization, the lock becomes weak, and consumer disengagement becomes a probability which is shown in figure 2.

Figure 2. Lock Mechanism Model Diagram

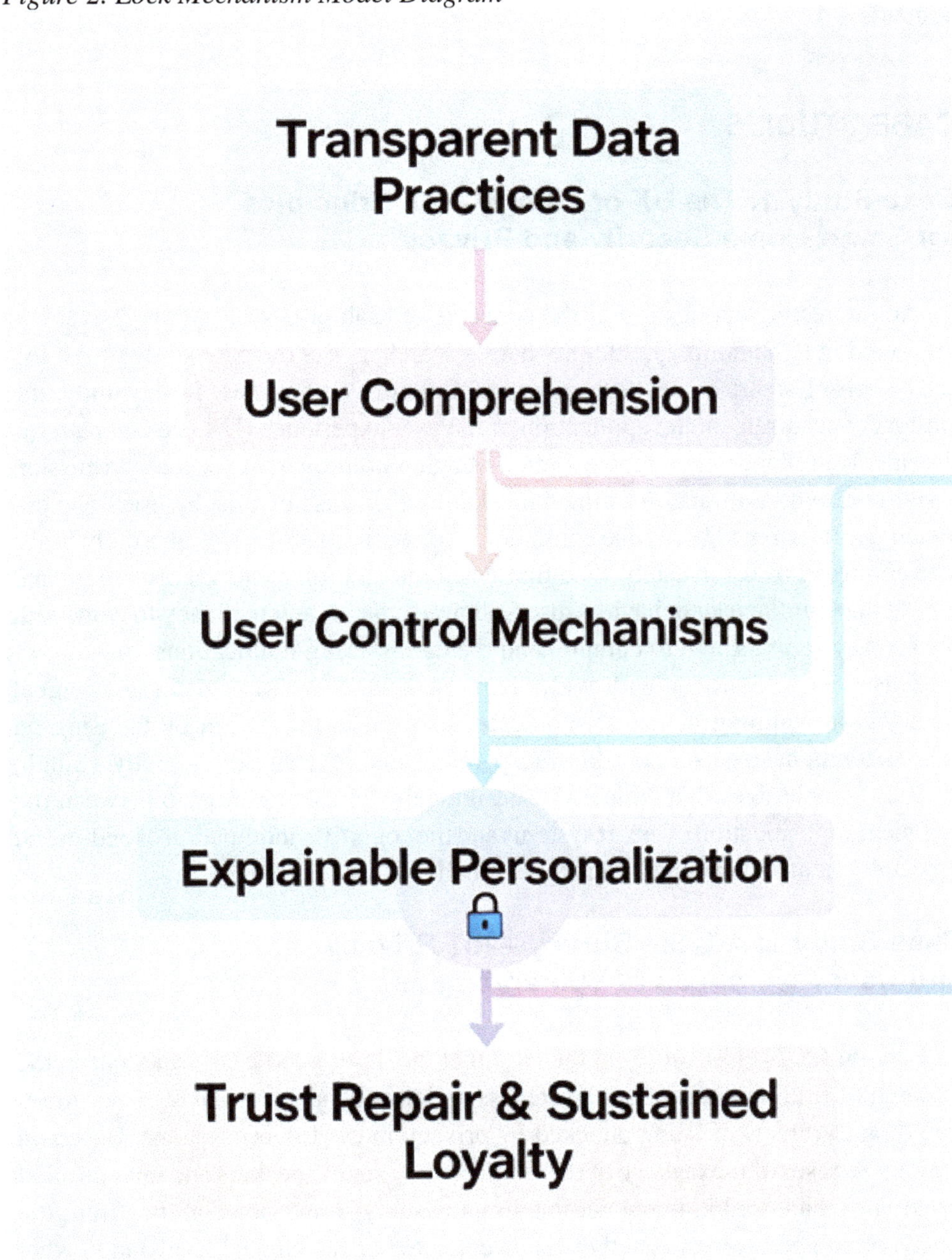

These pillars will not be in a vacuum and they will develop with the technology and with the social expectation. As an example, personalization works better when design is user-centric, and transparency is put forward. Similarly, when data infrastructures are secure and ethical, it is more credible to develop communication strategies.

CASE STUDIES

Case Study 1: The UX of Things – UX Principles for Smart Home Security and Privacy

An interesting application of the concepts of usability, security, and privacy is presented in (Chalhoub, G. 2022), where researchers use the case study of the IoT ecosystem of smart homes to provide the field-driven analysis. In the study, the authors concentrate on the application of the user experience (UX) design patterns that involve reliance on feedback provided by input, properly executed permission system or tiered notifications aimed at evoking the sense of trust by users and enhancing transparency in routine communication with smart devices on a daily basis. The empirical research established that when the controls were visibly salient and part of the familiar user behaviors, users showed a far greater tendency to work with the privacy settings, and to comprehend the data-sharing implications.

This is in consistency with wider ideas presented by (Russell, J., & Ajeigbe, K. 2022) in claiming that trust should be involved in the design by focusing on UXs that emphasize user control, transparency, and reversibility. Equally, (Singh, V. 2024) emphasizes that ethical UX design helps in closing the gap between the technical sophistication of smart systems and the cognitive anticipation of end-users, especially in an environment highly personalized.

Case Study 2: A Case Survey – IoT Privacy and User Awareness of Vulnerabilities

Lawson (2024) has surveyed the case that tackles a good case argument in the research of finding out the user awareness and user behavior when it comes to responding to threats of being attacked by privacy in the IoT ecosystems. Based on the known cases of the leakage of data collected by smart speakers and uncontrolled tracking of data used in home automation, the study shows one common trait: the user is often not aware of exactly what is collected on a technical level and in what level of detail after he or she expressed his or her supposed consent. It breaks the connection between the formalities of consent and the reality of how the users perceive it and decreases long-term brand loyalty.

The research shows the significance of such systems of trust mending, as immediate disclosure, user education and increasing transparency on interface level.

This is similar to what has been experienced in the work by (Caven, P. J. 2025), who highlighted the need to communicate proactive trust in the wake of failed trust. Also, (Dobre, J. 2025) agrees with the fact that integrating cybersecurity awareness into the UX lifecycle not only fixes any potential risks in the future but also improves the brand perception.

Case Study 3: Shaping User Privacy Experiences in Self-Tracking and Smart Homes

(Shalawadi, S. B. 2025) studies the transition of privacy preferences and trust relationships of self-monitoring devices and smart home technologies and gives in-depth contextual data on user-centred design and behavioral response to the ecosystems of enhanced information visibility. By way of participatory design and long-term observation, the study determined that users would develop consent fatigue, resulting in their agreeing to invasive terms by default, but then showing subsequent regret or distrust in opaque data flows or personalization results in adverse effect scenarios. This case shows how it is of critical importance to ESG-driven UX, which regards the aspect of privacy as an interactive interplay of communication

Most importantly, the study can show the benefits of modular consent systems, Data Usage Summaries, and user-configurable data-sharing settings as the means of enhancing user control, as well as shifting privacy out of the regulatory box into a collaborative providing value. This is consistent with the findings of (Siyadri & Sri, 2024) who also investigated the study of user-centric privacy design systems where ethical-by-design solutions in IoT are apparent. It also processes (Amil, Y. 2024) by stating that personalization can only be sustainable in case it is accompanied by a lot of visibility and real-time feedback loops of consent.

Case Study 4: Beyond the Screen – Cross-Platform UX for Wearables, IoT, and Emerging Technologies

The study presented by (Kose, B. O. 2025) proposes an in-depth overview of the cross-platform approach to user experience in wearables and Internet of Things ecosystem, with a particular focus on how it is possible to create a consistent and privacy-sensitive user experience across physical and virtual touchpoints. The applied study demonstrates in practice that the division of mobile interface, wearable device, and ambient smart environment will result in loss of user confidence-even in those cases when backend security itself is sound, the exploration and applications-focused testing. The feeling of anxiety was described when using health monitoring and location-based services as users lacked context when information was transferred between devices. The work by (Kose, B. O. 2025) provides a feasible roadmap of how security, personalization, and experience could be united on a higher level than the interface.

The study is beaded on three kinds of UX characteristics including cross-modal feedback, granular user privilege controls, and real-time explainability as the features, which are required to mitigate cognitive friction and reinstate trust. The steps are in tandem with the study done by (Chan-Olmsted et al., 2024) who state that device coherence is important and clarity on personalization logic is essential on trust-building.

Case Study 5: Ethical Data Practices in the Digital Age

(Yamuna, S. M., & Madhuvarsini, C. P. 2025) consider actual implementations of IoT-bases consumer technologies in the emerging markets with the focus on the lack of transparency of personalization and the lack of clear consent mechanisms that creates lack of trust despite the fact that the platforms are providing significant value to the users. Some of the implications described in the study include wearables and retail applications that excessively utilized behavioral data with no means to exercise control or interpretation by the consumer, leading to consumer backlash and regulatory caution.

This resonates with the conclusion of (Nafees, M., & Kumar, M. 2023) that the value of cybersecurity trust scaffolding within the digital ecosystem is the reliably green brand loyalty provided they put into practice the ethical data management. Similarly, (Moshed, A., & Al-Jabaly, S. 2024) observed that a combination of strategic IoT integration with an equivalent level of emotional relevance and transparency of privacy is necessary to maintain customer relationships in the case of a telecom product.

Case Study 6: The Internet of Things – Enabling Technologies, Platforms, and Use Cases

(Raj, P., & Raman, A. C. 2017) outlines IoT ecosystem structural architecture and describes real-life cases in which technologies have challenged the optimization aspect of the implementation of those systems at the expense of user confidence. The first example is about smart retail shelves that reactively and dynamically changed their offers according to the customer behavior data but not the fine consent and in-context disclosure. The mismatch resulted in pushback of the consumers and a sudden drop in the use of platforms a situation that however has had operational advantages.

The case resonates with the statements by (Saeed, S. 2023) who found how security transparency focused on customers significantly influences the trust building in the e-commerce environment, when automation and tracking are widespread. Along the same line, (Cheruku, H. K. 2025) underlines the point that the personalization should be acceptable to the customers, stressing that without proper communication, data-based optimization that often can be seen as aggressive damages the brand identity.

Case Studies 7: Studying the Integration of Everyday Objects with the Internet and Implications for Human Lives

It is an interdisciplinary case study conducted by (Manwaring et al., 2025) that concentrates on understanding the processes of mutual adaptation of introducing smart objects into everyday life and the reinforcement of user expectations, privacy practices, and emotional attachment to technology. In the studies on smart kitchen devices, wearable and environmental ambient sensors, the researchers realized that individuals embraced personalized UX, contrasting the visible consent processes, and clear feedback on how information is used.

One of the most important insights was that the perception of trust was positive when people had visibility over and control of data trails they left across the platforms (and when personalization engines also provided value and explainability). This is in agreement with (Bing et al. 2024) who affirmed that customer loyalty to products in consumer durable Internet of Things is not just about functionality, but also how fair and open bosses exercise communicating the brands.

In addition to this, the research concurs with (Singh, V. 2024) that ethical application of personalization technologies is not only the fulfillment of technical requirements but the mediation of cognitive disparities through communication that revolves around the needs of users. The results echo that trust is a two-way thing that is not established by automation but by dialogue.

Overview of Cases

Table 2. Overview of Cases

Case Study	Title/ Organization Focus	Context & Industry	Key Problem Identified	Ethical/UX Intervention Applied	Outcomes/ Results	Connection to Overall Topic
1	The UX of Things – UX Principles for Smart Home Security and Privacy	Smart home IoT ecosystem	Low user trust due to unclear data-sharing controls and lack of transparency	Applied UX design patterns emphasizing visible controls, permission systems, and layered notifications to foster trust	Improved user willingness to adjust privacy settings and understand data sharing; enhanced sense of security	Highlights ethical UX as key to minimizing perceived intrusion and increasing brand credibility
2	A Case Survey – IoT Privacy and User Awareness of Vulnerabilities	IoT devices and home automation	Low user awareness of what data is collected and consent misalignment	Introduced transparency mechanisms, disclosure prompts, and user education for better understanding of IoT data flows	Increased trust repair through immediate transparency and proactive trust communication	Underlines importance of ethical fidelity and user education in IoT privacy management
3	Shaping User Privacy Experiences in Self-Tracking and Smart Homes	Smart homes and self-tracking devices	Consent fatigue and subsequent privacy regret due to opaque data flows	Implemented modular consent systems, data usage summaries, and configurable privacy settings	Users gained greater control and satisfaction over personalization processes	Demonstrates ESG-driven, user-centric, ethical-by-design approach to data transparency
4	Beyond the Screen – Cross-Platform UX for Wearables, IoT, and Emerging Technologies	Cross-device IoT and wearables	Trust erosion due to inconsistent experiences across devices	Developed cross-modal feedback, granular privilege controls, and real-time explainability features	Restored user confidence and reduced cognitive friction across device ecosystems	Proves that coherence and transparency in UX foster security and trust across platforms
5	Ethical Data Practices in the Digital Age	IoT consumer technologies in emerging markets	Lack of consent transparency and overuse of behavioral data in personalization	Proposed situational consent, data impact mediation, and explicit interface transparency	Decreased user backlash and improved ethical alignment in personalization workflows	Reinforces need for value-based ethics in digital data management

continued on following page

Table 2. Continued

Case Study	Title/ Organization Focus	Context & Industry	Key Problem Identified	Ethical/UX Intervention Applied	Outcomes/ Results	Connection to Overall Topic
6	The Internet of Things – Enabling Technologies, Platforms, and Use Cases	IoT platform ecosystems	Over-optimization and automation leading to reduced user trust	Applied modular consent and interpretable algorithmic logic in UX frameworks	Enhanced trust and acceptance of IoT systems by aligning optimization with user understanding	Connects transparency-driven personalization with sustainable IoT adoption
7	Studying the Integration of Everyday Objects with the Internet and Implications for Human Lives	Everyday smart objects and ambient technologies	Inadequate visibility and emotional disengagement in IoT interactions	Introduced transparent consent, cross-platform data visibility, and user feedback on personalization	Positive trust perception, emotional engagement, and higher user satisfaction	Illustrates ethical personalization as a dialogue-based trust-building process

Strategic Imperatives and Policy Recommendations

a) Embed Ethical UX by Default

It is not an option to retrofit ethics design. Active involvement of transparent consent user interfaces, traceability of data flows, and integration of future layered privacy settings as an addition to the context of the IoT products ecosystems is to be pursued by the UX designers and the platform engineers. This is merely due to the fact that, according to (Chan-Olmsted, S., & Kim, H. J. 2024), the personalization should not come as a trade-off of user comprehension, when it is adaptive. Context-aware notifications, opt-in privacy modules, and progressive disclosures, as evidenced in (Chalhoub, G. 2022) of a UX study, have the capabilities of equipping users without getting in the way of performance. In addition, (Singh, V. 2024) also highlights the point that these design cues decrease the feeling of being monitored and increase the freedom of acting as a user.

b) Elevate Algorithmic Accountability through Visual Transparency

It is important that users are aware of the functioning of algorithms as they are more and more influencing the choices and the content. The platforms must insert explainable AI elements into the form of dynamic dashboards, user-facing data trails, and logic preview of the algorithms behind the algorithms, which demystify automated personalization. (Yamuna, S. M., & Madhuvarsini, C. P. 2025) warn the alienation of opacity, (Saeed, S. 2023) and (Cheruku, H. K. 2025) demonstrate the necessity of visibility being visual, participative, and cognitively lightweight in terms of use of data. The health, retail and smart mobility IoT developers will have to incorporate visual explainability processes that visualize to the user the data utilized, the time it occurred and the exchange purpose, transforming data flow into a transparent conversation, rather than an unnerving exchange.

c) Institutionalize Modular Consent Frameworks across Devices

One-time privacy agreement has disappeared because the demands of users and the need to abide by the rules pushed this aspect to rest and was static. To the contrary, the modular, contextual, and time-updated consent needs to be institutionalized by brands. Toggles in the device interactions such as real-time request of the permission in conjunction with the conditions of use warnings and the opt-out backup, enforce the ability on companies to meet the problem of the consent fatigue (Shalawadi, S. B. 2025) and likewise of personalization anxiety (Amil, Y. 2024). The other dynamic change (Hakiki et al., 2024) indicate on a global scale involves policy evolving towards adaptive consent where the interface builds on dynamic equities and legal concerns. This would not only be regulatory compliant but would also form a strong bond between the user and privacy providing environments through enabling attributes of privacy environments to be revisable, legible and human-centric. This is one of the necessities of every brand that targets longevity in terms of confidence and GDPR/CCPA reciprocity.

d) Bridge Tech–User Literacy Gaps through Participatory Design

The brands that will market their business in international IoT environments will have to understand the range of user knowledge about data habitat. Participatory design that involves collaborations with users when creating the flows of data, the layer of personalization, and the language the interface is spoken within, models of participatory design allay the elements of confusion and distrust. (Russell, J., & Ajeigbe, K. 2022) suppose that comprehensibility, like security, should be also provided, particularly in such spheres as smart homes and Health trackers. As it is verified by (Singh, V. 2024), a design language must be aligned not only with emotional concerns but also with cognitive ones.

e) Regulate UX-Level Privacy Through Cross-Sector Policy Innovation

Current privacy regulations are more and more inadequate when they are restricted to backend infrastructures or lawful disavowals. The regulation should be applicable to interface-level duties and avoid deceiving users and disempowering them due to misleading design. (Caven, P. J. 2025) continues to state that UX is no longer a design practice but is also a location where policy is being practiced.

New guidelines, which would define interface dark patterns, award transparency innovation, and endorse compliance-through-design toolkits should be adopted by brands in large ratios. It is congruent with the descriptive orientation provided by (Yamuna, S. M., & Madhuvarsini, C. P. 2025) about legal space-related ethics concerning design.

f) Integrate Trust Metrics into Brand Performance and Loyalty KPIs

Trust is not an emotion of the second type, trust is business, trust is a metric-to-pilot brand metric. The performance measures also have to incorporate perceived fairness, data respect, and platform transparency of users in interconnected ecosystems. It is seen that when brands treat the digital behavior of the consumers ethically, rather than efficiently, they continue to remain loyal to such brands (Bing et al. 2024). (Tamrakar et al. 2025) once again remind that ethical credibility is essential to make brand experience complete. The organizations are encouraged to implement trust indices, ethical design score, and the privacy perception analytics into brand performance dashboards.

g) Foster Interdisciplinary Trust Governance within IoT Organizations

The issue cannot be kept under compliance teams as trust governance. Instead, they need to be cross-function councils (including UX designers, legal professionals, C-levels in cybersecurity, AI engineers and consumer psychologists) whose work should be based on co-performing an evaluation of personalization functionality, consent models and ethical risks. According to (Dhiman & Dhote, 2025), the majority of the breakdown of trust falls between the lines: in the absence of policy transfer into design or the lack of engineering to pick up on social clues. (Gujar, P. 2025) supports this conclusion and states that sustainable IoT ethics can only be achieved through coordination of the system. Such internal review mechanisms are supposed to convene regularly to audit new product streams, track legal changes, and consider proximate user opinions so that trust management is not a crisis measure but part and parcel of design practice.

BENEFITS AND CHALLENGES OF POSITIONING TRUST, SECURITY, TRANSPARENCY, AND UX IN IOT BRANDING

Benefits

a. Collaborative Personalization that Enhances Loyalty to the Consumer

Planned personalization's which are carried out in an open fashion establish a more significant emotional attachment and behavioral loyalty. Personalization with the aid of a trust-based system underlines user satisfaction and reduces the issues related to privacy, as demonstrated by (Tamrakar et al. 2025).

b. Receiving a Competitive Differentiation by means of the Trust-based Branding

Trust becomes a distinguishing value when it comes to the saturated IoT markets. Ethical data treatment and secure UX practices (the example of aligning the model of consent with GDPR) put the companies into the position of responsible future-ready brands. This conforms to (Bing et al. 2024), who further assert that the trust sets apart even the commodity smart products.

c. The Strength of a Transparent interface to bring Gain by giving power to the user

Digital trust will be achieved through transparency and visibility of consent and will enable the user to start interacting with systems as opposed to waging war against them. In the study by (Singh, V. 2024), the main idea is an intuitive UX linked with data answerability which supports long term use through increasing digital literacy and perceived competence.

d. Regulatory Readiness and Reduced Legal Exposure

Brands regulations and safeguarded by secure-by-designing capabilities and methods are minimized through institutionalization. Advantage: It minimizes the struggles of modifying the cycles of getting used to new legislatures when all they do is present the pieces of legislatures (Hakiki et al., 2024).

e. Enhanced Cross-Platform User Retention

Reliable UX design maintains uniformity in associated gadgets. The users will be more willing to stick with an ecosystem when it is characterized by transparent, combined, and cross-platform data practices with less barriers when switching between devices and greater brand adhesion (Chan-Olmsted, S., & Kim, H. J. 2024).

f. Stronger Brand Equity and Ethical Perception

With an enhanced digital awareness of consumers, brand equity is becoming more and more dependent on what a value is beyond mere functionality. According to (Yamuna, S. M., & Madhuvarsini, C. P. 2025), the relationship between privacy-preserving technologies and reputation, word-of-mouth is also true of the trustworthiness of influencers.

Challenges

a. Balancing Personalization with Consent Complexity

To provide users with customized experiences and at the same time guarantee ethical consent design is a technical and mental challenge. According to (Shalawadi, S. B. 2025), complicating consent structures too much can result in the confusion or apathy of the users, whereas simplification can result in ignorant user consent. It is something that brands will continuously be rebalancing.

b. Overcoming Legacy Infrastructure and Design Debt

Resource demands can be created in legacy systems as transparency and modular privacy controls are added to legacy systems. Privacy-by-design foresight was not applied to many systems that were constructed and therefore their upgrades are expensive and also culturally disruptive within an organization (Gujar, P. 2025).

c. Navigating the Personalization–Privacy Paradox

Consumers are also predicting an individualized experience, and they are worried about who will use their information. The paradox presents a contradiction between marketing and law due to the insistence of segmentation since this issue and demand may contradict ethical rules of design (Saeed, S. 2023).

d. Scarcity of Ethical UX Talent and Governance Models

A significant number of already completed product teams do not have specialists who are trained in the aspect of UX, ethics, and regulation. Indeed, as noted by (Dhiman & Dhote, 2025), the world faces an increasing lack of talent in ethical design strategy, and the number of institutions providing interdisciplinary training specific to IoT eco-systems is still very low.

e. Interface-Level Policy Gaps and Regulatory Inertia

The majority of privacy regulations are centered on backend security with no influence on the front-end design manipulation. With such a loophole there may be the possibility of using dark patterns and deceiving opt-ins along with the personalization with no restrictions. According to (Caven, P. J. 2025), policies should be made up to UX realities to provide substantive protection to its users.

f. User Distrust from Past Breaches and Surveillance Cultures

When brands rebuild malpractices, recovery of trust may take a long time owing to the sustained doubts. Previous scandals, the black box nature of personalization and surveillance across applications creates a cultural backlash that makes re-engagement hard at least amongst Gen Z using the apps that are sensitive to issues regarding data ethics (Kollárová, S., & Niklová, M. 2025).

FUTURE DIRECTIONS FOR PILLARS OF DIGITAL TRUST AND LOYALTY IN IOT ECOSYSTEMS

1. Operationalize Consent as a Continuous Experience

The studies will have to shift to dynamic permissive to dynamic behaviour adaptive models of consent. According to (Rahman, P. 2025), this is crucial when it comes to persuasive interfaces particularly within a data driven scenario. These strategies resonate with what (Amil, Y. 2024) suggests, namely the focus on a solution of modular consent as a way to reduce fatigue and stimulate the continuation of trust in a smart ecosystem where it is possible.

2. Advance Emotionally Intelligent and Ethical AI Personalization

Emotional states should also be recognized by personalization systems of the future rather than being limited to behavioral cues. (Mitra. A., & Paul. S. 2025) urge the implementation of emotional intelligence in algorithmic decisioning especially in the field of finance and health to increase empathy-based loyalty. Such notions are reflected by (Singh, V. 2024), who stressed that ethical UX depends on how to create a connection between human emotionality and the AI writing code.

3. Integrate Algorithmic Transparency into UX Norms

Algorithmic explainability at the interface level ought to become standardized. (Selvakumar et al., 2025) demand AI audits, explainability dashboards, and displaying the information about inferences. This conforms to (Yamuna, S. M., & Madhuvarsini, C. P. 2025) who criticize black-box AI as a potential point of severe degradation in the trust between users and the brands.

4. Co-Design Trust Mechanisms with End-Users

The UX research should be made participatory to customize trust features according to the behavior of people in the real world. (Boni, E. K. 2024) accentuates that the perceptions of risk are divided along the horizons of age, gender, tribal, or cultural lines, and co-designed ethics are paramount. This corresponds to (Russell, J., & Ajeigbe, K. 2022), who emphasized user-centric design in order to guarantee credibility in connected systems, especially in situations where cognitive asymmetries occur.

5. Foster Regulatory UX Innovation

The UX design should become a regulatory field. Back-end requirements should be legislated along with interface manipulation (dark patterns, forced consent). (Caven, P. J. 2025) advocates policy-based policy innovation especially regarding AI-based personalization. This is consistent with (Hakiki et al., 2024) who argue that unity in frameworks has to be addressed by accounting to both law and design ethics.

6. Measure Trust Through Cross-Disciplinary Metrics

The ethical perception, privacy satisfaction, and trust sentiment should be included in the next-generational frameworks of loyalty. According to (Aldboush &

Ferdous, 2023), brands should not stop with engagement and start measuring emotional loyalty by perceiving data fairness. The same can be seen in (Bing et al. 2024) who identified that the concept of value alignment is currently a more important customer retention factor than price or utility.

7. Leverage Semantic Web and Web 3.0 for Trust Automation

Semantic data systems and decentralised identity tools will facilitate real-time user provable consent and AI traceability on the IoT. They are proposed to be intelligent infrastructure trust engines according to Melnyk (2024). Their ability to interoperate with the vision of (Gujar, P. 2025) in the form of interoperable and transparent systems is one example of how trust can be engineered on protocol level.

CONCLUSION

In the digital, interconnected world driven by the smart gadgets, creating brand loyalty and gaining trust is no longer a linear process that appears to relay only on the performance of the product, especially after COVID-19 (Ganesha, K.S., & Hemalatha, K.G. 2025). This chapter has traversed the field where information, morals and graphical aesthetics come together- where product loyalty is not only based on what a company provides, but how well and honestly and properly it interacts with people through technology.

Summarizing all the pillars separately is not a top priority anymore, and it is necessary to discuss what their convergence actually means the emergence of a new type of trust systems based on experiences. Whether IoT becomes trusted or untrusted, it comes more and more to the level of single-user interactions that either add to the trust of its process or to its loss. Here, trust should not be regarded as a passive output of usage, but a strategic deliverable that is developed by being ethical in personalization, proactive in communication and collective in control.

Never has a brand existed in an ecosystem that is influenced by digital intimacy like now. By allowing some brands into closed off areas in the literal and metaphorical sense, the user demands independence and integrity. The aspect, here, is that transparency is more than a value in the design: it is an indicator of moral compatibility. According to (Chan-Olmsted, S., & Kim, H. J. 2024), an evaluation of the utility of smart devices today, is now commonly based on not only functionality, but on how they make them feel about their own agency with data.

The actual struggle is not the technical or regulatory one in what lies ahead. It has something to do with the culture. It needs the companies to realize the emotional and ethical sides of IoT experience where users do not observe algorithms as a neutral tool but consider itself the demonstration of corporate personality. Over-personalizing or over-collecting or manipulating will not bode well into the future of brands. Alternatively, transparency is critical, as (Yamuna, S. M., & Madhuvarsini, C. P. 2025) warn: any resistance develops on the background of opacity, although legal regulations allow it.

Nonetheless, the situation is not that dark. A number of the frameworks, cases, and recommendations of this chapter indicate options that are directional, constructive, and actionable. There are blueprints in motion, such as ethical UX that is built in default (Singh, V. 2024), modular consent models that change across context (Amil, Y. 2024), trust governance boards that cut across legal and technical (Dhiman & Dhote, 2025) to name a few. All that is left is the desire to institutionalize these as fundamental business strategies and not just as compliance reactions.

In anticipation of future maturity, we would incorporate semantic AI, Web 3.0 trust layers; and what a challenge it would be to test the limits of user-brand relationships with emotional AI. Whether each of these technologies adopt a supporting or barring role in enforcing or eroding loyalty, will depend on the way organizations contextualize intelligence and empathy, automation and explanation and ethics.

Therefore, the future of IoT ecosystems regarding brand loyalty does not belong to the best but to the most responsible. The market makers will not only dominate markets; they will also establish the moral framework of the online world.

REFERENCES

Al-Mutawa, H. A., Sowailem, E. K., & Al Mubarak, M. (2025). Business Ethics in E-commerce: Ethical Concerns and Safeguarding Consumer Trust and Loyalty. In *Sustainable Digital Technology and Ethics in an Ever-Changing Environment* (Vol. 2, pp. 3–20). Springer Nature Switzerland. DOI: 10.1007/978-3-031-86708-8_1

Aldboush, H. H., & Ferdous, M. (2023). Building trust in fintech: An analysis of ethical and privacy considerations in the intersection of big data, AI, and customer trust. *International Journal of Financial Studies*, *11*(3), 90. DOI: 10.3390/ijfs11030090

Amil, Y. (2024). The impact of AI-driven personalization tools on privacy concerns and consumer trust in e-commerce (Master's thesis, University of Liège). http://hdl.handle.net/2268.2/21371

Bakator, M., Ćoćkalo, D., Makitan, V., Stanisavljev, S., & Nikolić, M. (2024). The three pillars of tomorrow: How Marketing 5.0 builds on Industry 5.0 and impacts Society 5.0? *Heliyon*, *10*(17), e36543. DOI: 10.1016/j.heliyon.2024.e36543 PMID: 39281657

Banerjee, S., Whig, P., & Parisa, S. K. (2024). Leveraging AI for Personalization and Cybersecurity in Retail Chains: Balancing Customer Experience and Data Protection. *Transactions on Recent Developments in Artificial Intelligence and Machine Learning*, *16*, 16.

Bing, G., Al Mughairi, B., Karim, A. M., & Karim, A. M. (2024). Study on Importance of Brand Loyalty for Customer Retention for Consumer Durable Products: New Era Viewpoint. *International Journal of Academic Research in Business & Social Sciences*, *14*(1), 453–464. DOI: 10.6007/IJARBSS/v14-i1/20464

Boni, E. K. (2024). Exploring perceived risk and digital ethics affecting consumer experiences and decision-making in smart retailing (Doctoral dissertation, Brunel University London).

Caven, P. J. (2025). Applying User-Centric Communication Strategies to Mitigate Cybersecurity Risks and Increase Transparency in Technology Markets (Doctoral dissertation, Indiana University).

Chalhoub, G. (2022). The UX of things: exploring UX principles to inform security and privacy design in the smart home (Doctoral dissertation, University of Oxford).

Chan-Olmsted, S., Chen, H., & Kim, H. J. (2024). In smartness we trust: Consumer experience, smart device personalization and privacy balance. *Journal of Consumer Marketing*, *41*(6), 597–609. DOI: 10.1108/JCM-12-2021-5072

Cheruku, H. K.Harsha Koundinya Cheruku. (2025). Data Privacy in E-commerce: Balancing Personalization with Customer Trust. *Journal of Computer Science and Technology Studies*, *7*(5), 680–687. DOI: 10.32996/jcsts.2025.7.5.75

Dhiman, H., & Dhote, T. (2025). IoT-driven digital marketing framework for enhanced consumer experience. Kronika Journal, 25(4), 37-50. https://kronika.ac/wp-content/uploads/4-KKJ2437.pdf

Dobre, J. (2025). Secure UX: Building cybersecurity and privacy into the UX lifecycle. UXMatters. https://www.uxmatters.com/mt/archives/2025/03/secure-ux-building-cybersecurity-and-privacy-into-the-ux-lifecycle.php

El-Annan, S. H., & Hassoun, R. (2025). Enhancing Consumer Trust Through Transparent Data Practices and Ethical Data Management in Business. In *Innovation Management for a Resilient Digital Economy* (pp. 105–148). IGI Global Scientific Publishing.

Ganesha, K. S., & Hemalatha, K. G. (2025). Digital Transformation in Advertising after COVID-19: Routing the New Landscape. In *Handbook of Digital Innovation, Transformation, and Sustainable Development in a Post-Pandemic Era* (pp. 384–406). CRC Press.

Gujar, P. (2025). Data Privacy and Security Concerns in Software and Data Usability. In *Data Usability in the Enterprise: How Usability Leads to Optimal Digital Experiences* (pp. 289–307). Apress. DOI: 10.1007/979-8-8688-1183-8_10

Hakiki, R., Nurlina, N., & Abaharis, H. (2024). Navigating Ethical Marketing: How Transparency Influences Brand Loyalty in the Digital Age. *YUME: Journal of Management*, *7*(3), 1644–1654.

. Iftikhar, S. M. (2024). A Critical Review of Personalization in Digital Marketing: Psychological, Technological and Ethical Perspectives. Technological and Ethical Perspectives (August 15, 2024).

John, B. (2025). The Impact of AI-Powered Chatbots on User Experience: Exploring Perceived Risks to Privacy, Loyalty, and Continued Usage. https://www.researchgate.net/publication/388615153_The_Impact_of_AI-Powered_Chatbots_on_User_Experience_Exploring_Perceived_Risks_to_Privacy_Loyalty_and_Continued_Usage

Kollárová, S., & Niklová, M. (2025). *The digital identity of Generation Z.* Matej Bel University., https://e-isbn.pl/IsbnWeb/record/show_cover.pdf?picture_id=186914

Kose, B. O. (2025). Beyond the Screen: Cross-Platform UX for Wearables, IoT, and Emerging Technologies. Navigating Usability and User Experience in a lti-PlatfoMurm World. United States, IGI Global, 2024.

Kwan, D., Cysneiros, L. M., & do Prado Leite, J. C. S. (2021, September). Towards achieving trust through transparency and ethics. In 2021 IEEE 29th International Requirements Engineering Conference (RE) (pp. 82-93). IEEE. DOI: 10.1109/RE51729.2021.00015

Lawson, M. N. (2024). A Case Survey: Internet of Things Privacy and User Awareness of Vulnerabilities (Doctoral dissertation, Marymount University).

Magrizos, S., Campora, M., Lamprinakos, G., Giovanis, A., & Christofi, M. (2025). Transparency by design: The effect of privacy policies visualisation on brand trust and perceived intrusion. *Behaviour & Information Technology*, •••, 1–13.

Manoj, G., Juliet, P. A., Mege, V. S., Devi, K. G., Gnanasekaran, C., & Indira, P. (2025). AI for Personalization: Transforming Customer Journeys in Self-Service Technology. In Practical Applications of Self-Service Technologies Across Industries (pp. 255-286). IGI Global Scientific Publishing.

Manwaring, P., Malakhatka, E., Fiore, E., Paradiso, J., Hill, D., & Wiberg, M. (2025). Internet of Things (IoT): Studying the Integration of Everyday Objects with the Internet and the Implications for Human Lives. In *Human-Technology Interaction: Interdisciplinary Approaches and Perspectives* (pp. 175–199). Springer Nature Switzerland. DOI: 10.1007/978-3-031-78357-9_6

Melnyk, A. (2024). Examining The Impact of Advanced Technologies and Semantic Web Integration in Web 3.0 And The Future of Strategic Digital Marketing. Publishing House "Baltija Publishing".

Mitra, A., & Paul, S. (2025). Harnessing AI-Driven Personalization for Financial Brand Loyalty: The Role of Emotional Intelligence in FinTech Marketing. In Intersecting Natural Language Processing and FinTech Innovations in Service Marketing (pp. 243-274). IGI Global Scientific Publishing.

Morales Sharp, T. (2023). Ethical guide for social media marketing: brand humanization, data privacy, and brand trust. Universitat Politècnica de València. https://riunet.upv.es/handle/10251/197971

Moshed, A., & Al-Jabaly, S. (2024). Enhancing marketing success in Jordanian telecom: Strategic IoT integration and brand relationship management for maximized consumer loyalty. Journal of Infrastructure. *Policy and Development*, *8*(6), 3858.

Nafees, M., & Kumar, M. (2023). Cybersecurity And Privacy Trust. In *Digital Data: Navigating The Digital Trust Landscape* (1st ed., p. 108). Noble Science Press., DOI: 10.52458/9789388996747.nsp2023.eb.ch-14

Ogawara, M. (2025). The influence of consumer privacy preferences on personalized marketing and multichannel CRM integration. *Frontiers in Management Science, 4*(1), 12–19. DOI: 10.56397/FMS.2025.01.03

Owen, A., & Moore, J. (2023). Ethical considerations in AI-driven personalization for eCommerce platforms. International Journal of Scientific Research in Computer Science. *Engineering and Information Technology, 11*(2), 287–294. DOI: 10.32628/CSEIT251112371

Prem, R. (2025). Hyper-Personalization in Digital Marketing: Evaluating Consumer Trust and Brand Loyalty in the Age of AI-Driven Campaigns. *Exploresearch, 02*(02), 106–115. DOI: 10.62823/ExRe/2025/02/02.62

Rahman, P. (2025). Exploring ethics and trust in persuasive technologies (Doctoral dissertation, University of British Columbia).

Raj, P., & Raman, A. C. (2017). *The Internet of Things: Enabling technologies, platforms, and use cases*. Auerbach Publications.

Russell, J., & Ajeigbe, K. (2022). User-centric networking: Designing for experience. https://www.researchgate.net/publication/389674597_User-Centric_Networking_Designing_for_Experience

. Sadiq, S., Sundar, & Devi, A. (2024). Consumer trust and ethical branding in E-Commerce 2.0. International Journal of Science, Engineering and Technology. DOI: 10.61463/ijset.vol.12.issue6.972

Saeed, S. (2023). A customer-centric view of E-commerce security and privacy. *Applied Sciences (Basel, Switzerland), 13*(2), 1020. DOI: 10.3390/app13021020

Selvakumar, P., Sudheer, P., & Kannan, N. (2025). Balancing Innovation and Privacy: Understanding AI in the Digital World. In Digital Citizenship and the Future of AI Engagement, Ethics, and Privacy (pp. 279-304). IGI Global Scientific Publishing.

Shalawadi, S. B. (2025). Shaping user privacy experiences in self-tracking and smart homes: A design artifact approach (Doctoral dissertation, Aalborg University). Aalborg University Open Publishing. https://vbn.aau.dk/files/784094476/PHD_SBS_ONLINE.pdf

Sharma, S. (2023). Data Privacy Concern Due to Information Personalization Technologies: A Quantitative Study, Utilizing Technology Acceptance Model (TAM) to Explore the Consumers' Experience in E-Commerce (Doctoral dissertation, University of the Cumberlands).

Singh, V. (2024). Fostering Effective Human-AI Collaboration: Bridging the Gap Between User-Centric Design and Ethical Implementation. *International Journal on Recent and Innovation Trends in Computing and Communication*, *12*(2), 22–30.

Siyadri, Y., & Sri, R. D. A. (2024). "Advancing User-Centric Privacy: A Comprehensive Research Roadmap For Ethical And Secure Technology Development." i-Manager's. *Journal of Information Technology*, *13*(3).

Tamrakar, S., Gupta, O. P., Gupta, M., & Katahare, G. N. (2025). Harnessing the power of brand experience to foster brand trust in the digital era. Samvakti Journal of Research in Business Management, 6(1), 184-204. https://www.samvaktijournals .com/sjrbm.2025.70/harnessing_power_brand_experience_foster_brand_trust _digital_era.pdf

. Velasco, C., Reinoso-Carvalho, F., Barbosa Escobar, F., Gustafsson, A., & Petit, O. (2024). Paradoxes, challenges, and opportunities in the context of ethical customer experience management. Psychology & Marketing, 41(10), 2506-2524.Haris, A. (2025). Consumer behaviours shifts in digital age: Impact on brand loyalty.

Vishwakarma, R. K., Pandey, A., Kundnani, M. P., Yadav, A. K., Singh, M. N., & Yadav, M. S. (2025). Personalization vs. privacy: Marketing strategies in the digital age. *Journal of Marketing & Social Research*, *2*, 177–191.

Yamuna, S. M., & Madhuvarsini, C. P. (2025). Ethical Data Practices in The Digital Age: Ensuring Privacy, Transparency, And Accountability. Proceedings of Emerging Trends in Technology and Digital Transformation for Sustainable Business Development. PSG College of Arts & Science, 59.

Yellanki, S. K. (2025). *Behavioral Intelligence and Operational Design: Exploring Modern Service Models, Customer-Centric Platforms, and Sustainable Digital Infrastructure*. Deep Science Publishing.

Chapter 9
Navigating Ethical, Legal, and Security Challenges in IoT Markets:
Building Trust in a Connected World

R. Vettriselvan
http://orcid.org/0009-0005-1097-0806
Academy of Maritime Education and Training, India

Palanivel Rathinasabapathi Velmurugan
http://orcid.org/0000-0002-0395-9060
Berlin School of Business and Innovation, Germany

C. Catherene Julie Aarthy
http://orcid.org/0000-0001-9353-5546
MEASI Institute of Management, Chennai, India

Richa Sirohi
Saraswathi Institute of Medical Sciences, Hapur, India

T. R. Kalai Lakshmi
School of Management Studies, Sathyabama Institute of Science and Technology, Chennai, India

ABSTRACT

Businesses and consumers benefit considerably from the IoT expansion while dealing with vital ethical as well as legal and security challenges. Trust becomes the essential factor for successful IoT implementation by addressing major issues about data

DOI: 10.4018/979-8-2600-1263-5.ch009

privacy as well as cybersecurity weaknesses together with regulatory requirements and algorithmic clarity standards. The method demonstrates how organizations should manage complex digital systems through data governance practices which combine ethical design capabilities with pro-active legal frameworks. The chapter conveys unique importance of CDR that establishes enduring consumer trust by maintaining ethical technological deployments. The paper demonstrates the need for transparency throughout IoT integration by presenting case studies that examine effective and unsuccessful deployments of IoT principles. Through comprehensive guidance the chapter presents an approach which helps institutions, regulators and technological experts build robust IoT facilities which respect both people's fundamental rights and community interests.

INTRODUCTION

Internet of Things (IoT) has not only become a reality since it does not exist in theory, but also a pillar of technological and social infrastructure that constantly redefines industries, the economy as a whole, and our daily lives across the globe. Be it intelligent homes and self-driving cars, precision agriculture, telemedicine, and connected manufacturing, IoT technologies provide unprecedented prospects of efficiency on operation, personalised services, sustainability, and innovation. The IDC (2022) estimates that in 2025, about 55.7 billion interconnected devices will be operational and generate over 73 zettabytes of data every year. This exponential growth is only the beginning of the technological revolution, but a complete change in relations between the human, institutions, and the environment. Nevertheless, it is the same interconnectivity that allows predictive analytics and automated decision-making that puts the society at risk of ethical, legal, and cybersecurity threats. The architecture of IoT is decentralised and connected, which puts physical and digital worlds into grey zones, and it provides the possibility to make decisions in real time and increases risks associated with privacy, integrity, accountability, and bias (Ajzen, 1991). The sheer volume of ongoing data gathering attracts cyberattacks and misuse of IoT systems, which results in unauthorised access, information manipulation and engaging in ethical misconduct. These insecurities pose acute challenges regarding the safety, fairness and responsibility of our online spaces that require multi-dimensional governance structures that incorporate technical, legal and moral regulations.

The IoT economy has thus been based on digital trust. Unless users can confirm the significant protection of their privacy, strong cybersecurity, and ethical practises, they are not ready to use new technologies (Dodiya et al., 2024). Trust is dependent on the ability of the users to control their personal data, transparency of corporate data management and enforceable data protection laws. The establishment of such trust presupposes the active ethical interaction, clear communication, and adherence to the ever-changing data-protection standards. Devices should not just be reliable, but also just, that is, secure, predictable, and respectful to user autonomy and dignity. Digital trust is not merely about technical performance, but it is about the emotional and the social aspects of human-technology interaction. Ethical concerns of IoT are much broader than breach of individual privacy. Opaque data processes, the loss of informed consent, and algorithmic bias are some of the structural inequities and surveillance practises that may adversely affect democratic participation and social justice (El-Khoury and Arikan, 2021). The adverse effects of the IoT are collective: discriminatory algorithms may discriminate against communities, and omnipresent surveillance can undermine civic privacy. To create an ethical system that reflects the conditions of hyper-connectivity, there is a necessity to work on both technological obscurity and the culture of surveillance normalisation.

In the meantime, the juridical environment finds it difficult to keep up with such inventions. Conventional principles of privacy, liability, and consumer protection were intended many years before the advent of autonomous cross-jurisdictional networks of the IoT. The questions of accountability in the case when the devices fail or participate without human control, and concerns the national legislations governing those data moving across the borders at the same time have become under the legal uncertainty. The end-users typically do not have significant control over the data gathered by devices on the common or semi-public premises. As a result, the regulatory mechanisms need to transform so that they can create adaptive equilibrating frameworks that safeguard users without crushing innovation (Vettriselvan et al., 2024). These hardships are further increased by cybersecurity vulnerability. The minimal protection of many IoT products is because of cost and short-cycle product development. Unsecured devices are weaponizable as evidenced by the Mirai botnet attack in 2016, which has caused havoc to critical infrastructure and endangered national security. The current threat environment has taken a new shape that is characterised by ransomware against hospitals, industrial controllers, and smart-city grids. Poor passwords, old firmware and lack of awareness are human factors that only increase the risks, showing that IoT security is as much a social as a technical problem.

It is in the light of such complexities that proper governance of IoT involves an interdisciplinary approach that integrates ethical foresight, legal flexibility, and technical strength. Innovation should be driven by ethics since design through deployment and law should provide accountability and cross border compliance. Security is not something that should be considered as an afterthought but rather a part of trustful design. These dimensions combined form the backbone of Corporate Digital Responsibility (CDR) - a new paradigm, which relates the corporate social responsibility to the digital realm. Organisations can make commitments through CDR to protect the rights of individuals, make algorithms transparent, and include privacy-by-design and cybersecurity-by-default in their operations. Trust in this dynamic environment is an asset that can be measured and an element of competitive advantage. When companies act as ethical custodians and have transparent governance, they are likely to win the loyalty of the users, access regulatory permission, and be legitimate to the society. Going beyond compliance regulations to proactive CDR is not only a moral obligation, but is also a strategic need to grow the business in a sustainable manner.

The chapter adopts an interdisciplinary and critical approach to the issue of exploring the relationship between ethical, legal, and security factors in influencing the levels of trust in IoT markets. It will focus on (1) elaborating a conceptual model of the interrelationship between these areas within a consistent governance structure; (2) examine empirical and theoretical evidence conducted by various fields such as healthcare, manufacturing, and smart cities; and (3) suggest ways in which the policymakers and institutions can institutionalize responsible IoT practices. The analysis has relied upon behavioural, ethical and socio-technical theories such as the Theory of Planned Behaviour as proposed by Ajzen (1991) to explain the role of the attitudes, perceived control and the social norms in shaping trust towards the adoption of ethical IoT systems. The chapter will also discuss case-based evidence of four large sectors of IoT applications, including consumer smart devices, industrial automation, digital health and urban infrastructure, and demonstrate the dynamics of trust within the sector (Wakili and Bakkali, 2024). The different fields present unique moral challenges and management requirements, but these all lead to the same concept: trust as the basis of co-existence on the net. To develop trustful IoT ecosystems, thus, collaboration between regulators, corporations, developers, and actors of civil-society is essential. After all, the future of the connected world is not only the technological progress but the human capability to maintain trust, justice and responsibility in the digital encounters. Holding on to such trust means that the IoT revolution will serve human dignity, social justice, and sustainable progress, and not destroy it.

CONCEPTUAL FRAMEWORK

The fast-growing Internet of Things (IoT) has brought us to the era when devices, systems, and services are linked to each other together, producing tremendous amounts of real-time data. This broad connectivity affords a significant business potential, encourages innovation, and introduces new business design opportunities, at the same time, questioning our established cultural values toward privacy, trust, ethics, and security. The conceptual aspects of the IoT ecosystem, the dynamics of digital trust, ethical concerns, risk-based stratification, and the security-trust-law relationship in the global digital economy are key to dealing with the complex issues. An IoT ecosystem is comprised of various types of devices, such as sensors, actuators, smartphones, wearables, autonomous machines, and cloud platforms working in harmony with big-data analytics software and user interfaces. They all combine to automate the data acquisition process, data processing and communication as well as make vital decisions. The ecosystem spans across the production sectors, including the healthcare, agriculture, manufacturing, transportation and urban management (smart cities), although the sector has its own operational needs and ethical risks.

The most important elements of an IoT ecosystem include data-gathering devices and sensors, communication networks (Wi-Fi, 5G, LPWAN), data-processing platforms, user interfaces, and security systems to maintain the stability of the system, the authenticity, and privacy of data. Since IoT gadgets are operating in distributed networks and have few resources, they create new threat levels to traditional security models and all the connected gadgets must be considered as entry points of vulnerability. The loosely connected IoT network topology creates numerous security points, making it hard to enforce the central control; hence, novel governance models are urgent. Digital trust is a basic market requirement in the IoT technology, which sums up the trust that the stakeholders have in the operations of digital systems coupled with protection of sensitive data, the autonomy of the user, and ethical standards. The future implementation and continued usage of the IoT systems thus depends on development of digital trust between all stakeholders. The building and upkeep of trust are critically dependent on a number of factors, such as the assurance of security by safeguarding devices and networks, the openness of information about the gathering and use of data, the dependability of the functionality of the devices, the ethical use of data, which leads to the informed consent and the dignity of the users, and the adherence to the changing privacy and cybersecurity rules, the GDPR, and the CCPA. The gaps in these dimensions trigger the loss of trust, resulting in the loss of user engagement and the need to face regulatory consequences and reputational damage to organisations. Digital trust development, therefore, should be regarded as a key strategic core that all stakeholders in the course of the IoT operations should focus on.

Ethical principles should be applied at all phases of the development of an IoT system, which is a significant prerequisite that will allow aligning the level of technological evolution with the tendencies accepted by society. The development of the IoT technology is based on the fundamental moral principles that incorporate autonomy with beneficence, justice, non-maleficence, transparency, and accountability. People need to be able to manage all their data, privacy, and interactions with their devices in order to maintain self-determination in the virtual world. The principle of beneficence requires the IoT technology to produce beneficial social effects, including better healthcare, better environmental management and safe city systems. Justice requires fair sharing of the benefits of innovation and this does not allow deep-rooted inequalities to be entrenched. Non-maleficence requires medical professionals to prevent intentional and unintentional harm which includes malfunctioning equipment use and sorting algorithms that are discriminatory. Users need full disclosure of decision making practises and data processing methods, on the other hand, institutions and individuals are accountable to ethical behaviour. Ethical violations such as cloudy surveillance, use of data to generate business profit, continuation of systematic biases by processing algorithmically are highly dangerous to civic trust and democracy. IoT ecosystems are saturated with multiple risk areas since they have large dynamic areas that fluctuate between security, privacy, operational, regulatory, and ethical threats. Security threats are in the form of unauthorised device access, chronic DDoS attacks, ransomware, and vulnerabilities to integrity and availability of the system. Data privacy is jeopardised when third parties unrelated to the individual perform surveillance, profiling, and data mining without any significant user approval. Operational risks include technical malfunctions, interoperability, and cyber-physical cyber-security threats that put critically important infrastructure at risk. Non-regulatory risks come about as a result of failure to meet protection standards which imposes financial fines and reputational losses. The presentation of biases in algorithms generates ethical risks that create discrimination and intrusive access of data that erode democratic rights. The impact of organisational resilience on these types of risks undermines user trust and changes adoption rates and market performance. Trust, law, security, and ethics require thorough insight into their interaction since their soundness and survival are the keys to constructing resilient and human-centred IoT ecosystems. The ethical design practises that show commitment by an organisation to the rights and social welfare of the individuals boost user confidence. The legislation provides the necessary safety requirements that set minimum data privacy requirements and share responsibility and security standards among consumers. These principles are realised through security implementations through system level resilience deployments that minimise the frequency and misuse of breaches. The intersection of ethics and legal standards and security controls is used to design user experiences that encourage trust-based engagement with the IoT technologies.

Digital trust develops on a gradual cycle that forces organisations to incorporate moral concepts in design (ethics by design) as well as making sure that legal acceptability is achieved throughout the project lifecycle (compliance by default) or making cybersecurity the most important aspect (security by design). Maintaining trust needs the active involvement of users and transparency in practises as well as the creation of channels of raising concerns. The development of an overall governance system to deal with the IoT issues is the most important in the modern world. Disjointed, responsive approaches to security, privacy, or ethics cannot meet the demands of modern times with the complex technology developments and growing social anxieties. A comprehensive approach should be based on a number of aspects: establishing an Ethical Impact Assessment (EIA) into product development process to disclose risks in advance and prevent them; conducting a continuous security risk assessment, as the lifecycle of the product progresses; involving a variety of stakeholders in the design and implementation, as well as evaluation to ensure inclusivity, cultural sensitivity, and equity; and conducting a strict regulatory compliance evaluation, in particular, in cross-border environments, when ambiguities in jurisdiction occur. These systems of integration allow organisations to move beyond simple levels of compliance, towards dynamic, value-based innovation, which is the connexion between technology development and human-rights defence, social equality, and environmental stewardship. The understanding of the basic concepts of the IoT ecosystem, digital trust, ethical standards, and the security threats should be in the focus of successful management of modern technologies. The success or failure of IoT initiatives will eventually depend on trust. Co-operation in the direction of governance structures will pre-empt arising problems, tolerate various stakeholders, follow ethical principles, and resilience. The governance standards are implemented strategically to ensure that the promises of IoT deliver positive results in the digital environment, which brings social and economic gains and promotes democratic activities.

THEORETICAL FRAMEWORK

The analysis of the ethical, legal, and security dilemmas in the Internet of Things (IoT) environment requires employing the theory of the issues that have been properly developed and which explain the interaction between technological progress, human behaviour, institutional organisation, and ethical responsibility. The input of behavioural science and organisational theory, risk perception, and normative ethics provide a multidimensional prism through which the reactions of people and the organisation to nascent digital technologies can be analysed. Here, to theorise sustainable digital trust and ethical governance in IoT markets, the chapter use six theories that are interconnected, including Diffusion of Innovation, Technology Acceptance Model, Stakeholder Theory, Theory of Planned Behaviour, Trust Theory, and Risk Perception Theory (Tzafestas, 2018).

Diffusion of Innovation Theory

The Diffusion of Innovation (DoI) Theory provides the temporal change in the social acceptance of new technologies with five categories of adopters; innovators, early adopters, early majority, late majority, and laggards. In the environment of the IoT, the first movers often appear to be more sceptical about the privacy, data security, and the stability of operations (Sasikala and Sachan, 2024). The available empirical data suggest that the first cases of ethical failures or cyberattacks may delay the further spread significantly by damaging social trust (Nastjuk et al., 2022). As a result, the pace of the IoT adoption is largely dependent on the development of trust as an essential social token. Organisations need to develop this trust by open communication, security performance that can be observed and ethical compliance that is active. With the formation of trust and perceived value, the diffusion process increases rapidly, and the principle of innovation becomes more acceptable in large social networks.

Technology Acceptance Model (TAM)

An alternative viewpoint that can be applied to understand the nature of user behaviour in IoT set-ups is the Technology Acceptance Model (TAM). It is a model that assumes that Perceived Usefulness (PU) and Perceived Ease of Use (PEOU) are critical factors of technology acceptance. In modern versions of TAM, Perceived Security and Perceived Privacy are equally emphasised as influential variables in the process of adopting IoT (Nastjuk et al., 2022). The users should feel that the IoT devices do not only work efficiently and easily, but also consider their autonomy and data integrity. The privacy-by-design and security-by-default features can be combined with explicit consent mechanisms by designers and developers in order to amplify the adoption. Failure to observe such qualities leads to user disappointment and backlash hence destroying organisational productivity and reputation. Therefore, the most common channel through which the IoT can be adopted in a sustainable manner is trust-based innovation, which is founded on accountability and transparency.

Stakeholder Theory

The Stakeholder Theory of Freeman (1984) is an extension of the analytical focus of individual acceptance to corporate responsibility, which holds that organisations need to take into account the interests of all the stakeholders, that is, users, regulators, advocacy groups, employees, suppliers, and the local communities. Ethical management in the IoT field involves economic incentive versus privacy and privacy protection, data stewardship, and equity in the society. The tension between profit-making goals and social responsibility requires governing structures that would reflect participatory ethics and decision-making. Cybersecurity priorities combined with data ethics as a multi-stakeholder governance framework can be used to promote resilience and trust in the population. Through institutionalisation of stakeholder communication and ethical control, IoT companies will be in a better position to solve regulatory difficulties and build credibility and digital trust systems.

Theory of Planned Behaviour (TPB)

The Theory of Planned Behaviour (TPB) by Ajzen (1991) provides a behavioural theory of the way people develop intentions to adopt IoT. TPB determines three behaviour determinants: attitude towards the action, subjective norms, and perceived behavioural control. Regarding the risks associated with the IoT, including surveillance or data exploitation, negative perceptions may breed negative attitudes, which are supported by the social discourse that highlights the dangers of technology. On the contrary, positive attitudes are achieved by offering ethical guarantees, open consent choices and control-awakening strategies. Perceived behavioural control is supported by user empowerment, which is accomplished by customisable privacy controls and understandable information, which increases trust and adoption levels. Therefore, TPB proves that ethical communication and transparency are moral requirements and drivers of long-term IoT participation.

Moral Principles of IoT Governance

Normative ethics provide the necessary guidelines on how to assess the IoT governance models. Kantian (deontological) ethics is based on the importance of duty, rights, and respect of the autonomy of a person (Nanda and Kumar, 2024). In this regard, IoT companies have a moral obligation to ensure informed consent, protect user privacy, and regard human dignity highly in lieu of profitability. Utilitarian ethics on the other hand focus on the common good and maximisation of social benefits. Data aggregation can be a matter of responsible management, such as in traffic optimisation in smart cities, and this would not be unjustified by utilising limited amounts of data so long as transparency and equity are ensured. The balance between the deontological duty and utilitarian results will be maintained so that the creation of the IoT can be considered to be ethically defensible and socially acceptable. This two-pronged ethic focuses policy makers and innovators towards sustainable innovation equity.

Theory of Trust in the Digital World

The psychological anchoring of digital adoption is trust. The Trust Theory states that users are willing to give vulnerability to a system when they think that the system behaves in a competent, honest, and benevolent way (Kounelis et al., 2014). Competence refers to functional reliability; integrity refers to observation of ethical and legal norms; benevolence refers to the perception that systems are concerned with the welfare of its users. Cases of trust quickly diminish in the event that any of these elements fails in IoT ecosystems. Therefore, to build trust, there is a need to conduct ethical audits on a regular basis, share information about data practises, and show responsibility. Organisations that implement ethical trust by implementing certified security measures and user-friendly design develop a robust relationship and long-term trust in the marketplace.

Risk Perception Theory

The Risk Perception Theory explains the way the users perceive the technological risks both in the rational and emotional perspective. Perceived risks are often larger than objective risks in the environment of the IoT because of media discourse and social amplification. Users might be more frightened by the possibility of being spied on or privacy violations than justified by the existence of vulnerable systems. The unresolved misconceptions might cause outburst of social anxiety and stall the growth of technology. The perceived risk and the actual risk are aligned through the effective communication of risks, which involves transparency reports, user education and quick crisis response. When trust is centralised on informed knowledge, users become more resilient and flexible towards the integration of the IoTs.

Ethical and Secure IoT Systems Integrated Framework

These theories together form a single point of analysis of trust and ethics in the governance of IoT. Diffusion of Innovation and TAM explain the role of perception and usability in determining adoption. Stakeholder Theory brings about the accountability in the corporate system and TPB sheds light on the behavioural processes between trust and control. These relationships are based on moral reasoning and founded on ethical theory, and they are explained by the Trust Theory and the Risk Perception Theory, which clearly shows the psychological and emotional aspects of digital trust. Collectively, they are a multistage model of governance that facilitates transparency, equity, and resilience (Karale, 2021; Ishmaev, 2020).

This combined model is a precursor to three pillars of sustainable IoT ecosystems:

- Safe and Visible Architecture: Integrating ethics and privacy into the technology lifecycle.
- Collaborative Governance: Making corporate responsibility consistent with multi-stakeholder involvement.
- Risk Literacy and Communication: Cloosing the gap between the general population and facts via open communication.

The IoT implementation and regulation thus requires a balance between morality and innovation. Digital ecosystems are growing, and the technological development has to be directed by ethical intelligence which is based on trust, fairness, and the autonomy of the user. The future of IoT does not only lie in the intelligent systems, but in systems that reflect integrity as well as accountability in such a way that the digital evolution is in line with the long held norms of dignity, justice and collective well-being of humans.

RESEARCH METHODOLOGY

This paper uses a systematic literature review (SLR) to question the ethical, legal and security predicaments plaguing the Internet of Things (IoT) and to offer formidable solutions that may strengthen the Internet of Things digital trust. The investigation will be methodologically rigorous, transparent, and reproducible by adopting the PRISMA 2020 guidelines (Page et al., 2021). Since IoT is an interdisciplinary subject (it intersects computer science, cybersecurity, law and behavioural ethics), an integrative review design is essential to bring together qualitative and quantitative evidence.

Research Design

The preference of an SLR was not by chance, since it is a strong tool in terms of locating, analysing, and synthesising a wide range of academic and industrial research and maintaining an acute vigilance on the influence of bias. The scope of the work, i.e., January 2020-April 2024, enabled us to capture the latest trends in the governance of IoT. PRISMA was our guidepost, and we used four consecutive steps:

- Identification- finding of appropriate literature by use of a well-tuned set of keywords.
- Screening- elimination of duplications and studies that were out of our scope.
- Eligibility - evaluation on strict inclusion criteria.

- Inclusion- ultimate choice of studies which satisfied our quality and relevance criteria.

The sources of data adopted Scopus, Web of Science, IEEE Xplore, ScienceDirect, ACM Digital Library, and Google Scholar where exhaustive coverage of academic works was guaranteed. To incorporate real and policy worldviews into the tapestry we also considered grey literature including reports, white papers published by Gartner, International Data Corporation (IDC), the World Economic Forum, and the European Commission. This two-source approach provided theoretical and practical information concerning IoT ethics and trust governance.

Data Selection and Search Strategy

We designed our search carefully, with the use of Boolean operators and controlled vocabulary to enable the search to be as precise as possible. The initial word Internet of Things or IoT combined with the operational words, such as, ethical challenges, privacy issues, surveillance, bias in IoT, legal compliance, law of data protection, GDPR, CCPA, cybersecurity risks, IoT vulnerabilities, digital trust, and adoption of IoT. The results were limited to peer-reviewed publications published 2020 -24 and truncated and filtered to focus on contemporary relevance. All candidate studies were reviewed manually to ensure that they all aligned in terms of themes. The inclusion criteria were: (a) explicit emphasis on an ethical, legal, or security aspect of IoT; (b) empirical or conceptual rigour; and (c) full-text accessibility. In order to maintain focus and clarity, we filtered out studies that had nothing to do with the governance of the IoT or were published in other languages other than English.

Data Synthesis and Quality Assessment

Quality appraisal was based on modified standards of the CASP and AMSTAR2 toolkits. All the chosen articles were analysed in terms of research design validity, methodological clarity, theoretical value, and relevance to digital trust. The final synthesis was carried out with only medium to high-quality rated. A synthesis of qualitative thematic analysis and quantitative pattern recognition through the integrative review approach facilitated the discovery of common problems, including privacy of the data, bias in the algorithm, lack of cybersecurity, and gaps in regulations.

Limitations

Although it has systematic rigour it had a number of limitations. The literature can be biassed in favour of successful IoT trust models by publication bias, whereas failures are being under-reported. A restriction to English only cuts out possibly useful non-English literature and the pace of technological change suggests that by April 2024 and beyond emerging regulatory or cybersecurity technology could be out of scope. To overcome these limitations, the modern policy briefs of industry were included to support the academic corpus and maintain its relevance to the context.

Ethical Considerations

Since this study was based on literature found publicly and did not involve any human or animal subjects, it did not have to be approved ethically. However, the research was conducted in the strictest practises of academic honesty, reference standards and extensive documentation transparency. Every one of the methodological procedures was captured to ensure reproducibility and verifiability. The approach described below will create a strong, cross-functional basis of the problem of ethical, legal, and security issues of IoT. The study builds on a credible domain of knowledge that underpins conceptualisations as well as practical suggestions about digital trust in IoT governance by rigorously incorporating PRISMA-guided principles, quality databases, and grey literature.

SOLUTIONS AND RECOMMENDATIONS

The security, ethical, and legal issues which have been defining the markets of the Internet of Things (IoT) require the joint, multidisciplinary strategy that would unite the technological progress, the legal update, the organisational control, the empowerment of consumers, and the cooperation between the multiple stakeholders. To ensure the continued digital trust in the IoT ecosystems, the innovation should be accompanied by the accountability, transparency, and moral vision. The recommendations below outline a controlled roadmap towards the realisation of resilient, trustful and human-centric IoT environments.

Privacy- and Security-by-Design (PbD and SbD)

The integration of Privacy-by-Design (PbD) and Security-by-Design (SbD) concepts at the initial stages of the development of IoT is inherent. Privacy and security can no longer be considered as a post-deployment feature but should be seen as part of product architecture. The functionality-based collection of data, the default privacy settings that are user-friendly, the end-to-end encryption, and the pre-release penetration testing should be established by the practitioners. These are measures that reduce vulnerability and guarantee adherence to international data protection laws, including GDPR and CCPA, as well as strengthen consumer trust. Organisations that incorporate PbD and SbD models have a long term investment in ethical development of technologies, which improves their reputations and competitive edge in the international market.

Open Data Governance

The transparency of data governance practices determines the level of trust in the IoT systems. Most existing platforms are using long and vague privacy terms that blur the goals of data use and puzzle customers. Firms need to substitute them with brief, consumer-friendly privacy statements, consent forms that are interactive and simplified data-handling choices to allow users access, amend, or erase their data. An example of best-practise model can be viewed in the case of Apple App Privacy Labels that allow having properly disclosed information on data and make an informed decision. Open data practises provide information symmetry between the consumer and firms, which results in higher levels of engagement and brand loyalty. In addition to compliance with regulations, the transparency in ethics promotes long-term sustainability because it brings the business practises closer to the expectations of fairness and responsibility in society.

Alignment With Regulations and Legal Conformance

The world is fast changing its existing legal systems to accommodate data and AI issues related to IoT. Data minimisation, explicit consent, and algorithmic accountability are highlighted in the EU General Data Protection Regulation (GDPR), California Consumer Privacy Act (CCPA) and the proposed EU Artificial Intelligence Act (2023). In order to be compliant, organisations ought to embrace the following measures:

- Complete Data Protection Impact Assessment (DPIAs) at every stage of development.
- Establish Data Protection Officers (DPOs) to control the compliance and risk management.
- Initiate other cross-border compliance regimes to harmonise global activities.
- Use risk-based AI regulation to provide fairness, explainable and redress to users.

Regulatory compliance is not only a way of reducing regulatory fines, but also enhancing stakeholder trust. Organisations that conform to new international standards become respectable online citizens who can maintain long-term international relationships.

Corporate Digital Responsibility (CDR)

Corporate Digital Responsibility (CDR) is a continuation of Corporate Social Responsibility (CSR) into the digital space, prioritising moral responsibility in data management and technology development. The CDR-based IoT company integrates the concepts of fairness, accessibility, sustainability, and privacy protection into each phase of digital processes.

A successful CDR model entails:

Conscience development of products that value inclusivity and accessibility-

- Accountable data management, which holds accountability at the supply chain.
- Sustainable development of devices, which lessens the influence of e-waste and carbon emissions.
- Community involvement by creating awareness and involving stakeholders.

Companies that use robust CDR policies develop a stronger brand reputation, become distinct in morally responsible markets, and help to build social resiliency to cyber threats. CDR therefore makes ethical behaviour a source of strategic competitiveness and innovation.

Cybersecurity and Risk Management

Due to the size and the interdependent nature of IoT networks, specialised cyber risk management models are necessary. Multi-layered defence strategy should be implemented by organisations and it should be founded on the following key practises:

- Apply the latest firmware patches after deployment to overcome emerging vulnerabilities.
- Device and user authentication systems of identity and access management.
- Cybersecurity certification (e.g. ISO/IEC 27001) to show compliance and reliability.
- Artificial intelligence-based anomaly detectors to detect suspicious behaviour.
- Audit of vendors and supply-chain to avoid breach due to third-party dependencies.

A resilient cybersecurity stance will convert IoT ecosystems into a reactive framework to a predictive and adaptive security framework. The inclusion of AI analytics will increase the promptness of threat detection and response, without violating privacy and functionality.

Data Minimization, Openness, and Safeguarding

User empowerment is another enabler of digital trust that is critical. The ethical, privacy, and cybersecurity issues of connected devices are not well known to many consumers even despite the rampant use of the IoT. In addressing this gap, governments, industrial associations and civil organisations need to liaise in setting up:

- Digital safety campaign on IoTs.
- Security guidelines to all IoT devices mandatory.
- Certification programmes to harmonise the ethical and safety standards.

As soon as users are informed of their rights to use digital space and their duties related to the security of such usage, confidence is promoted and safer use of technology can be achieved. Educated consumers, on their end, reward responsible corporations with loyalty, which creates a self-majority culture of trust and responsibility.

Multi-Stakeholder Governance and Public-Private Partnerships (PPP)

IoT ecosystems cannot be managed also by only corporate or government controls, but cross-sectoral partnerships. PPP is essential in setting ethical standards of IoT development and security measures that can be used in changing technologies. Self-regulatory measures adopted by industries with the assistance of government agencies can facilitate harmonisation of ethical practises in the industries. An example to the benchmark is the Siemens Charter of Trust, a global alliance of cybersecurity players that has included key players in the industry to set some common standards of data protection and transparency. Open-source partnerships also improve transparency based on peer review, which allows collective innovation and responsibility. Multi stakeholder governance means that the IoT trust should not be a property privilege but a collective good.

Sector Recommendations

Due to the industry-specific character of the IoT applications, the context-specific trust frameworks are required:

- Healthcare IoT: Should ensure that there is strict adherence to HIPAA (U.S.) and GDPR (EU) when dealing with patient data. Interoperability of medical devices should be encrypted, data transferred through them should be authenticated and monitored in real-time to maintain confidentiality and safety (Wakili & Bakkali, 2024).
- Smart Cities: It needs to be institutionally transparent by means of open standards of data, involving citizens in the governance and properly spelling out accountability provisions. The cities ought to embrace the public consultation paradigm to guarantee civic confidence in urban surveillance and information analytics frameworks.
- Industrial IoT: Needs a strong intellectual property protection, safe operational technologies, and implementation of ethical AI to eliminate safety and reputational risks. The accountability in automated manufacturing environments requires ISO/IEC-compliant infrastructure and supervision of the manufacturing process by people, who is known as a human-in-the-loop.
- Consumer IoT: It needs simplified consent interfaces, privacy labels, and adaptive encryption protocols to help secure house devices better. To increase the confidence of the product life, manufacturers are expected to offer after sales services and compulsory firmware updates.
- To address potential ethical issues, AI integration must be performed ethically.

Ethical Artificial Intelligence Integration

- To eliminate the possibility of ethical challenges, the AI integration should be conducted in an ethical manner.

With the increased use of artificial intelligence in IoT systems, the principles of ethical AI cannot be ignored. These are fairness, explainability, transparency and accountability. The IoT-AI convergence should be regulated by the frameworks that foster human-centred design and free decision-making. Organisations are to perform:

Algorithms of Audits to Identify and Reduce the Discriminatory Results

- Explainability reviews To make sure that decisions made in the system can be explained by users as well as regulators.
- Human-in-the-loop processes to maintain moral and contextual control in critical systems.

These principles are in-built as they ensure that the IoT ecosystems prevent algorithmic damage and encourage fair innovation. IoT combined with ethical AI is therefore a future of sustainable technological change: in which machine intelligence supplements, instead of compromising human judgement.

Developing Trust in IoT Ecologies

Figure 1. Trust in IoT Ecosystems

Responsible IoT innovation is built upon and achieved through trust. It is nurtured via open administration, moral leadership and frequent communication. Companies that will turn ethical, legal, and security threats into strategic value will be able to become the leaders in the digital trust economy. Developing the belief-based IoT systems goes beyond the technical design, but it is an ethical obligation to defend the human dignity, justice, and strength in the known connected world. The institutionalisation of the strategies of building trust at every level of the IoT lifecycle, i.e., conceptualisation, implementation, and post-market maintenance, will be the key to sustained competitiveness and well-being of the society. The approach of ethical foresight, constant checking of compliance and active governance will guarantee that the Internet of Things technologies will help build a safe, fair, and sustainable cyber society.

FUTURE RESEARCH DIRECTIONS

Internet of Things (IoT) remains the technology that is redefining technology, business and society at a very fast rate. Nevertheless, this rapid expansion adds to more complicated ethical, legal and security issues that require forward-thinking and multi-disciplinary studies. Although the present state of regulations and technical reactions implies countermeasures to immediate security risks, greater gaps exist in the measurement of trust, the harmonisation of governance, predictive cybersecurity, and the integration of artificial intelligence into human. The future studies need to establish robust, flexible models that ensure the long-term digital trust, compatibility with the changing environment, and enforcement of international governance criteria.

Figure 2. Future Research Needs for Trust in IoT Ecosystems

IoT Systems Trust Metrics and Measurement

One of the highest priorities of research is to establish and quantify, and standardise metrics of trust. Current research mostly depends on subjective survey or proxy measures, which are not cross-sectoral (Wang et al., 2023). Further studies ought to come up with universal evidence-based models of measuring trust that will incorporate technological and human aspects of trust.

Suggested trust indices should look at:

- Security and reliability of devices,

- Transparency in data and practises of ethics,
- Mechanisms of user autonomy and consent, and
- Control and protection of privacy.

An integrated, multi-layered metric system of the integration of technical performance metrics and socio-ethical metrics will enable organisations and regulators dynamically to assess trust in the IoT lifecycle - deployment to decommissioning. Longitudinal research ought to follow the development of trust in different phases of the device usage and determine which factors cause the decline or restoration of the user confidence. Also, cross-cultural models should be used in research in order to investigate the perception of various societies towards privacy, corporate responsibility, and surveillance by the government. The result will empower the policymakers and businesses to create culturally aware trust systems that improve worldwide IoT usage and moral stability.

Cross-Border Data Governance and Global Harmonisation

IoT networks are transnational and international by nature, but the frameworks of data governance are incomplete. The comparison of the GDPR in EU, sectoral strategies in the U.S., and the Cybersecurity Law in China, and the newly developed frameworks of emerging economies poses a significant challenge in compliance to multinational providers of IoTs. Comparative studies of these regimes should be given preference in future research so as to establish the possibility of convergence and the feasible harmony mechanisms. There are two possible directions that the studies can suggest:

- Mutual recognition agreements: National regulators acknowledge some common data protection standards,
- International adequacy frameworks- reflecting the GDPR model of adequacy of cross-border data transfer.

The advent of sovereign data space and federated data architecture (e.g., GAIA-X, European Commission, 2022) is a promising basis of global interoperability. The scholars need to examine how such structures can reconcile the straddling requirements of security, innovation, and data sovereignty. Finally, harmonised international governance will minimise regulatory conflicts, increase the efficiency of compliance, and augment digital trust across borders, which is essential in industries like logistics, finance, and smart cities that act within cross-national boundaries.

Cybersecurity Risk Anticipation Predictive Analytics

The majority of the currently existing IoT security measures are reactive, meaning they deal with vulnerabilities after they have taken place. Due to the increased complexity of the IoT ecosystems, reactive paradigms have to be substituted by predictive ones. Future works must be aimed at creating AI-based predictive analytics that can:

- Real time detection of anomalous behaviours,
- In the case of anticipation of a cyber-attack in terms of behavioural pattern recognition, and
- Defence countermeasures are deployed automatically, prior to attacks (Radanliev et al., 2022).

By combining internet of things risk management with machine-learning-powered behavioural analytics, the cybersecurity preparedness can be revolutionised. Additionally, the supply-chain security, yet to be taken into account in the internet of things risk modelling, necessitates predictive frameworks to detect vulnerabilities involving the third-party vendors and manufacturing channels. The creation of such predictive functions will guarantee that internet of things based infrastructures are no longer response based incident-blocking frameworks, but proactive and anticipatory defence networks, which will enhance user trust and regulatory adherence.

Decentralised Identity and Blockchain Trust Models

Centralised identity management places users at the risk of severe security dangers that include data breaches, identity theft, and control loss on personal data. The future research on the IoT security should, consequently, focus on the research of the Decentralised Identity (DID) systems, which run on blockchain and distributed ledger technologies (DLT) (Gillis et al., 2023). Such technologies may facilitate user-owned identities, resilient authentication, and verifications that do not rely on central authorities, so that they are not tampered with. Research should analyse:

- Scalability and interoperability of a blockchain identity system,
- Implications of the DLT operations on the environment and energy, and
- Models of integration between DID and the current IoT authentication infrastructures.

Through further development of decentralised trust architectures, future IoT ecosystems have the capability to mitigate systemic vulnerabilities, facilitate data sovereignty, and provide the privacy preserving collaboration between devices and users across the globe.

Trust Formation Emotional AI and Behavioural Analytics

Emotions and behavioural patterns have significant effects on human trust in the systems of IoT. With the integration of the IoT into everyday life, Emotional AI that deciphers human emotions based on speech, facial expression, and sensor data can provide a way to a more empathetic and more adaptable system. Ethical integration of Emotional AI in the IoT should be investigated in the future to support:

- Individualised trust communication,
- Responsive device interfaces, emotive, and
- User mood or stress-based adaptive system control.

Simultaneously, behavioural research needs to examine how users respond to a breach of trust, such as privacy invasion or technical failures to devise recovery strategies that restore trust following the occurrence of such events. Emotionally intelligent IoT design will guarantee that the IoT devices do not only increase efficiency but also human well-being and digital empathy.

International Standards of IoT Ethics and Compliance

The lack of global ethical guidelines to IoT technologies has contributed to a dissimilarity in the practises that are responsible. Companies often make speed of commercialisation more important than ethical design, posing the dangers of exploitation and inequality. The future research ought to be in coming up with global standards of IoT ethics, which are based on the current ISO and IEEE standards.

Proposals include:

- Ethical certification labels of IoT devices should be created, as in Fair Trade certifications, with references to the principles of privacy, transparency, inclusivity, and sustainability.
- Establishment of industry-specific ethical principles in order to cover the peculiarities of healthcare, transport, education, and industrial practise.

International ethics councils to ensure adherence to ethics and promote shared responsibility.

Global ethical standards will even the competition between responsible innovators and unscrupulous players as well as protecting the consumer using signals of trust that are internationally recognised.

Sector Specific Research Agendas

The diversity of the applications of IoT requires sector-specific approaches to research to respond to the context-dependent ethical and legal challenges:

- Healthcare IoT (H-IoT): Future studies should ensure the safety of patient autonomy and confidentiality and apply predictive analytics in optimising care. Research needs to come up with ethical consent systems, curb algorithmic biases in diagnosis, and make linked medical machines more secure.
- Smart Cities: It should undertake research on how the citizens can be involved in the governance of urban data and provide democratic methods of allowing the citizens to monitor the surveillance and data gathering. Preservation of privacy and safety will be the primary concern of the upcoming model of urban innovations.
- Industrial IoT (IIoT): Investigation should focus on protection of intellectual property, resilience in operations and ethical automation. The study in redundancy planning, recovery of risks and accountability of self-operating system will enhance the accountability and reliability of industry.
- Agricultural and Environmental IoT: Research on the area should explore how the IoT data can benefit sustainability objectives without compromising the rights of farmers and local data possession in rural ecosystems.

It is through the alignment of moral issues with the challenges unique to the industry that researchers can guarantee that innovation will bring about welfare to the society in addition to economic development.

Expectant and All-Inclusive IoT Governance

The next stage of IoT should be to shift to anticipatory governance rather than reactive regulation which is a proactive form that incorporates resilience, inclusivity, and ethical foresight. Studies are needed to overcome the gaps between technology creators, policy makers, ethicists, behavioural scientists, and civil society.

The main priorities in the future are:

- Trust assessment mechanisms with socio-technical measures,
- International harmonisation of laws on data governance,

- Enhanced cybersecurity analytics on risk proactive threat reduction,
- No central authentication models that encourage user control,
- Affectively intelligent artificial intelligence improving user device empathy, and
- Global ethical certification systems by industry.

The multidisciplinary research that involves researchers and other stakeholders around the world will create the intellectual and ethical base of a fair, safe and trusted digital world. The following layer of the IoT development needs to promote not only innovation and efficiency, but also justice, transparency, and human dignity..

CONCLUSION

Internet of Things (IoT) is one of the most disruptive technological innovations of the twenty-first century that are transforming industries, economies, and societies in terms of unprecedented interconnectedness, automation, and data-driven intelligence. It has redefined efficiency, personalization and connectedness, and at the same time, it has created significantly serious ethical, legal, and security issues that cannot be ignored. The sustainability and legitimacy of the IoT ecosystems do not solely rely on the fact that technical development is going to continue but instead a concerted effort to resolve those premises issues via the process of trust, transparency, and ethical governance. In this chapter, this chapter analysed critically the key role played by trust in both the success and acceptance of the impact of IoT systems to the society. Trust is the essential engine on which users interact, institutions become innovative and markets grow. In its absence, technology development is endangered of rejection by the population, government regulation, and loss of reputation. Trust construction and sustenance, therefore, has to be conceptualised as an ongoing, multi-dimensional affair enshrined in each phase of the IoT system design, implementation, and management. The relationships among technological reliability, moral leadership, legal compliance, and social responsibility influence the effect on the trust in the IoT ecosystems. Technology is not enough to create sustainable trust; it must be embedded within the organisation, where privacy protection, data security, fairness, and inclusiveness are pushing their systems to the core of their system design and governance. Privacy by Design (PbD), Security by Design (SbD), and Ethical Artificial Intelligence (AI) are the approaches that should be implemented as the cornerstones instead of the add-ons. Ethical foresight will enable developers to foresee the possible harms, respect human rights and make innovation relevant to the values and dignity of the people.

Reliable IoT systems can be based on four interdependent ethical principles, namely: autonomy, beneficence, non-maleficence, and justice. The principles offer empowerment to users, protect ownership of data, and enhance fair access to the advantages of technology among different communities. All stages of the IoT design and functioning should be associated with transparency, which will contribute to the popular awareness and trust in digital systems. Instead, ethical governance must be formalised as an organisational form of governance and not a corporate social responsibility issue or a form of compliance. Regulatory compliance is not sufficient to bring people trust whereas legal mechanisms like the GDPR, CCPA, and upcoming AI Acts stipulate essential protections to the privacy and accountability. Organisations need to surpass the legal requirements by adopting Corporate Digital Responsibility (CDR) models that consolidate ethical data management, sustainability, and inclusiveness. By having open operations and equitable innovation, the companies may turn the ethical behaviour into the reputational capital, thus attaining a competitive edge in the growing ethics-oriented international market. Ethical excellence has been made a business requirement in the digital economy.

Cybersecurity and infrastructural resilience is another foundation of IoT trust. The conventional model of responding to incidents of cyber threats by reactive means has been found to be insufficient in an environment where there are billions upon billions of interconnected, low-security devices. The future of cybersecurity needs to be more predictive and AI-enhanced defence features that can help in detecting vulnerabilities and curbing them prior to exploitation. This transformation implies secure-by-design production, active intrusion detection and enhanced supply-chain integrity. Organisational and human factors such as awareness of the employee, data processing and errors prevention should be given an equivalent weight as compared to technical protection. Protection to vulnerabilities on humans and systems should, therefore, be comprehensive to ensure that there is total spectrum protection. To obtain trust at scale, it is necessary to have multi-stakeholder governance, which involves governments, corporations, academia, and civil society. Every stakeholder has its own role: governments create protective regulation; corporations incorporate ethics and security in the product design and development; academic institutions produce evidence-based knowledge; and civil organisations promote the idea of digital rights and literacy. Cooperation structures promote transparency and accountability as well as collective responsibility in the management of IoT ecosystems. Different types of tools, including institutionalizing confidence in connected technologies, will be essential: public-private partnerships, open standards, and certification mechanisms, including ethical device trust labels.

Public education and awareness are also a source of sustainable trust. Connected devices have a high risk of vulnerability because users do not think of the ethical and security consequences of the technology used. Technological diffusion has to be accompanied by broad-based digital literacy programs, which will allow users to make the correct choice and implement safe digital habits. Educated users will be able to act in a more responsible manner and the circle of trust continues to thrive with a positive feedback loop. Priorities in research required in the future to maintain trust in the IoT are also identified in this chapter. To assess privacy, security, and ethical compliance in a transparent manner, standardised values of trust and evaluation systems should be created. The implementation of machine learning and behavioural analytics in predictive models of cybersecurity will allow detecting threats and vulnerabilities early. Similarly, decentralised identity systems based on blockchain provide some promising platforms to secure authentication, user-sovereignty, and distributed trust.

Moreover, Emotional AI and human-machine interaction research should enhance our knowledge about the mechanisms of the development, decline, and recovery of trust in the digital space. IoT systems with emotional intelligence can enhance the user experience with understanding and responding interfaces. Research in global data governance should be also able to follow the cross-border harmonisation or the goals of balancing innovation, sovereignty, and cultural diversity to facilitate responsible international data flows. Furthermore, specialised ethical standards are necessary in specialised areas of healthcare IoT, smart cities, and industrial automation, as each requires a specific moral and regulatory set of demands. In essence, this research will prove that the success of IoT ecosystems is not flowing entirely through the sophistication of the technology but human perception, values and relationships. Systems that seem opaque, unfair, or disempowering are not accepted by users irrespective of the functionality of the systems. Authentic innovation is thus required to be based on ethical design, open communication and cultural understanding that appeal to human needs and societal standards.

The future of IoT will be based on a compromise between innovation and integrity, autonomy and accountability, and efficiency and kindness. The development of reliable IoT systems needs collaboration between technical integrity, moral vision, legal safeguard, and social integration. Not only the governments, but also corporations and citizens should help to create the culture of accountability and respect in the digital sphere. Finally, the IoT era is based on trust and operates in a currency of trust. It is impossible to legislate or engineer it alone, it needs to be nurtured through incessant moral interaction and open cooperation. Our technological advancement will be limited to the collective capacity of the community to harmonise technology advancements with human dignity, justice, and social well-being in the future. With the incorporation of ethical, legal, and security concepts into each step of the IoT development, we will be able to make sure that innovation and humanity move in one direction, to the secure, inclusive, and sustainable digital future.

REFERENCES

Ajzen, I. (1991). The theory of planned behavior. *Organizational Behavior and Human Decision Processes*, *50*(2), 179–211. DOI: 10.1016/0749-5978(91)90020-T

Dodiya, K. R., Jha, M., & Jha, S. (2024). Fortifying the digital forge: unleashing cybersecurity in the interconnected world of digital manufacturing. In *Emerging Technologies in Digital Manufacturing and Smart Factories* (pp. 230–256). IGI Global Scientific Publishing. DOI: 10.4018/979-8-3693-0920-9.ch014

El-Khoury, M., & Arikan, C. L. (2021). From the internet of things toward the internet of bodies: Ethical and legal considerations. *Strategic Change*, *30*(3), 307–314. DOI: 10.1002/jsc.2411

IDC. (2022). *Worldwide Internet of Things Spending Guide*. International Data Corporation.

Ishmaev, G. (2020). The ethical limits of blockchain-enabled markets for private IoT data. *Philosophy & Technology*, *33*(3), 411–432. DOI: 10.1007/s13347-019-00361-y

Karale, A. (2021). The challenges of IoT addressing security, ethics, privacy, and laws. *Internet of Things : Engineering Cyber Physical Human Systems*, *15*, 100420. DOI: 10.1016/j.iot.2021.100420

Kounelis, I., Baldini, G., Neisse, R., Steri, G., Tallacchini, M., & Pereira, A. G. (2014). Building trust in the human? internet of things relationship. *IEEE Technology and Society Magazine*, *33*(4), 73–80. DOI: 10.1109/MTS.2014.2364020

Nanda, P., & Kumar, V. (2024). New generation technologies: Development vs. ethical challenges. *International Journal of Business Information Systems*, *46*(3), 411–434. DOI: 10.1504/IJBIS.2024.140437

Nastjuk, I., Trang, S., & Papageorgiou, E. I. (2022). Smart cities and smart governance models for future cities. *Electronic Markets*, *32*(4), 1917–1924. DOI: 10.1007/s12525-022-00609-0

Page, M. J., McKenzie, J. E., Bossuyt, P. M., Boutron, I., Hoffmann, T. C., Mulrow, C. D., & Moher, D. (2021). The PRISMA 2020 statement: an updated guideline for reporting systematic reviews. bmj, 372.

Sasikala, B., & Sachan, S. (2024). Decoding decision-making: embracing explainable AI for trust and transparency. Exploring the frontiers of artificial intelligence and machine learning technologies, 42.

Tzafestas, S. G. (2018). Ethics and law in the internet of things world. Smart cities, 1(1), 98-120.

Vettriselvan, R., Vijai, C., Patel, J. D., Sharma, P., & Kumar, N. (2024, March). Blockchain embraces supply chain optimization by enhancing transparency and traceability from production to delivery. In *2024 International Conference on Trends in Quantum Computing and Emerging Business Technologies* (pp. 1-6). IEEE. DOI: 10.1109/TQCEBT59414.2024.10545308

Wakili, A., & Bakkali, S. (2024). Internet of Things in healthcare: An adaptive ethical framework for IoT in digital health. Clinical eHealth, 7, 92-105.

Yadav, D., Yadav, A., & Singh, S. (2024). Concerns, Threats, and Ethical Considerations in Using Cloud of Things. In Cloud of Things (pp. 345-364). Chapman and Hall/CRC.

KEY TERMS AND DEFINITIONS

Blockchain in IoT: The application of blockchain technology to secure, authenticate, and manage IoT device communications and transactions through distributed ledgers that ensure transparency, immutability, and trust.

Corporate Digital Responsibility (CDR): The extension of corporate social responsibility into the digital sphere, emphasizing ethical data management, cybersecurity, privacy, digital sustainability, and stakeholder engagement in technological contexts.

Cross-Border Data Governance: The establishment of legal and operational frameworks that regulate the flow, storage, and protection of personal and industrial data across national borders, balancing sovereignty, privacy, and innovation.

Decentralized Identity (DID): A digital identity model in which users maintain ownership and control over their personal information through cryptographic mechanisms, reducing reliance on centralized authorities for authentication.

Digital Trust: The confidence stakeholders have in the reliability, integrity, and ethical behavior of digital technologies, systems, and providers, particularly regarding data protection, privacy, and security.

Ethical AI: Artificial intelligence systems designed and operated according to ethical principles, including fairness, accountability, transparency, and respect for human rights, particularly in contexts involving data-driven IoT applications.

Internet of Things (IoT): A network of interconnected physical devices embedded with sensors, software, and other technologies, enabling data collection, exchange, and remote control across digital and physical environments.

Predictive Cybersecurity: The use of artificial intelligence, machine learning, and behavioral analytics to anticipate and prevent cyber threats before they materialize, shifting from reactive to proactive security strategies.

Privacy by Design (PbD): An approach to system engineering that embeds privacy considerations and user data protection into technology design from the earliest stages, ensuring that privacy is proactive, not reactive.

Security by Design (SbD): A methodology where security features are integrated into systems and devices from inception, rather than being added after development, ensuring resilience against cyber threats.

Chapter 10
Navigating the Ethics of Big Data:
Responsible AI and Data Governance in IoT-Powered Marketing

Lenah Cleo Kelepile
http://orcid.org/0009-0006-3734-1839
University of Namibia, Namibia

Noble Pete-I Gotolph Eiaseb
http://orcid.org/0009-0002-0318-9761
University of Namibia, Namibia

ABSTRACT

The marketing environment has seen a dramatic transformation with the introduction of the Internet of Things (IoT), which has made data-driven tactics and highly tailored client experiences possible. However, there are also serious ethical questions that have been brought up by the incorporation of IoT technology into marketing strategies, especially in relation to the gathering, storing, and use of enormous volumes of personal data. The significance of ethical oversight, strong data governance, and responsible AI has increased as businesses use Big Data and AI more and more to improve their marketing skills. The extensive literature review in this chapter is based solely on peer-reviewed publications from 2015 to 2025. Moreover, the chapter also explores ethical challenges raised by IoT-enabled marketing, concentrating on problems pertaining to data governance, responsible AI, and big data. The chapter ends with a framework for moral decision-making and practical recommendations for legislators, engineers, and marketers.

DOI: 10.4018/979-8-2600-1263-5.ch010

1. INTRODUCTION

The integration of Artificial Intelligence (AI) with the Internet of Things (IoT) is transforming, enabling businesses to automate processes, gather valuable insights, and tailor personalised experiences (Vemuri et al., 2022). According to Abbasi et al. (2024), as personal data collection increases, so do the concerns regarding privacy, security, and ethics. Transparent data governance and responsible standards are essential to maintaining trust and complying with regulations (Kalla & Smith, 2024). Furthermore, Vemuri et al. (2022), Kalla and Smith (2024) maintain that as more companies adopt Big Data (BD) and AI, fairness, transparency, and accountability are essential.

An inference can be drawn that with globalisation and liberalisation of free trade, ensuring ethical integration of AI and IoT could further propel international marketing (Abbasi et al., 2024). This could result in developing countries getting into new developed markets. Moreover, this could increase the GDP, infrastructural development, and life expectancy of those living in emerging economies (Kalla & Smith, 2024; Abbasi et al., 2024; Vemuri et al., 2022). This chapter addresses key ethical issues, including data governance, consumer protection, and autonomous decision-making, providing a framework and guidance for the responsible use of AI in marketing.

1.1 Context and Background of AI and IoT in Marketing

The integration of Artificial Intelligence (AI) in marketing has significantly reshaped business-consumer interactions, enabling more data-driven, efficient, and personalised experiences (Galli & Ocampo, 2019). Key applications such as predictive analytics leverage machine learning and big data to forecast consumer behaviour, improve targeting, and boost campaign outcomes (Lee et al., 2022).

AI-powered predictive tools can increase conversion rates by up to 15%, as businesses can tailor offerings based on historical patterns (Analytics McKinsey Report, 2016). In supporting Lee et al. (2022) contend that AI also enhances pricing strategies and customer retention through dynamic adjustments and timely outreach. In addition to data analytics, Galli and Ocampo (2019) aver that AI-powered tools such as chatbots and virtual assistants enable 24/7 engagement, streamlining service delivery and reducing operational costs.

Shafique et al. (2024), Kar and Haldar (2016) maintain that these technologies provide instant, personalised support, which is highly valued by modern consumers. Furthermore, 60% of companies utilise chatbots, with 75% of users preferring immediate responses. AI also revolutionises content creation through automated, personalised messaging across platforms, boosting consumer loyalty and sales as demonstrated by Sephora's 25% sales increase through AI beauty recommendations (Mansouri & Bezgrari, 2022). Furthermore, AI promotes inclusive marketing by enhancing accessibility for users with disabilities through image recognition and voice-command features (Jayadatta, 2023).

Looking ahead, Jayadatta (2023) maintains that AI will continue to evolve, with emerging applications such as influencer analytics, real-time ROI measurement, and advanced attribution modelling offering deeper marketing insights. These innovations will enable firms to optimise their customer journey strategies while navigating ethical considerations in data usage (Lee et al., 2022). The future of AI in marketing thus demands a balance between technological advancement and responsible practice to maintain consumer trust and competitiveness in an increasingly digital landscape (Shafique et al., 2024).

1.2 Problem Statement

The rise of AI in marketing has called for a renewed emphasis on ethical principles, especially fairness and explain-ability (Kumar & Suthar, 2024). Explainable AI (XAI) strives to clarify algorithmic decisions by offering interpretable outputs that both marketers and consumers can easily grasp (Su et al., 2023; Hermann, 2022). Furthermore, Kumar and Suthar (2024) assert that this transparency is vital for building trust and accountability, particularly when AI systems influence customer targeting or pricing choices.

Additionally, fairness in AI involves actively removing biases that could lead to discriminatory outcomes, ensuring that AI-driven marketing does not unfairly affect specific demographic groups (Eid et al., 2024). Organisations must implement governance like regular AI audits to detect bias and ensure fairness, with ethics committees overseeing compliance and safeguarding against risks (Gonçalves et al., 2023). Consumer empowerment is also crucial: people should control their data via opt-in/opt-out and access transparency dashboards showing how their data is used in marketing (Hermann, 2022).

Ultimately, Oluwafemi et al. (2021) maintain that by balancing automation with human oversight is key to ethical AI. Furthermore, while AI boosts efficiency and personalization, it should not replace human judgment in critical decisions (Ejjami, 2024; Oluwafemi et al., 2021). Marketing teams need ongoing training in AI ethics, bias detection, and responsible use to assess and intervene in outputs (Floridi et al., 2018).

Subsequently, Ejjami (2024) further propounds that with ethical awareness and proper tools, businesses can ensure AI enhances consumer trust and brand strength. Consequently, without proper guidelines and data governance structures in place, exploitation of customers could possibly increase (Karami et al., 2024). As a result,

Karami et al. (2024), Ejjami (2024) assert that customers might lose money, personal information, reputational damage which could possibly end in depression, ill health and ultimate skyrocketing of suicide rates and ultimate death.

Moreover, the challenges associated with AI integration with IoT should be considered and dealt with promptly before adverse result manifest (Moradi, 2021; Rosário & Raimundo, 2025). Therefore, this paper sets out to undertake a comprehensive literature review to address major challenges and provide strategic actionable recommendations that could be used in ethical marketing the age of AI, BD and IoT.

2. LITERATURE REVIEW

2.1 Emerging AI-Driven Technologies in Digital Marketing

2.1.1 Predictive Analytics

Lee et al. (2022) found that predictive analytics, which are powered by AI are key to data-driven marketing and business strategy. Furthermore, predictive analytics uses machine learning to analyse historical and real-time data, detecting patterns and forecasting consumer behaviour to personalise experiences (Lee et al., 2022). Moreover, Galli and Ocampo (2019) assert that the growth of big data from transactions, social media, IoT, and browsing histories has made predictive analytics more effective. This is more especially evident in e-commerce where personalised recommendations boost engagement and loyalty (Galli & Ocampo, 2019).

In addition, these insights help target marketing, optimise inventory, and develop products. The rise of predictive analytics is attributed to increased access to data, enhanced computing power, and user-friendly platforms such as Hadoop and Spark (Raeesi-Vanani et al., 2025). Furthermore, Saleh et al. (2024) maintains that advanced algorithms, including deep learning, enhance prediction accuracy for unstructured data such as text, images, or video. In competitive markets, businesses utilise these tools to remain agile, responding quickly to shifts in consumer demand, preventing churn, and better matching products to their target markets (Saleh et al., 2024). Companies like Netflix and Amazon analyse data to segment audiences and suggest content, strengthening consumer ties.

Furthermore, Raeesi-Vanani et al. (2025) explicates predictive analytics offers benefits but faces challenges like data privacy, ethics, and model reliability. Compliance with regulations such as GDPR is vital to avoid legal and reputational risks. Model accuracy depends on high-quality data, but over-relying on past data can miss emerging trends, requiring regular updates. Skills shortages hinder deployment, emphasising the need for skilled professionals (Saleh et al., 2024). As AI and IoT evolve, future analytics will involve real-time data, natural language processing, and increased emphasis on ethics and transparency.

2.1.2 Automated Decision-Making

AI is transforming digital marketing by enabling real-time optimisation through data-driven decision-making. Moreover, companies leverage AI tools like machine learning, programmatic advertising, and predictive analytics to boost efficiency and engagement (Araujo et al., 2020). Additionally, with over 2.5 quintillion bytes of data daily, traditional methods are inadequate, prompting firms to adopt AI for precise targeting, dynamic content, and rapid responses (Ivanov, 2023).

Ivanov (2023) further assert that AI's ability to interpret complex data in real time gives businesses a competitive edge, helping them anticipate consumer behaviour and adapt strategies. Subsequently, AI enhances marketing through automated media buying with live data, improving targeting, and reducing costs, and through chatbots providing instant support and lead generation (Araujo et al., 2020). Sentiment analysis and social listening help assess public opinion for campaign adjustments, enabling hyper-personalisation that boosts loyalty and engagement (Waldman, 2019).

However, Waldman (2019) contends that reliance on large datasets raises privacy, bias, and transparency issues, demanding ethical oversight and responsible data use. In support, Lomborg et al. (2023) propound that AI will keep reshaping marketing with advances in natural language processing, voice search, and augmented reality, offering insights into consumer intent and engaging brand interactions. Additionally, AI's potential is vast, but should support rather than replace human creativity and emotional intelligence. Companies balancing AI's efficiency with ethics will lead in digital marketing (Lomborg et al., 2023). Maintaining consumer trust through transparency is crucial for sustainable AI marketing.

2.1.3 Smart Devices & Wearables

The IoT has emerged as a transformative force in marketing, enabling brands to gather real-time, high-volume data through interconnected smart devices. Moreover, by linking wearables, smartphones, and home automation systems, marketers gain access to granular insights into consumer behaviour, preferences, and lifestyle pattern (Dehghani & Dangelico, 2017). Shei et al. (2022) argue that this has allowed companies to move beyond traditional mass marketing toward hyper-personalised campaigns that resonate on an individual level, increasing relevance and conversion.

Furthermore, through two-way communication channels, brands can now interact dynamically with users, adjusting promotions based on contextual and behavioural triggers (Shei et al., 2022). Smart devices, especially wearables and mobile sensors, are crucial for tracking behaviour. They collect data like location, heart rate, and activity, allowing marketers to personalise offers in real time (Bathla et al., 2022). For example, fitness wearables can promote supplements or workout gear based on activity, creating targeted advertising.

Ultimately, Maiorescu et al. (2020) assert that data analytics and machine learning enhance IoT data by uncovering patterns and predicting behaviours, enabling companies to customise marketing and improve engagement and loyalty. Iot marketing offers benefits but raises privacy and ethical issues. Sensitive data, especially health info, needs safeguards and clear communication to build trust. Regulations like GDPR stress ethical data practices, requiring consent and opt-outs (Maiorescu et al., 2020). As IoT grows, trends like AI, AR, and voice devices will reshape marketing. Success depends on balancing innovation with responsible data handling.

2.1.4 Connected Retail Experiences

The integration of IoT in retail enhances customer engagement through real-time, context-specific interactions. Devices like beacons and sensors collect behavioural data to send personalised promotions via smartphones based on proximity and preferences (Gupta et al., 2025). Beacons, Bluetooth transmitters, deliver alerts like discounts or recommendations when customers enter store zones, enriching shopping (Hudson et al., 2025). These tools help retailers understand foot traffic, optimise layouts, and tailor marketing, boosting satisfaction and loyalty.

According to Gupta et al. (2025), real-time IoT insights let retailers quickly respond to consumer behaviour and market shifts. Sensors track dwell times and product interactions, aiding predictive models for inventory and sales. Data on co-purchases can inform bundling, while shelf sensors prevent stockouts with alerts (Rosário & Raimundo, 2025). Connecting in-store and online data provides a complete customer view, enhancing targeting and efficiency. This data-driven approach offers a competitive edge.

Deploying IoT in retail marketing faces challenges like consumer privacy concerns, especially around location tracking and data collection. Transparent policies, opt-in systems, and regulations like GDPR are vital for trust (Hudson et al., 2025). High costs, integration issues, and possible tech failures demand strategic planning and skilled staff. Future advances in AI, AR, and voice systems will enhance personalisation. Retailers adopting these innovations while managing ethical and operational issues will lead connected commerce.

2.1.5 Behavioural Tracking

The IoT is transforming digital marketing by enabling real-time behavioural tracking through interconnected devices like wearables, appliances, and sensors. These devices gather detailed data on consumer actions, preferences, and routines, providing marketers with insights into user engagement (Priyadharshini et al., 2024). Technologies such as fitness trackers and smart home appliances monitor lifestyle habits and product interactions. Cloud computing and real-time analytics process large data, allowing marketers to quickly adapt strategies.

Kravets et al. (2025) assert that IoT's behavioural tracking enables hyper-personalisation, predictive marketing, and better customer engagement. Behavioural tracking scales personalised experiences by tailoring content to behaviours and provides real-time feedback for prompt interactions, boosting loyalty (Kravets et al., 2025). Predictive models help marketers anticipate needs, optimise inventory, and create bundles to increase sales. This adaptive approach strengthens consumer-brand relationships and supports agile marketing.

However, Bădică and Mitucă (2021) state that balancing automation with human creativity is essential for authentic implementation. Despite its benefits, IoT marketing raises ethical and operational concerns. Continuous data collection challenges transparency, consent, and GDPR compliance (Bădică & Mitucă (2021). The rise of IoT devices increases cybersecurity risks, needing better protection. Relying too much on behavioural data may overlook emotional and cultural nuances crucial for marketing. As IoT and AI evolve, future strategies must focus on responsible data use, ethics, and user-centred design to sustain trust and long-term success (Lee, 2020).

2.2 Ethical Challenges in AI-Driven IoT Marketing

The convergence of AI, IoT, and marketing presents opportunities for personalisation but raises ethical concerns such as privacy, consent, bias, and manipulation as companies utilise AI to interpret IoT data (Fares & Jammal, 2023). This section reviews these challenges in AI-enabled IoT marketing. Understanding AI and IoT in marketing is key. IoT connects devices like smart appliances and health monitors, collecting data on preferences and interactions. Businesses use these data for targeted marketing, with AI analysing it to predict behaviour and customise messages. For example, a smart fridge might suggest recipes or ads based on food consumption. While enhancing personalisation, these practices also pose ethical concerns about data collection and use (Alam, 2025; Alhitmi et al., 2024).

2.2.1 Privacy and Data Security

According to Tasnim et al. (2025), one of the most urgent ethical issues is privacy. IoT devices naturally collect sensitive information about their users, often without their explicit consent or awareness. For example, a fitness tracker records an individual's daily activities and health metrics, which can be shared with third-party companies for marketing purposes. Consequently, without strict regulations, users may not be aware of how their data is being used, leading to a serious breach of privacy (Rosário & Raimundo, 2025).

Additionally, the storage and transmission of this data are vulnerable to cyberattacks, which can result in breaches exposing personal information. Businesses must strike a careful balance between utilising consumer data to enhance marketing and protecting consumers' privacy rights (Tasnim et al., 2025). Ethical considerations necessitate open communication about data collection, robust security measures, and transparent consent procedures.

2.2.2 Informed Consent

Linked closely to privacy issues is the concept of informed consent. As a result of the complexities of AI-driven IoT marketing, many consumers may not realise how much data is collected, analysed, and used. Traditional consent processes often fall short, as terms and conditions tend to be lengthy and filled with jargon that obscure the true implications of data sharing (Neisse et al., 2015; Tanczer et al., 2017). Marketers should prioritise clear and simple communication about consent. Subsequently, to ethically involve consumers, organisations should implement frameworks that allow for easily understandable consent procedures, making sure individuals know exactly what they agree to when using IoT devices. Moreover, consent should be an ongoing process, not a one-time event, allowing consumers to regularly manage their data sharing preferences (Pathmabandu et al., 2023)

2.2.3 Bias and Fairness

An important challenge in AI-driven IoT marketing is bias in AI algorithms. Machine learning models depend heavily on training data. Furthermore, Al-Hitmi and Sherif (2018) found that if this data contains biases related to race, gender, or socio-economic background, algorithms can reinforce these biases. For example, targeting certain demographics based on past purchasing behaviour without considering diversity can exclude marginalised groups. Addressing bias requires fairness and equity, with organisations prioritising diverse data collection and regular bias audits. Transparency in algorithm development and datasets is also crucial. An inclusive AI approach helps marketers serve diverse customers ethically (Al-Hitmi et al., 2024).

2.2.4 Manipulation and Autonomy

AI's predictive capabilities can lead to manipulation, raising ethical questions about consumer autonomy. According to Tokeley (2021), when marketing exploits personal data to influence behaviour, it risks undermining free choice. For example, if an AI predicts a user will buy a product based on IoT data, it might target them with tailored ads, pushing impulsive decisions. This raises the question of whether decisions are truly autonomous or shaped by algorithms (Tokeley, 2021). Ethical marketing should respect consumer autonomy, empowering rather than manipulating. Balancing this is key to maintaining trust and long-term loyalty (Janiesch et al., 2019).

2.2.5 Regulatory Compliance and Accountability

Given the ethical issues surrounding AI-driven IoT marketing, regulatory compliance is essential. Governments and organisations globally enacting laws address data and AI ethics. Europe's GDPR offers a framework to protect data and privacy (Chowdhury, 2019; Grant & Agoro, 2021). Meeting regulations is crucial for ethical business and customer trust. Accountability in AI deployment is key, involving legal adherence and internal ethical guidelines. Companies should form interdisciplinary teams with ethicists, technologists, and marketers to evaluate social impact and uphold ethical principles (Furfaro et al., 2022).

2.2.6 Consumer Advocacy and Education

Ultimately, the ethical considerations in AI-driven IoT marketing call for greater consumer advocacy and education. Consumers should be aware of their rights related to data privacy and the implications of using IoT devices (Al-Hogail, 2018). Additionally, by empowering consumers with this knowledge, they can make informed choices and hold companies accountable for maintaining ethical standards. Educating them on data usage and privacy management fosters a sense of control and promotes responsible behaviour (Dornak, 2025).

Moreover, Dornak (2025) assert that businesses can gain from partnering with advocacy groups and engaging consumers in discussions on data ethics, ensuring their marketing aligns with societal values. Ultimately, the ethical challenges of AI-driven IoT marketing are complex and require careful consideration from all stakeholders. In addition, as technological advancements continue, the importance of transparency, accountability, and fairness becomes even more critical (Suklabaidya, 2024).

Furthermore, Suklabaidya (2024) states that marketers must navigate issues such as privacy, consent, bias, manipulation, and regulatory compliance while fostering an environment that benefits consumers rather than exploits them. Therefore, by implementing ethical standards, companies can leverage AI and IoT to create personalised, impactful experiences, all while protecting customer trust and well-being (Harkin et al., 2022; Dornak, 2025). Finally, moving into an era driven by smart technology, a dedication to ethical practices will shape the future of marketing and its societal influence.

2.3 Responsible Data Governance in IoT Marketing

In the digital age, integrating IoT into marketing has transformed how businesses engage consumers. IoT devices generate vast data to improve customer experiences and optimise operations (Saluja et al., 2024). However, IoT marketing raises ethical concerns, making responsible data governance crucial to protect privacy and uphold standards. Ethical AI in IoT marketing helps businesses manage data use, ensure compliance, build trust, and promote sustainability (Collins et al., 2024). Responsible data governance refers to a framework that ensures the proper management, protection, and ethical use of data throughout its lifecycle.

In IoT marketing, this covers key aspects such as data collection, storage, analysis, sharing, and disposal. Furthermore, with the expected rise of over 75 billion IoT devices by 2025, the need for robust governance structures becomes even more critical (Trautman et al., 2020). Collins et al. (2024) maintain that companies must develop clear policies on data collection methods, access rights, processing procedures, and security measures to prevent unauthorised access or data breaches. Good data governance also guarantees compliance with laws like GDPR and CCPA, which require transparent data practices and inform consumers about what data is collected, used, stored, and shared. Non-compliance can result in heavy fines and reputational damage. Therefore, organisations should implement strict governance policies aligned with these regulations to foster customer trust (Saluja et al., 2024).

2.3.1 The Role of Ethical AI in IoT Marketing

AI analyses large IoT datasets and raises ethical issues in marketing, such as fairness, accountability, transparency, and privacy. Ethical AI ensures data analysis and decisions do not discriminate or manipulate consumers (Oladosu et al., 2024). In addition, while AI tailors marketing by scrutinising habits and demographics, biased data can perpetuate inequalities, leading to unfair targeting or neglect. Organisations should use diverse data and monitor results to prevent discrimination.

2.3.2 Key Principles of Responsible Data Governance in IoT Marketing

Responsible data governance is an integral part of ensuring that consumers are not taken advantage of or harmed. Additionally, with the advent of internationalisation and international trade, integrating IoT and marketing has helped organisations reach more customers in an effective and efficient manner (Sargiotis, 2024). Furthermore, to effectively implement responsible data governance and promote ethical AI practices within IoT-driven marketing, businesses should follow several core principles as stipulated hereunder.

2.3.2.1 Transparency

Organisations must be open about their data practices, informing customers about data collection methods, purposes, and usage. This not only builds trust but also allows consumers to make informed decisions regarding their data. Additionally, customers are more likely to spend more when they trust an organisation. An inference could be made that organisations that lack transparency are more likely to lose customer, competitive advantage, and eventual failure (Moradi, 2021).

2.3.2.2 Consent

Obtaining clear consent from consumers before data collection is essential. This fosters a sense of ownership and control for individuals over their personal information. Consent mechanisms should be straightforward, enabling users to opt-in or opt-out effortlessly. In addition, open consent protocols for consumers allows for a clear and transparent professional relationship between the organisation and the consumer (Sargiotis, 2024). Consequently, this could break down barriers and miscommunication. Thereby, allowing a higher customer retention rate.

2.3.2.3 Data Minimisation

Collecting only the necessary data for specific marketing objectives minimises the potential for misuse. Limiting the amount of data gathered reduces risks linked to data breaches and boosts consumer confidence. Data minimisation could also allow increased consumer awareness and ensure responsible data collection by organisations (Oladosu et al., 2024). However, many organisations collect huge amount of customer data without a sole specific purpose. This could lead to breakdown of customer trust and increase customer attrition and subsequent loss of lucrative markets.

2.3.2.4 Security

Employing robust security measures to protect consumer data from unauthorised access is crucial. This includes using encryption, conducting regular security audits, and providing employee training on data protection protocols. Cyber security risk has increased with hackers and illicit data breaches. As a result, it is quite evident that security protocols are implemented by organisations in order to ensure consumer data is protected (Das & Mitra, 2024).

2.3.2.5 Accountability

Organisations must be responsible for their data practices, ensuring all stakeholders understand their roles in upholding ethical standards. This accountability extends to third-party vendors involved in data processing (Sargiotis, 2024). Furthermore, accountability could possibly instil trust and ensure that customers data will be kept safe and only those entrusted have permission to access customer data.

2.3.2.6 Regular Audits and Assessments

Performing regular audits of data procedures helps identify potential ethical issues or compliance breaches early. Organisations should carry out self-assessments of their AI systems to confirm they function without bias and follow ethical principles (Collins et al., 2024).

2.4 Integrating Ethical AI into IoT Marketing Strategies

Ethical AI has become very critical in todays' volatile global technology landscape. This is further made more urgent by international marketing and globalisation. The emergence of new markets for emerging economies in developed countries has necessitated the need for integrating ethical AI into IoT marketing strategies (Trautman et al., 2024; Collins et al., 2024). However, integrating ethical AI practices into IoT marketing requires a strategic approach that encompasses several stages of the marketing process as provided below.

2.4.1 Data Collection and Processing

Organisations must start by establishing guidelines for data collection that align with ethical standards as a first step. Furthermore, businesses should prioritise quality data that is relevant and representative. Moreover, by utilizing automated tools with built-in ethical checks can help in collecting and processing data responsibly (Petrescu et al., 2020).

2.4.2 Algorithm Development

When developing AI algorithms, organizations must prioritize fairness and inclusivity. This can involve diverse teams in the design phase, ensuring varied perspectives contribute to the algorithm's development. Additionally, organizations should employ fairness metrics to assess and refine their algorithms regularly (Das & Mitra, 2024).

2.4.3 Consumer Engagement

Engaging with consumers regarding their preferences and perspectives on data usage fosters a sense of partnership. Surveys, feedback forms, and open channels for communication can provide valuable insights into consumer attitudes toward data practices. This could enable clear communication lines establishment and create transparency (Koul & Sabrina, 2019).

2.4.4 Monitoring and Evaluation

Continuous monitoring of AI systems is vital to ensure they operate ethically over time. This involves assessing the impact of marketing strategies on different consumer groups and adjusting practices based on feedback and outcomes (Bangui et al., 2023).

2.4.5 Collaboration and Knowledge Sharing

Organizations should collaborate with industry peers, regulatory bodies, and academic institutions to share knowledge and best practices on ethical AI and data governance. This collaboration can foster innovative solutions to common challenges in IoT marketing (Onu et al., 2025).

2.5 Challenges and Solutions in Responsible Data Governance

While the principles outlined above establish a solid foundation for responsible data governance and ethical AI in IoT marketing, several challenges may arise (Koul & Sabrina, 2019). Finding robust solutions for challenges in responsible data governance is very important to ensure customers are protected, data is safe and there are clear ethical guidelines that are followed. Challenges and solutions in responsible data governance are provided hereunder.

2.5.1 Complexity of IoT Ecosystems

The interconnectedness of IoT devices can complicate data governance. To tackle this, organisations should create detailed data maps that outline data flows, sources, and destinations, ensuring transparency and accountability (Alves et al., 2024).

2.5.2 Rapid Technological Advancements

The quick pace of technological innovation can outpace current regulations. Organisations should advocate for flexible regulations that adapt as technology evolves, keeping frameworks relevant and practical (Marinova, 2024)

2.5.3 Consumer Scepticism

Many consumers remain wary of data collection practices. Enhancing transparency and providing clear value, such as personalised services or rewards, can help build trust and reduce scepticism (Bangui et al., 2023).

2.5.4 Resource Constraints

Smaller companies may lack the resources to establish comprehensive data governance. Collaborating with external compliance specialists or using cost-effective technology solutions can help smaller organisations uphold ethical standards (Onu et al., 2025). As IoT technology advances in marketing, responsible data governance and ethical AI are essential. Businesses must protect consumer rights and promote ethical use by adhering to transparency, consent, and accountability (Koul & Sabrina, 2019). These measures build trust and maximise Iot marketing potential. Ethical AI throughout marketing ensures strategies are effective, fair, and respectful of privacy. Committing to responsible data governance and ethical AI helps businesses succeed and have a positive impact on society (Marinova, 2024).

2.6 Ethical and Explainable AI in Marketing

As AI becomes more integrated into marketing systems, questions about fairness, transparency, accountability, and human agency become increasingly urgent. The ethical use of AI is no longer optional but a fundamental principle for organisations seeking to build trust and long-term relationships with customers (Gaur & Sahoo, 2022). This section examines key pillars that define the ethical use of AI in marketing, including fair and explainable AI, ethical audits, consumer empowerment, and human oversight.

2.6.1 Fair and Explainable AI

A major concern in AI-powered marketing is the lack of transparency in how algorithms make decisions. Many sophisticated AI models, particularly deep learning ones, act as black boxes, thereby making it hard for stakeholders to understand their decision processes (Hermann, 2022). This lack of clarity can damage trust and cause issues like discrimination or biased targeting. To combat this, there is an increasing focus on developing explainable XAI systems.

These prioritise interpretability, helping marketers, regulators, and consumers understand why specific outputs occur. For example, an AI recommending personalised ads should clarify the reasons, such as user behaviour or preferences. Additionally, fairness needs to be a key consideration in designing and deploying AI (Gaur & Sahoo, 2022). Marketing strategies driven by AI should be thoroughly assessed for fairness to prevent discrimination based on gender, race, age, or socioeconomic factors. Techniques like fairness-aware machine learning and bias mitigation algorithms are now incorporated during model training to support this goal (Kumar & Suthar, 2024).

2.6.2 Ethical AI Audits

Using AI ethically involves more than just good intentions; it requires established frameworks for accountability. One effective approach is conducting regular ethical AI audits (Mökander, 2023). Mökander (2023) further notes that these involve systematic reviews of AI models to detect and address issues like biases, discrimination, or unfair targeting. Such audits, LaBrie and Steinke (2019) propose should be performed frequently and updated based on evolving data, market changes, and social values. To enhance audit effectiveness, organisations should create independent ethics committees composed of experts from fields such as data science, law, ethics, consumer behaviour, and diversity, equity, and inclusion (DEI). These committees serve as governance bodies, overseeing AI design, deployment, and impact (LaBrie & Steinke, 2019). They also set ethical standards, review high-risk projects, and ensure regulatory compliance.

2.6.3 Consumer Empowerment

Respecting user autonomy is essential for ethical AI practice. Consumers should be informed about data use and have direct control over how their personal data is collected, stored, and used by AI systems (Du & Xie, 2021). One practical solution is to implement opt-in and opt-out options for AI-driven personalisation and tracking. These should be presented in clear, user-friendly language and interfaces to ensure informed consent rather than passive acceptance (Lim & Kim, 2024). Additionally, transparency dashboards can empower consumers to monitor data flows, understand how their data influences algorithmic decisions, and adjust their privacy settings in real-time. Such transparency tools not only comply with emerging data protection laws, such as the EU's General Data Protection Regulation (GDPR) or California's Consumer Privacy Act (CCPA), but also build consumer trust and loyalty by demonstrating a commitment to ethical standards (Park, 2019; Blanke, 2020; Voss, 2021) .

2.6.4 AI and Human Oversight

AI can automate many marketing tasks like content customisation and predictive analytics but cannot replace human judgment. Implementing ethical AI requires collaboration, where technology helps but does not replace critical decisions. Human oversight is key for detecting anomalies, verifying results, and handling ethical issues AI cannot manage (Holzinger et al., 2025). Moreover, Enqvist (2023) found that to achieve this balance, marketers need AI literacy- understanding AI, its ethics, and best practices. Ongoing training enables responsible AI interpretation, questioning algorithms, and addressing ethical concerns. This minimises risks and promotes responsibility and ethics in the organisation (Enqvist, 2023).

Holzinger et al. (2025) argue that as marketing advances in the AI era, ethical principles must stay at the forefront of innovation. Prioritising fairness, transparency, and accountability goes beyond just meeting regulations it is vital for long-term business success. According to Sayles (2024), organisations can achieve this by adopting explainable models, conducting ethical audits, empowering consumers, and ensuring robust human oversight. Ethical AI has evolved from being a theoretical ideal to a practical requirement for building a future where technology and trust coexist harmoniously (Salgado-Criado, 2025).

3. RECOMMENDATIONS

3.1 Governance and Policy Recommendations

- Create national localised legal compliance protocols in order to ensure accountability.
- Ensure the implementation of protocols and mechanisms for opt-in and opt-out ease for users.
- Ensure implementation of data retention frameworks and limitations.
- Ensure human consent oversight of AI systems and processes by requiring documentation provision for automated decision making.

- Provide clear and transparent partnerships and collaborative efforts between government and private sector in order to create ethical AI standards in marketing.

3.2 Transparency and Accountability Recommendations

- Develop and enhance explainable AI systems that enable customers to interpret and understand information holistically.
- Provide users with the ability to check which of their data is collected and stored, thereby allowing them the ability to opt-out if they deem it unethical.
- Ensure that there is a mechanism that enables disclosure of third party data sharing so that customers are aware.
- Create a customer complaints procedure, whereby unethical data sharing practices or misuse of customer data are reported to ensure accountability.
- Implement prompt notifications for data breaches and remedies thereof so that there is a clear communication line between organisations and customers.

3.3 Security and Risk Management Recommendations

- Conduct comprehensive risk analysis by conducting threat modelling for AI systems in order to prepare, anticipate and act when risk occur.
- Ensure to regularly update and patch up IoT devices with latest security updates.
- Limit major damage to main corporate systems by isolating IoT devices from main systems.
- Implement authorisation requirement protocols for authorised personnel only to limit data breaches.
- Implement data protection task force that monitors, reacts and curbs data breaches by constantly evaluating unusual activity.

3.4 Consumer Rights and Empowerment

- Ensure customers have the ability to download and transfer their data to other IoT platforms.
- Implement fast tracked opt-out options that do not take too long nor are complicated.
- Provide quarterly reports to customers on their data usage and to enable them to give consent.
- Conduct customer awareness campaigns to promote data rights, digital landscape education and customer empowerment.

- Provide customers with real-time control over their data by enabling them to utilise interfaces to change permissions whenever possible.

4. CONCLUSION

As IoT and AI-powered data continue to transform marketing, they present significant ethical, legal, and societal issues in addition to previously unheard-of chances for tailored customer interaction. Real-time behavioural data collection and analysis from linked devices heralds a new era of contextually aware, intelligent marketing. Nevertheless, the dangers of widespread surveillance, algorithmic prejudice, data breaches, and the degradation of personal freedom and privacy temper this promise. The ethical use of big data in IoT-powered marketing has been critically analysed in this chapter using four key dimensions: consumer rights and empowerment, security and risk management, transparency and accountability, and governance and policy.

Every aspect is essential to creating human-centred, ethical marketing systems that are not only inventive and effective but also equitable, inclusive, and socially sustainable. Beyond merely adhering to regulations, responsible AI in marketing must represent a stronger dedication to moral rectitude and the welfare of society. In order to ensure data security and resilience against misuse, organizations must create data governance models that place a high priority on accountability, consent, and transparency. At the forefront of marketing innovation must be consumer empowerment via control, consent, and education. Furthermore, the legal and ethical frameworks that govern technology must also change as they do. In an IoT-driven future, ethical marketing necessitates constant introspection, stakeholder cooperation, multidisciplinary policymaking, and flexible norms.

Through proactive governance and inclusive design, organizations must not only address ethical issues but also foresee and avoid them. In the end, a balanced strategy that respects individual dignity and public trust while embracing innovation is essential to the future of ethical data-driven marketing. Businesses that include ethics into the foundation of their data and AI strategy can reduce risks and cultivate stronger, more reliable customer relationships. We can fully utilize IoT and AI technologies in a way that benefits companies, customers, and society at large by responsibly and strategically navigating the complexity of big data.

REFERENCES

Abbasi, M., Nishat, R. I., Bond, C., Graham-Knight, J. B., Lasserre, P., Lucet, Y., & Najjaran, H. (2024). A review of AI and machine learning contribution in business process management (process enhancement and process improvement approaches). *Business Process Management Journal.*

Al-Hitmi, H. K., Mardiah, A., Al-Sulaiti, K. I., & Abbas, J. (2024). Data security and privacy concerns of AI-driven marketing in the context of economics and business field: An exploration into possible solutions. *Cogent Business & Management, 11*(1), 2393743. DOI: 10.1080/23311975.2024.2393743

Al-Hitmi, M., & Sherif, K. (2018). Employee perceptions of fairness toward IoT monitoring. *VINE Journal of Information and Knowledge Management Systems, 48*(4), 504–516. DOI: 10.1108/VJIKMS-01-2018-0007

Al-Hogail, A. (2018). Improving IoT technology adoption through improving consumer trust. *Technologies, 6*(3), 64. DOI: 10.3390/technologies6030064

Alam, A. (2025). Ethical Challenges and Bias in AI-Driven Marketing: Educational Imperatives and Policy Perspectives. In *Impacts of AI-Generated Content on Brand Reputation* (pp. 55-108). IGI Global Scientific Publishing.

Alves, A. M., Chuma, E. L., Vaz, G. C., De Oliveira, G. G., Roger, L. L. B., & Lano, Y. (2024, July). AI Ethics in IoT: Involving Society in the Discussion. In *2024 International Conference on Electrical, Computer and Energy Technologies (ICECET* (pp. 1-4). IEEE. DOI: 10.1109/ICECET61485.2024.10698429

Araujo, T., Helberger, N., Kruikemeier, S., & De Vreese, C. H. (2020). In AI we trust? Perceptions about automated decision-making by artificial intelligence. *AI & Society, 35*(3), 611–623. DOI: 10.1007/s00146-019-00931-w

Bădică, A. L., & Mitucă, M. O. (2021). IOT-enhanced digital marketing conceptual framework. *BRAIN. Broad Research in Artificial Intelligence and Neuroscience, 12*(4), 509–531. DOI: 10.18662/brain/12.4/262

Bangui, H., Buhnova, B., & Ge, M. (2023). Social internet of things: Ethical AI principles in trust management. *Procedia Computer Science, 220*, 553–560. DOI: 10.1016/j.procs.2023.03.070

Bathla, D., Ahuja, R., Awasthi, S., & Santhosh, A. (2022). Analytical Impact of Digital Marketing on Smart Wearables in India. In *Institutions, Resilience, and Dynamic Capabilities of Entrepreneurial Ecosystems in Emerging Economies* (pp. 158-170). IGI Global Scientific Publishing. DOI: 10.4018/978-1-6684-4745-1.ch010

Blanke, J. M. (2020). Protection for 'Inferences drawn': A comparison between the general data protection regulation and the california consumer privacy act. *Global Privacy Law Review, 1*(2).

Chowdhury, N. (2019, September). An IoT and blockchain-based approach for ensuring transparency and accountability in regulatory compliance. In *Adjunct Proceedings of the 2019 ACM International Joint Conference on Pervasive and Ubiquitous Computing and Proceedings of the 2019 ACM International Symposium on Wearable Computers* (pp. 957-962). DOI: 10.1145/3341162.3349320

Collins, A., Hamza, O., Eweje, A., & Babatunde, G. O. (2024). Challenges and solutions in data governance and privacy: A conceptual model for telecom and business intelligence systems. *Telecom and Business Intelligence Journal, 9*(3), 110–125. DOI: 10.54660/.IJMRGE.2024.5.1.1064-1081

Das, S., & Mitra, A. (2024). Balancing the scale: ethical marketing in the age of big data-a comprehensive analysis of data governance standards and the role of effective technology. In *Ethical marketing through data governance standards and effective technology* (pp. 50–61). IGI Global Scientific Publishing. DOI: 10.4018/979-8-3693-2215-4.ch004

Dehghani, M., & Dangelico, R. M. (2017, March). Smart wearable technologies: Current status and market orientation through a patent analysis. In *2017 IEEE International Conference on Industrial Technology (ICIT)* (pp. 1570-1575). IEEE. DOI: 10.1109/ICIT.2017.7915602

Dornak, J. (2025). Fostering A Right to Repair for Consumer IoT: A community-based Participatory Design Approach.

Du, S., & Xie, C. (2021). Paradoxes of artificial intelligence in consumer markets: Ethical challenges and opportunities. *Journal of Business Research, 129*, 961–974. DOI: 10.1016/j.jbusres.2020.08.024

Eid, M. A. H., Hashesh, M. A., Sharabati, A. A. A., Khraiwish, A., Al-Haddad, S., & Abusaimeh, H. (2024). Conceptualizing ethical AI-enabled marketing: Current state and agenda for future research.

Ejjami, R. (2024). The Holistic AI-Enhanced Marketing Framework Theory: Bridging Human Creativity and AI for Ethical Marketing. *International Journal For Multidisciplinary Research, 6*(5), 1325.

Enqvist, L. (2023). 'Human oversight'in the EU artificial intelligence act: What, when and by whom? *Law, Innovation and Technology, 15*(2), 508–535. DOI: 10.1080/17579961.2023.2245683

Fares, N. Y., & Jammal, M. (2023). AI-Driven IoT Systems and Corresponding Ethical Issues. In *AI and Society* (pp. 233–248). Chapman and Hall/CRC.

Floridi, L., Cowls, J., Beltrametti, M., Chatila, R., Chazerand, P., Dignum, V., Luetge, C., Madelin, R., Pagallo, U., Rossi, F., Schafer, B., Valcke, P., & Vayena, E. (2018). AI4People—An ethical framework for a good AI society. *Minds and Machines, 28*(4), 689–707. DOI: 10.1007/s11023-018-9482-5 PMID: 30930541

Furfaro, A., Felicetti, C., Saccà, D., & Crupi, F. (2022). Accountability of IoT Devices. In *Security, Trust and Privacy Models, and Architectures in IoT Environments* (pp. 133–147). Springer International Publishing.

Galli, B. J., & Ocampo, L. A. (2019). Exploring the relationships between continuous improvement and predictive analytics. *International Journal of Advanced Operations Management, 11*(3), 189–210. DOI: 10.1504/IJAOM.2019.100709

Gaur, L., & Sahoo, B. M. (2022). Explainable AI in ITS: Ethical concerns. In *Explainable artificial intelligence for intelligent transportation systems: Ethics and applications* (pp. 79–90). Springer International Publishing. DOI: 10.1007/978-3-031-09644-0_5

Gonçalves, A. R., Pinto, D. C., Rita, P., & Pires, T. (2023). Artificial intelligence and its ethical implications for marketing. *Emerging Science Journal, 7*(2), 313–327. DOI: 10.28991/ESJ-2023-07-02-01

Grant, O., & Agoro, H. (2021). Trends in Network Compliance and Regulatory Challenges.

Gupta, R., Usman, M., Kashid, P. V., Mohan, M. L., Gaidhani, V. A., & Ghuge, M. A. R. (2025). Artificial Intelligence and IoT in Retail Marketing: Innovations in Smart Stores and Personalized Shopping. *Artificial Intelligence, 5*(2).

Harkin, D., Mann, M., & Warren, I. (2022). Consumer IoT and its under-regulation: Findings from an Australian study. *Policy and Internet, 14*(1), 96–113. DOI: 10.1002/poi3.285

Hermann, E. (2022). Leveraging artificial intelligence in marketing for social good—An ethical perspective. *Journal of Business Ethics, 179*(1), 43–61. DOI: 10.1007/s10551-021-04843-y PMID: 34054170

Holzinger, A., Zatloukal, K., & Müller, H. (2025). Is human oversight to AI systems still possible? *New Biotechnology, 85*, 59–62. DOI: 10.1016/j.nbt.2024.12.003 PMID: 39675423

Ivanov, S. H. (2023). Automated decision-making. *foresight, 25*(1), 4-19.

Janiesch, C., Fischer, M., Winkelmann, A., & Nentwich, V. (2019). Specifying autonomy in the internet of things: The autonomy model and notation. *Information Systems and e-Business Management, 17*(1), 159–194. DOI: 10.1007/s10257-018-0379-x

Jayadatta, S. (2023). A study on latest developments in artificial intelligence (AI) and internet of things (IoT) in current context. *Journal of Applied Information Science, 11*(2), 21–28.

Kalla, D., & Smith, N. (2024). Integrating IoT, AI, and big data for enhanced operational efficiency in smart factories. *Educational Administration: Theory and Practice, 30*(5), 14235–14245.

Kar, R., & Haldar, R. (2016). Applying chatbots to the internet of things: Opportunities and architectural elements. *arXiv preprint arXiv:1611.03799.*

Karami, A., Shemshaki, M., & Ghazanfar, M. (2024). *Exploring the ethical implications of ai-powered personalization in digital marketing. Data Intelligence*. In-Press.

Koul, A. S. N. A., & Sabrina, A. (2019). *A framework for fair and responsible data market ecosystems* (Doctoral dissertation, éditeur non identifié).

Kravets, O., Korolova, U., Nosachenko, O., Vasiltsova, O., & Koberniuk, S. (2025). AI-Powered Digital Marketing: Enhancing Customer Behaviour Predictions. *European Journal of Sustainable Development, 14*(2), 84–84. DOI: 10.14207/ejsd.2025.v14n2p84

Kumar, D., & Suthar, N. (2024). Ethical and legal challenges of AI in marketing: An exploration of solutions. *Journal of Information. Communication and Ethics in Society, 22*(1), 124–144. DOI: 10.1108/JICES-05-2023-0068

LaBrie, R. C., & Steinke, G. (2019). Towards a framework for ethical audits of AI algorithms.

Lee, C. S., Cheang, P. Y. S., & Moslehpour, M. (2022). Predictive analytics in business analytics: Decision tree. *Advances in Decision Sciences, 26*(1), 1–29. DOI: 10.47654/v26y2022i1p1-29

Lee, I. (2020). Internet of Things (IoT) cybersecurity: Literature review and IoT cyber risk management. *Future Internet, 12*(9), 157. DOI: 10.3390/fi12090157

Lomborg, S., Kaun, A., & Scott Hansen, S. (2023). Automated decision-making: Toward a people-centred approach. *Sociology Compass, 17*(8), e13097. DOI: 10.1111/soc4.13097

Maiorescu, I., Bucur, M., Georgescu, B., Moise, D., Strat, V. A., & Zgură, I. D. (2020). Social media and IOT wearables in developing marketing strategies. Do SMEs differ from large enterprises? *Sustainability (Basel), 12*(18), 7292. DOI: 10.3390/su12187292

Mansouri, C., & Bezgrari, A. (2022). Digital marketing as a mechanism to pursue the digital transformation: Case study of Sephora. *Revue des Economies financières bancaires et de management, 11*(1), 851-869.

Marinova, N. (2024). Advantages and ethical considerations of industrial iot artificial intelligence solutions usage. *Бизнес управление*, (2), 43-58.

Mökander, J. (2023). Auditing of AI: Legal, ethical and technical approaches. *Digital Society : Ethics, Socio-Legal and Governance of Digital Technology*, *2*(3), 49. DOI: 10.1007/s44206-023-00074-y

Moradi, M. (2021). Importance of internet of things (IoT) in marketing research and its ethical and data privacy challenges. *Business Ethics and Leadership*, *5*(1), 22–30. DOI: 10.21272/bel.5(1).22-30.2021

Neisse, R., Baldini, G., Steri, G., Miyake, Y., Kiyomoto, S., & Biswas, A. R. (2015, December). An agent-based framework for informed consent in the internet of things. In *2015 IEEE 2nd World Forum on Internet of Things (WF-IoT)* (pp. 789-794). IEEE. DOI: 10.1109/WF-IoT.2015.7389154

Oladosu, S. A., Ike, C. C., Adepoju, P. A., Afolabi, A. I., Ige, A. B., & Amoo, O. O. (2024). *Frameworks for ethical data governance in machine learning: Privacy, fairness, and business optimization*. Magna Sci Adv Res Rev.

Oluwafemi, I. O., Clement, T., Adanigbo, O. S., Gbenle, T. P., & Adekunle, B. I. (2021). A Review of Ethical Considerations in AI-Driven Marketing Analytics: Privacy, Transparency, and Consumer Trust. *International Journal Of Multidisciplinary Research and Growth Evaluation*, *2*(2), 428–435. DOI: 10.54660/.IJMRGE.2021.2.2.428-435

Onu, P., Pradhan, A., Madonsela, N. S., Ajayi, S. A., Osueke, C. O., Samuel, D. R., & Adebayo, S. (2025). Integration of ai and iot in smart manufacturing: Exploring technological, ethical, and legal frontiers. *Procedia Computer Science*, *253*, 654–660. DOI: 10.1016/j.procs.2025.01.127

Park, G. (2019). The changing wind of data privacy law: A comparative study of the European Union's General Data Protection Regulation and the 2018 California Consumer Privacy Act. *UC Irvine L. Rev.*, *10*, 1455.

Pathmabandu, C., Grundy, J., Chhetri, M. B., & Baig, Z. (2023). Privacy for IoT: Informed consent management in Smart Buildings. *Future Generation Computer Systems*, *145*, 367–383. DOI: 10.1016/j.future.2023.03.045

Petrescu, M., Krishen, A., & Bui, M. (2020). The internet of everything: Implications of marketing analytics from a consumer policy perspective. *Journal of Consumer Marketing*, *37*(6), 675–686. DOI: 10.1108/JCM-02-2019-3080

Priyadharshini, L., Gautam, K. K., Agrawal, S., Rao, D. M. K., & Natarajan, S., & LB, M. (2024, November). IoT-Enabled Consumer Behavior Tracking. In *2024 Second International Conference Computational and Characterization Techniques in Engineering & Sciences (IC3TES)* (pp. 1-5). IEEE.

Raeesi Vanani, I., Taghavifard, M. T., & Yalpanian, M. A. (2025). Predictive Analytics Solution for Digital Capabilities Identification Towards Business Performance Improvement. *SN Computer Science*, *6*(1), 85. DOI: 10.1007/s42979-024-03630-6

Rosário, A. T., & Raimundo, R. J. (2025). The Integration of AI and IoT in Marketing: A Systematic Literature Review.

Saleh, H. H., Chyad, A. K., Barakat, M., & Naamo, G. S. (2024). Enhancing Business Operations Efficiency Thorough Predictive Analytics. *J. Ecohumanism*, *3*(5), 700–714. DOI: 10.62754/joe.v3i5.3932

Salgado-Criado, J. (2025). Human oversight of artificial intelligence: An operations management perspective. *Journal of Industrial Engineering and Management*, *18*(2), 285–304. DOI: 10.3926/jiem.8567

Saluja, S., Nayyar, V., Rojhe, K., & Sharma, S. (Eds.). (2024). *Ethical Marketing Through Data Governance Standards and Effective Technology*. IGI Global. DOI: 10.4018/979-8-3693-2215-4

Sargiotis, D. (2024). Key Principles of Data Governance: Building a Strong Foundation. In *Data Governance: A Guide* (pp. 137–163). Springer Nature Switzerland. DOI: 10.1007/978-3-031-67268-2_3

Sayles, J. (2024). Human Oversight of AI Systems. In *Principles of AI Governance and Model Risk Management: Master the Techniques for Ethical and Transparent AI Systems* (pp. 267–276). Apress. DOI: 10.1007/979-8-8688-0983-5_12

Shafique, M., Mumtaz, G., Ahmad, S. Z., & Iqbal, S. (2024). A Comparative Analysis of AI Chatbot Performance in IoT Environments. *Journal of Computing & Biomedical Informatics*, *7*(02).

Shei, R. J., Holder, I. G., Oumsang, A. S., Paris, B. A., & Paris, H. L. (2022). Wearable activity trackers–advanced technology or advanced marketing? *European Journal of Applied Physiology, 122*(9), 1975–1990. DOI: 10.1007/s00421-022-04951-1 PMID: 35445837

Su, Y., Wang, E. J., & Berthon, P. (2023). Ethical marketing AI? A structured literature review of the ethical challenges posed by artificial intelligence in the domains of marketing and consumer behavior.

Suklabaidya, S. (2024). Towards inclusive societies: Leveraging IoT for community development and education.

Tanczer, L., Carr, M., Brass, I., Steenmans, I., & Blackstock, J. J. (2017). Iot and its implications for informed consent. *PETRAS IoT Hub, STEaPP: London.*

Tasnim, K., Abdullah, M. S., Karim, M. Z., & Hasan, R. (2025). AI-Driven Innovation, Privacy Issues, and Gaining Consumer Trust: The Future of Digital Marketing. *Business & Social Sciences, 3*(1), 1–7.

Tokeley, K. (2021). The Power of the" Internet of Things" to Mislead and Manipulate Consumers: A Regulatory Challenge. *Notre Dame J. on Emerging Tech., 2*, 111.

Trautman, L. J., Hussein, M. T., Ngamassi, L., & Molesky, M. J. (2020). Governance of the Internet of Things (IOT). *Jurimetrics, 60*(3), 315–352.

Vemuri, V. P., Naik, V. R., & Chaudhary, V. (2022). Analyzing the use of internet of things (IoT) in artificial intelligence and its impact on business environment. *Materials Today: Proceedings, 51*, 2194–2197. DOI: 10.1016/j.matpr.2021.11.264

Voss, W. G. (2021). The CCPA and the GDPR are not the same: Why you should understand both. *CPI Antitrust Chronicle, 1*(1), 7–12.

Waldman, A. E. (2019). Power, process, and automated decision-making. *Fordham Law Review, 88*, 613.

Zuboff, S. (2015). Big other. *Journal of Information Technology, 30*(1), 75–89. DOI: 10.1057/jit.2015.5

Compilation of References

Abbasi, M., Nishat, R. I., Bond, C., Graham-Knight, J. B., Lasserre, P., Lucet, Y., & Najjaran, H. (2024). A review of AI and machine learning contribution in business process management (process enhancement and process improvement approaches). *Business Process Management Journal.*

Abd Elaziz, M., Al-qaness, M. A., Dahou, A., Al-Betar, M. A., Mohamed, M. M., El-Shinawi, M., Ali, A., & Ewees, A. A. (2024). Digital twins in healthcare: Applications, technologies, simulations, and future trends. *Wiley Interdisciplinary Reviews. Data Mining and Knowledge Discovery, 14*(6), e1559. DOI: 10.1002/widm.1559

Abdulmalek, S., Nasir, A., Jabbar, W. A., Almuhaya, M. A., Bairagi, A. K., Khan, M. A. M., & Kee, S. H. (2022, October). IoT-based healthcare-monitoring system towards improving quality of life: A review. []. MDPI.]. *Health Care, 10*(10), 1993. PMID: 36292441

Addas, A. (2023). The concept of smart cities: A sustainability aspect for future urban development based on different cities. *Frontiers in Environmental Science, 11*, 1241593. DOI: 10.3389/fenvs.2023.1241593

Adibi, S., Rajabifard, A., Shojaei, D., & Wickramasinghe, N. (2024). Enhancing healthcare through sensor-enabled digital twins in smart environments: A comprehensive analysis. *Sensors (Basel), 24*(9), 2793. DOI: 10.3390/s24092793 PMID: 38732899

Adreani, L., Bellini, P., Fanfani, M., Nesi, P., & Pantaleo, G. (2024). Smart city digital twin framework for real-time multi-data integration and wide public distribution. *IEEE Access : Practical Innovations, Open Solutions, 12*, 76277–76303. DOI: 10.1109/ACCESS.2024.3406795

Ahmadi-Assalemi, G., Al-Khateeb, H., Maple, C., Epiphaniou, G., Alhaboby, Z. A., Alkaabi, S., & Alhaboby, D. (2020). Digital twins for precision healthcare. In *Cyber defence in the age of AI, Smart societies and augmented humanity* (pp. 133–158). Springer International Publishing. DOI: 10.1007/978-3-030-35746-7_8

Ahmed, A., Bhatti, S. H., Gölgeci, I., & Arslan, A. (2022). Digital platform capability and organizational agility of emerging market manufacturing SMEs: The mediating role of intellectual capital and the moderating role of environmental dynamism. *Technological Forecasting and Social Change*, *177*, 121513. DOI: 10.1016/j.techfore.2022.121513

Ahmed, S. F., Sharmin, S., Kuldeep, D. A., Lameesa, A., Bin Alam, M. S., Liu, G., & Gandomi, A. H. (2024). Internet of Medical Things (IoMT)-based healthcare technologies: Recent advances, taxonomy, and future outlook. *Results in Engineering*, *22*, 103787. DOI: 10.1016/j.rineng.2024.103787

Ajzen, I. (1991). The theory of planned behavior. *Organizational Behavior and Human Decision Processes*, *50*(2), 179–211. DOI: 10.1016/0749-5978(91)90020-T

Alalhareth, M., & Hong, S.-C. (2024). Enhancing the Internet of Medical Things (IoMT) security with meta-learning: A performance-driven approach for ensemble intrusion detection systems. *Sensors (Basel)*, *24*(11), 3519. DOI: 10.3390/s24113519 PMID: 38894310

Alam, A. (2025). Ethical Challenges and Bias in AI-Driven Marketing: Educational Imperatives and Policy Perspectives. In *Impacts of AI-Generated Content on Brand Reputation* (pp. 55-108). IGI Global Scientific Publishing.

Alazab, M., Khan, L. U., Koppu, S., Ramu, S. P., Boobalan, P., Baker, T., Maddikunta, P. K. R., Gadekallu, T. R., & Aljuhani, A. (2022). Digital twins for healthcare 4.0—Recent advances, architecture, and open challenges. *IEEE Consumer Electronics Magazine*, *12*(6), 29–37. DOI: 10.1109/MCE.2022.3208986

Alcaraz, C., Meskini, I. H., & Lopez, J. (2025). Digital twin communities: An approach for secure DT data sharing. *International Journal of Information Security*, *24*(1), 17. DOI: 10.1007/s10207-024-00912-1

Aldboush, H. H., & Ferdous, M. (2023). Building trust in fintech: An analysis of ethical and privacy considerations in the intersection of big data, AI, and customer trust. *International Journal of Financial Studies*, *11*(3), 90. DOI: 10.3390/ijfs11030090

Aldehim, G., Khan, S., Shahzad, T., Khan, M. A., Ghadi, Y. Y., Jiang, W., Mazhar, T., & Hamam, H. (2025). Balancing sustainability and security: A review of 5G and IoT in smart cities. *Digital Communications and Networks, 11*(6), 1722–1737. Advance online publication. DOI: 10.1016/j.dcan.2025.06.007

Al-Dulaimy, A., Jansen, M., Johansson, B., Trivedi, A., Iosup, A., Ashjaei, M., Galletta, A., Kimovski, D., Prodan, R., Tserpes, K., Kousiouris, G., Giannakos, C., Brandic, I., Ali, N., Bondi, A. B., & Papadopoulos, A. (2024). The computing continuum: From IoT to the cloud. *Internet of Things : Engineering Cyber Physical Human Systems, 27*, 101272. DOI: 10.1016/j.iot.2024.101272

Al-Fuqaha, A., Guizani, M., Mohammadi, M., Aledhari, M., & Ayyash, M. (2015). Internet of Things: A survey on enabling technologies, protocols, and applications. *IEEE Communications Surveys and Tutorials, 17*(4), 2347–2376. DOI: 10.1109/COMST.2015.2444095

Alghamdi, H. (2024). Assessing the impact of enterprise architecture on digital transformation success: A global perspective. *Sustainability (Basel), 16*(20), 8865. Advance online publication. DOI: 10.3390/su16208865

Al-Hitmi, H. K., Mardiah, A., Al-Sulaiti, K. I., & Abbas, J. (2024). Data security and privacy concerns of AI-driven marketing in the context of economics and business field: An exploration into possible solutions. *Cogent Business & Management, 11*(1), 2393743. DOI: 10.1080/23311975.2024.2393743

Al-Hitmi, M., & Sherif, K. (2018). Employee perceptions of fairness toward IoT monitoring. *VINE Journal of Information and Knowledge Management Systems, 48*(4), 504–516. DOI: 10.1108/VJIKMS-01-2018-0007

Al-Hogail, A. (2018). Improving IoT technology adoption through improving consumer trust. *Technologies, 6*(3), 64. DOI: 10.3390/technologies6030064

Ali, A., Laghari, A. A., Kandhro, I. A., Kumar, K., & Younus, S. (2024). Systematic analysis of on-premise and cloud services. *International Journal of Cloud Computing, 13*(3), 214–242. DOI: 10.1504/IJCC.2024.139604

Ali, A., Qureshi, M. A., Shiraz, M., & Shamim, A. (2021). Mobile crowd sensing based dynamic traffic efficiency framework for urban traffic congestion control. *Sustainable Computing : Informatics and Systems, 32*, 100608. DOI: 10.1016/j.suscom.2021.100608

Aljarrah, M. M., Zawaideh, F. H., Magableh, M., Al Wahshat, H., & Mohamed, R. R., & K V, A. (2023). Internet of Things and data analytics: Challenges and future applications. *2023 International Conference on Computer Science and Emerging Technologies (CSET)*. DOI: 10.1109/CSET58993.2023.10346664

Alkan, D. (2020). Re-shaping business strategy in the era of digitisation. In *Digital Transformation and Innovative Services for Business and Learning* (pp. 76–97). DOI: 10.4018/978-1-7998-1125-1.ch004

Alkemade, G., & Toet, J. (2020). Data protection regulation in the Netherlands. In *Data Protection Around the World: Privacy Laws in Action* (pp. 165–188). TMC Asser Press.

Almuhaya, M. A., Jabbar, W. A., Sulaiman, N., & Abdulmalek, S. (2022). A survey on Lorawan technology: Recent trends, opportunities, simulation tools and future directions. *Electronics (Basel)*, *11*(1), 164. DOI: 10.3390/electronics11010164

Al-Mutawa, H. A., Sowailem, E. K., & Al Mubarak, M. (2025). Business Ethics in E-commerce: Ethical Concerns and Safeguarding Consumer Trust and Loyalty. In *Sustainable Digital Technology and Ethics in an Ever-Changing Environment* (Vol. 2, pp. 3–20). Springer Nature Switzerland. DOI: 10.1007/978-3-031-86708-8_1

Al-Shetwi, A. Q., Atawi, I. E., El-Hameed, M. A., & Abuelrub, A. (2025). Digital Twin Technology for Renewable Energy, Smart Grids, Energy Storage and Vehicle-to-Grid Integration: Advancements, Applications, Key Players, Challenges and Future Perspectives in Modernising Sustainable Grids. *IET Smart Grid*, *8*(1), e70026. DOI: 10.1049/stg2.70026

Alves, A. M., Chuma, E. L., Vaz, G. C., De Oliveira, G. G., Roger, L. L. B., & Lano, Y. (2024, July). AI Ethics in IoT: Involving Society in the Discussion. In *2024 International Conference on Electrical, Computer and Energy Technologies (ICECET* (pp. 1-4). IEEE. DOI: 10.1109/ICECET61485.2024.10698429

Amalia, N., & Hindarto, D. (2024). Enterprise architecture for efficient integration of IoT lighting systems in smart city frameworks. *Sinkron*, *8*(2), 1091–1099. Advance online publication. DOI: 10.33395/sinkron.v8i2.13591

Amil, Y. (2024). The impact of AI-driven personalization tools on privacy concerns and consumer trust in e-commerce (Master's thesis, University of Liège). http://hdl.handle.net/2268.2/21371

Ammar, M. (2024). *Advanced Digital Twins for Current Real Time Condition Monitoring*. Diagnosis and Predictive Remaining Lifecycles.

Amosu, O. R., Kumar, P., Fadina, A., Ogunsuji, Y. M., Oni, S., & Adetula, K. (2024). Harnessing real-time data analytics for strategic customer insights in e-commerce and retail. *World Journal of Advanced Research and Reviews*, *23*(2), 880–889. Advance online publication. DOI: 10.30574/wjarr.2024.23.2.2407

Anttiroiko, A. V., Laine, M., & Lönnqvist, H. (2020). City as a growth platform: Responses of the cities of Helsinki metropolitan area to global digital economy. *Urban Science (Basel, Switzerland)*, *4*(4), 67. DOI: 10.3390/urbansci4040067

Araujo, T., Helberger, N., Kruikemeier, S., & De Vreese, C. H. (2020). In AI we trust? Perceptions about automated decision-making by artificial intelligence. *AI & Society*, *35*(3), 611–623. DOI: 10.1007/s00146-019-00931-w

Arseculαratne, B., Rodrigo, N., & Chang, R. (2024). Digital Twins for Reducing Energy Consumption in Buildings: A Review. *Sustainability (Basel)*, *16*(21), 9275. DOI: 10.3390/su16219275

Atmakuri, V. V., Lari, M. S. N., & Thangaraj, A. (2021). Design for sustainable smart cities. DOI: 10.1007/978-981-16-0041-8_79

Atzori, L., Iera, A., & Morabito, G. (2010). The internet of things: A survey. *Computer Networks*, *54*(15), 2787–2805. DOI: 10.1016/j.comnet.2010.05.010

Austin, M., Delgoshaei, P., Coelho, M., & Heidarinejad, M. (2020). Architecting smart city digital twins: Combined semantic model and machine learning approach. *Journal of Management Engineering*, *36*(4), 04020026. DOI: 10.1061/(ASCE)ME.1943-5479.0000774

Awaisi, K. S., Ye, Q., & Sampalli, S. (2024). A Survey of Industrial AIoT: Opportunities, Challenges, and Directions. *IEEE Access : Practical Innovations, Open Solutions*, *12*, 96946–96996. DOI: 10.1109/ACCESS.2024.3426279

Awasthi, M., Raghuvanshi, C. S., Dudhagara, C., & Awasthi, A. (2025). Exploring virtual smart healthcare trends using digital twins. In *Digital twins for smart cities and villages* (pp. 377–406). Elsevier. DOI: 10.1016/B978-0-443-28884-5.00017-8

Babu, C. S., Anniyappa, C. A., & Raut, A. (2025). Toward seamless mobility: Integrating connected and autonomous vehicles in smart cities through digital twins. In *Digital Twins for Smart Cities and Villages* (pp. 169–187). Elsevier. DOI: 10.1016/B978-0-443-28884-5.00008-7

Bachechi, C. (2022, August). Digital twins for urban mobility. In *European Conference on Advances in Databases and Information Systems* (pp. 657-665). Cham: Springer International Publishing.

Bădică, A. L., & Mitucă, M. O. (2021). IOT-enhanced digital marketing conceptual framework. *BRAIN. Broad Research in Artificial Intelligence and Neuroscience, 12*(4), 509–531. DOI: 10.18662/brain/12.4/262

Bakator, M., Ćoćkalo, D., Makitan, V., Stanisavljev, S., & Nikolić, M. (2024). The three pillars of tomorrow: How Marketing 5.0 builds on Industry 5.0 and impacts Society 5.0? *Heliyon, 10*(17), e36543. DOI: 10.1016/j.heliyon.2024.e36543 PMID: 39281657

Baker, S., & Xiang, W. (2023). Artificial Intelligence of Things for Smarter Healthcare: A Survey of Advancements, Challenges, and Opportunities. *IEEE Communications Surveys and Tutorials, 25*(2), 1261–1293. DOI: 10.1109/COMST.2023.3256323

Banerjee, S., Whig, P., & Parisa, S. K. (2024). Leveraging AI for Personalization and Cybersecurity in Retail Chains: Balancing Customer Experience and Data Protection. *Transactions on Recent Developments in Artificial Intelligence and Machine Learning, 16*, 16.

Bangui, H., Buhnova, B., & Ge, M. (2023). Social internet of things: Ethical AI principles in trust management. *Procedia Computer Science, 220*, 553–560. DOI: 10.1016/j.procs.2023.03.070

Barbone, A. S., Meftah, M., Markiewicz, K., & Dellimore, K. (2019). Beyond wearables and implantables: A scoping review of insertable medical devices. *Biomedical Physics & Engineering Express, 5*(6), 062002. DOI: 10.1088/2057-1976/ab4b32

Barney, J. (1991). Firm resources and sustained competitive advantage. *Journal of Management, 17*(1), 99–120. DOI: 10.1177/014920639101700108

Bathla, D., Ahuja, R., Awasthi, S., & Santhosh, A. (2022). Analytical Impact of Digital Marketing on Smart Wearables in India. In *Institutions, Resilience, and Dynamic Capabilities of Entrepreneurial Ecosystems in Emerging Economies* (pp. 158-170). IGI Global Scientific Publishing. DOI: 10.4018/978-1-6684-4745-1.ch010

Batty, M. (2018). Digital twins. *Environment and Planning. B, Urban Analytics and City Science, 45*(5), 817–820. DOI: 10.1177/2399808318796416

Belik, M., & Rubanenko, O. (2023). Implementation of digital twin for increasing efficiency of renewable energy sources. *Energies, 16*(12), 4787. DOI: 10.3390/en16124787

Ben-Daya, M., Hassini, E., & Bahroun, Z. (2019). Internet of things and supply chain management: A literature review. *International Journal of Production Research, 57*(15-16), 4719–4742. DOI: 10.1080/00207543.2017.1402140

Beniczky, S., Karoly, P., Nurse, E., Ryvlin, P., & Cook, M. (2021). Machine learning and wearable devices of the future. *Epilepsia, 62*(S2), S116–S124. DOI: 10.1111/epi.16555 PMID: 32712958

Benton, D. (1990). The impact of increasing blood glucose on psychological functioning. *Biological Psychology, 30*(1), 13–19. DOI: 10.1016/0301-0511(90)90087-D PMID: 2223932

Bernardo, B. M. V., de Sousa, M. C., Silva, M. M., & Azevedo, A. I. (2024). Data governance & quality management—Innovation and breakthroughs across different fields. *Journal of Innovation & Knowledge, 9*(4), 100598. DOI: 10.1016/j.jik.2024.100598

Berte, D. R. (2018, May). Defining the iot. In *Proceedings of the international conference on business excellence* (Vol. 12, No. 1, pp. 118-128). Pearson Educational. DOI: 10.2478/picbe-2018-0013

Bharadwaj, A. S. (2000). A resource-based perspective on information technology capability and firm performance: An empirical investigation. *Management Information Systems Quarterly, 24*(1), 169–196. DOI: 10.2307/3250983

Bibri, S. E., & Krogstie, J. (2020). The emerging data–driven Smart City and its innovative applied solutions for sustainability: The cases of London and Barcelona. *Energy Informatics, 3*(1), 5. DOI: 10.1186/s42162-020-00108-6

Bing, G., Al Mughairi, B., Karim, A. M., & Karim, A. M. (2024). Study on Importance of Brand Loyalty for Customer Retention for Consumer Durable Products: New Era Viewpoint. *International Journal of Academic Research in Business & Social Sciences, 14*(1), 453–464. DOI: 10.6007/IJARBSS/v14-i1/20464

Blanke, J. M. (2020). Protection for 'Inferences drawn': A comparison between the general data protection regulation and the california consumer privacy act. *Global Privacy Law Review, 1*(2).

Bokolo, A. J. (2023). Data driven approaches for smart city planning and design: A case scenario on urban data management. *Digital Policy. Regulation & Governance, 25*(4), 351–367.

Bolici, R., & Mora, L. (2016). The development process of smart city strategies: the case of Barcelona. In *RE-CITY Future City-Combining Disciplines* (pp. 155-181). Juvenes print.

Boni, E. K. (2024). Exploring perceived risk and digital ethics affecting consumer experiences and decision-making in smart retailing (Doctoral dissertation, Brunel University London).

Bonomi, F., Milito, R., Zhu, J., & Addepalli, S. (2012). Fog computing and its role in the Internet of Things. *Proceedings of the First MCC Workshop on Mobile Cloud Computing*, 13–16. https://doi.org/DOI: 10.1145/2342509.2342513

Borgia, E. (2014). The Internet of Things vision: Key features, applications and open issues. *Computer Communications*, *54*, 1–31. DOI: 10.1016/j.comcom.2014.09.008

Bortolini, R., Rodrigues, R., Alavi, H., Vecchia, L. F. D., & Forcada, N. (2022). Digital twins' applications for building energy efficiency: A review. *Energies*, *15*(19), 7002. DOI: 10.3390/en15197002

Bostrom, R. P., & Heinen, J. S. (1977). MIS problems and failures: A socio-technical perspective. Part I: The causes. *Management Information Systems Quarterly*, *1*(3), 17–32. DOI: 10.2307/248710

Bouguern, S. (2024). Designing the future: Exploring the smart manufacturing ecosystem and future landscape. *Journal of Novel Engineering Science and Technology*. DOI: 10.56741/jnest.v3i03.603

Broniarczyk, S. M., & Griffin, J. G. (2014). Decision difficulty in the age of consumer empowerment. *Journal of Consumer Psychology*, *24*(4), 608–625. DOI: 10.1016/j.jcps.2014.05.003

Butner, K. (2010). The smarter supply chain of the future. *Strategy and Leadership*, *38*(1), 22–31. DOI: 10.1108/10878571011009859

Cai, M., Kassens-Noor, E., Zhao, Z., & Colbry, D. (2023). Are smart cities more sustainable? An exploratory study of 103 US cities. *Journal of Cleaner Production*, *416*, 137986. DOI: 10.1016/j.jclepro.2023.137986

Calzada, I. (2018). (Smart) citizens from data providers to decision-makers? The case study of Barcelona. *Sustainability (Basel)*, *10*(9), 3252. DOI: 10.3390/su10093252

Cappon, G., Acciaroli, G., Vettoretti, M., Facchinetti, A., & Sparacino, G. (2017). Wearable continuous glucose monitoring sensors: A revolution in diabetes treatment. *Electronics (Basel)*, *6*(3), 65. DOI: 10.3390/electronics6030065

Capra, C. F. (2019). The Smart City and its citizens: Governance and citizen participation in Amsterdam Smart City. In *Smart Cities and Smart Spaces: Concepts, Methodologies, Tools, and Applications* (pp. 1407-1427). IGI Global Scientific Publishing.

Cavada, M., Tight, M. R., & Rogers, C. D. (2019). A smart city case study of Singapore—Is Singapore truly smart? In *Smart city emergence* (pp. 295–314). Elsevier. DOI: 10.1016/B978-0-12-816169-2.00014-6

Caven, P. J. (2025). Applying User-Centric Communication Strategies to Mitigate Cybersecurity Risks and Increase Transparency in Technology Markets (Doctoral dissertation, Indiana University).

Chai, P. R., Vaz, C., Goodman, G. R., Albrechta, H., Huang, H., Rosen, R. K., Boyer, E. W., Mayer, K. H., & O'Cleirigh, C. (2022). Ingestible electronic sensors to measure instantaneous medication adherence: A narrative review. *Digital Health, 8*. Advance online publication. DOI: 10.1177/20552076221083119 PMID: 35251683

Chalhoub, G. (2022). The UX of things: exploring UX principles to inform security and privacy design in the smart home (Doctoral dissertation, University of Oxford).

Chang, F., & Das, D. (2020). Smart nation Singapore: Developing policies for a citizen-oriented smart city initiative. In *Developing national urban policies: Ways forward to green and smart cities* (pp. 425–440). Springer Nature Singapore. DOI: 10.1007/978-981-15-3738-7_18

Chang, Z., Liu, S., Xiong, X., Cai, Z., & Tu, G. (2021). A Survey of Recent Advances in Edge-Computing-Powered Artificial Intelligence of Things. *IEEE Internet of Things Journal, 8*(18), 13849–13875. DOI: 10.1109/JIOT.2021.3088875

Chan, J. J., & Chye, S. W. C. (2023). Impact of Smart City Initiatives on urban planning strategies in Singapore: An in-depth analysis of technology-driven solutions and their influence on sustainable development and quality of life. *Journal of Strategy and Management, 7*(7), 11–21.

Chan-Olmsted, S., Chen, H., & Kim, H. J. (2024). In smartness we trust: Consumer experience, smart device personalization and privacy balance. *Journal of Consumer Marketing, 41*(6), 597–609. DOI: 10.1108/JCM-12-2021-5072

Chan, Y. E., & Reich, B. H. (2007). IT alignment: What have we learned? *Journal of Information Technology, 22*(4), 297–315. DOI: 10.1057/palgrave.jit.2000109

Charitonidou, M. (2022). Urban scale digital twins in data-driven society: Challenging digital universalism in urban planning decision-making. *International Journal of Architectural Computing, 20*(2), 238–253. DOI: 10.1177/14780771211070005

Chaudhary, J., Jain, U., Sudarshan, N., Pai, V., & Sutaria, K. & N. L. (2024). AI-driven digital mirror technology for securing IoT-enabled smart infrastructures. *2024 International Conference on Integrated Intelligence and Communication Systems (ICIICS)*. DOI: 10.1109/ICIICS63763.2024.10859436

Chaudhary, A., Meenakshi, M., Sharma, S., Rahman, M., & Srinivasan, S. (2025). Enhancing urban mobility: Machine learning-powered fusion approach for intelligent traffic congestion control in smart cities. *International Journal of System Assurance Engineering and Management*, •••, 1–8. DOI: 10.1007/s13198-024-02672-6

Cheng, R., Hou, L., & Xu, S. (2023). A review of digital twin applications in civil and infrastructure emergency management. *Buildings (Basel, Switzerland), 13*(5), 1143. DOI: 10.3390/buildings13051143

Cheruku, H. K.Harsha Koundinya Cheruku. (2025). Data Privacy in E-commerce: Balancing Personalization with Customer Trust. *Journal of Computer Science and Technology Studies*, *7*(5), 680–687. DOI: 10.32996/jcsts.2025.7.5.75

Chimene, D., Queener, K. M. K., Ko, B. S., McShane, M., & Daniele, M. (2024). Insertable Biosensors: Combining Implanted Sensing Materials with Wearable Monitors. *Annual Review of Biomedical Engineering*, *26*(1), 197–221. DOI: 10.1146/annurev-bioeng-110222-101045 PMID: 38346276

Chirumalla, K. (2021). Building digitalisation capabilities for innovation in manufacturing firms. *Technovation*. Advance online publication. DOI: 10.1016/j.technovation.2021.102215

Choi, T. Y., Rogers, D., & Vakil, B. (2020). Coronavirus, supply chains, and the future of manufacturing. *Harvard Business Review*.

Chowdhury, N. (2019, September). An IoT and blockchain-based approach for ensuring transparency and accountability in regulatory compliance. In *Adjunct Proceedings of the 2019 ACM International Joint Conference on Pervasive and Ubiquitous Computing and Proceedings of the 2019 ACM International Symposium on Wearable Computers* (pp. 957-962). DOI: 10.1145/3341162.3349320

Cioara, T., Anghel, I., Antal, M., Salomie, I., Antal, C., & Ioan, A. G. (2021). An overview of digital twins application domains in smart energy grid. *arXiv preprint arXiv:2104.07904*.

Collins, A., Hamza, O., Eweje, A., & Babatunde, G. O. (2024). Challenges and solutions in data governance and privacy: A conceptual model for telecom and business intelligence systems. *Telecom and Business Intelligence Journal*, *9*(3), 110–125. DOI: 10.54660/.IJMRGE.2024.5.1.1064-1081

Contreras, G., & Platania, F. (2019). Economic and policy uncertainty in climate change mitigation: The London Smart City case scenario. *Technological Forecasting and Social Change*, *142*, 384–393. DOI: 10.1016/j.techfore.2018.07.018

Cook, M., & Karvonen, A. (2024). Urban planning and the knowledge politics of the smart city. *Urban Studies (Edinburgh, Scotland)*, *61*(2), 370–382. DOI: 10.1177/00420980231177688

Coreynen, W., Matthyssens, P., & Van Bockhaven, W. (2017). Boosting servitization through digitization: Pathways and dynamic resource configurations for manufacturers. *Industrial Marketing Management*, *60*, 42–53. DOI: 10.1016/j.indmarman.2016.04.012

Coro, M. B. (2024). *Navigating digital transformation: Insights from recent studies on process automation and innovation*. International Seven Journal of Multidisciplinary., DOI: 10.56238/isevmjv2n1-011

Cowell, N. H., Chapman, L., Topping, D., James, P., Bell, D., Bannan, T., Murabito, E., Evans, J., & Birkin, M. (2025). Moving from monitoring to real-time interventions for air quality: Are low-cost sensor networks ready to support urban digital twins? *Frontiers in Sustainable Cities*, *6*, 1500516. DOI: 10.3389/frsc.2024.1500516

Cowley, R., Joss, S., & Dayot, Y. (2018). The smart city and its publics: Insights from across six UK cities. *Urban Research & Practice*, *11*(1), 53–77. DOI: 10.1080/17535069.2017.1293150

Dalenogare, L. S., Benitez, G. B., Ayala, N. F., & Frank, A. G. (2018). The expected contribution of Industry 4.0 technologies for industrial performance. *International Journal of Production Economics*, *204*, 383–394. DOI: 10.1016/j.ijpe.2018.08.019

Darley, W. K., Blankson, C., & Luethge, D. J. (2010). Toward an integrated framework for online consumer behavior and decision making process: A review. *Psychology and Marketing*, *27*(2), 94–116. DOI: 10.1002/mar.20322

Dasari, S. (2020). Ichor - An IoT, cloud, and mobile technologies based noninvasive glucose monitoring system. In *IEMTRONICS 2020 - International IOT, Electronics and Mechatronics Conference, Proceedings*. https://doi.org/DOI: 10.1109/IEMTRONICS51293.2020.9216345

Das, S., & Mitra, A. (2024). Balancing the scale: ethical marketing in the age of big data-a comprehensive analysis of data governance standards and the role of effective technology. In *Ethical marketing through data governance standards and effective technology* (pp. 50–61). IGI Global Scientific Publishing. DOI: 10.4018/979-8-3693-2215-4.ch004

De Vass, T., Shee, H., & Miah, S. J. (2018). The effect of "Internet of Things" on supply chain integration and performance: An organisational capability perspective. *AJIS. Australasian Journal of Information Systems*, *22*, 1734. Advance online publication. DOI: 10.3127/ajis.v22i0.1734

Deb, M., & Choudhury, A. (2021). Hybrid cloud: A new paradigm in cloud computing. *Machine Learning Techniques and Analytics for Cloud Security*, 3–23. DOI: 10.1002/9781119764113.ch1

Dehghani, M., & Dangelico, R. M. (2017, March). Smart wearable technologies: Current status and market orientation through a patent analysis. In *2017 IEEE International Conference on Industrial Technology (ICIT)* (pp. 1570-1575). IEEE. DOI: 10.1109/ICIT.2017.7915602

Del Campo, G., Saavedra, E., Piovano, L., Luque, F., & Santamaria, A. (2024). Virtual reality and internet of things based digital twin for smart city cross-domain interoperability. *Applied Sciences (Basel, Switzerland)*, *14*(7), 2747. DOI: 10.3390/app14072747

Deng, T., Zhang, K., & Shen, Z. J. M. (2021). A systematic review of a digital twin city: A new pattern of urban governance toward smart cities. *Journal of Management Science and Engineering*, *6*(2), 125–134. DOI: 10.1016/j.jmse.2021.03.003

Deren, L., Wenbo, Y., & Zhenfeng, S. (2021). Smart city based on digital twins. *Computational Urban Science*, *1*(1), 4. DOI: 10.1007/s43762-021-00005-y

Dhiman, H., & Dhote, T. (2025). IoT-driven digital marketing framework for enhanced consumer experience. Kronika Journal, 25(4), 37-50. https://kronika.ac/wp-content/uploads/4-KKJ2437.pdf

Dian, F. J., Vahidnia, R., & Rahmati, A. (2020). Wearables and the Internet of Things (IoT), applications, opportunities, and challenges: A survey. *IEEE Access : Practical Innovations, Open Solutions*, *8*, 69200–69211. Advance online publication. DOI: 10.1109/ACCESS.2020.2986329

Dickinson, D. L., McElroy, T., & Stroh, N. (2014). Impact of glucose on Bayesian versus heuristic-based decision making. *Journal of Neuroscience, Psychology, and Economics*, *7*(4), 237–247. DOI: 10.1037/npe0000030

Dirnfeld, R., De Donato, L., Somma, A., Azari, M. S., Marrone, S., Flammini, F., & Vittorini, V. (2024). Integrating AI and DTs: Challenges and opportunities in railway maintenance application and beyond. *Simulation*, *100*(9), 903–917. DOI: 10.1177/00375497241229756

Dobre, J. (2025). Secure UX: Building cybersecurity and privacy into the UX lifecycle. UXMatters. https://www.uxmatters.com/mt/archives/2025/03/secure-ux-building-cybersecurity-and-privacy-into-the-ux-lifecycle.php

Dodiya, K. R., Jha, M., & Jha, S. (2024). Fortifying the digital forge: unleashing cybersecurity in the interconnected world of digital manufacturing. In *Emerging Technologies in Digital Manufacturing and Smart Factories* (pp. 230–256). IGI Global Scientific Publishing. DOI: 10.4018/979-8-3693-0920-9.ch014

Domínguez-Bolaño, T., Campos, O., Barral, V., Escudero, C. J., & García-Naya, J. A. (2022). An overview of IoT architectures, technologies, and existing open-source projects. *Internet of Things : Engineering Cyber Physical Human Systems*, *20*, 100626. DOI: 10.1016/j.iot.2022.100626

Donohoe, R. T., & Benton, D. (1999). Cognitive functioning is susceptible to the level of blood glucose. *Psychopharmacology*, *145*(4), 378–385. DOI: 10.1007/s002130051071 PMID: 10460314

Dornak, J. (2025). Fostering A Right to Repair for Consumer IoT: A community-based Participatory Design Approach.

dos Santos, M. R. P., Callado, A. C., & Laurindo, L. E. C. (2024). Enhancing IoT conceptual, practical, and programming learning skills. *Anais do XXXII Workshop sobre Educação em Computação (WEI 2024)*. DOI: 10.5753/wei.2024.1944

Dremel, C., Wulf, J., Goutier, M., & Brenner, W. (2017). How AUDI is navigating the digital transformation. *MIS Quarterly Executive*, *16*(4), 289–306.

Duan, W., Eva, A., Andrews, L., & Liu, Y. (2024). The role of platform ecosystem configuration toward performance bifurcation. *Journal of Innovation & Knowledge*, *9*(2), 100490. DOI: 10.1016/j.jik.2024.100490

Dubey, A., & Yadav, S. K. (2024). Basics of Internet of Things. *International Journal of Scientific Research in Engineering and Management*. DOI: 10.55041/IJSREM37970

Dubey, P., Thinakaran, A., & Rewatkar, R. M. (2025). Digitizing Wellness: A Deep Dive Into EHR/EMR Systems. *The Impact of Algorithmic Technologies on Healthcare*, 375–396. DOI: 10.1002/9781394305490.ch17

Dubey, R., Bryde, D., Ali, S. M., & Papadopoulos, T. (2023). Dynamic digital capabilities and supply chain resilience. *International Journal of Production Economics*, *259*, 108790. DOI: 10.1016/j.ijpe.2023.108790

Dubey, R., Gunasekaran, A., Childe, S. J., Bryde, D. J., Giannakis, M., Foropon, C., Roubaud, D., & Wamba, S. F. (2019). Big data analytics and artificial intelligence pathway to operational performance under the effects of entrepreneurial orientation and environmental dynamism: A study of manufacturing organisations. *International Journal of Production Economics, 226*, 107599. DOI: 10.1016/j.ijpe.2019.107599

Dubey, R., Gunasekaran, A., Childe, S. J., Papadopoulos, T., Hazen, B., Giannakis, M., & Roubaud, D. (2020). Examining the role of big data and predictive analytics in the era of industry 4.0 and the COVID-19 pandemic on supply chain resilience. *International Journal of Logistics Management, 32*(1), 137–162. DOI: 10.1108/IJLM-05-2020-0205

Dubey, R., Gunasekaran, A., Childe, S. J., Papadopoulos, T., Luo, Z., Wamba, S. F., & Roubaud, D. (2019). Can big data and predictive analytics improve social and environmental sustainability? *Technological Forecasting and Social Change, 144*, 534–545. DOI: 10.1016/j.techfore.2017.06.020

Dudhe, P. V., Kadam, N. V., Hushangabade, R. M., & Deshmukh, M. S. (2017, August). Internet of Things (IOT): An overview and its applications. In *2017 International conference on energy, communication, data analytics and soft computing (ICECDS)* (pp. 2650-2653). IEEE. DOI: 10.1109/ICECDS.2017.8389935

Dureja, A., Dureja, A., Kumar, V., & Sabharwal, S. (2024). Combining digital twin technology and intelligent transportation systems for smart mobility. In *Transforming Industry using Digital Twin Technology* (pp. 281–296). Springer Nature Switzerland. DOI: 10.1007/978-3-031-58523-4_14

Du, S., & Xie, C. (2021). Paradoxes of artificial intelligence in consumer markets: Ethical challenges and opportunities. *Journal of Business Research, 129*, 961–974. DOI: 10.1016/j.jbusres.2020.08.024

Dwivedi, Y. K., Hughes, L., Ismagilova, E., Aarts, G., Coombs, C., Crick, T., Duan, Y., Dwivedi, R., Edwards, J., Eirug, A., Galanos, V., Ilavarasan, P. V., Janssen, M., Jones, P., Kar, A. K., Kizgin, H., Kronemann, B., Lal, B., Lucini, B., & Williams, M. D. (2021). Artificial Intelligence (AI): Multidisciplinary perspectives on emerging challenges, opportunities, and agenda for research, practice and policy. *International Journal of Information Management, 57*, 101994. DOI: 10.1016/j.ijinfomgt.2019.08.002

Dyer, J. H., & Singh, H. (1998). The relational view: Cooperative strategy and sources of interorganizational competitive advantage. *Academy of Management Review, 23*(4), 660–679. DOI: 10.2307/259056

Eddy, C. W., Castanier, M. P., & Wagner, J. R. (2024). Predictive Maintenance of a Ground Vehicle Using Digital Twin Technology. *SAE International Journal of Advances and Current Practices in Mobility, 7*(2024-01-2867), 865-876.

Eichhorn, K. (2022). *Content*. MIT Press. DOI: 10.7551/mitpress/13809.001.0001

Eid, M. A. H., Hashesh, M. A., Sharabati, A. A. A., Khraiwish, A., Al-Haddad, S., & Abusaimeh, H. (2024). Conceptualizing ethical AI-enabled marketing: Current state and agenda for future research.

Ejjami, R. (2024). The Holistic AI-Enhanced Marketing Framework Theory: Bridging Human Creativity and AI for Ethical Marketing. *International Journal For Multidisciplinary Research, 6*(5), 1325.

El Houari, M., El Haloui, M., & Ettaki, B. (2025). A new enterprise architecture-based approach for smart city value co-creation. [IJECE]. *International Journal of Electrical and Computer Engineering, 15*(1), 767. Advance online publication. DOI: 10.11591/ijece.v15i1.pp767-782

El-Annan, S. H., & Hassoun, R. (2025). Enhancing Consumer Trust Through Transparent Data Practices and Ethical Data Management in Business. In *Innovation Management for a Resilient Digital Economy* (pp. 105–148). IGI Global Scientific Publishing.

El-Khoury, M., & Arikan, C. L. (2021). From the internet of things toward the internet of bodies: Ethical and legal considerations. *Strategic Change, 30*(3), 307–314. DOI: 10.1002/jsc.2411

Elnour, M., Ahmad, A. M., Abdelkarim, S., Fadli, F., & Naji, K. (2024). Empowering smart cities with digital twins of buildings: Applications and implementation considerations of data-driven energy modelling in building management. *Building Services Engineering Research and Technology, 45*(4), 475–498. DOI: 10.1177/01436244241239290

Emvoliadis, A., Vryzas, N., Stamatiadou, M. E., Vrysis, L., & Dimoulas, C. (2024). Multimodal Environmental Sensing Using AI & IoT Solutions: A Cognitive Sound Analysis Perspective. *Sensors 2024, Vol. 24, Page 2755, 24*(9), 2755. DOI: 10.3390/s24092755

Engin, Z., van Dijk, J., Lan, T., Longley, P. A., Treleaven, P., Batty, M., & Penn, A. (2020). Data-driven urban management: Mapping the landscape. *Journal of Urban Management, 9*(2), 140–150. DOI: 10.1016/j.jum.2019.12.001

Enqvist, L. (2023). 'Human oversight'in the EU artificial intelligence act: What, when and by whom? *Law, Innovation and Technology, 15*(2), 508–535. DOI: 10.1080/17579961.2023.2245683

Ertürk, M. A. (2023). Time Series Prediction with Digital Twins in Public Transportation Systems. *Alphanumeric Journal, 11*(2), 183–192. DOI: 10.17093/alphanumeric.1402897

European Commission. (2021). Ethics guidelines for trustworthy AI. High-Level Expert Group on Artificial Intelligence. Brussels: European Commission.

Faisal, S. M., Ishrat, M., & Khan, W. (2025). Digital Twins in Healthcare: Revolutionizing Patient Care and Medical Operations. In *Digital Twins for Smart Cities and Urban Planning* (pp. 69-89). CRC Press.

Fan, C., Zhang, C., Yahja, A., & Mostafavi, A. (2021). Disaster City Digital Twin: A vision for integrating artificial and human intelligence for disaster management. *International Journal of Information Management, 56*, 102049. DOI: 10.1016/j.ijinfomgt.2019.102049

Fan, X., & Li, Y. (2023). Energy management of renewable based power grids using artificial intelligence: Digital twin of renewables. *Solar Energy, 262*, 111867. DOI: 10.1016/j.solener.2023.111867

Fares, N. Y., & Jammal, M. (2023). AI-Driven IoT Systems and Corresponding Ethical Issues. In *AI and Society* (pp. 233–248). Chapman and Hall/CRC.

Farsi, M., Daneshkhah, A., Hosseinian-Far, A., & Jahankhani, H. (Eds.). (2020). *Digital twin technologies and smart cities* (Vol. 32). Springer. DOI: 10.1007/978-3-030-18732-3

Fathy, Y., Jaber, M., & Nadeem, Z. (2021). Digital twin-driven decision making and planning for energy consumption. *Journal of Sensor and Actuator Networks, 10*(2), 37. DOI: 10.3390/jsan10020037

Fatorachian, H., & Kazemi, H. (2018). A critical investigation of Industry 4.0 in manufacturing: Theoretical operationalisation framework. *Production Planning and Control, 29*(8), 633–644. DOI: 10.1080/09537287.2018.1424960

Fatorachian, H., & Kazemi, H. (2021). Impact of Industry 4.0 on supply chain performance. *Production Planning and Control, 32*(1), 63–81. DOI: 10.1080/09537287.2020.1712487

Feng, H., Lv, H., & Lv, Z. (2023). Resilience towarded digital twins to improve the adaptability of transportation systems. *Transportation Research Part A, Policy and Practice*, *173*, 103686. DOI: 10.1016/j.tra.2023.103686

Ferré-Bigorra, J., Casals, M., & Gangolells, M. (2022). The adoption of urban digital twins. *Cities (London, England)*, *131*, 103905. DOI: 10.1016/j.cities.2022.103905

Filippova, E., Hedayat, S., Ziarati, T., & Manganelli, M. (2025). Artificial Intelligence and Digital Twins for Bioclimatic Building Design: Innovations in Sustainability and Efficiency.

Floridi, L., Cowls, J., Beltrametti, M., Chatila, R., Chazerand, P., Dignum, V., Luetge, C., Madelin, R., Pagallo, U., Rossi, F., Schafer, B., Valcke, P., & Vayena, E. (2018). AI4People—An ethical framework for a good AI society. *Minds and Machines*, *28*(4), 689–707. DOI: 10.1007/s11023-018-9482-5 PMID: 30930541

Ford, D. N., & Wolf, C. M. (2020). Smart cities with digital twin systems for disaster management. *Journal of Management Engineering*, *36*(4), 04020027. DOI: 10.1061/(ASCE)ME.1943-5479.0000779

Francisco, A., Mohammadi, N., & Taylor, J. E. (2020). Smart city digital twin–enabled energy management: Toward real-time urban building energy benchmarking. *Journal of Management Engineering*, *36*(2), 04019045. DOI: 10.1061/(ASCE)ME.1943-5479.0000741

Frank, A. G., Dalenogare, L. S., & Ayala, N. F. (2019). Industry 4.0 technologies: Implementation patterns in manufacturing companies. *International Journal of Production Economics*, *210*, 15–26. DOI: 10.1016/j.ijpe.2019.01.004

Frederico, G. F. (2021). From Supply Chain 4.0 to Supply Chain 5.0: Findings from a systematic literature review and research directions. *Logistics (Basel)*, *5*(3), 49. DOI: 10.3390/logistics5030049

Furfaro, A., Felicetti, C., Saccà, D., & Crupi, F. (2022). Accountability of IoT Devices. In *Security, Trust and Privacy Models, and Architectures in IoT Environments* (pp. 133–147). Springer International Publishing.

Furr, N., Shipilov, A., & Hagiu, A. (2022). What is digital transformation Core tensions facing established companies. *Global Strategy Journal*, *12*(3), 517–544. DOI: 10.1002/gsj.1442

Gadre, M., & Deoskar, A. (2020). Industry 4.0–digital transformation, challenges and benefits. *International Journal of Future Generation Communication and Networking*, *13*(2), 139–149.

Gailliot, M. T., Baumeister, R. F., DeWall, C. N., Maner, J. K., Plant, E. A., Tice, D. M., Brewer, L. E., & Schmeichel, B. J. (2007). Self-control relies on glucose as a limited energy source: Willpower is more than a metaphor. *Journal of Personality and Social Psychology*, *92*(2), 325–336. DOI: 10.1037/0022-3514.92.2.325 PMID: 17279852

Galbraith, J. R. (2014). *Designing the agile organization*. Jossey-Bass.

Galli, B. J., & Ocampo, L. A. (2019). Exploring the relationships between continuous improvement and predictive analytics. *International Journal of Advanced Operations Management*, *11*(3), 189–210. DOI: 10.1504/IJAOM.2019.100709

Galopoulou, K., & Varga, L. (2023). The role of digital twins in energy transition. *Energy Procedia*, *37*, 1–7.

Ganesha, K. S., & Hemalatha, K. G. (2025). Digital Transformation in Advertising after COVID-19: Routing the New Landscape. In *Handbook of Digital Innovation, Transformation, and Sustainable Development in a Post-Pandemic Era* (pp. 384–406). CRC Press.

Gao, P., Zhang, J., Gong, Y., & Li, H. (2020). Effects of technical IT capabilities on organizational agility: The moderating role of IT business spanning capability. *Industrial Management & Data Systems*, *120*(5), 941–961. DOI: 10.1108/IMDS-08-2019-0433

Gascó-Hernandez, M. (2018). Building a smart city: Lessons from Barcelona. *Communications of the ACM*, *61*(4), 50–57. DOI: 10.1145/3117800

Gaur, L., & Sahoo, B. M. (2022). Explainable AI in ITS: Ethical concerns. In *Explainable artificial intelligence for intelligent transportation systems: Ethics and applications* (pp. 79–90). Springer International Publishing. DOI: 10.1007/978-3-031-09644-0_5

Gebayew, C., Hardini, I. R., Panjaitan, G. H. A., & Kurniawan, N. B. (2018). A systematic literature review on digital transformation. *In 2018 International Conference on Information Technology Systems and Innovation (ICITSI)* (pp. 260–265). IEEE. DOI: 10.1109/ICITSI.2018.8695912

Gentner, T., Neitzel, T., Schulze, J., Gerschner, F., & Theissler, A. (2023). Data Lakes in Healthcare: Applications and Benefits from the Perspective of Data Sources and Players. *Procedia Computer Science*, *225*, 1302–1311. DOI: 10.1016/j.procs.2023.10.118

George, G., Haas, M. R., & Pentland, A. (2014). Big data and management. *Academy of Management Journal*, *57*(2), 321–326. DOI: 10.5465/amj.2014.4002

Ghaffari, K., Lagzian, M., Kazemi, M., & Malekzadeh, G. (2019). A socio-technical analysis of Internet of Things development: An interplay of technologies, tasks, structures and actors. *Foresight, 21*(6), 640–653. DOI: 10.1108/FS-05-2019-0037

Ghobakhloo, M. (2020). Industry 4.0, digitization, and opportunities for sustainability. *Journal of Cleaner Production, 252*, 119869. DOI: 10.1016/j.jclepro.2019.119869

Ghobakhloo, M., & Iranmanesh, M. (2021). Digital transformation success under Industry 4.0: A strategic guideline for manufacturing SMEs. *Journal of Manufacturing Technology Management, 32*(7), 1376–1397. DOI: 10.1108/JMTM-11-2020-0455

Ghorbanian, M. (2025). From Simulation to Reality: Using Digital Twin Technology (DT) to Design Sustainable Smart Cities. *International Journal of Architectural Engineering & Urban Planning, 35*(1).

Giaveno, S. (2021). Smart City and Digital Twins: Definitions, Methodologies, and Applications. In *Handbook of Research on Developing Smart Cities Based on Digital Twins* (pp. 243-264). IGI Global.

Gill, M., & VanBoskirk, S. (2016). The digital maturity model 4.0. *Forestry Research, 1*, 1–15.

Gobeawan, L., Lin, E. S., Tandon, A., Yee, A. T. K., Khoo, V. H. S., Teo, S. N., Yi, S., Lim, C. W., Wong, S. T., Wise, D. J., Cheng, P., Liew, S. C., Huang, X., Li, Q. H., Teo, L. S., Fekete, G. S., & Poto, M. T. (2018). Modeling trees for virtual singapore: From data acquisition to citygml models. *The International Archives of the Photogrammetry, Remote Sensing and Spatial Information Sciences, 42*(W10), 55–62. DOI: 10.5194/isprs-archives-XLII-4-W10-55-2018

Goel, A., Tamrakar, P., Lal, M., Bhende, M., Wani, M., & Saoji, S. (2024). Real-time medical IoT for continuous glucose monitoring. In *2024 International Conference on Intelligent Systems and Advanced Applications (ICISAA)*. IEEE. https://doi.org/ DOI: 10.1109/ICISAA62385.2024.10828888

Gokhale, P., Bhat, O., & Bhat, S. (2018). Introduction to IOT. *International Advanced Research Journal in Science. Engineering and Technology, 5*(1), 41–44.

Gonçalves, A. R., Pinto, D. C., Rita, P., & Pires, T. (2023). Artificial intelligence and its ethical implications for marketing. *Emerging Science Journal, 7*(2), 313–327. DOI: 10.28991/ESJ-2023-07-02-01

Gorantla, V. A. K., Gude, V., Sriramulugari, S. K., Yuvaraj, N., & Yadav, P. (2024). Utilizing Hybrid Cloud Strategies to Enhance Data Storage and Security in E-Commerce Applications. *2024 2nd International Conference on Disruptive Technologies, ICDT 2024*, 494–499. DOI: 10.1109/ICDT61202.2024.10489749

Goyal, N. K. (2025). Security and Privacy in IoT, Fog, and Blockchain Networks. In *Energy-Efficient Deep Learning Approaches in IoT, Fog, and Green Blockchain Revolution* (pp. 371-398). IGI Global Scientific Publishing.

Gramegna, N., Greggio, F., & Bonollo, F. (2020). Smart factory competitiveness based on real-time monitoring and a quality predictive model. DOI: 10.1007/978-3-030-57997-5_22

Grant, O., & Agoro, H. (2021). Trends in Network Compliance and Regulatory Challenges.

Gregori, N., & Holzmann, P. (2024). Same same, but different: Consumers' decision–making process and the role of digital context. *Journal of Interactive Marketing*, *66*, 24–37. DOI: 10.1080/10696679.2024.2361431

Gubbi, J., Buyya, R., Marusic, S., & Palaniswami, M. (2013). Internet of Things (IoT): A vision, architectural elements, and future directions. *Future Generation Computer Systems*, *29*(7), 1645–1660. DOI: 10.1016/j.future.2013.01.010

Gujar, P. (2025). Data Privacy and Security Concerns in Software and Data Usability. In *Data Usability in the Enterprise: How Usability Leads to Optimal Digital Experiences* (pp. 289–307). Apress. DOI: 10.1007/979-8-8688-1183-8_10

Guleria, P. (2022). Predictions on diabetic patient datasets using big data analytics and machine learning techniques. In *Big Data Analytics for Intelligent Healthcare Management*. IEE., DOI: 10.1016/B978-0-323-91907-4.00018-2

Guntha, R. (2019). IoT architectures for noninvasive blood glucose and blood pressure monitoring. In *Proceedings of the 2019 International Symposium on Embedded Computing and System Design (ISED)* (pp. 120–124). https://doi.org/DOI: 10.1109/ISED48680.2019.9096233

Gupta, R., Usman, M., Kashid, P. V., Mohan, M. L., Gaidhani, V. A., & Ghuge, M. A. R. (2025). Artificial Intelligence and IoT in Retail Marketing: Innovations in Smart Stores and Personalized Shopping. *Artificial Intelligence*, *5*(2).

Hakiki, R., Nurlina, N., & Abaharis, H. (2024). Navigating Ethical Marketing: How Transparency Influences Brand Loyalty in the Digital Age. *YUME: Journal of Management*, *7*(3), 1644–1654.

Hämäläinen, M. (2019). A framework for a smart city design: digital transformation in the Helsinki smart city. In *Entrepreneurship and the community: a multidisciplinary perspective on creativity, social challenges, and business* (pp. 63–86). Springer International Publishing.

Hämäläinen, M. (2021). Urban development with dynamic digital twins in Helsinki city. *IET Smart Cities*, *3*(4), 201–210. DOI: 10.1049/smc2.12015

Hameed, M., Jervis, M., & Ikushima, T. (2020). Intel® FPGAs in smart factory – A short case study. https://consensus.app/papers/intel-®-fpgas-in-smart-factor-y---a-short-case-study-hameed-al-doori/22cc4881be6e50d7aedf3393000a7c3d Ibrahimi, G., & Benchekroun, B. (2023). The contribution of agility to an organisation's digital transformation. *TEM Journal*. DOI: 10.18421/tem124-48

Haque, M. E., Tariq, F., Khandaker, M. R. A., & Wong, K.-K. (2023). *A survey of scheduling in 5G URLLC and outlook for emerging 6G systems*. IEEE., DOI: 10.1109/ACCESS.2023.3264592

Harkin, D., Mann, M., & Warren, I. (2022). Consumer IoT and its under-regulation: Findings from an Australian study. *Policy and Internet*, *14*(1), 96–113. DOI: 10.1002/poi3.285

Hartmann, P. M., Zaki, M., Feldmann, N., & Neely, A. (2016). Capturing value from big data – a taxonomy of data-driven business models used by start-up firms. *International Journal of Operations & Production Management*, *36*(10), 1382–1406. DOI: 10.1108/IJOPM-02-2014-0098

Hassan, M. U., Alaliyat, S., & Hameed, I. A. (2024). Towards the creation of a digital twin authoring tool: A smart mobility perspective in smart cities. *IEEE Access : Practical Innovations, Open Solutions*.

Heffernan, K. J., Vetere, F., & Chang, S. (2021). *Insertables: Beyond Cyborgs and Augmentation to Convenience and Amenity*. 185–227. DOI: 10.1007/978-3-030-30457-7_6

Helal, M. (2025). Current developments, applications, challenges and future trends in internet of things: A survey. *International Journal of Data and Network Science*. DOI: 10.5267/j.ijdns.2024.9.008

Helfat, C. E., Finkelstein, S., Mitchell, W., Peteraf, M. A., Singh, H., Teece, D. J., & Winter, S. G. (2007). *Dynamic Capabilities: Understanding Strategic Change in Organizations*. Blackwell Publishing.

Helo, P., & Thai, V. V. (2024). Logistics 4.0 – Digital transformation with smart connected tracking and tracing devices. *International Journal of Production Economics*, *275*, 109336. DOI: 10.1016/j.ijpe.2024.109336

Hemalatha, J., Balasubramanian, C., Sekar, M., Senthil Pandian, P., & Rajeswari, S. (2025). AIoT-powered proactive elderly healthcare: Wearable monitoring. *Rehabilitation Engineering, Assistive Technologies and the Future of Healthcare Using Robotics*, 165–182. DOI: 10.1016/B978-0-443-31624-1.00009-5

Hemdan, E. E. D., El-Shafai, W., & Sayed, A. (2023). Integrating digital twins with IoT-based blockchain: Concept, architecture, challenges, and future scope. *Wireless Personal Communications, 131*(3), 2193–2216. DOI: 10.1007/s11277-023-10538-6 PMID: 37360142

Henderson, J. C., & Venkatraman, N. (1993). Strategic alignment: Leveraging information technology for transforming organizations. *IBM Systems Journal, 32*(1), 4–16. DOI: 10.1147/sj.382.0472

Hermann, E. (2022). Leveraging artificial intelligence in marketing for social good—An ethical perspective. *Journal of Business Ethics, 179*(1), 43–61. DOI: 10.1007/s10551-021-04843-y PMID: 34054170

Holzinger, A., Zatloukal, K., & Müller, H. (2025). Is human oversight to AI systems still possible? *New Biotechnology, 85*, 59–62. DOI: 10.1016/j.nbt.2024.12.003 PMID: 39675423

Hossain, M., Islam, M. R., & Rahman, M. M. (2024). A holistic analysis of Internet of Things (IoT) security. *Future Internet, 16*(2), 40. DOI: 10.3390/fi16020040

Hu, W. (2024). Digital twin and AI enabled predictive maintenance in building industry.

Huang, K., Wang, K., Lee, P. K. C., & Yeung, A. C. L. (2023). The impact of industry 4.0 on supply chain capability and supply chain resilience A dynamic resource based view. *International Journal of Production Economics, 262*, 108913. DOI: 10.1016/j.ijpe.2023.108913

Huang, S., Wu, Q., Zhao, H., & Li, C. (2017). Distributed optimization-based dynamic tariff for congestion management in distribution networks. *IEEE Transactions on Smart Grid, 10*(1), 184–192. DOI: 10.1109/TSG.2017.2735998

Hughes, A., Shandhi, M. M. H., Master, H., Dunn, J., & Brittain, E. (2023). Wearable Devices in Cardiovascular Medicine. *Circulation Research, 132*(5), 652–670. DOI: 10.1161/CIRCRESAHA.122.322389 PMID: 36862812

Hui, Y., Wang, Q., Su, Z., Cheng, N., Chen, R., & Luan, T. H. (2024). Joint optimization of personalized route planning and global traffic scheduling: A dt-enabled integrated framework. *IEEE Transactions on Vehicular Technology, 73*(10), 14474–14485. DOI: 10.1109/TVT.2024.3408756

Iansiti, M., & Lakhani, K. R. (2014). Digital ubiquity: How connections, sensors, and data are revolutionizing business. *Harvard Business Review*, *92*(11), 91–99.

IDC. (2022). *Worldwide Internet of Things Spending Guide*. International Data Corporation.

Idowu, E. A. A., Teo, J., Salih, S., Valverde, J., & Yeung, J. A. (2023). Streams, rivers, and data lakes: An introduction to understanding modern electronic healthcare records. *Clinical Medicine*, *23*(4), 409–413. DOI: 10.7861/clinmed.2022-0325 PMID: 37524426

Ignatius, M., Wong, N. H., Martin, M., & Chen, S. (2019, July). Virtual Singapore integration with energy simulation and canopy modelling for climate assessment. [). IOP Publishing.]. *IOP Conference Series. Earth and Environmental Science*, *294*(1), 012018. DOI: 10.1088/1755-1315/294/1/012018

Iqbal, S. M. A., Mahgoub, I., Du, E., Leavitt, M. A., & Asghar, W. (2021). Advances in healthcare wearable devices. *Npj Flexible Electronics 2021 5:1*, *5*(1), 1–14. DOI: 10.1038/s41528-021-00107-x

Irfan, M. S., Dasgupta, S., & Rahman, M. (2024). Toward transportation digital twin systems for traffic safety and mobility: A review. *IEEE Internet of Things Journal*, *11*(14), 24581–24603. DOI: 10.1109/JIOT.2024.3395186

Ishmaev, G. (2020). The ethical limits of blockchain-enabled markets for private IoT data. *Philosophy & Technology*, *33*(3), 411–432. DOI: 10.1007/s13347-019-00361-y

Ishola, A. (2024). IoT applications in sustainability and sustainable community development. *World Journal of Advanced Research and Reviews _ Awaiting DOI.*

Issa, W., Moustafa, N., Turnbull, B., Sohrabi, N., & Tari, Z. (2022). Blockchain-based federated learning for securing IoT. *ACM Computing Surveys*, *55*(8). Advance online publication. DOI: 10.1145/3560816

Ivanov, S. H. (2023). Automated decision-making. *foresight, 25*(1), 4-19.

Ivanov, D. (2020). Predicting the impacts of epidemic outbreaks on global supply chains: A simulation-based analysis on the coronavirus outbreak (COVID-19/SARS-CoV-2) case. *Transportation Research Part E, Logistics and Transportation Review*, *136*, 101922. DOI: 10.1016/j.tre.2020.101922 PMID: 32288597

Ivanov, D. (2021). Supply Chain Viability and the COVID-19 pandemic: A conceptual and formal generalisation of four major adaptation strategies. *International Journal of Production Research*, *59*(12), 3535–3552. DOI: 10.1080/00207543.2021.1890852

Jacobides, M. G., Cennamo, C., & Gawer, A. (2018). Towards a theory of ecosystems. *Strategic Management Journal, 39*(8), 2255–2276. DOI: 10.1002/smj.2904

Jafari, M., Kavousi-Fard, A., Chen, T., & Karimi, M. (2023). A review on digital twin technology in smart grid, transportation system and smart city: Challenges and future. *IEEE Access : Practical Innovations, Open Solutions, 11*, 17471–17484. DOI: 10.1109/ACCESS.2023.3241588

Jaffrin, L. C., Nithya, T., & Divya, J. (2025, April). IoT for Sustainable Development: Enhancing Environmental Efficiency and Resource Optimization. In *2025 5th International Conference on Trends in Material Science and Inventive Materials (ICTMIM)* (pp. 1224-1230). IEEE.

Jagatheesaperumal, S. K., Rahouti, M., Ahmad, K., Al-Fuqaha, A., & Guizani, M. (2021). The duo of artificial intelligence and big data for industry 4.0: Applications, techniques, challenges, and future research directions. *IEEE Internet of Things Journal, 9*(15), 12861–12885. DOI: 10.1109/JIOT.2021.3139827

Jain, S., Yadav, N., Husain, M., Aggarwal, M., Arya, P., & Aggarwal, S. (2022). Internet of Underwater Things. *Internet of Things : Engineering Cyber Physical Human Systems*, 107–120. Advance online publication. DOI: 10.1201/9781003181613-9

Janapati, K. C., Vemula, Y. S., Chindam, V., & Bajjuri, A., & Koushik. (2024). IoT-based continuous glucose monitoring system. In *Proceedings of the 2024 International Conference on Expert Clouds and Applications (ICOECA)* (pp. 488–493). https://doi.org/DOI: 10.1109/ICOECA62351.2024.00091

Janiesch, C., Fischer, M., Winkelmann, A., & Nentwich, V. (2019). Specifying autonomy in the internet of things: The autonomy model and notation. *Information Systems and e-Business Management, 17*(1), 159–194. DOI: 10.1007/s10257-018-0379-x

Javaid, M., Haleem, A., Singh, R. P., & Suman, R. (2022). Artificial intelligence applications for industry 4.0: A literature-based study. *Journal of Industrial Integration and Management, 7*(01), 83–111. DOI: 10.1142/S2424862221300040

Javeed, D., Almusaylim, Z. A., Cuomo, S., Postolache, O., & Roman, R. (2024). Quantum-empowered federated learning and 6G wireless networks: Challenges, opportunities, and future directions. *Future Generation Computer Systems*. Advance online publication. DOI: 10.1016/j.future.2024.06.023

Jayachitra, S., Prasanth, A., Hariprasath, S., Benazir Begam, R., & Madiajagan, M. (2023). *AI Enabled Internet of Medical Things in Smart Healthcare*. 141–161. DOI: 10.1007/978-3-031-31952-5_7

Jayadatta, S. (2023). A study on latest developments in artificial intelligence (AI) and internet of things (IoT) in current context. *Journal of Applied Information Science*, *11*(2), 21–28.

Jiang, Z., Lv, H., Li, Y., & Guo, Y. (2022). A novel application architecture of digital twin in smart grid. *Journal of Ambient Intelligence and Humanized Computing*, *13*(8), 3819–3835. DOI: 10.1007/s12652-021-03329-z

John, B. (2025). The Impact of AI-Powered Chatbots on User Experience: Exploring Perceived Risks to Privacy, Loyalty, and Continued Usage. https://www.researchgate.net/publication/388615153_The_Impact_of_AI-Powered_Chatbots_on_User_Experience_Exploring_Perceived_Risks_to_Privacy_Loyalty_and_Continued_Usage

Kabir, M. R., Halder, D., & Ray, S. (2024). Digital twins for iot-driven energy systems: A survey. *IEEE Access : Practical Innovations, Open Solutions*, *12*, 177123–177143. DOI: 10.1109/ACCESS.2024.3506660

Kadiri, D., Pap, M., & Baletić, B. (2023). Smart Cities: London, Paris, Barcelona, Milan; Definitions and Strategies. *Prostor: znanstveni časopis za arhitekturu i urbanizam, 31*(2 (66)), 236-247.

Kahneman, D. (2011). *Thinking, fast and slow*. Farrar, Straus and Giroux.

Kalla, D., & Smith, N. (2024). Integrating IoT, AI, and big data for enhanced operational efficiency in smart factories. *Educational Administration: Theory and Practice*, *30*(5), 14235–14245.

Kamal, M. F. M., Yin, I., Muthuveeran, A. A. S., Affandi, H. M., & Nasir, N. M. (2025). Barriers in The Integration of Digital Twins (DTs) And Building Information Modelling (BIM) For Predictive Maintenance in Facility Management. *Journal of Design and Built Environment*, 112-125.

Kamari, M., Ismaili, A., & Gencel, C. (2019). The role of transparency in supply chains: A literature review. In *Proceedings of the 31st Annual Conference of the Nordic Logistics Research Network (NOFOMA).*

Kamble, S. S., Gunasekaran, A., & Gawankar, S. A. (2020). Achieving sustainable performance in a data-driven agriculture supply chain: A review for research and applications. *International Journal of Production Economics*, *219*, 179–194. DOI: 10.1016/j.ijpe.2019.05.022

Kamijo, H., & Ogasawara, H. (2023). Efforts to improve business agility in enterprise agile methodology. *IIAI-AAI, 2023*, 627–632. Advance online publication. DOI: 10.1109/IIAI-AAI59060.2023.00124

Kandt, J., & Batty, M. (2021). Smart cities, big data and urban policy: Towards urban analytics for the long run. *Cities (London, England)*, *109*, 102992. DOI: 10.1016/j.cities.2020.102992

Kane, G. C., Palmer, D., Phillips, A. N., Kiron, D., & Buckley, N. (2017). Achieving digital maturity. *MIT Sloan Management Review*, *59*(1), 1–20.

Kannisto, P., Hästbacka, D., Gutiérrez, T., Suominen, O., Vilkko, M., & Craamer, P. (2022). Plant wide interoperability and decoupled data driven process control with message bus communication. *Journal of Industrial Information Integration*, *26*, 100253. DOI: 10.1016/j.jii.2021.100253

Kao, L.-J., Chiu, C.-C., Lin, H.-T., Hung, Y.-W., & Lu, C.-C. (2024). Unveiling the dimensions of digital transformation: A comprehensive taxonomy and assessment model for business. *Journal of Business Research*, *176*, 114595. DOI: 10.1016/j.jbusres.2024.114595

Kar, R., & Haldar, R. (2016). Applying chatbots to the internet of things: Opportunities and architectural elements. *arXiv preprint arXiv:1611.03799.*

Karale, A. (2021). The challenges of IoT addressing security, ethics, privacy, and laws. *Internet of Things : Engineering Cyber Physical Human Systems*, *15*, 100420. DOI: 10.1016/j.iot.2021.100420

Karami, A., Shemshaki, M., & Ghazanfar, M. (2024). *Exploring the ethical implications of ai-powered personalization in digital marketing. Data Intelligence*. In-Press.

Katsoulakis, E., Wang, Q., Wu, H., Shahriyari, L., Fletcher, R., Liu, J., Achenie, L., Liu, H., Jackson, P., Xiao, Y., & Deng, J. (2024). Digital twins for health: A scoping review. *NPJ Digital Medicine*, *7*(1), 77. DOI: 10.1038/s41746-024-01073-0 PMID: 38519626

Kavitha, N., Nivethitha, T., Deebanchakkarawarthi, G., & Shakthipriya, P. (2025). Transforming Healthcare : Unleashing the Power of Artificial Intelligence of Things (AIoT). *AIoT*, 99–129. DOI: 10.1201/9781003482338-5

Kehl, P. E., Kramarz, T., Münch, F., Witt, L., Giebe, C., Peitz, C., & Cimdins, M. (2025). 5G-TSN integrated prototype for reliable industrial communication. *Electronics (Basel)*, *14*(4), 758. DOI: 10.3390/electronics14040758

Kennedy, D. O., & Scholey, A. B. (2000). Glucose administration, heart rate and cognitive performance: Effects of increasing mental effort. *Psychopharmacology*, *149*(1), 63–71. DOI: 10.1007/s002139900335 PMID: 10789884

Ketzler, B., Naserentin, V., Latino, F., Zangelidis, C., Thuvander, L., & Logg, A. (2020). Digital twins for cities: A state of the art review. *Built Environment*, *46*(4), 547–573. DOI: 10.2148/benv.46.4.547

Kharroubi, A. T., & Darwish, H. M. (2015). Diabetes mellitus: The epidemic of the century. *World Journal of Diabetes*, *6*(6), 850–867. DOI: 10.4239/wjd.v6.i6.850 PMID: 26131326

Kim, C. (2021). Evolution of Advanced Miniaturization for Active Implantable Medical Devices. *Nano-Bio- Electronic, Photonic and MEMS Packaging*, 407–415. DOI: 10.1007/978-3-030-49991-4_17

Kindström, D., Kowalkowski, C., & Sandberg, E. (2013). Enabling service innovation: A dynamic capabilities approach. *Journal of Business Research*, *66*(8), 1063–1073. DOI: 10.1016/j.jbusres.2012.03.003

Klonoff, D. C., & Kerr, D. (2016). Digital diabetes communication: There's an app for that. *Journal of Diabetes Science and Technology*, *10*(5), 1003–1005. DOI: 10.1177/1932296816660210 PMID: 27464752

Kolk, A. (2017). The social responsibility of international business: From ethics and the environment to CSR and sustainable development. *Journal of World Business*, *51*(1), 23–34. DOI: 10.1016/j.jwb.2015.08.010

Kollárová, S., & Niklová, M. (2025). *The digital identity of Generation Z*. Matej Bel University., https://e-isbn.pl/IsbnWeb/record/show_cover.pdf?picture_id=186914

Koohang, A., Paliszkiewicz, J., Nord, J. H., & Goluchowski, J. (2022). Internet of Things from awareness to continued use. *International Journal of Information Management*, *61*, 102442. DOI: 10.1016/j.ijinfomgt.2021.102442

Korada, L. (2022). Using Digital Twins of a Smart City for Disaster Management. *Journal of Computational Analysis and Applications*, *30*(1).

Kose, B. O. (2025). Beyond the Screen: Cross-Platform UX for Wearables, IoT, and Emerging Technologies. Navigating Usability and User Experience in a lti-PlatfoMurm World. United States, IGI Global, 2024.

Koul, A. S. N. A., & Sabrina, A. (2019). *A framework for fair and responsible data market ecosystems* (Doctoral dissertation, éditeur non identifié).

Kounelis, I., Baldini, G., Neisse, R., Steri, G., Tallacchini, M., & Pereira, A. G. (2014). Building trust in the human? internet of things relationship. *IEEE Technology and Society Magazine*, *33*(4), 73–80. DOI: 10.1109/MTS.2014.2364020

Koydemir, H. C., & Ozcan, A. (2018). Wearable and implantable sensors for biomedical applications. *Annual Review of Analytical Chemistry (Palo Alto, Calif.)*, *11*(1), 127–146. DOI: 10.1146/annurev-anchem-061417-125956 PMID: 29490190

Kravets, O., Korolova, U., Nosachenko, O., Vasiltsova, O., & Koberniuk, S. (2025). AI-Powered Digital Marketing: Enhancing Customer Behaviour Predictions. *European Journal of Sustainable Development*, *14*(2), 84–84. DOI: 10.14207/ejsd.2025.v14n2p84

Krotov, V. (2017). The Internet of Things and new business opportunities. *Business Horizons*, *60*(6), 831–841. DOI: 10.1016/j.bushor.2017.07.009

Kshetri, N. (2018). 1 Blockchain's roles in meeting key supply chain management objectives. *International Journal of Information Management*, *39*, 80–89. DOI: 10.1016/j.ijinfomgt.2017.12.005

Kühnel, K., & Au-Yong-Oliveira, M. (2022). Optimal distribution of current resources in a production environment. DOI: 10.1007/978-3-031-04829-6_55

Kumar, D., & Suthar, N. (2024). Ethical and legal challenges of AI in marketing: An exploration of solutions. *Journal of Information. Communication and Ethics in Society*, *22*(1), 124–144. DOI: 10.1108/JICES-05-2023-0068

Kumar, K. V. R., Kumar, K. D., Poluru, R. K., Basha, S. M., & Reddy, M. P. K. (2020). Internet of things and fog computing applications in intelligent transportation systems. In *Architecture and security issues in fog computing applications* (pp. 131–150). IGI Global. DOI: 10.4018/978-1-7998-0194-8.ch008

Kumar, T., & Kushwaha, D. S. (2019). An intelligent surveillance system based on IoT for internal security of a nation. [IJISP]. *International Journal of Information Security and Privacy*, *13*(3), 1–30. DOI: 10.4018/IJISP.201907010101

Kuppusamy, P. (2019). Smart education using internet of things technology. In *Emerging Technologies and Applications in Data Processing and Management* (pp. 385–412). IGI Global. DOI: 10.4018/978-1-5225-8446-9.ch017

Kušić, K., Schumann, R., & Ivanjko, E. (2023). A digital twin in transportation: Real-time synergy of traffic data streams and simulation for virtualizing motorway dynamics. *Advanced Engineering Informatics*, *55*, 101858. DOI: 10.1016/j.aei.2022.101858

Kwan, D., Cysneiros, L. M., & do Prado Leite, J. C. S. (2021, September). Towards achieving trust through transparency and ethics. In 2021 IEEE 29th International Requirements Engineering Conference (RE) (pp. 82-93). IEEE. DOI: 10.1109/RE51729.2021.00015

LaBrie, R. C., & Steinke, G. (2019). Towards a framework for ethical audits of AI algorithms.

Ladegourdie, G., Boydens, J., & Hennebert, J. (2022). OPC UA vs. MQTT: A performance evaluation for Industrial IoT applications. *IoT*, *3*(4), 465–484. DOI: 10.3390/iot3040027

Lamer, A., Saint-Dizier, C., Paris, N., & Chazard, E. (2024). Data Lake, Data Warehouse, Datamart, and Feature Store: Their Contributions to the Complete Data Reuse Pipeline. *JMIR Medical Informatics*, *12*(1), e54590. DOI: 10.2196/54590 PMID: 39037339

Larrañaga-Zumeta, A., Lucas-Estañ, M. C., Gozálvez, J., & Arriola, A. (2024). 5G configured grant scheduling for seamless integration with TSN industrial networks. *Computer Communications*, *226–227*, 107930. DOI: 10.1016/j.comcom.2024.107930

Lasi, H., Fettke, P., Kemper, H.-G., Feld, T., & Hoffmann, M. (2014). Industry 4.0. *Business & Information Systems Engineering*, *6*(4), 239–242. DOI: 10.1007/s12599-014-0334-4

Lawson, M. N. (2024). A Case Survey: Internet of Things Privacy and User Awareness of Vulnerabilities (Doctoral dissertation, Marymount University).

Lee, C. S., Cheang, P. Y. S., & Moslehpour, M. (2022). Predictive analytics in business analytics: Decision tree. *Advances in Decision Sciences*, *26*(1), 1–29. DOI: 10.47654/v26y2022i1p1-29

Lee, C., Kim, J., Ko, H., & Yoo, B. (2024). Addressing IoT storage constraints: A hybrid architecture for decentralized data storage and centralized management. *Internet of Things : Engineering Cyber Physical Human Systems*, *25*, 101014. DOI: 10.1016/j.iot.2023.101014

Lee, I. (2020). Internet of Things (IoT) cybersecurity: Literature review and IoT cyber risk management. *Future Internet*, *12*(9), 157. DOI: 10.3390/fi12090157

Lee, I., & Lee, K. (2015). The Internet of Things (IoT): Applications, investments, and challenges for enterprises. *Business Horizons*, *58*(4), 431–440. DOI: 10.1016/j.bushor.2015.03.008

Lee, J., Bagheri, B., & Kao, H.-A. (2015). A cyber-physical systems architecture for Industry 4.0-based manufacturing systems. *Manufacturing Letters*, *3*, 18–23. DOI: 10.1016/j.mfglet.2014.12.001

Le, T., & Fan, R. (2024). Digital twins for logistics and supply chain systems. *Computers & Industrial Engineering*, *187*, 109768. Advance online publication. DOI: 10.1016/j.cie.2023.109768

Li, S., Xie, H.-L., Zheng, P., & Wang, L. (2024). Industrial metaverse: A proactive human-robot collaboration perspective. *Journal of Manufacturing Systems*, *76*, 314–319. DOI: 10.1016/j.jmsy.2024.08.003

Litvinova, O., Klager, E., Tzvetkov, N. T., Kimberger, O., Kletecka-Pulker, M., Willschke, H., & Atanasov, A. G. (2022). Digital Pills with Ingestible Sensors: Patent Landscape Analysis. *Pharmaceuticals 2022, Vol. 15, Page 1025, 15*(8), 1025. DOI: 10.3390/ph15081025

Liu, X., Li, A., Fu, X., Luo, B., Du, X., & Guizani, M. (2021). Understanding digital forensic characteristics of smart speaker ecosystems. *IEEE Globecom Workshops*, 1–6. Advance online publication. DOI: 10.1109/GLOBECOM46510.2021.9685816

Li, W., Wang, B., Sun, R., Ai, L., & Lin, Z. (2025). Energy-efficient multimodal mobility networks in transportation digital twins: Strategies and optimization. *Energy*, *318*, 134587. DOI: 10.1016/j.energy.2025.134587

Llagostera-Brugarola, E., Corpas-Marco, E., Victorio-Vergel, C., Lopez-Aguilera, E., Vázquez-Gallego, F., & Alonso-Zarate, J. (2025). A Digital Twin for Intelligent Transportation Systems in Interurban Scenarios. *Applied Sciences (Basel, Switzerland)*, *15*(13), 7454. DOI: 10.3390/app15137454

Lomborg, S., Kaun, A., & Scott Hansen, S. (2023). Automated decision-making: Toward a people-centred approach. *Sociology Compass*, *17*(8), e13097. DOI: 10.1111/soc4.13097

Lu, L., Yin, M., Xie, Y., Pan, Y., Wang, M., & Brilakis, I. (2025). Development of A Trustworthy AI-supported Digital Twin Framework for Road Operation and Maintenance.

Lulla, G., Kumar, A., Pole, G., & Deshmukh, G. (2021, March). IoT based smart security and surveillance system. In *2021 international conference on emerging smart computing and informatics (ESCI)* (pp. 385-390). IEEE. DOI: 10.1109/ESCI50559.2021.9396843

Luthra, S., Kumar, A., Zavadskas, E. K., Mangla, S. K., & Garza-Reyes, J. A. (2020). Industry 4.0 as an enabler of sustainability diffusion in the supply chain: An analysis of influential strength of drivers in an emerging economy. *International Journal of Production Research*, *58*(5), 1505–1521. DOI: 10.1080/00207543.2019.1660828

Lu, Y. (2017). Industry 4.0: A survey on technologies, applications and open research issues. *Journal of Industrial Information Integration, 6*, 1–10. DOI: 10.1016/j.jii.2017.04.005

MacLachlan, A., Biggs, E., Roberts, G., & Boruff, B. (2021). Sustainable city planning: A data-driven approach for mitigating urban heat. *Frontiers in Built Environment, 6*, 519599. DOI: 10.3389/fbuil.2020.519599

Magrizos, S., Campora, M., Lamprinakos, G., Giovanis, A., & Christofi, M. (2025). Transparency by design: The effect of privacy policies visualisation on brand trust and perceived intrusion. *Behaviour & Information Technology*, •••, 1–13.

Mahdad, M., Hasanov, M., Isakhanyan, G., & Dolfsma, W. (2022). A smart web of firms, farms and IoT. *British Food Journal.* Advance online publication. DOI: 10.1108/BFJ-07-2021-0756

Mahmoodian, M., Shahrivar, F., Setunge, S., & Mazaheri, S. (2022). Development of digital twin for intelligent maintenance of civil infrastructure. *Sustainability (Basel), 14*(14), 8664. DOI: 10.3390/su14148664

Maiorescu, I., Bucur, M., Georgescu, B., Moise, D., Strat, V. A., & Zgură, I. D. (2020). Social media and IOT wearables in developing marketing strategies. Do SMEs differ from large enterprises? *Sustainability (Basel), 12*(18), 7292. DOI: 10.3390/su12187292

Maksimovic, M. (2017). Greening the future: Green Internet of Things (G-IoT) as a key technological enabler of sustainable development. In *Internet of things and big data analytics toward next-generation intelligence* (pp. 283–313). Springer International Publishing.

Mallioris, P., Aivazidou, E., & Bechtsis, D. (2024). Predictive maintenance in Industry 4.0: A systematic multi-sector mapping. *CIRP Journal of Manufacturing Science and Technology, 50*, 80–103. DOI: 10.1016/j.cirpj.2024.02.003

Manavalan, M. (2020). *Intersection of AI, ML, and IoT: An economic overview.* Global Disclosure of Economics and Business., DOI: 10.18034/gdeb.v9i2.584

Mancebo, F. (2020). Smart city strategies: Time to involve people. Comparing Amsterdam, Barcelona and Paris. *Journal of Urbanism, 13*(2), 133–152. DOI: 10.1080/17549175.2019.1649711

Manoj, G., Juliet, P. A., Mege, V. S., Devi, K. G., Gnanasekaran, C., & Indira, P. (2025). AI for Personalization: Transforming Customer Journeys in Self-Service Technology. In Practical Applications of Self-Service Technologies Across Industries (pp. 255-286). IGI Global Scientific Publishing.

Mansouri, C., & Bezgrari, A. (2022). Digital marketing as a mechanism to pursue the digital transformation: Case study of Sephora. *Revue des Economies financières bancaires et de management, 11*(1), 851-869.

Manwaring, P., Malakhatka, E., Fiore, E., Paradiso, J., Hill, D., & Wiberg, M. (2025). Internet of Things (IoT): Studying the Integration of Everyday Objects with the Internet and the Implications for Human Lives. In *Human-Technology Interaction: Interdisciplinary Approaches and Perspectives* (pp. 175–199). Springer Nature Switzerland. DOI: 10.1007/978-3-031-78357-9_6

March, H., & Ribera-Fumaz, R. (2018). Barcelona: From corporate smart city to technological sovereignty. In *Inside smart cities* (pp. 227-242). Routledge.

Marinova, N. (2024). Advantages and ethical considerations of industrial iot artificial intelligence solutions usage. *Бизнес управление*, (2), 43-58.

Mashat, B., Katircioglu, S., & Tanovic, E. (2024). Impact of Internet of Things adoption on organizational performance: A mediating analysis of supply chain integration, performance, and competitive advantage. *Sustainability (Basel), 16*(6), 2250. DOI: 10.3390/su16062250

Masicampo, E. J., & Baumeister, R. F. (2008). Toward a physiology of dual-process reasoning and judgment: Lemonade, willpower, and expensive rule-based analysis. *Psychological Science, 19*(3), 255–260. https://www.jstor.org/stable/40064920. DOI: 10.1111/j.1467-9280.2008.02077.x PMID: 18315798

Mathur, S., Kalla, A., Gür, G., Bohra, M. K., & Liyanage, M. (2023). A survey on role of blockchain for IoT: Applications and technical aspects. *Computer Networks, 227*, 109726. DOI: 10.1016/j.comnet.2023.109726

Matt, C., Hess, T., & Benlian, A. (2015). Digital transformation strategies. *Business & Information Systems Engineering, 57*(5), 339–343. DOI: 10.1007/s12599-015-0401-5

MAY. P. M. A., Savitha, V., Gayathri, S., & Mahalakshmi, S. (2025, April). Exploring Sustainable Computing: IoT, Big Data, and Energy-Efficient Solutions. In *2025 5th International Conference on Trends in Material Science and Inventive Materials (ICTMIM)* (pp. 1218-1223). IEEE.

Mayorova, K. S., & Balashova, E. (2021). Digital transition of industrial enterprises into the "smart" ecosystem. *Russian Journal of Industrial Economics*. DOI: 10.17073/2072-1633-2021-4-433-444

Mazzetto, S. (2024). A review of urban digital twins integration, challenges, and future directions in smart city development. *Sustainability (Basel), 16*(19), 8337. DOI: 10.3390/su16198337

McAfee, A., & Brynjolfsson, E. (2012). Big data: The management revolution. *Harvard Business Review*, *90*(10), 60–68. PMID: 23074865

McElroy, T., Dickinson, D. L., & Levin, I. P. (2020). Thinking about decisions: An integrative approach of person and task factors. *Journal of Behavioral Decision Making*, *33*(5), 538–555. DOI: 10.1002/bdm.2175

Mchirgui, N., Quadar, N., Kraiem, H., & Lakhssassi, A. (2024). The applications and challenges of digital twin technology in smart grids: A comprehensive review. *Applied Sciences (Basel, Switzerland)*, *14*(23), 10933. DOI: 10.3390/app142310933

Mekala, S. H., Bandara Ekanayake, T. N., & Jayaraman, P. P. (2023). Cybersecurity for industrial IoT threats, countermeasures, challenges and future directions. *Computer Communications*, *208*, 44–69. DOI: 10.1016/j.comcom.2023.06.020

Melnyk, A. (2024). Examining The Impact of Advanced Technologies and Semantic Web Integration in Web 3.0 And The Future of Strategic Digital Marketing. Publishing House "Baltija Publishing".

Messier, C., Pierre, J., Desrochers, A., & Gravel, M. (1998). Dosedependent action of glucose on memory processes in women: Effect on serial position and recall priority. *Brain Research. Cognitive Brain Research*, *7*(2), 221–233. DOI: 10.1016/S0926-6410(98)00041-X PMID: 9774737

Metzger, M. M. (2000). Glucose enhancement of a facial recognition task in young adults. *Physiology & Behavior*, *68*(4), 549–553. DOI: 10.1016/S0031-9384(99)00215-2 PMID: 10713296

Miorandi, D., Sicari, S., De Pellegrini, F., & Chlamtac, I. (2012). Internet of things: Vision, applications and research challenges. *Ad Hoc Networks*, *10*(7), 1497–1516. DOI: 10.1016/j.adhoc.2012.02.016

Mishra, S.. (2024). A survey on security and cryptographic perspective of IIoT. *Internet of Things : Engineering Cyber Physical Human Systems*, *26*, 101037. DOI: 10.1016/j.iot.2023.101037

Mithas, S., Ramasubbu, N., & Sambamurthy, V. (2011). How information management capability influences firm performance. *Management Information Systems Quarterly*, *35*(1), 237–256. DOI: 10.2307/23043496

Mitra, A., & Paul, S. (2025). Harnessing AI-Driven Personalization for Financial Brand Loyalty: The Role of Emotional Intelligence in FinTech Marketing. In Intersecting Natural Language Processing and FinTech Innovations in Service Marketing (pp. 243-274). IGI Global Scientific Publishing.

Mohammadi, N., & Taylor, J. E. (2017, November). Smart city digital twins. In *2017 IEEE symposium series on computational intelligence (SSCI)* (pp. 1-5). IEEE. DOI: 10.1109/SSCI.2017.8285439

Mökander, J. (2023). Auditing of AI: Legal, ethical and technical approaches. *Digital Society : Ethics, Socio-Legal and Governance of Digital Technology*, *2*(3), 49. DOI: 10.1007/s44206-023-00074-y

Monostori, L. (2014). Cyber-physical production systems: Roots, expectations and R&D challenges. *Procedia CIRP*, *17*, 9–13. DOI: 10.1016/j.procir.2014.03.115

Moradi, M. (2021). Importance of internet of things (IoT) in marketing research and its ethical and data privacy challenges. *Business Ethics and Leadership*, *5*(1), 22–30. DOI: 10.21272/bel.5(1).22-30.2021

Morales Sharp, T. (2023). Ethical guide for social media marketing: brand humanization, data privacy, and brand trust. Universitat Politècnica de València. https://riunet.upv.es/handle/10251/197971

Moshed, A., & Al-Jabaly, S. (2024). Enhancing marketing success in Jordanian telecom: Strategic IoT integration and brand relationship management for maximized consumer loyalty. Journal of Infrastructure. *Policy and Development*, *8*(6), 3858.

Moyne, J., & Iskandar, J. (2017). Big Data Analytics for Smart Manufacturing: Case Studies in Semiconductor Manufacturing. *Processes (Basel, Switzerland)*, *5*(3), 39. DOI: 10.3390/pr5030039

Mukherjee, S., Suleman, S., Pilloton, R., Narang, J., & Rani, K. (2022). State of the Art in Smart Portable, Wearable, Ingestible and Implantable Devices for Health Status Monitoring and Disease Management. *Sensors 2022, Vol. 22, Page 4228, 22*(11), 4228. DOI: 10.3390/s22114228

Muntés-Mulero, V., Ripolles, O., Gupta, S., Dominiak, J., Willeke, E. R., Matthews, P., & Somoskoi, B. (2019). Agile risk management for multi-cloud software development. *IET Software*, *13*(3), 172–181. Advance online publication. DOI: 10.1049/iet-sen.2018.5295

Murugan, K., Shaheen, N., Kumar, P. S., Homera, D. S., Saketh, M., & Sivaji, P. (2024). Development of an IoT based sugar tracker diabetic monitoring system. In *Proceedings of the 5th International Conference on IoT Based Control Networks and Intelligent Systems (ICICNIS)* IEEE (pp. 481–486). https://doi.org/DOI: 10.1109/ICICNIS64247.2024.10823123

Mu, X., & Antwi-Afari, M. F. (2024). The applications of Internet of Things (IoT) in industrial management: A science mapping review. *International Journal of Production Research, 62*(5), 1928–1952. Advance online publication. DOI: 10.1080/00207543.2023.2290229

Nafees, M., & Kumar, M. (2023). Cybersecurity And Privacy Trust. In *Digital Data: Navigating The Digital Trust Landscape* (1st ed., p. 108). Noble Science Press., DOI: 10.52458/9789388996747.nsp2023.eb.ch-14

Nag, D., Brandel-Tanis, F., Pramestri, Z. A., Pitera, K., & Frøyen, Y. K. (2025). Exploring digital twins for transport planning: A review. *European Transport Research Review, 17*(1), 15. DOI: 10.1186/s12544-025-00713-0

Nagy, J., Oláh, J., Erdei, E., Máté, D., & Popp, J. (2018). The role and impact of Industry 4.0 and the Internet of Things on the business strategy of the value chain—The case of Hungary. *Sustainability (Basel), 10*(10), 3491. DOI: 10.3390/su10103491

Nahavandi, S. (2019). Industry 5.0: A human-centric solution. *Sustainability (Basel), 11*(16), 4371. DOI: 10.3390/su11164371

Nambisan, S. (2017). Digital Entrepreneurship: Toward a Digital Technology Perspective of Entrepreneurship. *Entrepreneurship Theory and Practice, 41*(6), 1029–1055. DOI: 10.1111/etap.12254

Nambisan, S., Lyytinen, K., Majchrzak, A., & Song, M. (2017). Digital Innovation Management: Reinventing innovation management research in a digital world. *Management Information Systems Quarterly, 41*(1), 223–238. DOI: 10.25300/MISQ/2017/41:1.03

Nanda, P., & Kumar, V. (2024). New generation technologies: Development vs. ethical challenges. *International Journal of Business Information Systems, 46*(3), 411–434. DOI: 10.1504/IJBIS.2024.140437

Nastjuk, I., Trang, S., & Papageorgiou, E. I. (2022). Smart cities and smart governance models for future cities. *Electronic Markets, 32*(4), 1917–1924. DOI: 10.1007/s12525-022-00609-0

Nativi, S., Kotsev, A., Scudo, P., Pogorzelska, K., Vakalis, I., Dalla, B. A., & Perego, A. (2020). IoT 2.0 And The Internet Of Transformation (Web of Things and Digital Twins).

Nechesov, A., Dorokhov, I., & Ruponen, J. (2025). Virtual cities: From digital twins to autonomous ai societies. *IEEE Access : Practical Innovations, Open Solutions, 13*, 13866–13903. DOI: 10.1109/ACCESS.2025.3531222

Neisse, R., Baldini, G., Steri, G., Miyake, Y., Kiyomoto, S., & Biswas, A. R. (2015, December). An agent-based framework for informed consent in the internet of things. In *2015 IEEE 2nd World Forum on Internet of Things (WF-IoT)* (pp. 789-794). IEEE. DOI: 10.1109/WF-IoT.2015.7389154

Niu, B., Dai, Z., Liu, Y., & Jin, Y. (2022). The role of Physical Internet in building trackable and sustainable logistics service supply chains: A game analysis. *International Journal of Production Economics, 247*, 108438. DOI: 10.1016/j.ijpe.2022.108438

Noori, N., Hoppe, T., & de Jong, M. (2020). Classifying pathways for smart city development: Comparing design, governance and implementation in Amsterdam, Barcelona, Dubai, and Abu Dhabi. *Sustainability (Basel), 12*(10), 4030. DOI: 10.3390/su12104030

Nuerk, J., & Dařena, F. (2023). Activating supply chain business models' value potentials through systems engineering. *Systems Engineering, 26*(5), 660–674. DOI: 10.1002/sys.21676

Nzimakwe, T. I. (2020). Urbanisation and future smart cities: challenges of water and sanitation services. In *Reflections on African Cities in Transition: Selected Continental Experiences* (pp. 231–246). Springer International Publishing. DOI: 10.1007/978-3-030-46115-7_11

Ogawara, M. (2025). The influence of consumer privacy preferences on personalized marketing and multichannel CRM integration. *Frontiers in Management Science, 4*(1), 12–19. DOI: 10.56397/FMS.2025.01.03

Oladosu, S. A., Ike, C. C., Adepoju, P. A., Afolabi, A. I., Ige, A. B., & Amoo, O. O. (2024). *Frameworks for ethical data governance in machine learning: Privacy, fairness, and business optimization*. Magna Sci Adv Res Rev.

Oluwafemi, I. O., Clement, T., Adanigbo, O. S., Gbenle, T. P., & Adekunle, B. I. (2021). A Review of Ethical Considerations in AI-Driven Marketing Analytics: Privacy, Transparency, and Consumer Trust. *International Journal Of Multidisciplinary Research and Growth Evaluation, 2*(2), 428–435. DOI: 10.54660/.IJMRGE.2021.2.2.428-435

Omar, O. (2025). Digital Twins for Climate-Responsive Urban Development: Integrating Zero-Energy Buildings into Smart City Strategies. *Sustainability (Basel), 17*(15), 6670. DOI: 10.3390/su17156670

Omrany, H., Al-Obaidi, K. M., Husain, A., & Ghaffarianhoseini, A. (2023). Digital twins in the construction industry: A comprehensive review of current implementations, enabling technologies, and future directions. *Sustainability (Basel)*, *15*(14), 10908. DOI: 10.3390/su151410908

Onu, P., Pradhan, A., Madonsela, N. S., Ajayi, S. A., Osueke, C. O., Samuel, D. R., & Adebayo, S. (2025). Integration of ai and iot in smart manufacturing: Exploring technological, ethical, and legal frontiers. *Procedia Computer Science*, *253*, 654–660. DOI: 10.1016/j.procs.2025.01.127

Oproiu, M. I., Ileana, M., & Marian, C.-V. (2024). Architectural framework for IoT ecosystem. *2024 IEEE ECAI*. DOI: 10.1109/ECAI61503.2024.10607423

Orquin, J. L., & Kurzban, R. (2016). A meta-analysis of blood glucose effects on human decision making. *Psychological Bulletin*, *142*(5), 546–567. DOI: 10.1037/bul0000035 PMID: 26653865

Owen, A., & Moore, J. (2023). Ethical considerations in AI-driven personalization for eCommerce platforms. International Journal of Scientific Research in Computer Science. *Engineering and Information Technology*, *11*(2), 287–294. DOI: 10.32628/CSEIT251112371

Page, M. J., McKenzie, J. E., Bossuyt, P. M., Boutron, I., Hoffmann, T. C., Mulrow, C. D., & Moher, D. (2021). The PRISMA 2020 statement: an updated guideline for reporting systematic reviews. bmj, 372.

Palmaccio, M., Dicuonzo, G., & Belyaeva, Z. S. (2021). The internet of things and corporate business models: A systematic literature review. *Journal of Business Research*, *131*, 610–618. DOI: 10.1016/j.jbusres.2020.09.069

Pandita, N., Nand, S., Pathak, P., & Bhatt, V. (2023, October). Safeguarding Business Intelligence in Industrial IoT Using Blockchain-Enhanced Security. In *2023 4th International Conference on Data Analytics for Business and Industry (ICDABI)* (pp. 309-314). IEEE. DOI: 10.1109/ICDABI60145.2023.10629300

Panichakarn, B., Pochan, J., Shafiq, M., Saleem, I., Wang, Y., & Nazeer, S. (2024). Interplay of digital transformation, agility, and innovation. *Journal of Open Innovation*. Advance online publication. DOI: 10.1016/j.joitmc.2024.100408

Parker, S. K., & Grote, G. (2022). Automation, algorithms, and beyond: Why work design matters more than ever in a digital world. *Applied Psychology*, *71*(4), 1171–1204. DOI: 10.1111/apps.12241

Park, G. (2019). The changing wind of data privacy law: A comparative study of the European Union's General Data Protection Regulation and the 2018 California Consumer Privacy Act. *UC Irvine L. Rev.*, *10*, 1455.

Parviainen, P., Tihinen, M., Kääriäinen, J., & Teppola, S. (2017). Tackling the digitalization challenge: How to benefit from digitalization in practice. *International Journal of Information Systems and Project Management*, *5*(1), 63–77. DOI: 10.12821/ijispm050104

Pasmore, W. A., Francis, C., Haldeman, J., & Shani, A. (1982). Sociotechnical systems: A North American reflection on empirical studies of the seventies. *Human Relations*, *35*(12), 1179–1204. DOI: 10.1177/001872678203501207

Pathmabandu, C., Grundy, J., Chhetri, M. B., & Baig, Z. (2023). Privacy for IoT: Informed consent management in Smart Buildings. *Future Generation Computer Systems*, *145*, 367–383. DOI: 10.1016/j.future.2023.03.045

Patil, B. S. (2024). *The role of the Internet of Things in the telecom sector*. IJRASET., DOI: 10.22214/ijraset.2024.66194

Pee, L. G., & Pan, S. L. (2022). Climate-intelligent cities and resilient urbanisation: Challenges and opportunities for information research. *International Journal of Information Management*, *63*, 102446. DOI: 10.1016/j.ijinfomgt.2021.102446

Pelletier, C., L'Écuyer, F., & Raymond, L. (2025). Building organisational agility through digital transformation. *Industrial Management & Data Systems*. Advance online publication. DOI: 10.1108/IMDS-05-2024-0488

Peng, G. C. A., Nunes, M. B., & Zheng, L. (2017). Impacts of low citizen awareness and usage in smart city services: The case of London's smart parking system. *Information Systems and e-Business Management*, *15*(4), 845–876. DOI: 10.1007/s10257-016-0333-8

Pervez, F., Shoukat, M., Suresh, V., Farooq, M. U., Sandhu, M., Qayyum, A., Usama, M., Girardi, A., Latif, S., & Qadir, J. (2024). Medicine's New Rhythm: Harnessing Acoustic Sensing via the Internet of Audio Things for Healthcare. *IEEE Open Journal of the Computer Society*, *5*, 491–510. DOI: 10.1109/OJCS.2024.3462812

Petrescu, M., Krishen, A., & Bui, M. (2020). The internet of everything: Implications of marketing analytics from a consumer policy perspective. *Journal of Consumer Marketing*, *37*(6), 675–686. DOI: 10.1108/JCM-02-2019-3080

Petrova-Antonova, D., & Ilieva, S. (2020, August). Digital twin modeling of smart cities. In *International Conference on Human Interaction and Emerging Technologies* (pp. 384-390). Cham: Springer International Publishing.

Pettit, C., Bakelmun, A., Lieske, S. N., Glackin, S., Thomson, G., Shearer, H., & Newman, P. (2018). Planning support systems for smart cities. *City, Culture and Society*, *12*, 13–24. DOI: 10.1016/j.ccs.2017.10.002

Pillai, S. V., Purandare, P., & Jain, R. (2023). Digital Twin-Enabled Solutions for Smart City Applications. In *Handbook of Research on Network-Enabled IoT Applications for Smart City Services* (pp. 19–37). IGI Global. DOI: 10.4018/979-8-3693-0744-1.ch002

Pise, A. A., Almuzaini, K. K., Ahanger, T. A., Farouk, A., pant, K., Pareek, P. K., & Nuagah, S. J. (2022). Enabling Artificial Intelligence of Things (AIoT) Healthcare Architectures and Listing Security Issues. *Computational Intelligence and Neuroscience*, *8421434*(1), 1–14. DOI: 10.1155/2022/8421434 PMID: 36911247

Pise, A., Yoon, B., & Singh, S. (2023). Enabling Ambient Intelligence of Things (AIoT) healthcare system architectures. *Computer Communications*, *198*, 186–194. DOI: 10.1016/j.comcom.2022.10.029

Pivoto, D. G. S., de Almeida, L. F. F., da Rosa Righi, R., Rodrigues, J. J. P. C., Lugli, A. B., & Alberti, A. M. (2021). Cyber-physical systems architectures for industrial internet of things applications in Industry 4.0: A literature review. *Journal of Manufacturing Systems*, *58*, 176–192. DOI: 10.1016/j.jmsy.2020.11.017

Poongodi, T., Krishnamurthi, R., Indrakumari, R., Suresh, P., & Balusamy, B. (2020). Wearable Devices and IoT. *Intelligent Systems Reference Library*, *165*, 245–273. DOI: 10.1007/978-3-030-23983-1_10

Porter, M. E., & Heppelmann, J. E. (2014). How smart, connected products are transforming competition. *Harvard Business Review*, *92*(11), 64–88.

Powell, J., McCafferty-Leroux, A., Hilal, W., & Gadsden, S. A. (2024). Smart grids: A comprehensive survey of challenges, industry applications, and future trends. *Energy Reports*, *11*, 5760–5785. Advance online publication. DOI: 10.1016/j.egyr.2024.05.051

Prasad, A., Rastogi, T., Paolo, T., Tyagi, U., & Benedetto, F. (2023). Optimization of outcomes: Professional perspectives on mastering data-driven marketing. In Smith, E., & Doe, J. (Eds.), *Data engineering for data-driven marketing* (pp. 217–234). Springer.

Prasad, P. N. S. B. S. V., Hussain, S. A., Singha, A. K., Jana, B., Mandal, P., & Sanki, P. K. (2025). An advanced IoT-based non-invasive in vivo blood glucose estimation exploiting photoacoustic spectroscopy with SDNN architecture. *Sensors and Actuators. A, Physical, 162*, 116391. Advance online publication. DOI: 10.1016/j.sna.2025.116391

Prem, R. (2025). Hyper-Personalization in Digital Marketing: Evaluating Consumer Trust and Brand Loyalty in the Age of AI-Driven Campaigns. *Exploresearch, 02*(02), 106–115. DOI: 10.62823/ExRe/2025/02/02.62

Priyadharshini, L., Gautam, K. K., Agrawal, S., Rao, D. M. K., & Natarajan, S., & LB, M. (2024, November). IoT-Enabled Consumer Behavior Tracking. In *2024 Second International Conference Computational and Characterization Techniques in Engineering & Sciences (IC3TES)* (pp. 1-5). IEEE.

Putra, Z. D. W., & Van der Knaap, W. G. (2018). Urban innovation system and the role of an open web-based platform: The case of Amsterdam smart city. *Journal of Regional and City planning, 29*(3), 234-249.

Qian, L., Luo, Z., Du, Y., & Guo, L. (2009, December). Cloud computing: An overview. In *IEEE international conference on cloud computing* (pp. 626–631). Springer Berlin Heidelberg.

Qi, Q., Xu, Z., & Rani, P. (2023). Big data analytics challenges to implementing intelligent IIoT systems in sustainable manufacturing operations. *Technological Forecasting and Social Change, 190*, 122401. DOI: 10.1016/j.techfore.2023.122401

Qureshi, K. N., & Newe, T. (2024). Artificial Internet of Things : A New Paradigm of Connected Networks. *Artificial Intelligence of Things (AIoT)*, 3–20. DOI: 10.1201/9781003430018-2

Raeesi Vanani, I., Taghavifard, M. T., & Yalpanian, M. A. (2025). Predictive Analytics Solution for Digital Capabilities Identification Towards Business Performance Improvement. *SN Computer Science, 6*(1), 85. DOI: 10.1007/s42979-024-03630-6

Rahaman, S. U., Kumar, S., & Puchakayala, P. R. A. (2021). Data-driven customer segmentation: Advancing precision marketing through analytics and machine learning techniques. *Journal of Artificial Intelligence. Machine Learning and Data Science, 1*(1), 1–7. DOI: 10.51219/JAIMLD/shafeeq-ur-rahaman/309

Rahman, P. (2025). Exploring ethics and trust in persuasive technologies (Doctoral dissertation, University of British Columbia).

Rajbhar, R. (2022). *World of IoT and its challenges*. Data Analytics and Artificial Intelligence., DOI: 10.46632/daai/2/6/6

Raj, P., & Raman, A. C. (2017). *The Internet of Things: Enabling technologies, platforms, and use cases*. Auerbach Publications.

Ramachandran, K. K. (2018). Enhancing customer experience with real-time marketing analytics. *Eurasian Journal of Analytical Chemistry, 13*(6), 406–413.

Rao, A., Hu, H., & Nobre, A. C. (2013). The effects of combined caffeine and glucose drinks on attention in the human brain. *Psychopharmacology, 227*(1), 141–153. DOI: 10.1080/10284150500096994 PMID: 16117181

Razavi, H., Titidezh, O., Asgary, A., & Bonakdari, H. (2024). Building resilient smart cities: The role of digital twins and generative AI in disaster management strategy. In *Digital Twin Computing for Urban Intelligence* (pp. 95–118). Springer Nature Singapore. DOI: 10.1007/978-981-97-8483-7_5

Rejeb, A., Keogh, J. G., & Treiblmaier, H. (2019). Leveraging the Internet of Things and Blockchain Technology in Supply Chain Management. *Future Internet, 11*(7), 161. DOI: 10.3390/fi11070161

Rejeb, A., Zailani, S., Rejeb, K., Seuring, S., & Treiblmaier, H. (2022). The Internet of Things and the circular economy: A systematic literature review and research agenda. *Journal of Cleaner Production, 350*, 131439. DOI: 10.1016/j.jclepro.2022.131439

Rezazadegan, R., & Sharifzadeh, M. (2022). Applications of artificial intelligence and big data in industry 4.0 technologies. *Industry 4.0 Vision for Energy and Materials: Enabling Technologies and Case Studies*, 121-158.

Rikala, P., Braun, G., Järvinen, M., Stahre, J., & Hämäläinen, R. (2024). Understanding and measuring skill gaps in Industry 4.0 — A review. *Technological Forecasting and Social Change, 201*, 123206. DOI: 10.1016/j.techfore.2024.123206

Rodríguez-Rodríguez, I., Campo-Valera, M., Rodríguez, J.-V., & Lok Woo, W. (2024). IoMT innovations in diabetes management: Predictive models using wearable data. *Expert Systems with Applications, 238*, 121994. DOI: 10.1016/j.eswa.2023.121994

Rodríguez-Rodríguez, I., Zamora-Izquierdo, M.-A., & Rodríguez, J.-V. (2018). Towards an ICT-based platform for type 1 diabetes mellitus management. *Applied Sciences (Basel, Switzerland), 8*(4), 511. Advance online publication. DOI: 10.3390/app8040511

Rosário, A. T., & Raimundo, R. J. (2025). The Integration of AI and IoT in Marketing: A Systematic Literature Review.

Rothenbühler, M., Lizoain, A., Rebeaud, F., Perotte, A., Stoffel, M., & DeVries, J. H. (2025). A prospective pilot study demonstrating noninvasive calibration-free glucose measurement. *medRxiv*. https://doi.org/DOI: 10.1101/2024.08.17.24312052

Roy, S., Padmakumar, R., Jeganathan, S., & Kumaraguru, K. (2015). Personalization and consumer engagement in digital marketing. *Journal of Interactive Advertising*, *15*(1), 35–46.

Russell, J., & Ajeigbe, K. (2022). User-centric networking: Designing for experience. https://www.researchgate.net/publication/389674597_User-Centric_Networking_Designing_for_Experience

Rymaszewska, A., Helo, P., & Gunasekaran, A. (2017). IoT powered servitization of manufacturing–an exploratory case study. *International Journal of Production Economics*, *192*, 92–105. DOI: 10.1016/j.ijpe.2017.02.016

Saarikko, T., Westergren, U. H., & Blomquist, T. (2020). Digital transformation: Five recommendations for the digitally conscious firm. *Business Horizons*, *63*(6), 825–839. DOI: 10.1016/j.bushor.2020.07.005

Saberi, S., Kouhizadeh, M., Sarkis, J., & Shen, L. (2019). Blockchain technology and its relationships to sustainable supply chain management. *International Journal of Production Research*, *57*(7), 2117–2135. DOI: 10.1080/00207543.2018.1533261

Saeed, S. (2023). A customer-centric view of E-commerce security and privacy. *Applied Sciences (Basel, Switzerland)*, *13*(2), 1020. DOI: 10.3390/app13021020

Saeed, Z. O., Mancini, F., Glusac, T., & Izadpanahi, P. (2022). Future city, digital twinning and the urban realm: A systematic literature review. *Buildings (Basel, Switzerland)*, *12*(5), 685. DOI: 10.3390/buildings12050685

Sahu, Y., & Upadhyay, V. K. (2024). Environmental application of digital twins: A review. *Environmental Risk and Resilience in the Changing World: Integrated Geospatial AI and Multidimensional Approach*, 287-295.

Saksena, N. (2024). Hyper-personalization in retail: Leveraging data science and real-time streaming. *International Journal of Scientific Research in Computer Science Engineering and Information Technology*, *10*(6), 1382–1392. DOI: 10.32628/CSEIT241061179

Saleh, H. H., Chyad, A. K., Barakat, M., & Naamo, G. S. (2024). Enhancing Business Operations Efficiency Thorough Predictive Analytics. *J. Ecohumanism*, *3*(5), 700–714. DOI: 10.62754/joe.v3i5.3932

Salgado-Criado, J. (2025). Human oversight of artificial intelligence: An operations management perspective. *Journal of Industrial Engineering and Management, 18*(2), 285–304. DOI: 10.3926/jiem.8567

Saluja, S., Nayyar, V., Rojhe, K., & Sharma, S. (Eds.). (2024). *Ethical Marketing Through Data Governance Standards and Effective Technology*. IGI Global. DOI: 10.4018/979-8-3693-2215-4

Sanjay, A., Vijarania, M., & Jaglan, V. (2020). Security surveillance and home automation system using IoT. *EAI Endorsed Transactions on Smart Cities*, *5*(15), e1.

Sapienza, S., Palmirani, M., & Greco, S. (2024, August). Data Sharing Governance in Digital Twins and Smart Cities: The European Data Strategy. In *International Conference on Electronic Government and the Information Systems Perspective* (pp. 184-197). Cham: Springer Nature Switzerland. DOI: 10.1007/978-3-031-68211-7_15

Sargiotis, D. (2024). Key Principles of Data Governance: Building a Strong Foundation. In *Data Governance: A Guide* (pp. 137–163). Springer Nature Switzerland. DOI: 10.1007/978-3-031-67268-2_3

Sasikala, B., & Sachan, S. (2024). Decoding decision-making: embracing explainable AI for trust and transparency. Exploring the frontiers of artificial intelligence and machine learning technologies, 42.

Sathya, U., Hashini, S., Lakshmipriya, C., Varun, C. M., & Nalini, M. (2024, December). Emerging Trends and Future Prospects in Internet of Things (IoT) Technology. In *2024 International Conference on Sustainable Communication Networks and Application (ICSCNA)* (pp. 79-85). IEEE.

Satka, Z., Ashjaei, M., Fotouhi, H., Daneshtalab, M., Sjödin, M., & Mubeen, S. (2023). A comprehensive systematic review of integration of time sensitive networking and 5G communication. *Journal of Systems Architecture*, *138*, 102852. DOI: 10.1016/j.sysarc.2023.102852

Sayles, J. (2024). Human Oversight of AI Systems. In *Principles of AI Governance and Model Risk Management: Master the Techniques for Ethical and Transparent AI Systems* (pp. 267–276). Apress. DOI: 10.1007/979-8-8688-0983-5_12

Schächinger, H., Cox, D., Linder, L., Brody, S., & Keller, U. (2003). Cognitive and psychomotor function in hypoglycemia: Response error patterns and retest reliability. *Pharmacology, Biochemistry, and Behavior*, *75*(4), 915–920. DOI: 10.1016/S0091-3057(03)00167-9 PMID: 12957236

Schianchi, M. (2023). IoT-based framework for agile supply chains. *International Journal of Innovation in Engineering*. DOI: 10.59615/ijie.3.1.63

Schlömer, I. (2022). Agility as a driver of digital transformation – A literature review. DOI: 10.1007/978-3-031-15342-6_19

Scholey, A. B., Harper, S., & Kennedy, D. O. (2001). Cognitive demand and blood glucose. *Physiology & Behavior, 73*(4), 585–592. DOI: 10.1016/S0031-9384(01)00476-0 PMID: 11495663

Schöpf, V., Fischmeister, F. P. S., Windischberger, C., Gerstl, F., Wolzt, M., Karlsson, K. Æ., & Moser, E. (2013). Effects of individual glucose levels on the neuronal correlates of emotions. *Frontiers in Human Neuroscience, 7*, 212. Advance online publication. DOI: 10.3389/fnhum.2013.00212 PMID: 23734117

Schroeder, J. P., & Packard, M. G. (2003). Systemic or intra-amygdala injections of glucose facilitate memory consolidation for extinction of drug-induced conditioned reward. *The European Journal of Neuroscience, 17*(7), 1482–1488. DOI: 10.1046/j.1460-9568.2003.02578.x PMID: 12713651

Selvakumar, P., Sudheer, P., & Kannan, N. (2025). Balancing Innovation and Privacy: Understanding AI in the Digital World. In Digital Citizenship and the Future of AI Engagement, Ethics, and Privacy (pp. 279-304). IGI Global Scientific Publishing.

Seng, K. P., Ang, L. M., & Ngharamike, E. (2022). Artificial intelligence Internet of Things: A new paradigm of distributed sensor networks. *International Journal of Distributed Sensor Networks, 18*(3). Advance online publication. DOI: 10.1177/15501477211062835

Senna, P. P., Barros, A. C., & Bonnin Roca, J.. (2023). Development of a digital maturity model for Industry 4.0 based on the technology-organization-environment framework. *Computers & Industrial Engineering, 185*, 109645. DOI: 10.1016/j.cie.2023.109645

Senna, P. P., Ferreira, L. M. D. F., Barros, A. C., Bonnin Roca, J., & Magalhães, V. (2022). Prioritizing barriers for the adoption of industry 4.0 technologies. *Computers & Industrial Engineering, 171*, 108428. DOI: 10.1016/j.cie.2022.108428

Shafique, M., Mumtaz, G., Ahmad, S. Z., & Iqbal, S. (2024). A Comparative Analysis of AI Chatbot Performance in IoT Environments. *Journal of Computing & Biomedical Informatics, 7*(02).

Shahab, H., Iqbal, M., Sohaib, A., Ullah Khan, F., & Waqas, M. (2024). IoT-based agriculture management techniques for sustainable farming: A comprehensive review. *Computers and Electronics in Agriculture, 220*, 108851. DOI: 10.1016/j.compag.2024.108851

Shalawadi, S. B. (2025). Shaping user privacy experiences in self-tracking and smart homes: A design artifact approach (Doctoral dissertation, Aalborg University). Aalborg University Open Publishing. https://vbn.aau.dk/files/784094476/PHD_SBS_ONLINE.pdf

Shao, D., Calo, F., & Bryan-Kinns, N. (2023). Integration of IoT into e government. *Foresight*, *25*(6), 495–514. DOI: 10.1108/FS-04-2022-0048

Sharma, S. (2023). Data Privacy Concern Due to Information Personalization Technologies: A Quantitative Study, Utilizing Technology Acceptance Model (TAM) to Explore the Consumers' Experience in E-Commerce (Doctoral dissertation, University of the Cumberlands).

Sharma, N., Shamkuwar, M., & Singh, I. (2018). The history, present and future with IoT. In *Internet of things and big data analytics for smart generation* (pp. 27–51). Springer International Publishing.

Shei, R. J., Holder, I. G., Oumsang, A. S., Paris, B. A., & Paris, H. L. (2022). Wearable activity trackers–advanced technology or advanced marketing? *European Journal of Applied Physiology*, *122*(9), 1975–1990. DOI: 10.1007/s00421-022-04951-1 PMID: 35445837

Shen, S., Xiao, J., He, Y., He, Z., & Yahya, K. (2024). Construction of Smart Transportation City System Based on Digital Twins.

Shi, D., Meyer, O., Oberle, M., & Bauernhansl, T. (2024). Interoperable information modelling leveraging asset administration shell and large language model for quality control toward zero defect manufacturing. *Journal of Manufacturing Systems*, *77*, 678–696. DOI: 10.1016/j.jmsy.2024.10.011

Shi, W., Cao, J., Zhang, Q., Li, Y., & Xu, L. (2016). Edge computing: Vision and challenges. *IEEE Internet of Things Journal*, *3*(5), 637–646. DOI: 10.1109/JIOT.2016.2579198

Sicari, S., Rizzardi, A., Grieco, L. A., & Coen-Porisini, A. (2015). Security, privacy and trust in Internet of Things: The road ahead. *Computer Networks*, *76*, 146–164. DOI: 10.1016/j.comnet.2014.11.008

Singh, V. (2024). Fostering Effective Human-AI Collaboration: Bridging the Gap Between User-Centric Design and Ethical Implementation. *International Journal on Recent and Innovation Trends in Computing and Communication*, *12*(2), 22–30.

Siyadri, Y., & Sri, R. D. A. (2024). "Advancing User-Centric Privacy: A Comprehensive Research Roadmap For Ethical And Secure Technology Development." i-Manager's. *Journal of Information Technology*, *13*(3).

Sony, M., & Naik, S. (2020). Industry 4.0 integration with socio-technical systems theory: A systematic review and proposed theoretical model. *Technology in Society, 61*, 101248. DOI: 10.1016/j.techsoc.2020.101248

Soon, K. H., & Khoo, V. H. S. (2017). CityGML modelling for Singapore 3D national mapping. *The International Archives of the Photogrammetry, Remote Sensing and Spatial Information Sciences, 42*(W7), 37–42. DOI: 10.5194/isprs-archives-XLII-4-W7-37-2017

Soori, M., Arezoo, B., & Dastres, R. (2023). Internet of things for smart factories in Industry 4.0: A review. *Internet of Things and Cyber-Physical Systems, 3*, 192–204. DOI: 10.1016/j.iotcps.2023.04.006

Soto-Acosta, P., & Meroño-Cerdán, Á. L. (2008). Analyzing e-business value creation from an RBV perspective. *International Journal of Information Management, 28*(1), 49–60. DOI: 10.1016/j.ijinfomgt.2007.05.001

Soumyalatha, S. G. H. (2016, May). Study of IoT: Understanding IoT architecture, applications, issues and challenges. In *1st International Conference on Innovations in Computing & Net-working (ICICN16), CSE, RRCE. International Journal of Advanced Networking & Applications, 478*, 14.

Souri, A., Al-Masri, E., & Kumari, S. (2023). Blockchain architecture and methodologies for IoT. *Security and Privacy, 6*. Advance online publication. DOI: 10.1002/spy2.299

Srivastava, M., & Ghazala, S. (2025). Future-Proofing Sustainable Urban Development: Harnessing Fuzzy Logic for Smart Cities. In *Fuzzy Logic in Smart Sustainable Cities* (pp. 215-257). Jenny Stanford Publishing.

Stergiou, C. L., Bompoli, E., & Psannis, K. E. (2023). Security and privacy issues in IoT-based big data cloud systems in a digital twin scenario. *Applied Sciences (Basel, Switzerland), 13*(2), 758. DOI: 10.3390/app13020758

Su, Y., Wang, E. J., & Berthon, P. (2023). Ethical marketing AI? A structured literature review of the ethical challenges posed by artificial intelligence in the domains of marketing and consumer behavior.

Suh, W., Henclewood, D., Guin, A., Guensler, R., Hunter, M., & Fujimoto, R. (2017). Dynamic data driven transportation systems. *Multimedia Tools and Applications, 76*(23), 25253–25269. DOI: 10.1007/s11042-016-4318-x

Suklabaidya, S. (2024). Towards inclusive societies: Leveraging IoT for community development and education.

Sullivan, Y., Wamba, F., & Dunaway, M. (2023). Internet of Things and Competitive Advantage: A Dynamic Capabilities Perspective. *Journal of the Association for Information Systems*, *24*(3), 745–781. DOI: 10.17705/1jais.00807

Sunram-Lea, S. I., Foster, J. K., Durlach, P., & Perez, C. (2001). Glucose facilitation of cognitive performance in healthy young adults: Examination of the influence of fast-duration, time of day and preconsumption plasma glucose levels. *Psychopharmacology*, *157*(1), 46–54. DOI: 10.1007/s002130100771 PMID: 11512042

Su, Y., & Fan, D. (2023). Smart cities and sustainable development. *Regional Studies*, *57*(4), 722–738. DOI: 10.1080/00343404.2022.2106360

Talukder, A., & Haas, R. (2021). AIoT: AI meets IoT and Web in Smart Healthcare. *ACM International Conference Proceeding Series*, 92–98. DOI: 10.1145/3462741.3466650

Tambare, P., Meshram, C., Lee, C.-C., Ramteke, R. J., & Imoize, A. L. (2022). Performance measurement system and quality management in data-driven Industry 4.0: A review. *Sensors (Basel)*, *22*(1), 224. DOI: 10.3390/s22010224 PMID: 35009767

Tamrakar, S., Gupta, O. P., Gupta, M., & Katahare, G. N. (2025). Harnessing the power of brand experience to foster brand trust in the digital era. Samvakti Journal of Research in Business Management, 6(1), 184-204. https://www.samvaktijournals.com/sjrbm.2025.70/harnessing_power_brand_experience_foster_brand_trust_digital_era.pdf

Tanczer, L., Carr, M., Brass, I., Steenmans, I., & Blackstock, J. J. (2017). Iot and its implications for informed consent. *PETRAS IoT Hub, STEaPP: London.*

Tariq, B., Taimoor, S., Najam, H., Law, R., Hassan, W., & Han, H. (2020). Generating marketing outcomes through Internet of Things (IoT) technologies. *Sustainability (Basel)*, *12*(22), 9670. DOI: 10.3390/su12229670

Tasnim, K., Abdullah, M. S., Karim, M. Z., & Hasan, R. (2025). AI-Driven Innovation, Privacy Issues, and Gaining Consumer Trust: The Future of Digital Marketing. *Business & Social Sciences*, *3*(1), 1–7.

Teece, D. J. (2007). Explicating dynamic capabilities: The nature and microfoundations of (sustainable) enterprise performance. *Strategic Management Journal*, *28*(13), 1319–1350. DOI: 10.1002/smj.640

Teece, D. J. (2018). Business models and dynamic capabilities. *Long Range Planning*, *51*(1), 40–49. DOI: 10.1016/j.lrp.2017.06.007

Teece, D. J. (2018). Profiting from innovation in the digital economy: Enabling technologies, standards, and licensing models in the wireless world. *Research Policy, 47*(8), 1367–1387. DOI: 10.1016/j.respol.2017.01.015

Teece, D. J., Pisano, G., & Shuen, A. (1997). Dynamic capabilities and strategic management. *Strategic Management Journal, 18*(7), 509–533. DOI: 10.1002/(SICI)1097-0266(199708)18:7<509::AID-SMJ882>3.0.CO;2-Z

Tekin, H., & Dikmen, I. (2024). Inclusive smart cities: An exploratory study on the London smart city strategy. *Buildings (Basel, Switzerland), 14*(2), 485. DOI: 10.3390/buildings14020485

Tenkanen, H., & Toivonen, T. (2020). Longitudinal spatial dataset on travel times and distances by different travel modes in Helsinki Region. *Scientific Data, 7*(1), 77. DOI: 10.1038/s41597-020-0413-y PMID: 32132539

Thamik, H., Cabrera, J. D. F., & Wu, J. (2024). The Digital Paradigm: Unraveling the Impact of Artificial Intelligence and Internet of Things on Achieving Sustainable Development Goals. *Lecture Notes on Data Engineering and Communications Technologies, 192*, 21–40. DOI: 10.1007/978-3-031-53433-1_2

Tjahjono, B., Esplugues, C., Ares, E., & Pelaez, G. (2017). What does Industry 4.0 mean to supply chain? *Procedia Manufacturing, 13*, 1175–1182. DOI: 10.1016/j.promfg.2017.09.191

Tokeley, K. (2021). The Power of the" Internet of Things" to Mislead and Manipulate Consumers: A Regulatory Challenge. *Notre Dame J. on Emerging Tech., 2*, 111.

Tomàs, M. (2024). The smart city and urban governance: The urban transformation of Barcelona, 2011–2023. *Urban Research & Practice, 17*(4), 588–605. DOI: 10.1080/17535069.2023.2277205

Topping, D., Bannan, T. J., Coe, H., Evans, J., Jay, C., Murabito, E., & Robinson, N. (2021). Digital twins of urban air quality: Opportunities and challenges. *Frontiers in Sustainable Cities, 3*, 786563. DOI: 10.3389/frsc.2021.786563

Torre, D., Chennamaneni, A., & Rodriguez, A. (2023). Privacy preservation techniques for IoT devices A systematic mapping study. *IEEE Access : Practical Innovations, Open Solutions, 11*, 26429–26453. DOI: 10.1109/ACCESS.2023.3245524

Trautman, L. J., Hussein, M. T., Ngamassi, L., & Molesky, M. J. (2020). Governance of the Internet of Things (IOT). *Jurimetrics, 60*(3), 315–352.

Trifonov, H., & Heffernan, D. (2023). OPC UA TSN: A next-generation network for Industry 4.0 and IIoT. *International Journal of Pervasive Computing and Communications, 19*(3), 386–411. DOI: 10.1108/IJPCC-07-2021-0160

Trist, E. (1981). The evolution of socio-technical systems. In Van de Ven, A. H., & Joyce, W. F. (Eds.), *Perspectives on Organization Design and Behavior* (pp. 19–75). Wiley.

Trocin, C., Mikalef, P., Papamitsiou, Z., & Conboy, K. (2023). Responsible AI for Digital Health: A Synthesis and a Research Agenda. *Information Systems Frontiers, 25*(6), 2139–2157. Advance online publication. DOI: 10.1007/s10796-021-10146-4

Tzachor, A., Sabri, S., Richards, C. E., Rajabifard, A., & Acuto, M. (2022). Potential and limitations of digital twins to achieve the sustainable development goals. *Nature Sustainability, 5*(10), 822–829. DOI: 10.1038/s41893-022-00923-7

Tzafestas, S. G. (2018). Ethics and law in the internet of things world. Smart cities, 1(1), 98-120.

U.S. Department of Health and Human Services (HHS). (1996). *Health Insurance Portability and Accountability Act of 1996 (HIPAA), Public Law 104–191*. U.S. Government Publishing Office.

Uchirova, M., Baurina, S., & Khudyakov, S. (2021). *Industrial technologies in digital transformation*. Modern Global Economic System., DOI: 10.1007/978-3-030-69415-9_114

Vallée, A. (2024). Envisioning the future of personalized medicine: Role and realities of digital twins. *Journal of Medical Internet Research, 26*, e50204. DOI: 10.2196/50204 PMID: 38739913

Valsalan, P., Baomar, T. A. B., & Baabood, A. H. O. (2020). IoT based health monitoring system. *Journal of critical reviews, 7*(4), 739-743.

Van 't Schip, M. (2025). The Internet of Forgotten Things: European cybersecurity regulation and the cessation of Internet-connected consumer devices. *Computer Law & Security Review, 57*, 106152. DOI: 10.1016/j.clsr.2025.106152

Vemuri, V. P., Naik, V. R., & Chaudhary, V. (2022). Analyzing the use of internet of things (IoT) in artificial intelligence and its impact on business environment. *Materials Today: Proceedings, 51*, 2194–2197. DOI: 10.1016/j.matpr.2021.11.264

Verago, J. L., Grassi-Kassisse, D. M., & Spadari-Bratfisch, R. C. (2001). Metabolic markers following beta-adrenoceptor agonist infusion in footshock-stressed rats. *Brazilian Journal of Medical and Biological Research = Revista Brasileira de Pesquisas Médicas e Biológicas, 34*(9), 1197–1207. DOI: 10.1590/S0100-879X2001000900014 PMID: 11514845

Verhoef, P. C., Broekhuizen, T., Bart, Y., Bhattacharya, A., Dong, J. Q., Fabian, N., & Haenlein, M. (2021). Digital transformation: A multidisciplinary reflection and research agenda. *Journal of Business Research, 122*, 889–901. DOI: 10.1016/j.jbusres.2019.09.022

Vettriselvan, R., Vijai, C., Patel, J. D., Sharma, P., & Kumar, N. (2024, March). Blockchain embraces supply chain optimization by enhancing transparency and traceability from production to delivery. In *2024 International Conference on Trends in Quantum Computing and Emerging Business Technologies* (pp. 1-6). IEEE. DOI: 10.1109/TQCEBT59414.2024.10545308

Vial, G. (2019). Understanding digital transformation: A review and a research agenda. *The Journal of Strategic Information Systems, 28*(2), 118–144. DOI: 10.1016/j.jsis.2019.01.003

Villani, V., Pini, F., Leali, F., & Secchi, C. (2018). Survey on human–robot collaboration in industrial settings: Safety, intuitive interfaces and applications. *Mechatronics, 55*, 248–266. DOI: 10.1016/j.mechatronics.2018.02.009

Vishwakarma, R. K., Pandey, A., Kundnani, M. P., Yadav, A. K., Singh, M. N., & Yadav, M. S. (2025). Personalization vs. privacy: Marketing strategies in the digital age. *Journal of Marketing & Social Research, 2*, 177–191.

Voss, W. G. (2021). The CCPA and the GDPR are not the same: Why you should understand both. *CPI Antitrust Chronicle, 1*(1), 7–12.

Vrchota, J., Řehoř, P., Maříková, M., & Pech, M. (2021). Critical success factors of project management in relation to Industry 4.0 for sustainability of projects. *Sustainability (Basel), 13*(1), 281. DOI: 10.3390/su13010281

Wade, M., & Hulland, J. (2004). The resource-based view and information systems research: Review, extension, and suggestions for future research. *Management Information Systems Quarterly, 28*(1), 107–142. DOI: 10.2307/25148626

Wakili, A., & Bakkali, S. (2024). Internet of Things in healthcare: An adaptive ethical framework for IoT in digital health. Clinical eHealth, 7, 92-105.

Waldman, A. E. (2019). Power, process, and automated decision-making. *Fordham Law Review, 88*, 613.

Wamba, S. F., Akter, S., Edwards, A., Chopin, G., & Gnanzou, D. (2017). How 'big data' can make big impact: Findings from a systematic review and a longitudinal case study. *International Journal of Production Economics, 165*, 234–246. DOI: 10.1016/j.ijpe.2014.12.031

Wang, J., Xu, C., Zhang, J., & Zhong, R. Y. (2021). Big data analytics for intelligent manufacturing systems: A review. *Journal of Manufacturing Systems, 62*, 738–752. DOI: 10.1016/j.jmsy.2021.03.005

Wang, M., Sun, Y., Sun, H., & Zhang, B. (2023). Security Issues on Industrial Internet of Things: Overview and Challenges. *Computers, 12*(12), 256. DOI: 10.3390/computers12120256

Wang, X. T., & Huangfu, G. (2017). Glucose-specific signaling effects on delay discounting in intertemporal choice. *Physiology & Behavior, 169*, 195–201. DOI: 10.1016/j.physbeh.2016.12.001 PMID: 27940144

Wang, X.-T. (2018). Resource signaling via blood glucose in embodied decision making. *Frontiers in Psychology, 9*, 1965. DOI: 10.3389/fpsyg.2018.01965 PMID: 30374322

Weber, R. H. (2010). Internet of Things – New security and privacy challenges. *Computer Law & Security Review, 26*(1), 23–30. DOI: 10.1016/j.clsr.2009.11.008

Weber, R. H., & Weber, R. (2010). *Internet of Things: Legal perspectives*. Springer Science & Business Media. DOI: 10.1007/978-3-642-11710-7

Werbińska-Wojciechowska, S., Giel, R., & Winiarska, K. (2024). Digital twin approach for operation and maintenance of transportation system—Systematic review. *Sensors (Basel), 24*(18), 6069. DOI: 10.3390/s24186069 PMID: 39338814

Wernerfelt, B. (1984). A resource-based view of the firm. *Strategic Management Journal, 5*(2), 171–180. DOI: 10.1002/smj.4250050207

Westerman, G., Bonnet, D., & McAfee, A. (2014). *Leading digital: Turning technology into business transformation*. Harvard Business Press.

Whitmore, A., Agarwal, A., & Da Xu, L. (2015). The Internet of Things—A survey of topics and trends. *Information Systems Frontiers, 17*(2), 261–274. DOI: 10.1007/s10796-014-9489-2

Wu, D., Zheng, A., Yu, W., Cao, H., Ling, Q., Liu, J., & Zhou, D. (2025). Digital twin technology in transportation infrastructure: A comprehensive survey of current applications, challenges, and future directions. *Applied Sciences (Basel, Switzerland), 15*(4), 1911. DOI: 10.3390/app15041911

Xiao, M., Chen, L., Feng, H., Peng, Z., & Long, Q. (2024). Sustainable and robust route planning scheme for smart city public transport based on multi-objective optimization: Digital twin model. *Sustainable Energy Technologies and Assessments*, *65*, 103787. DOI: 10.1016/j.seta.2024.103787

Xu, H., Seng, K. P., Ang, L. M., & Smith, J. (2024). Decentralized and Distributed Learning for AIoT: A Comprehensive Review, Emerging Challenges, and Opportunities. *IEEE Access : Practical Innovations, Open Solutions*, *12*, 101016–101052. DOI: 10.1109/ACCESS.2024.3422211

Xu, L. D., Xu, E. L., & Li, L. (2018). Industry 4.0: State of the art and future trends. *International Journal of Production Research*, *56*(8), 2941–2962. DOI: 10.1080/00207543.2018.1444806

Yadav, D., Yadav, A., & Singh, S. (2024). Concerns, Threats, and Ethical Considerations in Using Cloud of Things. In Cloud of Things (pp. 345-364). Chapman and Hall/CRC.

Yadav, J. (2025). The Role of Edge Computing in Enhancing IoT Efficiency and Security. *Technology Perception*, *1*(1), 14–18.

Yammanur, V., & Chowdhury, R. H. (2024). *Leveraging enterprise architecture for digital transformation*. AJSTEME., DOI: 10.69593/ajsteme.v4i04.135

Yamuna, S. M., & Madhuvarsini, C. P. (2025). Ethical Data Practices in The Digital Age: Ensuring Privacy, Transparency, And Accountability. Proceedings of Emerging Trends in Technology and Digital Transformation for Sustainable Business Development. PSG College of Arts & Science, 59.

Yan, D. (2022). *Innovative talent ecosystem under digital transformation*. Lecture Notes in Electrical Engineering., DOI: 10.1007/978-981-16-4258-6_98

Yang, B., Lv, Z., & Wang, F. (2022). Digital twins for intelligent green buildings. *Buildings (Basel, Switzerland)*, *12*(6), 856. DOI: 10.3390/buildings12060856

Yellanki, S. K. (2025). *Behavioral Intelligence and Operational Design: Exploring Modern Service Models, Customer-Centric Platforms, and Sustainable Digital Infrastructure*. Deep Science Publishing.

Ylipulli, J., & Luusua, A. (2020). Smart cities with a Nordic twist? Public sector digitalization in Finnish data-rich cities. *Telematics and Informatics*, *55*, 101457. DOI: 10.1016/j.tele.2020.101457

Yoo, Y., Henfridsson, O., & Lyytinen, K. (2010). The new organizing logic of digital innovation: An agenda for information systems research. *Information Systems Research, 21*(4), 724–735. DOI: 10.1287/isre.1100.0322

Zak, P. J. (2015). Why Inspiring Stories Make Us React: The Neuroscience of Narrative. *Cerebrum : the Dana Forum on Brain Science, 2015*(2). PMID: 26034526

Zelenkov, Y. (2023). Enterprise agility in the era of smart IoT systems. *Business Informatics*. DOI: 10.17323/1998-0663.2023.3.52.69

Zhao, X., & Zhang, Y. (2024). Integrated management of urban resources toward Net-Zero smart cities considering renewable energies uncertainty and modeling in Digital Twin. *Sustainable Energy Technologies and Assessments, 64*, 103656. DOI: 10.1016/j.seta.2024.103656

Zhivkov, P., Fidanova, S., & Dimov, I. (2025). Digital Twin-Based Framework for Real-Time Monitoring and Analysis of Urban Mobile-Source Emissions. *Atmosphere (Basel), 16*(6), 731. DOI: 10.3390/atmos16060731

Zhong, R. Y., Xu, X., Klotz, E., & Newman, S. T. (2017). Intelligent manufacturing in the context of Industry 4.0: A review. *Engineering (Beijing), 3*(5), 616–630. DOI: 10.1016/J.ENG.2017.05.015

Zhou, W., Piramuthu, S., Chu, F., & Chu, C. (2017). RFID-enabled flexible warehousing. *Decision Support Systems, 98*, 99–112. DOI: 10.1016/j.dss.2017.05.002

Zimmermann, A., Schmidt, R., Jugel, D., & Möhring, M. (2020). Evolution of enterprise architecture for intelligent digital systems. DOI: 10.1007/978-3-030-50316-1_9

Zorrilla, M. E., & Yébenes, J. (2022). A reference framework for the implementation of data governance systems for Industry 4.0. *Computer Standards & Interfaces, 81*, 103595. DOI: 10.1016/j.csi.2021.103595

Zuboff, S. (2015). Big other. *Journal of Information Technology, 30*(1), 75–89. DOI: 10.1057/jit.2015.5

Zuehlke, D. (2010). SmartFactory—Towards a factory-of-things. *Annual Reviews in Control, 34*(1), 129–138. DOI: 10.1016/j.arcontrol.2010.02.008

About the Contributors

Johanna Pangeiko Nautwima is an accomplished economist and business strategist with a strong background in international economics, trade policy, regional integration, and business development. She holds a Doctor of Business Administration from the Namibia Business School, University of Namibia, where she investigated the impact of blue ocean strategy on the sustainable business performance of manufacturing SMEs. She is currently pursuing a PhD in Economics at Nelson Mandela University, South Africa, focusing on the impact of trade liberalisation and renewable energy consumption on industrial development and carbon emissions in Namibia. Dr. Nautwima is a Consultant - Economist and Trade Data Analyst at the African Development Bank Group, where she contributes to regional development and integration initiatives. Her work includes producing key knowledge products such as the Africa Visa Openness Index and the Africa Regional Integration Index, as well as engaging in policy formulation, trade, and investment strategy. With a strong academic background spanning Africa, Europe, and Asia, Dr. Nautwima has earned multiple degrees, including an MA in Economics from Savitribai Phule Pune University (India) and an MSc in Energy Policy from the Pan African University Institute of Water and Energy Sciences (Algeria). Her expertise extends to research in financial integration, entrepreneurship, and industrial development. Dr. Nautwima has published extensively in peer-reviewed journals, contributing to the fields of economic policy, sustainability, and strategic management. She has also been recognised with various academic scholarships and awards for her excellence in research and higher education. Her commitment to data-driven decision-making and policy analysis continues to shape discussions on regional economic growth and business innovation.

Asa Romeo Asa is an accomplished academic and industry expert with extensive experience in management science, logistics, and entrepreneurship. He earned his PhD in Management Science (Management Strategy) from Wuhan University of

Technology, China. He also holds an MSc in International Business Law from the University of Salford, UK, and an MBA from Wuhan University of Technology. Prof. Asa is the Director of the Namibian-German Institute for Logistics and an Associate Professor of Business Management at the Namibia University of Science and Technology. He has held several leadership roles in academia, including Head of Department and Associate Dean, where he played a pivotal role in research development, curriculum innovation, and institutional strategy. His research focuses on logistics, sustainability, entrepreneurship, and business strategy. He has supervised numerous master's and PhD students and has contributed to scholarly publications, academic reviews, and policy discussions in these fields. Prof. Asa is also an experienced consultant, advising businesses and institutions on strategic management, process improvement, and research-driven decision-making. With a passion for business research, data analytics, and lifelong learning, Prof. Asa continues to shape the discourse on sustainable business practices and technological advancements in logistics and supply chain management.

***

Munir Ahmad is a seasoned professional in the realm of Spatial Data Infrastructure (SDI), Geo-Information Productions, Information Systems, and Information Governance, boasting over 25 years of dedicated experience in the field. With a PhD in Computer Science, Dr. Ahmad's expertise spans Spatial Data Production, Management, Processing, Analysis, Visualization, and Quality Control. Throughout his career, Dr. Ahmad has been deeply involved in the development and deployment of SDI systems specially in the context of Pakistan, leveraging his proficiency in Spatial Database Design, Web, Mobile & Desktop GIS, and Geo Web Services Architecture. His contributions to Volunteered Geographic Information (VGI) and Open Source Geoportal & Metadata Portal have significantly enriched the geospatial community. As a trainer and researcher, Dr. Ahmad has authored over 50 publications, advancing the industry's knowledge base and fostering innovation in Geo-Tech, Data Governance, and Information Infrastructure, and Emerging Technologies. His commitment to Research and Development (R&D) is evident in his role as a dedicated educator and mentor in the field.

A. Arunprakash, M.Com., M.F.A., Ph.D., is an Assistant Professor in the Department of Commerce, School of Commerce at Jain (Deemed-to-be University), Bangalore. As a marketing specialist, he is a passionate reader and an academician by profession, thriving in bringing out excellence in teaching and learning. With 5 years of research experience and 5 years of teaching experience, he excels in his field to foster and inspire young minds with his innovative approach towards learning.

Anorgul Ashirova is working as an Associate Professor at the Department of General Professional Sciences, Mamun University, Khiva, Uzbekistan

Muralidhar B is a professionally qualified dental surgeon. He holds Ph.D. from Canara Bank School of Management Studies, Bangalore University after his MBA from Christ University. He has 18 years of total teaching experience spanning across dental education, healthcare management and general management and 4 years of corporate experience. He has worked as research associate in Institute for Social and Economic Change, Bangalore in a project entitled as "Management By and For Common Man: An Exploration of the Concept and Direction for Future"post Ph.D. He had secured 28th rank in S.S.L.C examination for Karnataka State in 1993. His 21 patents have been published and 2 design patents have been granted. He has 32 research publications to his credit out of which 6 are Scopus-indexed and 5 are ABDC indexed. He has co-authored 5 books. He is currently working as Assistant Professor in Department of Business Management Studies, School of Commerce, Jain Deemed to be University, Bangalore.

Muthamma B.U. has an impressive academic and professional background. Her 5 years of experience as an Assistant Professor, coupled with her pursuit of a Ph.D. in entrepreneurship at CMR University, Bangalore, reflects a strong commitment to academia and research. The fact that she actively participates and presents papers at both national and international conferences suggests her engagement with the broader academic community. Muthamma graduate degree in M. Com from Mangalore University provides her with a solid foundation in commerce, which likely contributes to her expertise in entrepreneurship. Her dedication to research is evident in her contributions to reputed journals, showcasing her commitment to advancing knowledge in her field. Additionally, her active involvement in workshops and webinars not only highlights her enthusiasm for professional growth but also suggests a proactive approach to staying updated on the latest developments in her area of expertise.

Catherene Julie Aarthy C is an Assistant Professor (Selection Grade) with over 23 years of experience in the education industry. Her expertise spans curriculum design, academic intervention, and integrated instruction. She has published 30 research articles in Scopus, WOS, ABDC, and other peer-reviewed journals, with a citation count of 161. Dr. Catherene holds a Ph.D. in Management from Hindustan Institute of Technology and Science, India, and a prestigious Data Science for Business Analytics (DSBA) certification from the McCombs School of Business, University of Texas at Austin. Her research interests include marketing management, business analytics, Marketing Analytics IoT, Predictive Analytics. She has guided several projects and presented her research works at national and international conferences.

Simeon Hamukoshi is a dynamic professional with a PhD in Chemistry and cross-disciplinary expertise. As a Strategic Projects Coordinator at NCRST, he advises the CEO, leads policy research, and guides AI integration. Formerly Head of Research on Green Hydrogen Applications at the Namibia Green Hydrogen Research Institute, he managed projects and supervised students. He has taught at the University of Namibia and worked as a Laboratory Chemist, ensuring quality control. His strategic impact is evident through roles on boards and taskforces focused on green hydrogen and procurement. Dr. Hamukoshi brings strong leadership, communication, research, and project management skills, along with active community engagement.

Ganesha K S is an Assistant Professor in the Department of Management Studies, at Dayananda Sagar College of Engineering, Bangalore, India. He has 15 years of experience in Corporate, Teaching and Research. He is a Member of the International Safety Quality Environment Management Association (ISQEM), UK. His primary research interests are tourist behavior, social media, sentiment analysis, human resource management, and labor studies. He has presented at multiple conferences and published articles in Scopus and other International Indexed journals. He has conducted FDP, workshops, and training in the areas of Digital Marketing, Statistical Analysis using SPSS, Project Management, Research Methodology, Entrepreneurship etc.

Nivas Kumar is affiliated with R.M.K Engineering College, Tamil Nadu, where he is actively involved in engineering research. His academic interests include emerging technologies and applied science. He regularly contributes to collaborative research and scholarly publications.

A. Maheshwari is an Associate Professor in the Department of CINTEL at SRM Institute of Science and Technology (SRMIST). She is associated with the SRM Nagar campus, Kattankulathur, Chengalpattu District, Tamil Nadu, India. Her academic work focuses on teaching, research, and interdisciplinary initiatives in her field.

Zokir Mamadiyarov is working in the Department of Finance and Tourism at Termez University of Economics and Service, Termez, Uzbekistan.

Ponnuviji N. P. is a faculty member in the Department of Computer Science and Engineering at R M K College of Engineering and Technology, Puduvoyal,

Tamil Nadu, India. She is engaged in teaching core computer science subjects and supporting students' academic development. Her interests focus on strengthening technical knowledge and practical problem-solving skills among learners.

Raja Suganya P V is an Assistant Professor in the Department of Artificial Intelligence and Data Science at Velammal Engineering College, Chennai. Her academic interests include machine learning, data analytics, and intelligent systems. She is dedicated to teaching excellence and research-oriented learning.

Abitha R. is an Assistant Professor in the Department of Artificial Intelligence and Data Science at Vel Tech Multi Tech Dr. Rangarajan Dr. Sakunthala Engineering College, Avadi, Chennai. She is dedicated to teaching and guiding students in AI, data science, and emerging intelligent technologies. Her academic interests focus on building strong analytical skills and practical knowledge among learners.

Vettriselvan R, an Associate Professor, AMET University, specialized in HRM and Marketing. He is acting as Mentor, Saraswathi Institute of Medical Sciences, Hapur. He served as Review Board member, National Council for Higher Education, Malawi, Head of the Department, School of Commerce and Management Studies, St. Eugene University, Zambia, and Director, Research and Publication, St. John the Baptist University, Malawi. He has published 28 books and 86 articles in peer reviewed journals and edited book chapters. Under his guidance two have completed and five are pursuing their PhD.

Varanasi Rahul, an Assistant Professor at JAIN University, Bangalore, holds three postgraduate degrees (M.Com in Accounting & Taxation, M.Com in Management, and MA in History) and is a semi-qualified Cost Accountant. He has cleared UGC NET in Commerce twice, AP SET in Commerce, History, and Management, and TS SET in Commerce. With 3 years of teaching experience and 6 months at PwC, he is also a freelance archaeologist, epigraphist, and numismatist. He has authored 3 books, published 6 research articles, contributed 9 book chapters, and written 30+ newspaper articles. Rahul has applied for 11 patents, with 1 granted and 09 published.

Palanivel Rathinasabapathi Velmurugan is associated with BSBI, Berlin as Lecturer in Human Resource Management & Finance Stream. Prior to joining BSBI, he held the designation "Head" Faculty of Management in Sharda University, Uzbekistan, Central Asia and "Dean of Arts" assignments in DMI St John the Baptist University, Malawi, Central Africa. Also, he has associated earlier with the DMI St Eugene University in Zambia, MAM Business School and various Engineering Colleges in India. He has done his Ph.D. in Management from Mannonmanium

Sundaranar University in India. Besides this, he holds an MBA Degree from SRM University in India and a BE Chemical Engineering degree from Annamalai University in India. Also, he completed six NPTEL Certificate Programs conducted by various IITs in India. He brings with him 16 years of rich working experience in teaching and research. Furthermore, he has a keen interest in the Case Method of teaching and research. He is an academic out of passion. Not only that, but he also takes keen interest in guiding Ph.D. students. He has supervised three Ph.D. research scholars under his supervision at DMI St Eugene University in Zambia.

José De Jesús Reyes-Sánchez, Ph.D. in senior management, has six master's degrees, in education, in management, professional soccer technique, in physical preparation, in professional soccer, in physical rehabilitation sciences, in sports sciences, as well as in coaching and integral well-being, who is a research professor at the TECNM Instituto Tecnológico Superior De Fresnillo, with more than 20 years of teaching experience, PRODEP profile and coordinator of the academic body with vast experience in conferences and workshops, currently novelist and writer.

K. Saravanan is an Associate Professor at SRM Institute of Science and Technology (SRMIST), SRM Nagar, Kattankulathur, Chengalpattu District, Tamil Nadu, India. He is actively engaged in teaching, research, and academic administration in the field of electrical and electronics engineering. His research interests include modern power systems, electrical machines, and intelligent control techniques.

N Sathyanarayana has over 15 years of teaching experience at both undergraduate and postgraduate levels. He holds a Master of Business Administration degree from Visvesvaraya Technological University (VTU) and a Master of Commerce degree from Periyar University. He has completed his Ph.D. in Banking and Finance from Dayananda Sagar University. Currently, he serves as an Assistant Professor in the School of Commerce at Jain (Deemed-to-be University), Bangalore. He has published 24 research papers in international journals, including three indexed in Scopus, and seven papers in national journals. Additionally, he has presented 14 research papers at international conferences and 11 at national conferences. He has co-authored two books at the national level and contributed 10 Scopus-indexed book chapters.

Sankar T C is an Assistant Professor in the Department of Computer Science and Engineering at JNN Institute of Engineering, Tamil Nadu. His academic interests include computer science education and emerging technologies. He is dedicated to fostering innovation and guiding students in research and technical development.

Kalai Lakshmi T. R. is an Associate Professor at the School of Management Studies, Sathyabama Institute of Science and Technology, Chennai. Her expertise includes marketing, human resource management, and soft skills. She has published in IEEE Xplore, contributed to ResearchGate, and serves as a reviewer for IJIRT and other academic journals.

Tatiana Tolusso is a PhD candidate in Communication, Markets and Society at IULM University. Her research focuses on consumer behaviour, innovation, neuromarketing, and marketing strategies. Lecturer and marketing professional, collaborating with Universities and Research Centres on projects at the intersection of behaviour, decision-making, sustainability, social and innovation.

Index

A

B

C

D

E

G

I

M

N

O

P

R

www.ingramcontent.com/pod-product-compliance
Lightning Source LLC
LaVergne TN
LVHW081536300926
849161LV00006B/1458